Early Buddhist Oral Tradition

Early Buddhist Oral Tradition

Textual Formation *and* Transmission

Bhikkhu Anālayo

Wisdom

Wisdom Publications
199 Elm Street
Somerville, MA 02144 USA
wisdomexperience.org

Library of Congress Cataloging-in-Publication Data
Names: Anālayo, 1962– author.
Title: Early Buddhist oral tradition: textual formation and transmission / Bhikkhu Anālayo.
Description: First. | Somerville: Wisdom Publications, 2022. | Includes bibliographical references and index.
Identifiers: LCCN 2021054630 (print) | LCCN 2021054631 (ebook) | ISBN 9781614298274 (hardcover) | ISBN 9781614298519 (ebook)
Subjects: LCSH: Buddhist education. | Buddhism—Study and teaching. | Oral tradition. | Monastic and religious life (Buddhism)
Classification: LCC BQ167 .A53 2022 (print) | LCC BQ167 (ebook) | DDC 294.3/75—dc23/eng/20220222
LC record available at https://lccn.loc.gov/2021054630
LC ebook record available at https://lccn.loc.gov/2021054631

ISBN 978-1-61429-827-4 ebook ISBN 978-1-61429-851-9

26 25 24 23 22
5 4 3 2 1

Cover design by Gopa & Ted 2. Interior design by James Skatges. Set in DGP 11.25/14.9. Cover art courtesy of The Metropolitan Museum of Art, New York, Gift of Daniel Slott, 1980, www.metmuseum.org.

As an act of Dhammadāna, Bhikkhu Anālayo has waived royalty payments for this book.

Wisdom Publications' books are printed on acid-free paper and meet the guidelines for permanence and durability of the Production Guidelines for Book Longevity of the Council on Library Resources.

Printed in Canada.

What is well transmitted orally
can still be empty, vain, and false,
and, too, what is not well transmitted orally
can still be factual, true, and not otherwise. (MN 95)

Contents

Introduction

In the following pages I examine the early Buddhist oral tradition from the viewpoint of its formation and transmission. The central question I intend to explore is how best to understand its dynamics: What is the most appropriate model for interpreting the existence of numerous variations between versions of a discourse preserved by different reciter lineages, given that these same parallels also show a remarkable degree of similarity and correspondence (together with exhibiting features of memorization that point to a concern with accurate transmission)? The present book is meant to express my current understanding of this topic in a way accessible to the general reader.

The presentation in what follows is the outcome of some twenty years of studying the relevant textual records, leading to about four hundred publications mainly based on comparative studies of parallel versions of these texts as transmitted by different oral recitation lineages. Central among these publications is my habilitation research, a comparative study of some one hundred fifty Pāli discourses of medium length in the light of a broad range of parallels extant in Chinese, Gāndhārī, Sanskrit, Tibetan, and at times even other languages.[1] Taking up such a range of texts in a single study had the obvious disadvantage that the sheer amount of material prevents the precision regarding details that is possible when doing a comparative study of a single text, ideally based on translating the different parallels. In this respect, my habilitation research can only offer a humble starting point for those wishing to do a closer study of a single discourse.

The advantage, however, is that surveying a broad range of parallels evidences general patterns of orality. This does not happen in a comparable way when doing only a few selected and more detailed comparative studies, where quite naturally the at times erratic nature of variations between parallels can leave a puzzling impression. It is only through an examination of many such cases that patterns behind the apparent muddle become clearer.

My exploration in the following pages begins with the key text recited regularly at fortnightly monastic observances, the code of rules (Pāli *pātimokkha*, Sanskrit *prātimokṣa*), and its relation to the narratives purporting to record the circumstances under which a particular rule was promulgated.

Patterns that emerge when studying the code of rules and the respective narratives recur in relation to verses embedded in prose narrations that similarly relate the circumstances believed to have led to the proclamation of the verse(s) in question. I explore these in the second chapter, after providing a brief overview over the different discourse collections. The third to fifth chapters are dedicated to various oral aspects of the early discourses, surveying evidence for memory errors, the impact of attempts at systematization, and instances of additions and innovations. Based on the material examined in this way, in the sixth chapter I explore the implications of the nature of these texts as the final product of centuries of oral transmission and evaluate the type of conclusions that can (and cannot) be drawn based on them, followed by presenting a sketch of the dynamics of early Buddhist orality.

A chief problem in studying the evidence provided by the early texts is the almost inevitable tendency to think in terms of modern modes of producing written texts. Yet, textual production in an oral setting differs substantially and needs to be considered on its own terms. My attempts to do justice to this requirement have benefitted from my experience of living many years in Sri Lanka, where the oral dimension of communication is still considerably more important than in the West, as well as from staying for some time on another occasion with tribal people living in the traditional way of hunting and gathering, a way of life in which communications were still entirely oral. Such personal experiences have helped me in my struggle to step out of the framework of thinking exclusively in terms of the written medium.

My presentation here is meant to provide an introduction to the relevant themes rather than an exhaustive survey, which within the limitations of a single monograph is not possible. Based on excerpts from my own more detailed studies of the respective points, I present a few selected examples to illustrate patterns of more general relevance. My aim throughout is to render academic research by myself and others more widely accessible, for which reason I try my best to explain ideas and concepts that are not necessarily familiar to the general reader. I have also endeavored to keep the main text as accessible as possible by relegating the more academic type of information to annotation. In addition, each chapter concludes with a brief summary of the main points of my discussion. In this way I trust it will be possible for the general reader to ignore the annotation and just read the main text, whereas my academic colleagues will hopefully still find in the annotations the information required to substantiate my presentation.

Whatever worth there may be in the following pages, none of it would have come into existence without the help of innumerable friends and colleagues over the past twenty years. Adequately naming each is no longer possible, hence I here express my deep gratitude in general to all and everyone who has, directly or indirectly, contributed to the growth of my understanding and the continuity of my research leading up to the present publication.

I. The Recital of the Monastic Rules

In what follows I begin by surveying the role and significance of the regular fortnightly recitation of the code of rules (Pāli *pātimokkha*, Sanskrit *prātimokṣa*) for the functioning of a monastic community. I also relate the coming into existence of different versions of this code of rules to the arising of distinct monastic ordination traditions and hence distinct oral transmission lineages. Then I explore the development of narratives that report the circumstances believed to have led to the promulgation of the rules against breaches of celibacy and against homicide (including assisted suicide). The material surveyed in this way affords me an occasion to take up the topic of memorization and improvisation, which are of continuous relevance for subsequent chapters.

1. After the Buddha's Demise

The role of the regular recitation of the code of rules as a crucial element in the functioning of the Buddhist monastic community (*saṅgha*) is aptly reflected in a Pāli discourse titled Discourse to Gopaka Moggallāna (*Gopakamoggallānasutta*) and narratively situated at a time shortly after the Buddha's demise. The relevant passage explains how the early Buddhist monastic community was able to remain in harmony despite the circumstance that the Buddha had not appointed a successor, none of his disciples was regarded by others as similar to the Buddha, and no one had been appointed by them as their leader. The explanation provided by Ānanda, a chief disciple who according to tradition served for a long time as the Buddha's attendant, takes the following form:[2]

> Brahmin, there are the guidelines of training laid down and the code of rules set forth for the monastics by the Blessed One who knows and sees, the arahant, the fully and rightly awakened one. As many of us as live in reliance on a certain village district all gather in the same place on an observance day; having gathered, we request one who has maintained [the code of rules to recite it]. When it is being recited, if there is an offence or a transgression, we make the monastic act in accordance with the teaching, in accordance with the instruction.

The Discourse to Gopaka Moggallāna has a parallel extant in Chinese translation, which presents a comparable explanation:[3]

> Suppose we dwell in reliance on a village or town. On the fifteenth day, when it is the time to recite the code of rules, we come together to sit in one place. If a monastic knows the teaching [of the code of rules], we invite that monastic to recite the teaching to us. If that assembly is pure, we all delight in and respectfully receive the recitation of that monastic. If that assembly is not pure, we instruct and deal with it according to the teaching that has been recited.

The differences that can be observed between these two passages are typical of what emerges on comparative study of parallel versions of an early Buddhist text. In the present case, alongside some variations the two parallels agree in highlighting the role of the teaching encapsulated in the code of rules as a central reference point to ensure harmony in the absence of anyone serving as a successor to the Buddha. Commenting on this passage, Eltschinger (2020, 138) notes that "the genuine successor of the Buddha is not one of his monks, not even a person, but the law, equated here with the *prātimokṣa*." Regarding the continuous role of this type of successor to the Buddha, Gombrich (1988, 110) observes that

> the *pātimokkha* ritual's *communal* function . . . was the one thing which held the Sangha together . . . since monks moved between communities, these regular compulsory meetings bound the Sangha together as a whole. We must remember that there was nothing else to do so, both because of the difficulty of communications and because there was no hierarchy, no structure of command, after the Buddha's death.

The importance of participation in the regular recitation of the code of rules finds illustration in a story reported in the different *Vinaya*s, the texts on "discipline" for monastics. According to the story in question, a monastic reflected on whether his presence was actually needed, given that he was pure. The narrative continues with the Buddha, who had become aware of the monastic's reflection, approaching him to clarify that his presence was indeed needed.[4] The story enshrines the basic principle that participation in the group recital of the code of rules was not negotiable, reflecting its importance in holding the monastic community together.

In order to serve this role in fostering communal harmony, there needs to be agreement among the gathered monastics on the contents of the code of rules. In an oral setting and in the absence of written records, the code of rules must have been regarded as a fixed text to be memorized with accuracy. In the words of McGovern (2019, 463), who otherwise argues in favor of viewing improvisation as a central element influencing the early texts, "no one would seriously doubt that this list of rules was memorized."[5] As pointed out by Allon (2018, 234),

> group recitation requires that the wording of the text and the arrangement of the textual units within a collection be fixed . . . a text—a *sūtra*, verse or textual unit or a collection of them—is fixed as long as it is memorized, repeated and communally recited without being intentionally changed, which of course allows for unintentional change.

2. The Growth and Recitation of the Code of Rules

Judging from the textual records, the code of rules in its present form appears to be the result of a gradual accretion of regulations promulgated on various occasions. Such a process may be reflected in a reference in a Pāli discourse to over one hundred and fifty rules,[6] thereby giving a number that falls short of the full count of the Theravāda code of rules for monks.[7] A gradual growth of the number of rules also appears to stand in the background of a regulation found similarly in the different *Vinaya*s. The regulation concerns the case of monastics pretending to be surprised on hearing a particular rule being mentioned. In the narrative setting, such a pretense serves to avoid being considered guilty of a breach.

The regulation in question makes best sense in a situation where the code of rules had not yet reached its final form. In such a setting, it could indeed happen that one suddenly comes to hear a rule being recited, which presumably has just been included in the code of rules, due to having only recently been promulgated. In other words, the attempt to pretend ignorance of a particular rule would only really work in a situation where this could in principle have occurred. The report of the Buddha's censure of this type of pretense comes with the indication that, once someone has participated in (the latest version of) the recital at least two or three times, such a person is expected to know its contents and any pretense of ignorance should not be accepted.[8] With a continuously expanding set of rules, one could indeed only be sure these are known once a particular monastic has at least a few times participated in their recital, after this has been updated to include the latest promulgation. In this way, the early stages in the recitation of the code of rules exemplify the inherent fluidity of the early Buddhist oral material in general, depicted by Davidson (1990/1992, 293) in this way:

> During the more than forty years of the Buddha's teaching career, there were many monks acting as authoritative teachers of the doctrine throughout the kingdom of Magadha and its border areas. They would cross paths with the master from

> time to time and receive new information as his doctrine and teaching style developed. They would also receive new information from one another during the fortnightly congregations, the summer rains retreats, and whenever they met as their mendicant paths crossed.

Visualizing the situation in this way, there would have been a continuous need for updating the body of texts a particular reciter had memorized, including the rules themselves.

Another development can be discerned regarding the carrying out of such recital. During an early period, the actual recitation of this continuously expanding code of rules apparently served as the occasion for admitting an offense.[9] This is evident in an injunction found in the motion that introduces a recital of the different codes of rules, which enjoins that all assembled monastics should pay careful attention to what is being recited. Offenders should reveal their transgressions, whereas those who are pure should remain silent.[10] In support of keeping in mind this function, the actual recital includes recurrent inquiries as to whether the assembled monastics are pure in regard to the particular set of rules just recited. Such questioning would have afforded a natural occasion for admitting a transgression. Kieffer-Pülz (2021, 48) explains that

> even though the question of the reciter is posed in the assembly in a general manner, each of the participating monks needs to understand it as if they had been personally asked, and, therefore, each has to respond to this question—if they have committed an offence—before the question has been asked for a third time.

In the course of time, this procedure appears to have been modified such that the revelation of transgressions instead took place before the recital of the code of rules began. As Gombrich (1991, 35) notes, "the procedure was changed: monks paired off and confessed to each other before the public recitation."[11] The net result was a shift of the nature of the fortnightly observance toward becoming more formalized and avoiding any disruption in the continuity of the recitation. I will return below to this shift, which is of relevance to an appreciation of the impact of memorization errors on the transmission of the code of rules in different reciter lineages.

A recital of the code of rules can be considered to involve a "group recitation." In principle, such a group recitation can take different forms: everyone recites together, one person recites and the others repeat, or one person recites and the others just follow mentally, possibly intervening to correct if a mistake should occur. The last of these models is the one particularly relevant to the fortnightly observance. From a normative perspective, as explained by Ñāṇatusita (2014, xlviii):

> While the Pātimokkha [code of rules] is recited, meticulous attention is paid to the recitation by the reciter as well as the other bhikkhus who are present so that no word is omitted and that the pronunciation of every word and syllable is correct.

In addition to the fortnightly observance, another occasion for recital is when teaching the code of rules to others. In such a setting, other modalities of group recitation would be relevant. At first, a senior monastic knowledgeable in the code of rules would teach newly ordained monks by reciting it for them portion by portion, with the others repeating until they have well memorized the relevant part. Lacking a written reference point, such a step-by-step procedure can enable students of differing memorization capacities to byheart the code of rules. Once this has been achieved at least to some degree, they could all recite together, the teacher leading by reciting louder and the others reciting at the same time, thereby gaining a chance to correct what they may have wrongly memorized or to be reminded of the proper sequence. Eventually, the teacher may invite individuals to do their own recitation, stepping in to correct should an error occur.

Although in principle the pattern of potential intervention to correct errors would be relevant to the fortnightly observance as well, the situation changes if the reciting monastic is the most senior one or the one who usually teaches the code of rules to others. Given the pervasive emphasis on respect for seniority in monastic protocol and the high regard for teachers in the ancient Indian setting, it is considerably less likely that others would have the courage to interrupt and correct if a mistake occurred. Moreover, the actual carrying out of the fortnightly observance need not conform to the normative expectation of meticulous attention paid by all those who are present, as boredom can easily set in and lead to participants no longer attending carefully to the details of what is being recited. In other words, correction of a mistake requires first of all that its occurrence is clearly noticed and in addition that the one who notices it feels entitled to point it out. A preference for keeping quiet must have become further strengthened once the nature of the fortnightly observance changed in the manner described above, whereby the actual recitation no longer served as an occasion for revealing transgressions. In such a setting of uninterrupted recitation, chances increase that errors remain uncorrected because speaking up to note a mistake will be more embarrassing as it interrupts the smooth performance of the ritual observance.

A problem here is in particular the lack of an external reference point to decide disagreements on what should be recited. In an entirely oral setting, perceptions of correctness depend very much on the authority exerted by a particular monastic. If a monastic of considerable seniority and good repute should have a slip of memory, which in view of the nature of human memory can easily happen, chances that this will not be corrected are fairly high. After all, someone who may have noticed this error would have no way to double-check, as there is no written testimony to what had up to then been the "correct" version.[12] If the reciting monastic should be the one who teaches the code of rules to newly ordained monastics, what until then would have been considered an "error" will morph into becoming part of what from now on will be considered the "correct" version among the disciples in the lineage of this teacher.

3. Concatenation and Waxing Syllables

The group recital of the code of rules can rely on a feature called "concatenation" to facilitate recall of the rules in order. Such concatenation, which is a feature of ancient Indo-Iranian orality,[13] is one of two patterns that I would like to introduce briefly at this point. In the present case, concatenation involves an arrangement of the sequence of the rules, whenever this is possible, in such a way that an item mentioned in one rule recurs in the next rule. Such arranging could be the result of a conscious application of the principle of concatenation. Alternatively, it could also be that rules just happened to be ordered in a way that results in their being more easily memorized, which would in turn strengthen the tendency for this particular sequence to become the standard one in a particular reciter tradition. In fact, since the basic working mechanism of memory is by way of association, the occurrence of concatenation could at times simply result from the way human memory stores information. Besides the code of rules, the same principle of concatenation can be seen at work in other early Buddhist texts, a topic to which I will return in the next chapter.[14]

The way concatenation functions can be exemplified with a few rules from the Theravāda *Vinaya*,[15] taken from the class of rules whose transgression requires being disclosed to a fellow monastic (*pācittiya*).[16] In the translation below, the terms that serve to link rules are alternatively in italics or in capital letters. In each case, a breach of the rule occurs if the following happens:

- If any monk should make *someone not fully ordained* recite the teaching word-by-word (4)
- If any monk should for more than two or three nights LIE DOWN TO SLEEP TOGETHER with *someone not fully ordained* (5)
- If any monk should LIE DOWN TO SLEEP TOGETHER with *a woman* (6)
- If any monk should impart a teaching to *a woman* in more than six or five sentences, except when a knowledgeable male [is also present] (7)

In this way, the reference to someone who is not fully ordained connects rules 4 and 5, the action of lying down to sleep together connects rules 5 and 6, and the mention of a woman connects rules 6 and 7 (in the corresponding rules for nuns, the corresponding reference is instead to a man). The same pattern continues beyond the rules presented above, as the term "teaching" in rule 7 recurs in a compound in rule 8, which shares with rule 9 a reference to "someone not fully ordained" (a reference thus shared by rules 4, 5, 8, and 9).

The application of such concatenation can considerably facilitate the challenging task of remembering the rules in order, once their sequence has been established. At the same time, such application is naturally limited by the formulation of the rules. If rules do not share terminological similarities of the type mentioned above, they need to be remembered without recourse to such aids to memorization. Moreover, the ordering of rules that do share some terminology can be done in different ways. In the example above, since rules 4, 5, 8, and 9 share the same term, they could in principle have been connected to each other in various ways.

Another pattern of considerable impact on the formation of early Buddhist oral texts is the principle of "waxing syllables." Application of this principle takes the form of ordering a list of synonyms or otherwise related items in such a way that words with fewer syllables are followed by words with the same number or more syllables.

Such listings of synonyms are a recurrent feature of the early Buddhist texts, related to the pervasive use of repetition in various forms (a topic to which I will turn in a subsequent chapter). Simply said, the tendency is to state a particular quality or item not just once but several times by giving similar terms, somewhat comparable to a thesaurus that lists words in groups of synonyms. The main point appears to be simply to make sure that the meaning shared by these alternative expressions sufficiently impresses itself on the listeners. In particular in the case of listings of near-synonyms, appreciating the underlying message need not be taken to require identifying minor differences of meaning between individual terms in such a series of words. Instead, it would probably do more justice to the oral nature of the texts to focus on what the listed expressions share in common, in the understanding that their purpose is to ensure that this common meaning will not be missed by the listener.

The crescendo effect that results from the application of the principle of waxing syllables to such lists of synonyms facilitates memorization. If a particular list is rather long, the same principle can be applied to subunits, usually grouping together items that have some relationship to each other. An example would be the first part of a rather long Pāli list used to describe irrelevant types of conversations undertaken by not particularly well-behaved monastics.[17] Based on discerning somewhat distinct themes, this description can be divided into six subunits. The sequence of individual words in each subunit in turn follows the principle of waxing syllables:[18]

First subunit, talk related to government: kings, robbers, ministers;
rājakathaṃ, corakathaṃ, mahāmattakathaṃ,
syllable count: 4+4+6.

Second subunit, talk related to war: armies, dangers, battles;
senākathaṃ, bhayakathaṃ, yuddhakathaṃ,
syllable count: 4+4+4.

Third subunit, talk related to monastic requisites: food, drink, clothing, beds;
annakathaṃ, pānakathaṃ, vatthakathaṃ, sayanakathaṃ,
syllable count: 4+4+4+5.

Fourth subunit, talk on lay life: garlands, perfumes, relatives, vehicles;
mālākathaṃ, gandhakathaṃ, ñātikathaṃ, yānakathaṃ,
syllable count: 4+4+4+4.

Fifth subunit, talk on localities: villages, towns, cities, counties;
gāmakathaṃ, nigamakathaṃ, nagarakathaṃ, janapadakathaṃ,
syllable count: 4+5+5+6.

Sixth subunit, talk on gossip: women, heroes, streets, wells, the departed;
itthikathaṃ, sūrakathaṃ, visikhākathaṃ, kumbaṭṭhānakathaṃ, pubbapetakathaṃ,
syllable count: 4+4+5+6+6.

Recitation of such a list has an almost musical quality, with the ending of each subunit allowing for a brief pause to catch one's breath before rhythmically reciting the next. This makes it easier and also to some extent more pleasant to memorize and rehearse a rather long list of different types of conversations.

The application of this principle is not confined to series of synonyms. This can be seen in the wording of the seventh rule taken up above, which concerned teaching in "more than six or five sentences." The corresponding Pāli phrase is *uttarichappañcavācāhi*, where the term for "six," *cha*, occurs before the term for "five," *pañca*. My literal translation as "six or five sentences," rather than "five or six sentences," is on purpose to reflect this peculiarity. In this way, the sequence of Pāli numerals follows the principle of waxing syllables even though this goes against the natural tendency to adopt an ascending order by listing "five" first and only then "six."[19] I will come back to the two patterns of concatenation and waxing syllables in the next chapter.

4. Different Monastic Lineages

The different *Vinaya*s regulate in much detail the fortnightly recital of the code of rules, whose correct recall can be aided by the two patterns surveyed above. The undertaking of such fortnightly recital is a requirement when more than three monastics live in the same designated area. Alternative modes of recital are recognized, where a fairly simple version requires just reciting the introductory motion and the most important rules (Pāli and Sanskrit *pārājika*),[20] whose intentional breaking results in an irreversible loss of the status of being a fully ordained monastic.[21] The next alternative adds rules whose breach requires a formal process of rehabilitation on the part of the offender (Pāli *saṅghādisesa*, Sanskrit *saṃghāvaśeṣa* or *saṃghātiśeṣa*).[22] Another alternative adds two rules known as "undetermined" (Pāli and Sanskrit *aniyata*), and the last alternative recognized is a full recitation of the entire code of rules.[23]

After the Buddha's demise, with the gradual spread of monastic communities over different parts of India, various memorization errors would have naturally led to the emergence of different versions of this code of rules. The occurrence of variations as such is an integral feature of orality. As pointed out by Vansina (1985, 161) in the context of a study of oral tradition in general, at "any moment in time the corpus of any community is in fact not totally homogeneous."

In the case of the oral transmission of the Buddhist code of rules, at times differences are merely a matter of minor variations in wording, at other times they affect the sequence of rules, and occasionally they can even result in a particular rule not appearing in all traditions.[24] Notably, as evident in a comparative survey of the code of rules for male monastics provided in the groundbreaking work by Waldschmidt (1926, 3) and in an excellent survey of *Vinaya* literature by Clarke (2015, 62), differences in the actual number of rules for monks between various *Vinaya* traditions affect in particular those rules that only come up for recitation when the entire code of rules is recited. In the case of the rules for nuns, however, variations in count also affect the rules involving a temporary loss of one's monastic status.

The adherence to distinct codes of rules is characteristic of the different monastic traditions that came into existence in the course of the history of Indian Buddhism. One of the three monastic lineages still alive today is the Dharmaguptaka tradition, found in China, Korea, Taiwan, Vietnam, etc. Another monastic lineage is the Mūlasarvāstivāda tradition, found in Tibet and Mongolia.[25] Yet another such monastic lineage, extant in South and Southeast Asian countries like Myanmar, Sri Lanka, Thailand, etc., is usually referred to as Theravāda.[26]

Each of these three traditions follows different codes of rules embedded in different *Vinaya*s; they employ different languages to carry out monastic procedures and wear different monastic robes. Several other such monastic lineages came into existence in India but died out at some point. A convenient referent to such diversity takes the form of speaking of "eighteen" such lineages, where the number eighteen is best taken in a figurative sense, rather than as accurately reflecting the situation on the ground in ancient India.[27]

The emergence of these different monastic traditions is often conceptualized as the result of schisms. The occurrence of a schism (*saṅghabheda/saṃghabheda*) requires that at least four fully ordained monastics decide to carry out monastic observances on their own rather than continuing to participate in these with the community of which they had been, up to that point, an integral part. The prototype for such a procedure is the narrative of the first schism involving Devadatta, situated at a time when the Buddha was still alive.[28] Such a procedure does not necessarily involve a difference on doctrinal grounds, but much rather concerns a different attitude regarding what type of conduct should be binding for all monastics.

The arising of the so-called eighteen Buddhist monastic lineages in ancient India, however, need not invariably have followed the precedent set by the story of Devadatta, in the sense of being eighteen occasions when groups of monastics intentionally decided to form a tradition of their own. To my mind it seems considerably more plausible that the arising of distinct monastic lineages could at times have resulted simply from the gradual increase of differences between the codes of rules recited in different parts of India. Monastics wandering from one particular community to another could be expected to tolerate some minor differences in wording when participating in the fortnightly observance (provided they even noted them). But after major differences had appeared, which are more easily noticed, such participation would become considerably more challenging. After all, a central purpose of such a recital, as explicitly stated at the end of the different versions of the code of rules, is to train in concord in the rules that have just been recited.[29] This requires having the same set of rules. Once this requirement no longer holds, it becomes rather difficult to carry out the fortnightly observance together.[30]

The manifestation of variations is of course not a one-time event, but something that must have kept occurring time and again during successive stages of oral transmission and institutional development. Hence to some degree such variations must have manifested continuously even within a particular ordination lineage, when this had formed.

With distinct ordination lineages in existence, probably resulting from an early stage in the spread of Buddhist monastics over different geographical areas in ancient India, differences between their respective corpora of orally transmitted texts would have tended to increase, due to substantially fewer opportunities for "correction" during group recital in the presence of participants trained in another reciter lineage. When members of different *Vinaya* traditions, after these had been formed, eventually came to live in close vicinity to each other, by then it must have become rather difficult or even no longer possible for them to carry out monastic observances together.

When reciters ordained in a particular tradition perform the recitation of the code of rules mainly with their peers who are familiar with the same version of the text, they will be prone to do the same for other texts. In this way, distinct monastic ordination lineages tend to result in different oral transmission lineages. Such natural correlation need not be considered to result in a rigid and impenetrable separation of textual transmission lineages. This is hardly plausible, given the fluidity of oral transmission. For the same reason, variations between parallel versions do not invariably align with distinct transmission lineages (or school affiliation). It also does not mean that monastics of a particular local tradition might not at times approach a famous teacher ordained in a different lineage to receive teachings. But it does imply general trends of collections of texts being orally transmitted by groups of reciters who belong to the same ordination tradition.

From the emic perspective of a particular tradition, after awareness of differences has set in, the impression can easily arise that the other ordination traditions somehow got things wrong. After all, their code of rules differs from the "right version," which is obviously one's own. From this viewpoint, then, it becomes understandable why a Theravāda chronicle considers the other "seventeen" monastic lineages to be schismatics.[31] If the position taken here should exemplify the general trend of affairs, which seems to me fairly probable, the idea of a "schism" forming the background for the emergence of different monastic lineages would be the result of polemics rather than reflecting actual occurrences of intentionally carried out splits of monastic communities in ancient India.

A proper appreciation of the ancient setting can benefit considerably from developing sensitivity for appropriate terminology, such as not referring to a monastic lineage (*nikāya*) as a "sect."[32] As pointed out succinctly by Boucher (2005, 292n10),

> the word "sect" is used among sociologists of religion to denote a movement that has broken from its parent body (the "church") and remains in tension with it, often with overt hostility to existing social institutions with which the church has accommodated itself. Buddhist *nikāya*s are monastic ordination lineages which overlap hardly, if at all, with such a definition.

Rather than thinking in terms of sects that result from schisms due to doctrinal disputes, it would be preferable to envisage the situation in terms of monastic lineages that differ from each other in their respective codes of rules. Such differences could have developed in a considerably more accidental manner than dissidents intentionally splitting off from their parent body.

The perspective that emerges in this way is of considerable relevance for the transmission of the early Buddhist texts in general. In view of the fluctuating nature of oral transmission over centuries, some degree of variation among textual collections transmitted by reciters who belong to the same transmission lineage is only to be expected. In other words, individual instances of lack of conformity need not invariably reflect the influence of the school affiliation of the transmitters of a particular text. In fact, emphasis on particular textual collections as a product of a certain Buddhist "school" needs to be combined with an awareness that the respective texts have come into being well before the arising of self- and other-identified Buddhist "schools." Salomon (2008, 14) comments that it is open to question

> how meaningful such supposed 'school affiliations' really are, especially in the contexts of earlier periods for which it is by no means certain that we are dealing with canonically fixed texts associated with specific schools . . . for we do not know with any confidence that the distribution of recensions of Buddhist texts in early times strictly followed sectarian, as opposed to, for example, geographical patterns.

In other words, distinctions of school affiliation are useful predominantly in terms of attempting to discern individual transmission lineages as a basis for evaluating the significance of correspondences and variations in comparative studies of the received versions. Similarities between closely related transmission lineages are less significant than similarities between transmission lineages that appear to have been operating independently for a considerable time. This potential, however, should not lead to the assumption that variations must invariably reflect sectarian agendas. Boucher (2008, 190) rightly points out:

> The problem with always seeing *nikāya* as at the heart of . . . differences is that it occludes other possible explanations . . . we might do well to consider explanations for their distinctiveness that goes [sic] beyond our modern proclivity for school affiliation.

5. Communal Recitation

A shift of perspective from viewing the early Buddhist texts as the products of sectarian agendas also enables a better appreciation of the term *saṅgīti/saṃgīti*, which stands for a "communal recitation" rather than for a "council." Tilakaratne (2000, 175) explains that

> the fundamental purpose of the act of *saṅgāyana* [reciting together] and therefore of the events described as *saṅgīti* [communal recitation] is the assurance of the unity of the Buddhist monastic organization . . . the key activity was to recite together the Dhamma and the *Vinaya* . . . [which], first and foremost, was meant to be a public expression of one's allegiance to the organisation which was represented by the Dhamma and the *Vinaya* . . . the recital of the Pātimokkha by the members of the Saṅgha every fortnight serves virtually the same purpose.

In sum, "we need to view these acts of communal recitals as determined, first and foremost, by a very important communal requirement, namely, the assurance of the solidarity of the Saṅgha, as a group, to one way of behaviour (the *Vinaya*)" (196).

The different *Vinaya*s report that the convocation of the first communal recitation (*saṅgīti/saṃgīti*), held according to tradition near the town of Rājagaha/Rājagṛha soon after the Buddha's demise, was occasioned by the perceived need to ensure adherence to the monastic rules. The introductory narrative reports that news of the Buddha's recent decease had motivated a particular monastic to voice his relief, thinking that from now on he would be free to act as he wished.[33] In order to forestall a diffusion of such attitudes, the first communal recitation was reportedly held. Whatever the historical value of this narrative, it complements the indication made in the Discourse to Gopaka Moggallāna and its parallel, taken up at the outset of this chapter, in that adherence to the code of rules was perceived as a crucial principle enabling a harmonious continuity of the monastic community after the Buddha had passed away.

The narrative of the first communal recitation reports a decision taken by the assembled monastics not to implement a permission believed to have been given by the Buddha, according to which the minor rules can be abolished after his demise. A chief factor reportedly influencing this decision was uncertainty among the members of the congregation regarding the precise implication of the reference to "minor rules." Moreover, the decision not to abolish any existing rule and not to allow for new rules to be promulgated follows a principle believed to have been taught by the Buddha himself, according to a passage found in the Discourse on the [Buddha's] Final Nirvana (*Mahāparinibbānasutta*) and several of its parallels. The passage in question presents, as one of several principles preventing decline, the principle that existing rules should not be abolished and new rules should not be established.[34] This is precisely the attitude that according to the first communal recitation was considered binding on all Buddhist monastics.

According to a basic pattern evident in the different *Vinaya*s, if the Buddha promulgated rules in response to a particular problem and such first promulgation was insufficient to settle the matter, he is shown to make adjustments by changing the formulation or pronouncing additional stipulations. In this way, the *Vinaya* narratives on the promulgation of rules present these as ad hoc regulations open to amendments if this should be required. As explained by von Hinüber (1995, 7), "rules are derived from experience and based on the practical need to avoid certain forms of behavior in future . . . consequently there is no [pre-]existent system of Buddhist law." At the same time, however, from an emic perspective the Buddha "is the only law giver, and thus all rules . . . are thought to go back to the Buddha." After the decease of the Buddha, the regulations believed to have been promulgated by him became unalterable law that no longer admits any change, a status all the more evident with the decision reportedly taken at the first communal recitation even not to take a step sanctioned by the Buddha.

The notion of the impossibility to change any rule appears to have continued down the centuries. The different *Vinaya*s report the occurrence of a second communal recitation, held a century after the Buddha's demise in response to the monks in Vesālī/Vaiśālī accepting monetary donations, which they considered allowable.[35] This could hardly have become an issue worth explicit reporting in the different *Vinaya*s if the rule that prohibits accepting such donations had been viewed as amenable to change. A simple intentional adjustment of that rule, agreed on by the local group of Vesālī/Vaiśālī monks, would have left no room for others to intervene. The very report of a second communal recitation implies that even a century later an intentional change of a rule was not considered a viable option.

The degree to which the emic perception of the monastic regulations disallows their intentional adjustment can be illustrated with the example of how Theravāda monks handle the ruling according to which they should use only three robes. These are the two relatively long outer robes (*uttarāsaṅga* and *saṅghāṭi*), one of which is of double-layer cloth and thus considerably warmer than the other, and the shorter inner garment (*antaravāsaka*). Originally the first two appear to have been much shorter.[36] The interpretation of the relevant measurement appears to have changed at a relatively early stage, as a result of which the "correct" size of these two became considerably longer. The difference in size between the three robes becomes inconvenient when one robe has just been washed and is still wet. With three robes of similar size, one can be washed and left to dry while the other two can be worn to cover the lower and upper body. Once the sizes differ, however, this simple procedure no longer works so well. With three robes of dissimilar size, it would be much easier if one were not restricted to these three and could have an extra robe that can be worn while one of the three is left somewhere to dry.

A way of solving the situation within the parameters of keeping to the letter of the rule is to give another name altogether to an additional robe, formally determining it for use by calling it a "requisite cloth" (*parikkhāracoḷa*). No number limitations apply for requisite cloths, hence in this way a monk can have more than the traditionally allowed three robes without infringement of the rule. As documented by Kieffer-Pülz (2007, 35–45) in a detailed study of this monastic procedure, textual discussions of this option seem to have perdured from an opinion voiced by someone who apparently lived in the environs of the first century BC all the way to the seventeenth century; the same practice is still in use in contemporary times.

Two millennia of such concerns to fulfill the literal sense of the rule could easily have been avoided through a single intentional adjustment of this rule. This evidently did not happen, testifying to the continuity of the attitude showcased in the account of the first communal recitation.

From an emic perspective, monastics are comparable to police officers who are expected to keep and protect the law but are unable to change it. Evaluating the behavior of a local group of police officers in response to a particular accident based on the assumption that they could have adjusted the law to facilitate resolving the situation would not be reasonable, as it would fail to give proper recognition to their role. The same holds for assuming that a local group of monastics could have just adjusted monastic law to help resolve a particular situation; such an assumption similarly fails to give proper recognition to the evidence we have regarding the emic perception of the role of monastics. Both police officers and monastics have no legislative prerogatives but can only execute the law.

An expression of this fundamental attitude toward the rules, believed to have been originally promulgated by the Buddha, can be seen in a statement by the eminent and otherwise quite progressive Theravāda monk

Ajāhn Buddhadāsa at the sixth communal recitation,[37] held in Myanmar in 1956. He explains that Theravāda monastics are in principle

> against the revoking, changing or altering of the original even in its least form . . . we have no warrant of addition in such a manner that would make Buddhism develop according to [the] influence of the . . . locality, or to any other circumstances . . . we are afraid of doing such a thing.

Precisely this type of attitude toward the rules, which is not confined to Theravādins, makes it so difficult to establish an order of nuns in those monastic traditions where it does not exist.[38] At a conference on the revival of full ordination for nuns, held in 2007 in Hamburg under his auspices, the Dalai Lama (2010, 268) explained: "If I were a Buddha, I could decide [to grant ordination to nuns]; but that is not the case. I am not a Buddha. I can act as a dictator regarding some issues, but not regarding matters of Vinaya."

The endurance of the notion that *Vinaya* rules are not open to being changed by local communities (or even highly respected leaders, such as the Dalai Lama) makes it unconvincing to assume that variations between different codes of rules must be the outcome of a series of intentional decisions taken by local monastic communities. Instead of adopting such a perspective, a mode of understanding the arising of such variations needs to be found that takes into account the function of the code of rules and the attitude toward it among monastic reciters.

It appears to have been precisely the reverential attitude of the reciters toward the material they passed on from generation to generation that has endowed oral transmission with an aura of reliability and prestige, ensuring that it continued for centuries even once writing had been introduced.[39] A contributive factor here may well have been the circumstance that, unlike the writing down of a text, oral transmission tends to be a communal effort, due to the role of repeated group recitation as a means of correction. In a cultural setting that overall tends to grant importance to the group over the individual much more than is the case nowadays, oral transmission could easily have been perceived as more reliable than written manuscripts, even though this runs counter to the way we may regard the matter in this day and age.

According to Vansina (1985, 31), from the viewpoint of oral tradition "information coming from more people to more people has greater built-in redundancy [i.e., is more reliable] than if it were to flow in one channel of communication. Multiple flow does not necessarily imply multiple distortion only, rather perhaps the reverse." Karttunen (1998, 116) comments on medieval Vedic literature that "frequent copying seems to have introduced textual corruption more easily than the traditional method of oral transmission founded on careful training applying special mnemotechniques." As noted by Killingly (2014, 126–27) in a discussion of Vedic recitation:

> The notion that oral texts are fluid and written texts are stable, though it holds true in many instances, is a simplification which ignores the fact that oral and written transmission can each have various forms and purposes . . . while writing can ensure the stability of a text, it can also facilitate change . . . Oral and written transmission may facilitate either fluidity or stability, depending on how they are used; neither necessitates the one or the other.

Hence, "we need to recognize that the crucial difference is not between writing and oral transmission, but between the presence and absence of a technique for stabilizing a text" (129).

The continuous relevance of, and reliance on, oral transmission can be seen in the travel records of the pilgrim Faxian, who had gone to India in search of *Vinaya* material to be translated into Chinese. According to his report, the texts he was searching for were still transmitted entirely by oral means in fourth- to fifth-century North India, as a result of which he was unable to find written versions that he could have copied.[40] Commenting on fragment findings from the Northern Silk Road, Sander (1991, 142) reasons that the continuity of oral transmission "may explain the total absence of . . . Vinaya and Sūtra texts [in Sanskrit] before the fifth century AD." The same apparent reluctance to shift over completely to written material applies to the Pāli tradition.[41] The attitudes evident in this way align with the improbability of the idea that intentional changes introduced by local groups of monastics were a generally acceptable mode of dealing with the texts. Had this indeed been the case, it would make it less probable for the orally transmitted material to be perceived as being to such an extent trustworthy and reliable.

I will return to the topic of intentional changes in subsequent parts of my exploration, as this is an important topic related to the need to step out of modes of thinking influenced by textual production in the West, where intentional changes are indeed the main reason for the occurrence of variations. In contrast, a proper understanding of the early Buddhist oral tradition requires taking fully into account the dynamics of orality and the functions of the relevant texts, in the way these are documented by the available evidence.

6. The Group of Six

The above-suggested conclusion, regarding the improbability that intentional change is the main factor responsible for variations, concerns the formulation of the monastic rules themselves. The situation differs considerably with the narratives describing the circumstances believed to have led to the promulgation of a rule, where intentional change appears to have indeed been a factor of considerable relevance.

In the case of the tale mentioned earlier in this chapter, according to which monastics pretended to be surprised on hearing a particular rule being mentioned, the different versions of the relevant narrative agree in attributing such behavior to member(s) of a group of monks known as the "group of six."[42] Such a reference to the "group of six" is not without some ambiguity, as Sarvāstivāda and Theravāda texts provide differing lists of the members of this group, agreeing on only two out of the altogether six names listed in each version.[43]

References to this group of six monks are a recurrent trope in *Vinaya* narrative, with a similar trope involving a group of misbehaving nuns found in narratives concerning the promulgation of rules for nuns. Although in the case just mentioned the parallel versions agree in referring to the six monks, this is not invariably the case. An example is the rule forbidding recitation word-by-word to someone who has not taken full ordination, taken up earlier in this chapter. Only some *Vinaya*s explicitly mention the group of six in their account of what led to the promulgation of this rule.[44]

Another example is a rule that forbids partaking of food at the wrong time. Whereas the Theravāda *Vinaya* mentions the group of six in its version of the events leading up to the promulgation of this rule,[45] such a reference is not found in other accounts.[46] The topic of the wrong time comes up again in the context of a rule against entering a village at a time considered to be inappropriate. Here, again, there is no agreement among the different *Vinaya*s on relating the promulgation of this rule to something done by members of the group of six.[47]

In this way, the extant *Vinaya*s disagree on the specific role played by the group of six. Such disagreements also extend to other aspects of the stories that purport to record the circumstances behind the promulgation of rules, which shows that the accurate recording of historical events was not the main purpose of such *Vinaya* narratives.[48] In other words, instead of being an attempt to provide an exact reflection of what happened in ancient India, this type of text is probably best considered from the viewpoint of its literary function. This literary function can be illustrated with the help of a closer look at two major rules concerning a breach of celibacy and the killing of a human being. These two rulings are of considerable significance, as their intentional breach implies, as briefly mentioned above, an irrevocable loss of the condition of belonging to the community of fully ordained monastics.

7. The Ruling on a Breach of Celibacy

The first of the two regulations to be studied in more detail concerns celibacy, which can safely be assumed to have been a topic of central importance for the early Buddhist monastic tradition. Although the ruling itself is closely similar in the different *Vinaya* traditions, the narrative of its promulgation exhibits substantial differences.[49] The basic story line depicts a monk who is persuaded by his mother to have intercourse with his former wife in order to ensure the continuity of the family line and its inheritance. Whereas several *Vinayas* just present this story without providing much information about the protagonist's personal background,[50] another two *Vinayas* relate in detail how the monk in question, called Sudinna, went forth.[51]

According to their report, hearing a talk by the Buddha had made Sudinna, the only son of a wealthy household, become quite intent on going forth, so as to dedicate himself wholeheartedly to the practice of the Buddha's teaching. When conveying his wish to the Buddha, he found out that his parents' permission was needed for him to be granted ordination. On returning home he expressed his aspiration to his parents, who refused to give their consent. Sudinna was so keen on the monastic life that he went on a hunger strike to force his parents to grant him the needed permission.[52] Faced by the prospect of the death of their only child, the parents finally relented and let him go forth.[53]

This tale shows Sudinna defying the wishes of his parents and forcing them to consent to his plan to go forth by threatening to starve himself to death. The description of such an attitude does not tally too well with the report, subsequent to his ordination, of his willingness to accommodate his parents' wish to ensure the continuity of the family line by having sex with his former wife. Already at the time of his going forth, his parents' concern for the family lineage and the bequest of their wealth to the next generation would have been natural considerations for an only son in the ancient Indian social setting. This could hardly have been something he had not been aware of from the outset.

The story of his inspiration to go forth on hearing a teaching by the Buddha, the need to get the parents' permission, their refusal, the decision to go on a prolonged hunger strike, and the final relenting of the parents also occur in a Pāli discourse and its parallels, whose protagonist is instead called Raṭṭhapāla/Rāṣṭrapāla.[54] The similarity between the two stories gives the impression that the two *Vinaya* traditions under discussion might have adopted this story to enhance the narrative explaining the promulgation of the ruling against breaches of celibacy.[55]

The suggested enhancement can best be understood by turning to the function of *Vinaya* narrative. Unlike the actual rule, the story of its promulgation does not come up every fortnight for recitation in order to express and ensure communal harmony.[56] Instead, a narrative is relevant to the situation of teaching *Vinaya*, in particular when introducing newly ordained monastics to the rule or when counseling other monastics who are apprehensive of yielding to a temptation. A teacher of *Vinaya* needs above all to make sure that those he instructs are fully aware of what can cause them to lose their status as fully ordained members of the monastic community. To achieve that, he has to clarify when and under what circumstances a breach of celibacy can occur. Failing to do this properly would make him partly responsible for a loss of their monkhood, owing to their lack of awareness about how this should be preserved. This endows the employment of a good story in a teaching context with considerable importance, in view of the dire repercussions of a potential transgression.

Executing this teaching task requires inculcating a keen awareness in other monastics that they may easily be drawn into doing something that has rather grave consequences. From this perspective, precisely the gravity of this rule would have encouraged some enhancement, rather than ensuring that the same tale was handed down with only minimal variations by successive generations of monastic reciters in the different Buddhist traditions.

Integrating elements from the tale of Raṭṭhapāla/Rāṣṭrapāla adds more weight to the warning to be given, as in this way the one who breaches the rule of celibacy is an otherwise outstanding and exemplary monk. This monk is so keen on going forth that he is willing to risk death in order to get his parents' permission to exchange a life of luxury and affluence for that of a mendicant; a tale that could easily make monastics sitting in the audience wonder if they would be capable of a similar degree of renunciation. The message to a monastic audience hearing this story seems quite to the point: even a monk with such a strong and sincere inspiration is not beyond danger. The stark example provided in this way would go a long way in driving home to other monastics that they should not presume themselves to be beyond the possibility of infringement of the regulation on celibacy, just because they are sincerely dedicated to the monastic life.

In this way, an apparent tendency to improve the story can be appreciated from the viewpoint of its teaching function in the context of monastic education, where it serves as an integral part of the *Vinaya* project of inculcating moral values, believed to be enshrined in the rules, in order to foster the corresponding behavior among monastics. The evolved tale of the Sudinna episode thereby contrasts the Buddhist ideal of renunciation to the Brahminical notion of a man's duty in procreation, reinforcing the message that, when having to negotiate this tension, a Buddhist monastic should stay firmly on the side of renunciation.

8. The Ruling Against Killing a Human Being

The apparent concerns in the background of origination stories of rules can be further appreciated by turning to another rule whose breach also results in a loss of one's status as a fully ordained monastic. This is the third of the rules for monks that come up every fortnight for recitation,[57] which concerns killing a human being or else assisting someone in committing suicide. The narrative depicting the promulgation of this rule takes up the case of assisting other monastics in committing suicide, motivated by disgust with their own bodies.[58] The story leading up to the mass suicide of monastics is particularly noteworthy, as they developed disgust with their own bodies after hearing an injunction given by the Buddha. The injunction recommends cultivating the perception of the lack of attractiveness of the human body. Besides being found in different *Vinayas*,[59] the report of such a brief teaching with disastrous consequences also occurs in two discourses.[60]

It is remarkable that the reciters would pass on a story that certainly does not place the Buddha in a particularly good light. A mass suicide of disciples is a rather alarming outcome of a teaching given by the one who, according to the standard formula for recollection, is a "supreme trainer of persons to be tamed."[61] Moreover, in some *Vinaya* versions the dramatic features of the story increase. Three *Vinayas* report that a particular person assisted the monks in committing suicide and eventually killed altogether up to sixty monks.[62] The same number occurs in another three *Vinayas*, with the decisive difference that this is the maximum number of monks killed in a single day.[63] As a result, the overall count of casualties becomes substantially higher.[64] One of these *Vinayas* describes that the whole monastery had become filled with a disarray of corpses, a stinking and impure place that was comparable to a cemetery.[65]

The tendency to increase the dramatic effects of the tale, which in this case runs directly counter to the tendency to exalt the Buddha,[66] is best understood from the viewpoint of a *Vinaya* teaching context aimed at inculcating the need to avoid such suicidal behavior. The more dramatic the tale, the better the lesson will be learned. In the present case, this lesson covers not only the avoidance of a breach of the rule as such (by way of assisting suicide) but also conveys the inappropriateness of committing suicide oneself. The tale thereby points to the need of the early Buddhist tradition to define its position in the ancient Indian context vis-à-vis attitudes toward the body promoted by competing ascetic practices and ideologies. The vivid details of the drama throw into relief the importance of a balanced attitude that leads beyond sensuality without resulting in self-destructive tendencies.

As explained by Schopen (1994, 61), if "*vinaya* cases are neither fables nor historical accounts, but rather the forms that *vinaya*-masters chose narratively to frame the issues that concerned them, then they do provide us a record of such concerns." The above two cases do indeed provide evidence for such concerns. The same is also fairly apparent in the accounts, given in the different *Vinaya*s, of how the order of nuns was founded. These provide ample evidence for the impact of negative attitudes toward nuns on those responsible for the shaping and transmission of this particular narrative.[67]

The two tales briefly examined here can in turn be seen to negotiate a felt need of the early Buddhist monastic community to carve out a clear-cut identity in distinction to contemporary brahmins and to ascetically inclined recluses. The two narrations throw into relief two extremes to be avoided: sensuality and excessive concern with the expectations of one's family on the one hand, and self-destructive asceticism on the other. They thereby reiterate the contrast between the two extremes to be avoided that stands at the outset of what according to tradition was the first discourse spoken by the Buddha.[68] With these two *Vinaya* narratives, the two extremes come alive in a *Vinaya* teaching context through showcasing monastics going off the middle path.

9. *Vinaya* and Discourse Literature

From the viewpoint of oral transmission, an intriguing feature of the narrative concerning the mass suicide of monks is that it occurs in discourse as well as *Vinaya* literature. In the case of the Theravāda tradition, this results in two somewhat different reports of the same event, as the discourse version does not mention the person who, according to the *Vinaya* account, assisted the monks in committing suicide. An absence of a reference to this person is understandable in the discourse version, since here the narrative does not lead up to the promulgation of a rule. Instead, this version occurs among discourses on the topic of mindfulness of breathing, hence the context only requires the mass suicide as such and the Buddha's subsequent recommendation that the monastics should better practice mindfulness of breathing, without further concern about how exactly the suicides happened.

Nevertheless, even the parts shared by the two versions, before the possible mention of this person, show some divergences.[69] The discourse describes the recommendation reportedly given by the Buddha with three phrases, to which the *Vinaya* version adds a fourth.[70] The same *Vinaya* version stands alone in illustrating the disgust developed by the monks with the example of a youthful person being repelled on finding the carcass of a dead animal has been hung on their necks.[71] Together with various small variations found in what is, after all, just a short portion of text, such differences are evidently the result of these two tales being transmitted for some time individually, even though this happened within the same circle of Theravāda reciters. Such variations are a natural occurrence in oral transmission and, as the present case clearly shows, need not be read as reflections of sectarian agendas.

The present case also shows that discourse and *Vinaya* literature were not kept strictly separate. As noted by Gethin (2014, 64):

> While the contents of the *Vinaya* and Sūtra Piṭakas [baskets] broadly fit the categories of "monastic discipline" (*vinaya*) and "teaching" (*dharma*) respectively, there is some overlap. For example, the *Vinaya* contains an account of the career of

> the Buddha incorporating material that is found in the Sūtra Piṭaka ... Likewise, the Sūtra Piṭaka includes discussion of specific *Vinaya* rules as well as more general *Vinaya* issues. There is also material in the Sūtra Piṭaka that touches on the basic principles of the *Vinaya* legal code that is absent from the Vinaya Piṭaka itself.

The Great Discourse on the [Buddha's] Final Nirvana, for example, could be the result of an importation of what originally was a *Vinaya* narrative.[72] Another discourse records the promulgation of a new type of rule against an obstinate monastic, the application of which is then reported in the Theravāda *Vinaya*.[73] The promulgation of this rule is also found in discourse parallels to this Pāli discourse.[74]

A similar pattern can be observed in relation to a different discourse, whose depiction of another obstinate monastic recurs twice in the Theravāda *Vinaya*.[75] His obstinate behavior is also taken up in a Chinese parallel to this discourse, as well as in several *Vinaya*s.[76] Again, seven ways of settling a litigation occur in a Pāli discourse, its parallels, and in the various codes of rules (I will return to these seven in a subsequent chapter).[77] Similarly, the reasons for promulgating monastic rules are covered in a Pāli discourse, its parallel, and in different *Vinaya*s.[78] Evidently, those responsible for the oral transmission of the texts did not consider *Vinaya* and discourse material as something to be kept strictly separate.

The lack of a sharp distinction between discourse and *Vinaya* literature in turn makes it meaningful to assume that patterns of orality evident in the material taken up in this chapter could in principle be similarly relevant when turning to discourse material, to be surveyed in the remainder of this book.

10. Memorization and Improvisation

The promulgation narratives studied above indicate that this type of text received a treatment different from the rules themselves.[79] In other words, two modalities of oral transmission appear to be identifiable here. One of these involves an attempt at precise memorization of the actual rules to ensure the proper execution of their fortnightly recital. The other of the two appears to have a more fluctuating character, in that some intentional improvement of the tale appears to be quite acceptable, if it can serve to enhance the function of the narrative in the context of teaching *Vinaya*. Such interests can even supersede the concern in the early texts to cast the Buddha in the role of an ideal teacher, as evident in the tale of the mass suicide of monks. These two modalities are of considerable relevance to discourse literature as well, wherefore I will return to them in subsequent chapters.

Although a narrative was evidently open to improvement, this does not necessarily imply a process of free improvisation. Instead, the tale of an exemplary monk willing to go on hunger strike to become a Buddhist mendicant seems to have been taken from its original setting in a discourse concerned with a different protagonist. In this way, an already existing tale appears to have been employed to enhance the *Vinaya* narrative reporting the circumstances of the promulgation of the rule on celibacy. In other words, the apparent license taken by the reciters to improve on the narrative operates within the framework of already existing textual material that is reused and adapted. Or else an improvement of a tale can be achieved through minimal means, such as when the description of killings reaching up to sixty persons becomes considerably more dramatic once this number of casualties occurred "daily."

When viewed from the perspective of the historical and cultural context, an attempt by the early Buddhist reciters to transmit with precision the code of rules would have had a precedent in the Vedic oral tradition. This type of oral transmission had acquired a high degree of precision based on a systematic training of reciters from their early youth onward. The existence of young brahmins who by the age of sixteen had already memorized the Vedas is in fact reflected in the discourses.[80]

The early Buddhist oral tradition differs in this respect, as Buddhist monastics would start training in recitation of the texts only after ordination. This usually would have taken place when they were older than young brahmins embarking on a course of training in Vedic lore.[81] Lack of training in memorization among at least those Buddhist reciters who did not come from a brahmin family would provide a background for understanding why variations can occur even in relation to the code of rules.

As briefly mentioned earlier, in the case of the codes of rules for nuns such variations are more pronounced. Suppose a monk who comes from a brahmin background takes part in transmitting the code of rules.[82] In such a case it is quite possible that he was trained in memorization in his youth. The situation of a nun would be different, however, since even if she should come from a brahmin family, as a woman she would not have stood a comparable chance of receiving such a training. For this reason, it would only be natural if a lack of memorization skills among nuns should adversely affect their transmission of the code of rules for nuns. Moreover, in the ancient setting nuns were more restricted in their movements and for this reason could not wander as freely from one monastic community to another, compared to the monks. In terms of oral transmission, this implies less of a chance for a memory error to be corrected through participation in group recitations with different nun reciters or by paying a visit to specialist monks who had memorized both codes of rules.

In this way, taking into consideration the ancient setting provides a perspective on the oral transmission of the codes of rules as a type of text which, from an emic viewpoint, was considered to be fixed rather than being open to intentional change or improvisation. Nevertheless, due to the vicissitudes of orality such a text was inevitably subject to memorization errors. Another dimension of the same oral transmission, however, concerns narrative texts that were amenable to intentional change and improvement. In the next chapter, I turn to a similar pattern evident in relation to verses and the narrative purporting to record the circumstances of their delivery.

11. Summary

The fortnightly recitation of the monastic code of rules served as the hub of the wheel of Buddhist monasticism after the death of its founder. This requires a fixed code of rules to be memorized, for which purpose the principle of concatenation can offer help by ensuring the maintenance of a particular sequence of the rules. A group recital of the code of rules led by a senior and respected monastic could result in a slip of memory not being corrected and eventually passed on to the next generation. A steady increase of such errors among different monastic communities, spread over various parts of India, appears to have been a significant factor in the gradual emergence of local and eventually separate monastic lineages that ultimately were no longer able to execute monastic observances together.

The need to inculcate proper behavior in other monastics stands in the background of the narratives that purport to record the circumstances under which a particular rule was promulgated. These narratives were evidently not seen as fixed in a manner comparable to the respective rules, leaving room for embellishment to enhance their function in a teaching context. In this way, two complementary modalities of oral transmission can be identified, with a core text (here the code of rules) of a more fixed type embedded in an explanatory text (here the promulgation narrative) of a more fluent type.

Variations occurring even in the apparently more fixed type of text can best be understood from the viewpoint of the ancient Indian setting, where Buddhist reciters for the most part would have lacked the thorough training in memorization skills that enabled Vedic reciters to transmit their texts with a remarkable degree of precision.

II. Discourse and Verse Collections

With this chapter my exploration shifts from texts on monastic discipline to the discourses. First, I introduce the four main discourse collections. Then I turn to verse collections found in addition to these four; in particular I study the relationship between verses and the prose description of the circumstances believed to have led to their delivery.

1. The Four Discourse Collections (*Āgama*)

The textual accounts of the first communal recitation (*saṅgīti/saṃgīti*), found in the different *Vinaya*s, report that the teachings given by the Buddha and his chief disciples were compiled into four collections. Although these accounts must have been influenced by later conceptions of scriptural canonicity and are preferably not read as conveying definite historical facts, their agreement on this basic fourfold division makes it probable that such a way of arranging the discourse material for oral transmission is relatively early.

The division adopted in this way assembles discourses according to length: long discourses, medium-length discourses, and short discourses. Furthermore, short discourses are collected according to two principles, placing together either those that share a particular topic or else those that share the employment of a particular number in their exposition. The purpose of portioning off discourses in this way is to facilitate their oral transmission, as it enables training reciters to memorize just one of these collections. As noted by Salomon (2011, 175),

> just as the Vedic tradition involved a division of labor whereby separate groups of specialists were responsible for the study,

> teaching, and ritual application of different classes of Vedic mantras, so too did the Buddhists develop the *bhāṇaka* [reciter] system whereby different monks specialized in the recitation of different *nikāya*s or sub-groupings of the vast corpus of *sūtra*s.

Most *Vinaya*s refer to the resultant four discourse collections as "what has come down," *āgama*, which could less literally be translated as "tradition." The Theravāda *Vinaya* instead employs the term "collection," *nikāya*.[83] Each of these two terms is attested in epigraphic evidence.[84]

The term *āgama* occurs regularly in Pāli discourses, although in such instances it appears in the singular, apparently serving as a referent to the entire corpus of orally transmitted texts.[85] This suggests a transition from a single corpus of such texts, "the *āgama*," to a division into four *āgama*s (or *nikāya*s) for the purpose of facilitating oral transmission.

In most *Vinaya*s, the Buddha's attendant Ānanda recites these discourse collections in reply to repeated questioning by Mahākassapa/Mahākāśyapa, another senior disciple reportedly still alive when the Buddha passed away.[86] Although this description is found in several *Vinaya*s, it needs be kept in mind that its depiction could be part of a fairly evident tendency in the different accounts of the first communal recitation to set a contrast between Mahākassapa/Mahākāśyapa and Ānanda, throwing into relief the eminence of the former at the expense of the latter.[87]

An alternative description in one *Vinaya* instead reports that Ānanda recited the texts on his own. According to this version, before the actual recital he had requested the assembled monastics to correct him if they noticed he had made an error, encouraging them to have no hesitation to speak up because of their respect for him.[88] This depiction more closely resembles the procedure relevant at an early stage for the group recitation of the code of rules. Another *Vinaya* offers a depiction of similar relevance to the recital of the rules, reporting that the textual collections were recited by the assembled monastics and the role of Ānanda was just to help out if they should have a lapse of memory.[89] In this way, in these two *Vinaya*s Ānanda has a more authoritative role that is better in keeping with the motif, portrayed in other texts, of his eminence in learning and his constant close association with the Buddha. Whatever may be the last word on these variations, taken together they exemplify different modalities of group recitation.

2. The Long Discourse Collections

In what follows I introduce each of the four main discourse collections, beginning with the long discourses. Complete collections of such long discourses by three distinct transmission lineages are still in existence. One of these three is extant in the Pāli language, this being the Theravāda "Collection of Long [Discourses]" (*Dīghanikāya*). This collection groups discourses into three main divisions, beginning with a Chapter on the Aggregate of Morality (*Sīlakkhandavagga*), which contains thirteen discourses.

The rationale behind grouping these discourses together appears to be based on the sharing of a description of the gradual path of training by twelve of the thirteen discourses assembled in this way. The gradual path account describes in detail the progress of a disciple from going forth via various practices and meditative attainments to the final goal.[90] In an oral setting, grouping together discourses that share such a substantial portion of text facilitates memorization, because the whole portion needs to be committed to memory only once. Such grouping is still advantageous when transmission shifts to the written medium, as the full text needs to be written out only at its first occurrence and afterward can be abbreviated, saving time and writing material (the latter being probably an important concern in a manuscript culture). Although the first discourse in this chapter of the collection does not have the gradual path account, it has a long exposition on morality which overlaps with sections of the standard description of the gradual path and to that extent similarly facilitates memorization and later writing out.

Next in the same collection comes the Great Chapter (*Mahāvagga*), in which seven out of ten discourses carry the qualification "great" in their titles. This thus appears to have served as the reference point for the emergence of this chapter. The final and third division is the Chapter [Beginning with] Pāṭika (*Pāṭikavagga*), named after the title of the first of its eleven discourses, the Discourse on Pāṭika[putta] (*Pāṭikasutta*). This chapter serves for allocating miscellaneous long discourses not included in the previous two chapters.

The Pāli collection of long discourses has a counterpart in another such collection extant in Sanskrit fragments, whose reciters appear to have been members of the Mūlasarvāstivāda monastic tradition(s). According to the reconstruction, based on the fragment remains,[91] this collection begins with a Section on Six Discourses (*Ṣaṭsūtrakanipāta*). Then comes a Section on Pairs (*Yuganipāta*) with eighteen discourses, and a Section on the Aggregate of Morality (*Śīlaskandhanipāta*), which comprises twenty-three discourses.

The reconstruction of the order of discourses in this collection from fragmentary manuscript remains relies in particular on summary verses (*uddāna*). Such summary verses are found frequently at the end of sections of the various discourse collections, listing key words that reflect the title or content of the discourses included in such a section. The main purpose of compiling such lists of key words appears to have been to serve as a memory aid for recitation, making sure that no discourse was left out and that their proper sequence was maintained. This function is comparable to the concatenation of rules discussed in the previous chapter. As with the grouping together of texts that share standardized descriptions, the employment of such summary verses continues to be of relevance once transmission shifts to the written medium.

The collection of long discourses extant in Sanskrit fragments shares with its Pāli counterpart the idea of grouping discourses on the aggregate of morality together. However, the actual sequence of arranging the discourses and their overall count differ. The Pāli collection has thirty-four discourses, whereas the collection extant in Sanskrit fragments contains altogether forty-seven discourses.

A third collection of long discourses, transmitted by Dharmaguptaka reciters, is extant in a Chinese translation done in 413 CE by the local monk Zhu Fonian, based on what appears to have been a Prakrit original recited from memory by the Indian monk Buddhayaśas. Besides this collection, some long discourses have also been translated individually into Chinese.[92] This state of affairs appears to reflect the way in which texts arrived in China and were then translated, in the sense that the Indic originals of these individual long discourses could have been part of a discourse collection.

Rendering an Indic text into Chinese involves bridging two languages that are substantially different from each other. This makes it a rather demanding task to transform a text from one language to the other without a change or even loss of meaning. At the same time, however, the extant *Āgama* translations can serve as important testimonies to early Buddhist thought.

Of the three extant collections of long discourses, the collection of long discourses extant in Chinese translation is the shortest one in terms of number of texts, as it has only thirty discourses. Unlike its two counterparts surveyed above, this collection falls into four divisions, which contain four, fifteen, ten, and finally only a single discourse. This single discourse is exceedingly long and without a known counterpart in any of the other extant discourse collections. It contains detailed cosmological descriptions that reflect a type of thought characteristic of later times, making it probable that this text was added at some point to the collection now extant in Chinese.[93] If this should indeed have been the case, then the three collections would previously have shared the adoption of a basic tripartite structure. Another similarity is the grouping together of discourses containing the gradual path account, which in the case of the Chinese version is the task of the third division of ten discourses. Whereas the tripartite division (if the lateness of the last discourse in the Chinese collection is granted) and the grouping together of discourses covering the gradual path point to a shared origin, the final count and order of discourses differ substantially, showing that each of these collections has been evolving in its own way during the prolonged period of transmission.

Although the assembling of discourses into four collections relies in principle on the idea of respective length, the resultant collections can nevertheless be seen to reflect a somewhat specific emphasis or characteristic coverage of topics. This has been recognized in later exegesis, according to which the collection of long discourses has the specific function of refuting non-Buddhist philosophies.[94] The Buddha's ability to convert and stand his ground in debate are indeed prominent themes in the discourses found in these three collections, together with the inspiration to be gained from his exceptional qualities. Given that debates and eulogies easily become prolonged, it is perhaps not surprising if a collection of long discourses should end up containing a considerable amount of such material. According to a complementary perspective provided by the Pāli commentarial tradition, the collection of long discourses was transmitted by the disciples of the Buddha's attendant Ānanda.[95] The early discourses tend to characterize Ānanda as having a deeply devoted attitude toward the Buddha, which would fit with a prominent theme in the long discourse collections, presumably making its memorization particularly appealing to those who were of a similar inclination.

3. The Collections of Discourses of Medium Length

Collections of discourses of medium length have survived from two different transmission lineages. One of these is extant in the Pāli language as one of the four Theravāda collections, the only transmission lineage of which a complete set of the four discourse collections has been preserved. The Collection of Medium-Length [Discourses] (*Majjhima-nikāya*) groups its 152 discourses into fifteen chapters that fall into three main divisions.

The other collection of medium-length discourses has been preserved in a Chinese translation carried out by the Indian monk Saṅghadeva in 398 CE, apparently based on a written Prakrit original transmitted by monastics who were members of a Sarvāstivāda reciter lineage.[96] Despite sharing an affirmation of the doctrine that everything exists with the Mūlasarvāstivāda lineage, the respective *Vinaya*s and discourse collections differ, so that these two are better treated as separate transmission lineages.[97] The Sarvāstivāda collection of medium-length [discourses] (*Madhyamāgama*) contains altogether 222 discourses. Ninety-six of the discourses found in the Sarvāstivāda collection have a parallel in the Theravāda medium-length collection;[98] most of its other discourses have instead parallels in other Pāli discourse collections. In addition to this complete collection, several medium-length discourses of various provenances have been translated individually into Chinese,[99] and Sanskrit as well as Gāndhārī fragments of such medium-length discourses have also been preserved.[100]

One of the discourse parallels found in the two complete collections of medium-length discourses has a monastic named Bakkula/Vatkula as its protagonist, who reports having been ordained for eighty years.[101] The indication given in this way implies that the discourse could only have come into existence much later than the Buddha's demise after forty-five years of teaching activity and for this reason could not have been part of the first communal recitation (*saṅgīti/saṃgīti*).[102] This discourse is not the only such instance, reflecting a clear awareness in the tradition itself that the texts reportedly recited by Ānanda at the first communal recitation could not have been an exact match of the extant collections.[103] In the words of Silk (2015, 11), within the tradition itself there is "explicit acknowledgement that canonicity is not coextensive with recitation at the First Council." Once again, the fluidity of oral tradition becomes apparent.

Sarvāstivāda exegesis considers the collection of discourses of medium length to have an emphasis on profound doctrines for intelligent audiences.[104] A related indication can be found in the Pāli commentarial tradition, according to which this collection was transmitted by the disciples of Sāriputta/Śāriputra,[105] who in the early discourses features as a disciple outstanding in wisdom. The perspectives provided by these two later sources can be seen to converge on the idea that a memorization of this discourse collection would have been particularly relevant for reciters with a propensity for the cultivation of wisdom.

4. Topic-wise Collections

The Theravāda collection of topic-wise assembled [discourses] (*Saṃyuttanikāya*) has five main chapters, which cover fifty-six sub-chapters. The first of these five is the Chapter with Verses (*Sagāthavagga*), whose title reflects the fact that its discourses tend to include verses. Then come three chapters associated with doctrinal topics, which are the Chapter on Conditionality (*Nidānavagga*), the Chapter on the [Five] Aggregates (*Khandhavagga*), and the Chapter on the Six Sense Spheres

(*Saḷāyatanavagga*). The final chapter is the Great Chapter (*Mahāvagga*), which covers various aspects of the path (and for this reason could also have been called Chapter on the Path, *Maggavagga*, instead). The Pāli commentarial tradition attributes the transmission of this collection to the disciples of Mahākassapa/Mahākāśyapa,[106] who features in the early discourses as an austere monastic with a predilection for ascetic practices. According to Sarvāstivāda exegesis, this type of collection is particularly appropriate for providing topics for meditation.[107]

The overall count of discourses in the Pāli collection of topic-wise assembled discourses is not easily determined due to the recurrent use of abbreviation,[108] an important feature of the early Buddhist oral tradition to be explored in more detail in a subsequent chapter. Suffice it for now to say that the relevant type of abbreviation takes the form of indicating, at the end of a discourse, that the same exposition should be repeated with some specific variations. The resultant number of permutations can at times be difficult to determine with exactitude, so that counts of the discourses in the collection can range from approximately 2,900 to 7,600.

A collection of topic-wise assembled [discourses] (*Saṃyuktāgama*) has been preserved in Chinese translation by the local monk Baoyun, begun in 435 CE and based on a text stemming from a Mūlasarvāstivāda transmission lineage.[109] The original used for this translation appears to have been acquired by the Chinese pilgrim Faxian during his sojourn in Sri Lanka in the Abhayagiri monastery,[110] which at that time seems to have had lively contact with the Indian mainland and hence could have had acquired texts from other reciter traditions to be kept in its library. The Chinese translation of this topic-wise collection is nearly complete, except that the twenty-third and twenty-fifth fascicles were lost due to an accidental exchange with two fascicles containing a translation of a different text.[111] The order of the collection also fell into disarray, although this has been reconstructed based on a partial commentary on the collection found in the *Yogācārabhūmi*. Variations in the count of discourses are even more pronounced in the case of this topic-wise collection, ranging from less than about 1,400 to over 13,400.

In addition to this (nearly) complete collection, two partial translations of collections of discourses arranged topic-wise are extant, as well as several discourses translated individually.[112] Sanskrit and Gāndhārī fragments of discourses from topic-wise assembled discourse collections have also been preserved.[113] In addition, a substantial number of topic-wise discourses are extant in Tibetan translation, found in a repertoire of canonical quotations compiled by Śamathadeva.[114] Śamathadeva's work takes the form of supplementing substantial parts or even the whole discourse to brief quotations found in the *Abhidharmakośabhāṣya*. The same work by Śamathadeva also has parallels to discourses found in the other collections, although those paralleling topic-wise assembled discourses are clearly in the majority.

No entire discourse collection is extant in Tibetan translation and, besides the work just mentioned, only a few discourses translated individually into Tibetan can still be consulted.[115] It seems that early discourse collections did reach Tibet, but these appear to have been lost during a period of persecution of Buddhism,[116] which presumably did not lead to efforts to procure originals again for translation. This would reflect a gradual decline of interest in the early discourses also evident elsewhere, which ostensibly were no longer studied for their own sake but mainly served as an authoritative backup for scriptural quotations found in other texts.

5. Numerical Discourse Collections

Two complete collections of numerically assembled discourses are extant: a Theravāda collection (*Aṅguttaranikāya*) and a collection translated into Chinese (*Ekottarikāgama*) by the local monk Zhu Fonian in 384, based on what appears to have been a Prakrit original recited from memory by Dharmanandin (or Dharmananda). Several individual discourses have also been preserved in Chinese, in addition to which there is an anthology of such discourses translated by An Shigao.[117] Parts of a collection of numerical discourses are also extant in Sanskrit and Gāndhārī fragments.[118]

The basic principle of arrangement in these two collections is to assemble discourses that in some way or another refer to a particular number, beginning with Ones and proceeding in an ascending order until coming to Elevens. Numerical topics like the four noble truths, for example, are not included in this collection. In such cases the reciters evidently preferred to group relevant discourses under their topic rather than their number, with the result that these were included in the topic-wise discourse collections.[119] The division between the numerical and the topic-wise collections is in fact not always clear-cut. Some overlap can also be seen between the other collections, as the collections of long discourses can at times accommodate relatively short discourses (at least compared to those in the remainder of the collection) just as the collections of medium-length discourses have a few long specimens.

As a result of discourses on central doctrinal matters having for the most part found inclusion in the topic-wise collections, the numerical collections tend to cover more everyday issues and practical matters, without, of course, being limited to that. Sarvāstivāda exegesis indicates that this type of collection is particularly appropriate for teaching celestials and humans.[120] The Pāli commentarial tradition attributes the transmission of this collection to the disciples of Anuruddha, famous in the early discourses for his exercise of the supernormal ability called the divine eye.[121] According to tradition, direct observation of events far away, even in various celestial realms, becomes possible through the exercise of the divine eye.

The collection translated by Zhu Fonian appears to have gone through a process of revision and addition of extraneous material in China.[122] Although some of its discourses have preserved features that appear to be earlier than their Pāli parallels, other texts in this collection are distinctly late. Material of such lateness is not found in the other discourse collections in a comparable manner, showing that this collection remained open for the incorporation of later texts and ideas for a substantially longer time. This holds even though it was the first of the four main *Āgama* collections to be translated into Chinese.

As far as the Indic original is concerned, it seems possible but not certain that this was transmitted by Mahāsāṅghika reciters,[123] a tradition which formed at a relative early point in the history of the different Buddhist traditions. Texts preserved by Mahāsāṅghika transmission lineages can at times be markedly different from their counterparts.

Even though the collection of numerical discourses extant in Chinese translation appears to have gone through some substantial changes, it is important to keep in mind that the discourses in the Chinese *Āgama*s in general are not themselves products of Chinese culture.[124] Instead, except for some later additions, they are testimonies of Indian Buddhism. By way of illustration, such discourses could be compared to an Indian wearing traditional Chinese dress. However much the clothing is Chinese, the person inside remains an Indian.

I will return to the four discourse collections from the viewpoint of their oral features in the chapter after the next.

6. Discourses Without Parallels

Before examining another early classificatory scheme that distinguishes different textual limbs (*aṅga*), in what follows I first take a brief look at a feature that manifests with considerably more frequency between discourses than in the case of the codes of rules: namely, the absence of a parallel. The methodology for identifying parallels, which stands at the background of noting such absence, relies on the same basic principle for both rules and discourses. Taking as an example the rule on a breach of celibacy: from the viewpoint of the Pāli version, the rules in other *Vinaya*s that treat the same matter are parallels; those that treat other matters are not parallels. That is, the notion of a parallel intends to identify different reports of the same promulgation believed to have been made by the Buddha. Similarly, parallels to the Discourse on Pāṭika[putta], the Pāli text mentioned above, can be identified in the Chinese collection of long discourses and among Sanskrit fragments based on the same notion that, at the endpoint of their transmission that we can still access nowadays, these are different reports of a particular teaching believed to have been given by the Buddha on a certain occasion.

The binary distinction between what counts as a parallel and what does not is at times insufficient to capture the situation. A way of approaching this, based on a conceptual framework taken from the same cultural setting within which these texts came into being, can be found by relying on the ancient Indian tetralemma.[125] The tetralemma goes beyond the dual logic familiar to Western thought by allowing that, in addition to affirmation and negation, both or neither of these two options could adequately reflect the situation. In this way, in addition to the distinction between the colors black and white, for example, something could be both (namely grey) or neither (namely, for example, blue).

Applied to the case of parallelism, two discourses could be "both a parallel and not a parallel" if they share a substantial portion of text, but in addition to that, each has a substantial portion that is completely unrelated to the other. The fourth alternative, "neither a parallel nor not a parallel," then applies to cases where it does not seem possible to decide if two discourses intend to report the same instance of teaching or not. At an early stage in my research, I tried to keep these two categories distinct, but since both possibilities occur relatively rarely, it soon became clear that for the sake of simplicity and practicability it makes more sense to assemble both under the single heading of "partial" parallelism. This then results in a taxonomy of three categories: parallel, partial parallel, not a parallel. In addition to introducing this taxonomy, more remains to be said on the notion of parallelism in relation to comparative studies. Since this would take me too far away from the main concerns of the present chapter, however, I will explore this topic in more detail in a subsequent chapter (see below p. 151).

The third of the three categories just mentioned came up above in relation to the last discourse in the Chinese collection of long discourses, which is without any parallel. Although in this case the content of the discourse in question points to lateness, the very fact of lacking a parallel is not sufficient evidence for drawing such a conclusion. This is due to two factors in combination: the substantially differing distribution of discourses over the four collections in various transmission lineages and the fact that only in the case of the Theravāda tradition do we still have access to a complete set of these four collections. Discourse collections extant in Chinese translation stem from distinct transmission lineages and the available Sanskrit and Gāndhārī fragments or Tibetan translations do not provide access to a complete collection, let alone all four.

The resultant situation can be illustrated with the help of a few examples, taken from a chapter of the Theravāda collection of medium-length discourses, the Chapter on Householders (*Gahapativagga*). Several Pāli discourses in this chapter have no counterpart in the Chinese *Āgama*s. One such case is the Discourse to Jīvaka (*Jīvakasutta*).[126] Although the Chinese *Āgama* collection of medium-length discourses has no parallel to this discourse, discoveries of Sanskrit fragments belonging to a collection of long discourses contain remnants of a version of this discourse.[127] In other words, whereas the Theravāda reciters placed their version of this discourse in their medium-length collection, other reciter traditions allocated this discourse to their long discourse collection. This exemplifies that lack of a parallel can be the result of differences in the distribution of discourses among the four discourse collections, transmitted by various Buddhist schools.[128]

Another example is the Discourse on What Is Sure (*Apaṇṇakasutta*); a few parts of a version of this Pāli text have been preserved in Sanskrit fragments.[129] Another example from the same chapter is the Discourse to Prince Abhaya (*Abhayarājakumāra-sutta*).[130] Even though no parallel is known in the Chinese *Āgama*s, a Sanskrit fragment and a quotation in a later work reflect the existence of other versions of this discourse.[131] Yet another example is the Discourse on the Observance [of Behaving Like] a Dog (*Kukkuravatikasutta*), for which no parallel is known either in the Chinese *Āgama*s or in Sanskrit fragments. Nevertheless, an exposition in an early Abhidharma work on the four types of action covered in this discourse explicitly refers by name to the protagonist of the discourse, who was observing the ascetic practice of behaving like a cow.[132] There can be little doubt that this reference reflects acquaintance with a version of this discourse.

In this way, even within a single chapter (which contains altogether only ten discourses), four instances can be identified of Pāli discourses that are without counterpart in the Chinese *Āgama*s, yet Sanskrit fragments or discourse quotations preserved in later sources document the existence of parallel versions. Needless to say, the obverse also applies, in that the circumstance that a particular discourse is without a Pāli parallel does not automatically imply that it must be late. Skilling (2020b, 338) points out:

> The notion that a text must have a Pali counterpart to be authentic, that a text without any Pali counterpart is inauthentic, did not exist in early, or even pre-modern, India. It is a modern idea, developed during the nineteenth-century colonial encounter and elaborated up to the present. It developed by default because the Pali collection was the sole surviving canon, and because, when the British colonized Lanka and Burma, it was this canon that the Orientalists encountered and studied.

7. The Textual "Limbs"

The early discourses on several occasions mention a list of *aṅga*s, which literally refer to "limbs" or "members." In the present context this could be understood to mean a limb of a particular text, in the sense of being an aspect or characteristic of this text, or else a limb of the whole corpus of teachings, in the sense of a textual collection (as is the case for the term *aṅga* in the Jain tradition). Rather than considering these textual limbs to have had such a function,[133] which would make them comparable to the textual collections surveyed above, the majority of scholars tends to favor the alternative option of considering these *aṅga*s to intend types of texts or styles of textual composition.[134]

A Pāli discourse passage mentions these textual limbs and at the same time also refers to the term *āgama* in the singular. Below I translate this passage, where my rendering of the textual limbs reflects my (necessarily limited) understanding of their significance, rather than being an attempt to provide a literal translation:[135]

> A monastic masters the teaching: prose with a list, prose mixed with verse,[136] an explanation,[137] a verse, an inspired utterance, a quotation, a tale of the past,[138] a marvel, and question-and-answer (between disciples).[139] They teach others in detail the

> teaching as they have heard and byhearted it. They make others recite in detail the teaching as they have heard and byhearted it. They rehearse in detail the teaching as they have heard and byhearted it. They reflect, ponder, and consider in their minds the teaching as they have heard and byhearted it.
>
> They enter the rainy season in a residence in which elder monastics live who are of much learning, have acquired the transmission (*āgama*), who know by heart the teaching, know by heart the discipline, and know by heart the summaries. Approaching them from time to time, they inquire and ask questions: "Venerable sir, how is this, what is its meaning?"

In the above passage, the (singular) *āgama* occurs alongside the listing of nine textual limbs,[140] giving the impression that these two were not seen as conflicting with each other. Instead, they seem to stand for complementary perspectives on the corpus of teachings to be memorized. The passage conveniently spells out key aspects of orality in the ancient setting. On the assumption that the nine textual limbs stand for textual types, the passage would begin by highlighting mastery of the variety of teachings. This in turn forms the basis for contributing to the continuity of oral transmission by passing on the texts to others, as well as making others rehearse these texts. In addition, there is of course also the need to rehearse regularly oneself in order to counter the failings of memory, a topic to be taken up again at the end of this chapter. Such memorization has its complement in cultivating an understanding of what those teachings convey, by reflecting and pondering on them. The understanding gained in this way can be developed further by approaching learned reciters who are versed in "the *āgama*," in order to ask questions and get the meaning of the teachings clarified.

If the nine textual limbs listed above did not refer to textual collections for apportioning discourses, what could have been their function? A survey of references to these textual limbs yields the impression that they tend to convey a sense of the variety of the teachings and thereby serve as a convenient reference to the acquisition of oral learning.[141] At the same time, however, it seems that the textual limbs only performed their function during an early period of oral transmission and apparently fell out of use relatively soon, as by the time of the commentaries their overall role and individual significance is no longer clear.

When considered from the perspective of the beginning stages in the evolution of the early Buddhist oral tradition, a circumstance of relevance could be that discourse titles appear to have come into being only gradually, often showing a considerable degree of variety.[142] Although some titles appear to be early, something to be taken up again below in relation to two early verse collections, others can be quite late. Such fluidity can be seen even with records of the same discourse in separate collections or even in various Pāli editions of the same collection, where at times otherwise closely similar texts carry different titles. An example involving separate discourse collections is the Pāli Discourse on Many Feelings, which recurs in another Pāli collection as the Discourse to Pañcakaṅga,[143] a change of title that shifts attention from the content of the exposition to one of its protagonists. A few examples for variations between Pāli editions of the same collection are the Discourse on the Noble Quest, which in the Burmese and Siamese editions becomes the Discourse on the Snare, the Discourse with an Instruction to Rāhula [given at] Ambalaṭṭhika, which in the Siamese edition becomes the Lesser Discourse with an Instruction to Rāhula, and the Great Discourse on the Six Sense Spheres, which in the Siamese edition becomes the Discourse with an Analysis of the Six Sense Spheres.[144] The same type of fluidity can also be seen in reports of the Buddha concluding a discourse by giving it a set of several different titles rather than just one.[145]

If during an early stage of oral transmission discourses were memorized without necessarily having a definite title, the question arises how the monastic described in the passage translated above would have formulated a question to be posed to the learned elders. To do that, some way of referencing a particular teaching would have been required. In such a setting, perhaps the textual limbs served as an additional tool to specify a particular teaching. The monastic might inquire about the "inspired utterance" spoken by the Buddha at such and such a place or about the "explanation" given by a particular eminent disciple to such and such a person, etc. On this hypothesis, the textual limbs could have provided a way of distinguishing different teachings. Such a function would then have become obsolete once the corpus of orally transmitted texts became more formally organized, with discourses receiving a title and, perhaps even more importantly, a placing in some discourse collection that can serve as an additional identifier. To the degree to which such organizational principles became finalized, to that degree the textual limbs would have lost individual importance, with only the full list still serving as a referent to the variety of the teachings.

From the viewpoint of this hypothesis, it is of interest to turn to a feature of the actual listing of these textual limbs in relation to the principle of "waxing syllables," introduced in the last chapter. The list of nine textual limbs can be seen to fall into three subunits:

> First subunit, basic modes of exposition: prose with a list, prose mixed with verse, explanations;
> *sutta geyya veyyākaraṇa*,
> syllable count; 2+2+5.
>
> Second subunit, shorter textual pieces: verse, inspired utterance, quotation;
> *gātha udāna itivuttaka*,
> syllable count: 2+3+5.
>
> Third subunit, other textual elements: a tale of the past, question-and-answer, marvel;
> *jātaka vedalla abbhutadhamma* (order emended),
> syllable count: 3+3+5.

In the case of the last subunit, I have emended the Pāli order on the assumption that the last two members may have exchanged their places. Support for this suggestion can be garnered from a range of listings of the textual limbs in other traditions, in which these two occur in the sequence opposite to the Pāli version.[146] This emendation supports the application of the principle of waxing syllables. Beyond that, however, it is of no further relevance to my present discussion, as it does not affect the division into three subunits.

The three subunits evident in this way could indeed have facilitated identifying particular expositions. The first subunit would enable discerning between a discourse that revolves around a particular list, one that repeats verse in prose, and one that provides explanations. The second subunit of more specific items further increases the ability to classify, by offering the possibility to refer to a verse, an inspired utterance, or a quote of what has been said on another occasion. Still more specific, in the sense of occurring with considerably less frequency, would be a tale of the past (of the type that eventually was considered to involve a past life of the Buddha), a question-and-answer exchange between disciples, and a marvel.

Understood in this way, the three subunits of textual limbs described above would have fulfilled a meaningful function, namely to identify a particular teaching at a time when these had not yet acquired a definite placing in a particular textual collection nor received a finalized title. Although this fits my hypothesis developed above, it needs to be kept in mind that, unlike the case of most conclusions drawn elsewhere in this study, in the present instance I am not able to marshal direct textual evidence in support of the suggested function of the textual limbs. In other words, what I have presented here is, after all, just a hypothesis.

8. Verse Collections

In addition to verses occurring as part of an exposition given in a discourse, verses gathered on their own have also occasioned the emergence of textual collections. In the Theravāda tradition these are found in the fifth "collection," *nikāya*, which contains a miscellany of texts, some of which are distinctly late.[147] Several verse collections found in this fifth collection, however, appear to reflect roughly the same period in the development of Buddhist thought as the discourses in the four main collections, surveyed above. Perhaps the most famous of these verse collections has the title "Words of the Teaching," generally known under its Pāli name *Dhammapada* (Sanskrit: *Dharmapada*). This Pāli collection contains 423 verses arranged in 26 chapters, which are often but not exclusively related to a particular topic, such as the "fool" (the fifth chapter), the "wise" (the sixth), and the arahant/arhat (the seventh), for example.[148] Prakrit and Gāndhārī versions of this collection are extant,[149] as well as two versions translated into Chinese.[150] Notably, one of these collections extant in Chinese combines the verses with prose narrations reporting the circumstances leading to the delivery of the verse(s) in question,[151] something that in the Pāli tradition is found rather in a commentary on the *Dhammapada*.[152]

Another Pāli collection brings together various "inspired utterances," *udāna*, to be examined in more detail below. Notably, this collection thereby takes as its title one of the nine textual limbs. The same holds for a collection of texts titled "This Was Said," *Itivuttaka*. The Pāli version of this collection contains 112 short discourses, each ending in a verse, arranged numerically proceeding from Ones to Fours. According to the Pāli commentary, the discourses in this collection had originally been heard by a lay woman named Khujjutarā, who in turn passed these on to the women in the royal harem of King Udena of Kosambī.[153]

Although it is of course no longer possible to verify this indication, it is noteworthy that the *Itivuttaka* stands out for adopting an introductory formula for its texts that differs from the standard formulation found in other discourses. The standard Pāli formulation is "thus have I heard" (*evaṃ me sutaṃ*), followed by providing information about the location where the discourse was believed to have been originally delivered.[154] The introduction to discourses in the *Itivuttaka*, however, has the following beginning: "This was said by the Blessed One, said by the arahant, so I have heard."[155] This departure from the standard formulation is not an idiosyncrasy of the Theravāda tradition, as a Sanskrit fragment version and a Chinese parallel to the *Itivuttaka* also have unique opening formulas, additionally also sharing with the Pāli version the feature of not mentioning any location.[156] From the viewpoint of the Pāli background story, the lack of such a mention would be natural, since the discourses in this collection were invariably given when the Buddha was staying at Khujjutarā's native town Kosambī/Kauśāmbī. Once the location was understood to be invariably the same, the reciters did presumably not feel any need to furnish explicit indications in this respect for each discourse.

The same pattern of unique formulas recurs again in the standard transition from prose to verse, which is similarly peculiar to the *Itivuttaka*: "This is the meaning of what the Blessed One said; in regard to this, it was said like this."[157] The Sanskrit and Chinese parallels also have such peculiar transition formulas.[158] The same pattern even extends to the concluding formula in *Itivuttaka* discourses: "This meaning was also said by the Blessed One, so I have heard it," a peculiarity also reflected in the Sanskrit version (the Chinese parallel lacks conclusions).[159]

These peculiar features evidently resisted the natural tendency of oral transmission to stereotype formulaic parts like the introduction and conclusion of a discourse or the transition from prose to verse in line with the phrasing used in other discourses. It follows that some degree of formalization of the material for oral transmission already took place at a very early stage, in line with what is in fact typical for orally formed text in traditional societies. In the present case, such formal aspects were apparently passed on unchanged by subsequent generations of reciters, without being adjusted to fit the form of other discourses. Moreover, the different compass of the parallel versions of this collection points to the integration of material from other discourse collections,[160] which appears to have been adjusted to the new setting by way of application of these peculiar formulations. In other words, a stereotyping of some such formulas took place, but this happened in line with the peculiar characteristics of this collection rather than adopting the procedure used elsewhere.

If one were to assume that the formalization of the discourses had only begun at a comparatively late point in time, the procedure used in the case of other discourses should have been applied similarly to the discourses in the *Itivuttaka* and its counterparts. The evidence available in this way does not support the idea of an early stage of free textual fluctuation followed after some time by a period of formalization resulting in fixed texts. Instead, the impression is one of a continuous and complex process of negotiation between formal elements and the natural fluctuations of orality, leading to the combination of stability and alteration that comparative study shows to be so characteristic of the early discourses.

9. Two Early Verse Collections

Another Pāli verse collection is the Section of Discourses (*Suttanipāta*), which falls into five chapters that are for the most part in verse, with occasional prose sections. The last two chapters appear to have been transmitted independently for some time before becoming part of the collection—yet another pointer to the fluidity of oral transmission.

One indication relevant to the nature of these chapters is that commentaries on just these two, providing explanations of expressions used in them, came into existence so early that they were included in the fifth collection (*nikāya*) alongside the text on which they comment.[161] Moreover, each of these two chapters is quoted as a stand-alone collection in other discourses.[162] One such quotation occurs in the two collections of topic-wise assembled discourses; the reference speaks of the Query by Māgandiya and indicates its placing to be the Chapter of Eights (*Aṭṭhakavagga*), the first of the two chapters under discussion here.[163] The different versions of this quote continue with a discussion of the significance of the passage quoted from this discourse. Another reference occurs in the collection of inspired utterances, *Udāna* (to be discussed below), as well as in a range of *Vinayas*.[164] According to the narrative context, the Buddha had asked a monastic by the name of Soṇa to recite some teachings, to which the latter complied by reciting the complete Chapter of Eights. The reference is of additional interest as it depicts the Buddha himself checking whether a particular monastic had memorized the teachings. Allon (2021, 22) comments that this episode "suggests that the initial training for Soṇa and probably also for other new monastics included memorizing and learning to recite texts."

The other of the two chapters under discussion is the Chapter on Going Beyond (*Pārāyanavagga*).[165] A reference that explicitly mentions this collection names the relevant discourse as the Query by Metteyya.[166] Other discourses record the Buddha quoting himself by referring to the Query by Puṇṇaka or to the Query by Udaya, and to the collection in which these are found.[167]

These instances can be contrasted with the case of two references to discourses found in the collections of long and topic-wise discourses, respectively. Both just mention the name of the discourse, without providing further indications regarding its location.[168] Yet another instance, which involves the quotation of a verse now found in the collection of Inspired Utterances (*Udāna*), appears without either name or location and thus only specifies that the verse was spoken by the Buddha.[169]

The explicit indications regarding title and location in the Chapter of Eights and the Chapter on Going Beyond could of course be later additions. However, in such a case it could reasonably well be expected that comparable indications would also have been added to other quotations of discourses or verses found elsewhere.

From an emic viewpoint, the Chapter of Eights and the Chapter on Going Beyond had already come into existence during the Buddha's lifetime. Although the historical accuracy of the picture that emerges in this way can no longer be verified, at least it seems to offer a reasonable scenario. For the purpose of oral transmission, the grouping together of verses into collections would have come in handy. In the case of the Chapter on Going Beyond, this would also have been quite natural, given that all its verses are associated with the same time and location.

A grouping of the discourses into four collections, however, could in turn have been motivated by the Buddha's passing away, as a result of which the continuously growing body of new teachings emerging in the course of his various instructions and encounters had come to something of a concluding point. In such a situation, the idea to create a more formalized body of the extant texts to be transmitted to future generations, by way of allocating discourses to four distinct collections, would have been a convenient way to proceed. Whatever may be the final word on this scenario, the gradually evolving and complex nature of the early Buddhist oral tradition can hardly be doubted.

10. The Chapter on Eights

Besides Sanskrit and Gāndhārī fragment parallels,[170] the Pāli version of the Chapter of Eights (*Aṭṭhakavagga*) has a Chinese counterpart preserved as a text on its own.[171] Whereas the Pāli version is entirely in verse, its parallels embed their verses in prose narrations. These narrations, fully preserved only in the Chinese version, have a function similar to the origination stories of monastic rules surveyed in the previous chapter, in the sense of reporting the circumstances believed to have led to the set of verses in question. The same holds for the stories found in a Chinese parallel to the *Dhammapada*, mentioned above, as well as in the Pāli commentary on the *Dhammapada*. Similar to the case of the *Dhammapada*, the stories that are believed to stand in the background of the verses of the Chapter of Eights are found in the Pāli commentarial tradition (different from the commentaries already mentioned that are now found in the fifth canonical collection).

At times, the information provided in the prose sections found in the Chinese version and the Pāli commentary is required to be able to understand a particular verse in the Chapter of Eights. A case in point is the first verse in the Discourse to Māgandiya (*Māgandiyasutta*),[172] presented below by giving first the Pāli version and then the Chinese parallel:[173]

> Having seen Craving, Discontent, and Lust,
> Even then there was no desire for sexual intercourse.
> What, then, about this, full of urine and feces,
> Which even with my foot I would not wish to touch?
>
> When I formerly saw the three deceptive females,
> Still, there was no passion for improper sexual intercourse.
> Now, what about embracing urine and feces?
> Even with the foot it should not be touched.

Acquaintance with early Buddhist thought enables deciphering the reference to "Craving, Discontent, and Lust" and its Chinese counterpart in the "three deceptive females" as intending the three daughters of Māra. However, since these three are celestials, which according to ancient Indian thought do not partake of solid food and have no digestive system, the ensuing reference to urine and feces could not apply to them and is somewhat baffling.

The narrative common to the Chinese version and the Pāli commentary reports that the brahmin Māgandiya wanted to marry his beautiful daughter to the Buddha. In other words, the reference to urine and feces serves as the Buddha's rather strongly worded rejection of this offer, conveying his total disinterest in Māgandiya's daughter. It seems fair to assume that the basic idea of such an offer, common to the two traditions, would have accompanied the verse from an early period onward, simply because an oral performance of the verse without some such explanation would have failed to be understood.

The probably close relationship between prose and verse evident in this way can be contrasted with the case of the Discourse on Quarrels and Disputes (*Kalahavivādasutta*), which offers a penetrative analysis of the mental roots of quarrels and disputes. The Pāli commentary considers this to be one of several instances when the Buddha had an exchange with another mind-made Buddha created by himself for the purpose of holding a discussion in front of a large gathering of celestials.[174] The same commentary recurrently employs this trope for quite different discourses in the Chapter of Eights. This gives the impression that this tale may have served to furnish the missing context for verses that were originally handed down without further indications about their setting and what prompted their delivery. At the same time, the repeated use of the same story as the background narration for quite different verses also points to an element of conservatism, comparable to the origination stories discussed in the previous chapter (see above p. 30).

Although the Chinese version also employs the trope of the Buddha creating another mind-made Buddha,[175] its background story differs substantially, as it depicts the Buddha defeating six contemporary teachers through the performance of miraculous feats.[176] Such a framing hardly does justice to verses whose concern is overcoming the inner roots of dispute rather than conquering opponents in a contest of supernormal powers.

Overall, according to Bapat (1950, 98) "no less than seven . . . of the sixteen Chinese stories introducing these sūtras are quite different" from the stories found in the Pāli commentary. The resultant combination of divergences and similarities suggests a gradual process of development. Some prose commentary would have come into existence relatively early and for this reason is shared between the Chinese version and the respective Pāli commentary. Other instances of such prose commentary, however, appear to have emerged only later and for that reason differ substantially in the two extant traditions.

The integration of narrative material that according to tradition stands in the background to the delivery of the verses in question can also be seen in the case of the Chapter on Going Beyond. The first part of this chapter has an introductory narration in verse that is later than the actual collection.[177] This gives the impression that, comparable to the case of the Chinese counterpart to the Chapter of Eights, here the Pāli collection has incorporated such later textual material. The main difference is only that, since the verses collected in the Chapter on Going Beyond were believed to have been spoken on a single occasion, the depiction of the setting occurs only once at the outset, rather than serving as an introduction to each single discourse.

11. Inspired Utterances

A pattern similar to the one just discussed can be seen in the Pāli collection of "Inspired Utterances," *Udāna*. The *Udāna* collection falls into eight chapters, with ten discourses in each. The resultant eighty discourses come with a prose narration reporting the circumstances believed to have led to the respective inspired utterance(s). Parallels to this collection extant in other languages, however, for the most part do not provide such prose narrations.[178] The main exception is a collection extant in Chinese translation, which shows a similar combination of inspired utterances with prose material.[179] However, rather than presenting a background narration, the prose portions in this work often take the form of a word commentary, in the sense of quoting selected words from the inspired utterance and then offering explanations of their significance. A comparative study shows that in only three cases do the Pāli version and its Chinese parallel provide a similar prose narration to a particular verse.[180]

From the viewpoint of oral transmission, this points to a pattern of prose material being added to an existing collection of inspired utterances.[181] At times, such later addition can result in a misfit. A case comparable in this respect to the Discourse on Quarrels and Disputes, discussed above, occurs in relation to the following inspired utterance:[182]

> What is the use of a well,
> If water is there all the time?
> Having cut craving at its root,
> What would one go searching for?

Whereas the stanza uses the image of the well as an illustration, the prose reports that brahmins of a particular village had blocked a well with chaff to prevent the Buddha and his disciples from drinking. When the Buddha requested his attendant to fetch some water for him, the well threw up all chaff by itself and was filled with clean water to the brim. This miracle is then supposed to be the occasion for the delivery of the above stanza. Pande (1957, 75) comments that "the author of the prose . . . seems to have grossly misunderstood the final verse, which intends 'water' in no more than a merely figurative sense." The Chinese parallel in fact does not mention any such incident and instead provides an interpretation of the well imagery.[183]

Closer inspection of the Pāli *Udāna* collection points to a gradual process of associating prose material with the inspired utterances, rather than a onetime combination of these two types of text.[184] One of the relevant features supporting such an impression concerns thematic continuity among inspired utterances collected in each chapter of the collection. During oral transmission, such thematic continuity helps to keep a series of verses or stanzas together. In the case of the first four chapters, all of the ten inspired utterances in each chapter share the same theme: a "brahmin," "happiness," a "monastic," and the "mind." In chapters 5 and 6 such thematic continuity holds only for four out of ten inspired utterances, and in chapters 7 and 8 for only two out of ten. Thus, the degree to which thematic continuity among inspired utterances serves its role of facilitating oral transmission decreases gradually.

Another relevant feature is concatenation, a principle already discussed in the previous chapter in relation to the sequence of the rules (and to be discussed again in a later chapter in relation to the sequence of discourses in a collection). Just as concatenation can ensure that the rules are recited in order, the same principle can also facilitate the recitation of a verse collection in order. The way this works can be illustrated with the example of the third chapter in the *Udāna* collection. The extracts below present only the part of each verse that relates to the next.[185]

> A monastic . . . is firm (3.1),
> A monastic is not perturbed (3.2).
>
> A monastic has crushed the thorn of sensuality . . . and is not perturbed by pleasure and pain (3.2),
> A monastic has overcome the thorn of sensuality . . . and is not perturbed by pleasure and pain (3.3).
>
> Firm like a mountain (3.3),
> Like a solid mountain . . . like a mountain (3.4).
>
> Unshakeable and well established (3.4).
> With mindfulness of the body established (3.5).

From the viewpoint of the whole collection, instances of such concatenation are a recurrent feature in the first three chapters of the *Udāna*, still evident in the fourth, hardly noticeable in the sixth and seventh, and completely absent in the fifth and eighth chapters. In this way, only in the first few chapters of the collection does concatenation offer strong support for an accurate recall of individual inspired utterances in their proper sequence.

In the case of prose material, the inverse situation to the above can be observed. In the first four chapters, similar or related narratives can at times occur at considerable distance from each other. In contrast, in the fifth to eighth chapters such narrations tend to occur in close proximity. In other words, whereas thematic continuity and concatenation point to the inspired utterances on their own being the central point of reference for the formation of the first four chapters, in the case of the fifth to eighth chapters the content of the prose narration appears to have been the central factor for determining the sequence of the discourses and thereby ensuring the maintenance of the "correct" sequence (in the sense of being the sequence adopted by a particular reciter tradition) during oral transmission.

The overall impression is one of a gradual and complex growth of the collection, whose first chapters must have been based on assembling just inspired utterances. At that time, thematic continuity and concatenation among the actual inspired utterances were central tools to facilitate oral transmission. When prose was subsequently added, the linkage between the inspired utterances no longer had as strong an effect as earlier, because the inspired utterances came to be separated from each other through at times long sections of prose text. Nevertheless, the sequence initially established through the verses continued to be transmitted. During the gradual growth of the collection, in the later part of the collection the role of facilitating accurate recall was taken by similarities among the prose narrations. This gives the impression that the inspired utterances in these chapters would have already been embedded in their accompanying prose when this part of the collection was formed.

12. Textual Memory

The perspectives that emerge from a study of the Chapter of Eights and the collection of Inspired Utterances points to patterns of oral transmission similar to those evidenced in the previous chapter. A core text, be this the code of rules or verses/inspired utterances, comes embedded in a prose narration purporting to record the circumstances leading to the delivery of the core text itself. Comparative study shows that such prose narrations were considerably more open to change than the corresponding core texts.

At the same time, comparative study of the verse collections surveyed above brings to light differences comparable to those observed among various codes of rules. It seems fair to propose that this reflects again the impact of lack of memorization training among Buddhist reciters compared to their Vedic predecessors. Of additional significance here is that, in the Vedic model, young brahmin reciters trained in memorizing texts whose meaning they only learned later. Bronkhorst (2016, 164) explains:

> Vedic memorization, which a youngster acquires in his teens or even before, uses special techniques to make sure that no syllable of the text committed to memory be lost. Understanding the content of what is learnt by heart is not part of this training, and is sometimes claimed to be a hindrance rather than a help.

The idea of considering an understanding of the text a hindrance to memorization acquires further significance in view of research on textual memory in cognitive psychology. The relevant experiment presented instructions about the use of Microsoft Word and Microsoft Excel to three groups of readers, asking them to remember the text. Subsequently, memory was tested through a recognition task in which the participants had to decide if a particular statement had been made in the original text. Of these participants, the first group had no experience with computer software at all, the second group had some experience, and the third group had advanced knowledge of computer software. Contrary to the expectations of the researchers, those who had no experience with computer software at all were more rapidly able to recognize sentences correctly than members of the other two groups.[186]

This finding on the workings of human memory helps to appreciate the nature and limitations of the early Buddhist oral transmission. Situated in their historical and cultural context, the early Buddhist reciters would naturally have tried to follow their precedent in the Vedic oral tradition. Yet, the oral transmission of the Vedic texts had acquired a high degree of precision not only based on a systematic training of reciters from their early youth onward, but also because these at first did not understand what they were memorizing. The reason why this worked so well for the Vedic reciters was precisely because they did not comprehend the content of what they were byhearting, in line with what the experiment with

Microsoft Word and Excel suggests. Understanding the text would have hindered their ability to memorize it with high precision.

This makes it even more understandable why the early Buddhist oral transmission did not arrive at a level of precision comparable to the Vedic reciters. As the passage translated earlier on the textual limbs clearly conveys, the reciters were expected to proceed from memorizing to reflecting on what they had learned and even approach elders to get the meaning clarified. In view of this basic difference in approach, compared to their Vedic brethren, one would indeed expect variations to arise during successive generations of Buddhist reciters. Their attempt to memorize with precision must have been hampered, if I may use this word, by their understanding.

Awareness within the tradition that a lack of understanding makes for a more trustworthy memorization can be seen in a range of exegetical-type passages collected by Silk (2020), which emphasize Ānanda's inability to understand fully the teachings of the Buddha that he had memorized and, according to the traditional account, recited at the first communal recitation.[187] In light of the Vedic precedent and contemporary research on textual memory, it becomes understandable why attributing a lack of understanding to Ānanda would enhance his status as the one who was believed to have had such a central role at the outset of the early Buddhist oral transmission. His want of comprehension would have made it appear more probable that he transmitted accurately what he had heard.

13. Summary

The oral transmission of the teachings believed to have been given by the Buddha and his disciples appears to have evolved from a continually growing corpus, the single *āgama*, to taking the form of four discourse collections mainly assembled based on the length of a discourse, with short discourses further allocated according to topic or else numerical theme.

Although the *Vinaya*s associate the division into four discourse collections with a communal recitation held soon after the Buddha's demise, tradition clearly recognizes that the collections that have come down to us could not have been finalized at that time.

References to textual limbs do not appear to have served a comparable function of providing a scaffolding for apportioning discourses. Instead, listings of nine or twelve such textual limbs seem to have functioned as references to textual types. Perhaps the identification of such textual limbs served as an aid for identifying a particular teaching, be it for the purpose of recitation or teaching, at a time when the respective discourses had not yet received a fixed placing in some collection and perhaps not even a definite title.

Alongside the four main discourse collections, the evolving corpus of oral texts also comprises several verse collections. Some of these combine verses with prose narrations that purport to record the circumstances of the poetic utterance in question. The relationship that emerges in this way, between a more stable core text and its more fluid prose embedding, appears to be similar to the case of the monastic rules and their promulgation narratives. In both cases, it seems fair to assume that the lack of thorough training in memorization skills influenced the attempt of Buddhist reciters to pass on their oral heritage, affecting even those textual portions that were perceived as comparatively more fixed.

III. Memory Errors

This chapter is the first of three in which I take a closer look at differences between parallel discourse versions.[188] I begin by taking up a central question, namely the assumption, which is in itself natural, that variations should in principle be attributed to intentional interventions, a topic already explored in relation to the code of rules in the first chapter. The evidence surveyed here makes the applicability of this assumption to the early discourses appear rather doubtful.

In order to explore this point, I focus on various memory errors, covering instances of what I have chosen to refer to as "innocent variations," "sequence errors," "meaningless additions," "conflations," "loss of text," and "lack of homogenization." Then I contrast these instances with explicit expressions in some passages of a concern with accurate transmission. A key to bridge this contrast, in my view, lies in a closer look at textual memory. Before embarking on this whole trajectory, however, I need to start off by articulating the key question underlying this chapter—the scope of validity of the explanatory model of intentionality—which needs to be held in such a way as to be in principle falsifiable by contradictory evidence.

1. The Explanatory Model of Intentionality

Even a short dip into the world of comparative studies, be this between parallel rules or verses or discourses, will bring to light the existence of minor and major variations. This inevitably leads to the question of how such differences should best be explained. Given the typical experience of scholars when writing and publishing books and articles, it is in a way natural to assume that comparable patterns must have impacted ancient

Indians as well. Nevertheless, there is a need to allow room for questioning the heartfelt certainty that differences obviously must be due to some intentional intervention. The possibility of alternative explanations is best left open, at least in principle.

This in turn leads to the question: What type of evidence would counter the impression that changes must be the result of intentional intervention? The answer would seem to be the identification of a substantial body of variations that, in one way or another, fail to make sense if conceived of as having been done intentionally. It is to such evidence that the present chapter is mainly dedicated.

Before delving into a closer exploration of relevant textual material, however, I wish to make it clear that my position is definitely not to deny that some changes must indeed be the outcome of intentional intervention. As would have already become evident in the first chapter of my study, I certainly do not intend to reject intentional change *in toto*. My point in what follows is only to counter the assumption that intentional activity by so-called editors or redactors is the default explanation.

An injunction clearly sanctioning intentional intervention occurs in two *Vinaya*s, according to which a reciter who has forgotten the location of a discourse should feel free to allocate it to one of the main places where the Buddha regularly stayed.[189] This instruction reflects the lack of importance accorded in the ancient Indian setting to such details. As noted by Coward (1986, 305–6), "the early Buddhists shared . . . the Indian indifference to historical details. Historical events surrounding a text are judged to be unimportant in relation to the unchanging truth the text contains." From the viewpoint of assessing the early Buddhist oral tradition, a remarkable aspect, already noted by Scharfe (2002, 25n93), is that in the ruling under discussion "no such 'creativeness' was allowed where the contents of the lesson is concerned."

Although not explicitly envisaged in the ruling under discussion, the possibility of intentional intervention can also affect the contents of a particular teaching and is thus not confined to the allowable supplementation of the name of a location (or a person) that has been forgotten. Such a case can be identified through comparative study of the Discourse with an Analysis of Offerings (*Dakkhiṇāvibhaṅgasutta*). The passage in question comes right after a list detailing seven types of offerings that could be made to the monastic community. The relevant Pāli passage reports the Buddha giving the following explanation to his attendant Ānanda:[190]

> Ānanda, in the future there will then be clan members, with yellow robes around their necks, who are immoral and of bad character. [People] will make offerings to those immoral ones for the sake of the community. Ānanda, I say that in that case as well a gift made to the community is incalculable and immeasurable. Ānanda, I say that even then a gift to an individual person is in no way of greater fruit than a gift to the community.

Right after the suggestion that a gift to an immoral recipient will be fruitful as long as it is given to the community, the Pāli discourse continues with an exposition of four purifications of a gift, according to which an offering becomes fruitful (literally "purified") on account of the donor, the recipient, both, or neither. In each case, such fruitfulness depends on the moral character of the person in question (although strictly speaking this leaves open the possibility of being overruled by a gift dedicated to the whole community).

The importance of the recipient's ethical purity also comes up in another discourse, according to which endowment with pure moral conduct is one of the qualities that makes the services and support received by a monastic recipient become fruitful.[191] For this reason, yet other discourses recommend purity of conduct and purity of the mind to ensure that the gifts monastics receive become fruitful for their donors.[192] As already noted by de Silva (1990, 33), the position taken in the above-translated passage from the Discourse with an Analysis of Offerings "is contradictory to ideas expressed elsewhere, that what is given to the virtuous is greatly beneficial but not what is given to the immoral. It is evident here that a later interpolation cannot be altogether ruled out." Similarly, Witanachchi (2006, 701) comments that the position taken in this Pāli passage "is a far cry from the place given to moral discipline and spiritual development in [other] early discourses."

The suggestion of a possible interpolation receives support from a closer inspection of the context of the above passage, which is preceded by listing offerings to various types of communities. The final part of the passage translated above would fit well as the conclusion to such an exposition, summing up that "a gift to an individual person is in no way of greater fruit than a gift to the community." In its present position, however, this sentence fits less well, since the description of an immoral individual recipient does not naturally call up the idea that a gift to an individual recipient could be of greater fruit than one given to the community. This makes it fair to assume that the description of immoral clan members could indeed be an interpolation, inserted after the last of the previously mentioned types of communities and before the indication, found at the end of the paragraph translated above, that a gift to an individual can never best a gift to the community.

The impression that a later change has taken place can be further corroborated through comparative study, which brings to light that one parallel to this Pāli discourse does not refer at all to future monastics.[193] A discourse quotation extant in Tibetan does not provide any further qualification of the monastic in question.[194] A Chinese *Āgama* discourse merely indicates that such future monastics are not energetic.[195] All of this is a far cry from qualifying them to be "immoral and of bad character," as is the case for the Pāli version.

In sum, it seems fair to conclude that "the need to ensure a constant supply of gifts even for less well-behaved monks . . . led to a conscious change of the wording of this discourse" (Anālayo 2005b, 103). The situation in the parallels suggests a gradual growth of a concern with encouraging offerings to monastics who fail to inspire the donors. The relevance of this agenda manifests also in a text belonging to a different genre, extant in Old Uighur (an ancient Turkic language), where the same idea can be found.[196] Although this is no longer a discourse parallel, the relevant passage clearly takes its inspiration from some version of the Discourse with an Analysis of Offerings, in line with a pervasive tendency of later texts to incorporate ideas found among the early discourses.

Moving on from this fairly clear case of intentional change of the content of a Pāli discourse passage for quite obvious motivations, in the remainder of this chapter I survey evidence that much rather suggests changes taking place without being necessarily the result of an intentional intervention.

2. Innocent Variations

By way of warming up to my topic, I first take up a type of variation that comes up with considerable frequency in comparative study, which I have chosen to refer to as "innocent variations." These are innocent in the sense that, unlike the case of promoting gifts to immoral monastics, no reason appears evident for preferring one version over another. Such variations often occur in relation to the sequence in which a particular set of topics are listed. One example is a list of seven methods for abandoning the influxes (*āsava/āsrava/āśrava*),[197] described with considerable similarity in a Pāli discourse with three Chinese *Āgama* parallels and a parallel extant in Tibetan translation.[198] Despite agreeing on the content of each method and on which of these should be listed first and last, the parallel versions show considerable differences in the sequence in which they present the other five methods. Below I list the seven methods in the sequence in which they occur in the Pāli version, followed by variant sequences in the parallels.

1. seeing,
2. restraining,
3. using,
4. enduring,
5. avoiding,
6. removing,
7. developing.

1, 2, 5, 3, 4, 6, 7 (two Chinese *Āgama* parallels),
1, 2, 5, 3, 6, 4, 7 (Tibetan parallel),
1, 4, 3, 5, 6, 2, 7 (third Chinese *Āgama* parallel).

The first and last methods concern positive qualities, namely "seeing" the four noble truths and "developing" the seven factors of awakening.

Whereas these positive qualities form the beginning and ending part of all lists, the other five, which are concerned with various forms of restraint, occur in different sequences. From the viewpoint of the doctrinal teaching given, such differing sequences do not appear to have a discernible repercussion. It does not really matter so much whether one mentions "restraining" of the six senses as the second or the penultimate in the list, as this practice will still have to be done continuously from the beginning to the end of the path to freedom from the influxes. The same applies to the other types of restraint. It is in this sense that the above variations appear to be of an innocent type, in that there does not seem to be an agenda behind their occurrence, such as is evident in the case of authenticating the giving of offerings to immoral monastics.

Comparative studies provide ample evidence for the occurrences of such variations. Another example is a discussion between a king and a Buddhist monastic on four themes, which in the Pāli sequence are (1) old age, (2) disease, (3) poverty, and (4) loss of kin. The same four themes are taken up in parallel versions with the following variations of order:[199]

1, 2, 4, 3.
2, 1, 3, 4.
4, 3, 2, 1.

Another such case involves different types of rebirth as an animal, listed similarly but with the following differences in sequence, compared to the Pāli version's sequence (1, 2, 3, 4, 5):[200]

1, 3, 4, 5, 2.
3, 5, 4, 1, 2.

Alternatively, such variations can result from pairing a set of similes in different ways. For example, a set of four different similes to illustrate wrong as well as right forms of practice can proceed presenting together the four wrong instances and the four right instances. Instead of adopting such a procedure, however, it is also possible to take up a simile from the wrong perspective and then immediately contrast it with the right perspective, before proceeding to the next simile. Here are two examples involving a sevenfold and an eightfold listing, respectively, that adopt such an alternative pattern. The sevenfold list serves to illustrate the potential of mindfulness of the body and the eightfold list highlights the contrast between right and wrong approaches to liberation. The two listings in the parallel versions, compared to the corresponding Pāli versions' sequences, proceed as follows:[201]

1, 4, 7, 2, 5, 3, 6.

2, 6, 3, 7, 1, 5, 4, 8.

The same employment of alternative patterns can also apply to expositions that do not involve similes. Here are three examples, each time compared to the sequence adopted in the respective Pāli versions. These examples stem from expositions taking up the topics of the relationship of karma to rebirth in a fourfold manner, the causes for experiencing pleasure and pain in a fivefold manner, and an analysis of sensory experience in a twelvefold manner.[202]

2, 4, 1, 3.

1, 3, 4, 5, 2.

1, 7, 2, 8, 3, 9, 4, 10, 5, 11, 6, 12.

The occurrence of such variations can even happen among discourses belonging to the same reciter tradition. An example in case concerns an exposition of four ways of undertaking things, distinguished according to whether these are either pleasant or else painful at the time of being done and again at the time of experiencing their result. This is a topic of two consecutive Pāli discourses, which adopt different sequences in listing these four, whereas their Chinese *Āgama* parallels adopt the same sequence.[203] Below I take the Chinese *Āgama* parallels as the starting point, followed by presenting sequential variations in Pāli discourses:

1. pleasant → painful
2. painful → pleasant
3. painful → painful
4. pleasant → pleasant

1, 3, 2, 4 (first of two consecutive Pāli discourses),
3, 1, 2, 4 (second of two consecutive Pāli discourses),
3, 2, 1, 4 (unrelated Pāli discourse).

As in the case of the first example of seven methods for abandoning the influxes, in the other cases surveyed here there does not seem to be any evident reason for preferring one sequence over another. Particularly noteworthy in the present case is the degree of variation found among discourses of the same reciter tradition, where even two Pāli discourses that follow each other directly in the same collection still differ in the basic sequence of their exposition. From the viewpoint of oral transmission, it would have been quite convenient to adopt the same sequence throughout, making it easier to remember the exposition. That this has not happened is one of several instances that point to a lack of homogenization of the discourse collections.

3. Sequence Errors

Another type of variation that emerges regularly from comparative studies involves instances of lack of coherence that result from variations in sequence. In a way, these are already evident within the relevant passage itself, as its progression somehow fails to make sense or seems unclear. Consulting the parallel version can help to confirm that there is indeed a problem with the sequence, leading to the impression that at some point in the course of oral transmission a "sequence error" occurred.

One example for such an apparent sequence error occurs in the Discourse on Two Types of Thought (*Dvedhāvitakkasutta*), which describes the Buddha's pre-awakening division of thoughts into wholesome and unwholesome types. The exposition of the latter type highlights the harmful nature of unwholesome thoughts and concludes with the Buddha stating that, whenever an unwholesome thought arose, in awareness of its detrimental repercussions he abandoned it.[204] The discourse continues by explaining that frequent thinking in unwholesome or wholesome ways will lead to a corresponding inclination of the mind, followed by a simile which describes how a cowherd has to guard and restrain the cows closely to prevent them from straying into ripe crop and eating it, in awareness of the fact that failing to do so will lead to punishment.

It is not clear in what way the cowherd's fear of punishment illustrates that frequent thinking leads to a corresponding inclination of the mind, as these seem to be different topics. The solution to this problem can be found in the Chinese *Āgama* parallel, which has the simile at an earlier point of its exposition, before broaching the topic of what leads to a mental inclination. In this version, the simile comes right after the depiction of how the Buddha-to-be dealt with an unwholesome thought:[205]

> I abandoned it, removed it, and vomited it out. Why is that? I saw that countless bad and unwholesome states will certainly arise because of it. It is just like, in the last month of spring when, because the fields have been sown, the area where cows can graze is consequently limited. The cowherd boy sets the cows free in uncultivated marshland. To prevent the cows from straying into others' fields, the cowherd boy promptly wields a cane on approaching them. Why is that? Because the cowherd boy knows that he will certainly be scolded, beaten, or imprisoned for their trespassing.

In this way, consulting the Chinese *Āgama* parallel makes it fair to propose that at some point in the transmission of the Pāli discourse the simile ended up in the wrong place. This holds not only for unwholesome thoughts, but also for wholesome ones. In this case both versions have a second version of the same simile, which depicts the cowherd being at ease when the crop has been harvested. Once that has happened, the cowherd can just let the cows graze wherever they want, as there is no longer anything to fear. In the Pāli version, this simile occurs after the exposition of how frequently thinking wholesome thoughts leads to a corresponding inclination of the mind.[206] Yet, a better placing would rather be before this exposition, where it could serve as an illustration for the experience of wholesome thoughts that do not call for an intervention through abandoning, removing, and making an end of them.

In their present position, the similes in the Pāli version are no longer able to perform their explanatory function properly. It is difficult to conceive of a reason that could have motivated an intentional change in position. Instead, it seems considerably more reasonable to envisage an accidental shift in position during oral transmission.[207] The double occurrence of the same type of shift is also most meaningfully envisaged as an error in oral transmission, as a copyist's error or a shuffling around of manuscripts would not result in reproducing twice the same effect. A shifting around of textual portions during oral transmission is in fact a frequent occurrence (which is precisely why the use of concatenation comes in handy) and at times can also affect the sequence within a series of similes.[208]

A shift of a textual portion to an incongruous position can also happen with material that does not involve a simile. A case illustrating this possibility occurs in the Discourse to Saṅgārava (*Saṅgāravasutta*), in relation to a question posed by the brahmin Saṅgārava to the Buddha. The question is whether celestials (*devas*) exist.[209] The placing of this question is puzzling, as it comes after the Buddha had given a detailed account of his pre-awakening practices, which comes with explicit references to celestials.[210] Norman (1977, 331) reasons that

> the question is asked immediately after the Buddha's statement that devatās [celestials] had approached him and shown great concern about his weak condition during his pre-enlightenment ascetic stage . . . the story he had told about the devatās necessarily implies that he admitted some sort of existence for them.

In a version of this discourse extant in Sanskrit fragments, the corresponding question occurs *before* the Buddha's autobiographical report of his quest for awakening.[211] With this different placing, the question makes much more sense.

Of further interest here is also the Pāli commentary, which explains that the reply Saṅgārava received to this question gave him the impression that the Buddha was speaking without actually knowing whether celestials exist.[212] Such a comment also becomes more meaningful once the question occurs at an earlier junction of the text, rather than with its present position in the Pāli discourse. In sum, it seems fair to propose that the placing of this question in the Pāli version would be the result of an error that occurred at a point in its oral or written transmission after the coming into existence of the relevant portion in the Pāli commentary. Notably, this error was never rectified.

Another instance of an apparent shifting of a textual portion can be identified in relation to a discussion of the ten qualities of an awakened one, found in the Discourse to Samaṇamaṇḍikā[putta] (*Samaṇamaṇḍikā-sutta*). The Pāli exposition of this topic departs from an otherwise pervasive pattern in the early discourses of first naming a topic, following that with a detailed examination, and finally concluding with a repetition of the first statement, which again names the topic at hand. In the Discourse to Samaṇamaṇḍikā[putta], however, the initial naming occurs at the outset of the discourse,[213] whereas its detailed exposition and a repetition of the initial statement are found only toward the end of the discourse.[214] In the Chinese *Āgama* parallel, in contrast, the initial statement occurs only in the final part of the discourse and directly leads over to the corresponding detailed explanation and concluding statement.[215] The separation in the Pāli version of the initial statement from the remainder of the exposition appears to be an error. The misplaced passage seems too short for its present placing to result from a jumbling of manuscripts during copying. It also occurs before its appropriate placing and thus could not be the result of a copyist's oversight and subsequent addition. Instead, the present state of affairs in the Pāli discourse appears to be attributable to an error during oral transmission.

Another example of a similar pattern concerns an account of the gradual path of training to be undertaken by a monastic in quest of awakening, found in the Lesser Discourse to Sakuludāyin (*Cūḷasakuludāyisutta*).

In the Pāli discourse, the gradual path of training occurs after the Buddha, in the course of a discussion about what constitutes an entirely pleasant world, had described the attainment of the four absorptions. The account of the gradual path also covers the four absorptions, qualifying each of them as a state superior to the entirely pleasant world discussed earlier.[216] In this way, the first absorption discussed now ends up being qualified as superior to all four absorptions discussed earlier. This fails to make sense. A Chinese *Āgama* parallel adopts a different sequence by having the gradual path account lead up to the discussion of absorption attainment as an entirely pleasant world.[217] This avoids the incoherent presentation in the Pāli version, whose present state can with considerable probability be considered the result of a transmission error.

Each of the cases surveyed here involves a loss of context that fails to make sense if envisaged as the result of an intentional intervention by so-called redactors or editors. Why would anyone want to shift a question about the existence of celestials to a point in the discourse where this has already been clarified, or separate an initial statement from the exposition it is meant to introduce, or position an account of gradual path in such a way that it leads to an incoherent presentation?

As mentioned above, my discussion here is not meant to imply that intentional change never happened, the acknowledgment of which is precisely the reason for beginning with the example provided by the Discourse with an Analysis of Offerings. But other evidence makes it hardly convincing to assume that variations must in principle be the result of some intentional activity by redactors or editors.

4. Meaningless Additions

Some cases of sequential errors leave it open to question whether the apparent error occurred during oral transmission or due to a copying mistake once the texts were transmitted in writing. As evidenced in Indic manuscript traditions, it can easily happen that a scribe accidentally jumps a line or more when preparing a copy of a text. However, such an explanation does not seem to work for two cases of meaningless addition to be taken up now.

One of these two cases involves the Discourse on Stilling Thought (*Vitakkasaṇṭhānasutta*), the twentieth discourse in the middle-length collection, which describes five methods for overcoming unwholesome thoughts. The discourse concludes with the following assessment of someone who has successfully employed these five methods to remove unwholesome thought and collect the mind:[218]

> Whatever thought they will want, they will think that thought; whatever thought they will not want, they will not think that thought. They cut off craving, did away with [any] fetter, and by rightly penetrating conceit made an end of *dukkha*.

This is rather puzzling, since the employment of the five methods in this discourse has mainly the potential of leading to mental composure (*samādhi*). Yet, the references to cutting off craving and making an end of *dukkha/duḥkha* are standard references to full awakening. The problem is not merely doctrinal, as the grammar also does not work. The ability to think stands in the future tense, whereas the remainder of the passage is in the past tense. This just fails to make sense. The Chinese *Āgama* parallel has a counterpart to the first part of the above passage, regarding mastery over thoughts, but does not continue after that with any reference to full awakening.[219]

A passage corresponding to the apparent addition to the Discourse on Stilling Thought can be found in another discourse that occurs previously in the same collection, being its second member. This discourse concludes by stating that, as a result of having implemented the instructions, practitioners "cut off craving, did away with [any] fetter, and by rightly comprehending conceit made an end of *dukkha*."[220] In this case, the statement is doctrinally meaningful, as it occurs after an exposition that according to early Buddhist thought can indeed lead to full awakening, and it also does not involve a grammatical problem. Moreover, the position taken in the Pāli version of this discourse receives support from its four *Āgama* parallels, which similarly conclude by referring to full awakening.[221] Since the two Pāli discourses are the second and the twentieth discourses in the collection, they occur at a considerable distance from each other (over a hundred pages in the PTS edition), making it improbable that the present error should be considered a copying mistake. Instead, it seems more probable to consider the addition of the unfitting passage in the Discourse on Stilling Thought to result from an error during oral transmission.

Another example concerns an exposition of ways of arriving at stream entry, discussed in the Discourse on Right View (*Sammādiṭṭhisutta*). The Pāli version concludes each of its descriptions of how to arrive at right view in this way:[222]

> Having completely removed the underlying tendency to lust, having dispelled the underlying tendency to aversion, having terminated the underlying tendency to the view and conceit "I am," having removed ignorance and aroused knowledge, [a noble disciple] is one who here and now makes an end of *dukkha*.
>
> Friend, to that extent as well a noble disciple is one of right view, whose view has become straight, who is endowed with experiential confidence and has arrived at this true teaching.

Whereas the context and the part translated in the second paragraph are about stream entry, the first paragraph is a description of full awakening. This is again a misfit. The attainment of stream entry does not require a removal of the underlying tendencies to lust and aversion and fails to be in itself the making of an end of *dukkha/duḥkha*. What the early discourses regularly do associate with stream entry is the gaining of right view and the possession of experiential confidence (*aveccappasāda/avetyaprasāda*). The parallels to the Pāli version have indeed only a counterpart to the second passage translated above, thereby confirming the impression that the first paragraph would be an addition.[223] This addition is fully integrated in its surrounding text and happens repeatedly with each exposition of ways of arriving at stream entry, making it hardly possible to consider it a copyist's error. Moreover, this first paragraph appears to be without a counterpart in this wording among other Pāli discourses, so that it could not be considered the outcome of some form of borrowing from elsewhere. Since the overall result is incoherent, it would also not make much sense to assume an intentional intervention.

It seems to me that the best way to make sense of this instance is to posit an error of memory caused by a lack of attention to meaning combined with an accidental association with some unrelated material. The one to have made such a blunder must have been a respected teacher of recitation, as a result of which this obviously incoherent presentation was not corrected and eventually managed to become the version transmitted to subsequent generations of Theravāda reciters.

5. Conflations

Another type of error that also conflicts with the assumption that intentional editorial intervention should be considered the default mode of explaining variations between discourse parallels involves what I would refer to as instances of conflation.

One example for what I have in mind with this expression involves ways of addressing the Buddha in the Greater Discourse to Sakuludāyin (*Mahāsakuludāyisutta*). The narrative context for the relevant passage, addressed to a non-Buddhist wanderer, concerns qualities of the Buddha that motivate his disciples to respect him. In the Pāli passage in question, the Buddha describes his own disciples referring to him with the expression "recluse Gotama":[224]

> Udāyin, suppose my disciples were to honor me, respect me, revere me, and venerate me [thinking]: "The recluse Gotama takes little food and commends taking little food."

In the early discourses, the expression "recluse Gotama" is regularly used to refer to the Buddha by non-Buddhists, but not by his disciples. Nevertheless, the usage in this case could in principle be a way of quoting a statement that has previously been made by the wanderer Sakuludāyin. However, Sakuludāyin's actual statement instead employs the respectful form of address normatively used by disciples of the Buddha:[225]

> Venerable sir, the Blessed One indeed takes little food and commends taking little food.

The same pattern continues for another four qualities, where in each case the non-Buddhist wanderer uses the expressions appropriate for a disciple of the Buddha, whereas the Buddha himself describes his own disciples employing the expression "recluse Gotama." A Chinese *Āgama* parallel supports the impression that a conflation has taken place, as here the wanderer and the report of the disciples use the more appropriate forms of address.[226] The presentation in the Pāli version can hardly be considered an intentional change, as to depict disciples as acting disrespectfully by being shown to use the expression "recluse Gotama" runs counter to a fairly pervasive tendency, evident in both versions, to exalt the Buddha.[227] Instead, it seems as if at some point during oral transmission the two modes of address got mixed up without the resultant incoherence being corrected on a subsequent occasion.

Another instance involving a conflation of modes of address can be seen in the Discourse on a Summary and an Analysis (*Uddesavibhaṅga-sutta*), which reports the Buddha giving a short teaching and then withdrawing. Uncertain about how to understand the implications of this teaching, the members of the audience approach a senior disciple by the name of Mahākaccāna, report the teaching, and request him to elucidate it. Mahākaccāna's explanation introduces a recapitulation of the short teaching by the Buddha as something given "to us."[228] Since he had not been present at the time of the original delivery, it would have been more fitting for him to be shown to refer to that statement without qualifying it as something given "to us." The Chinese *Āgama* parallel employs no such qualification at all.[229] The wording employed by Mahākaccāna in the Pāli version appears to be simply a result of the reciters repeating the formulation that occurred earlier when the monastics requested him to explain the short teaching by the Buddha.[230] The circumstance that the earlier request by the monastics appropriately employed the term "to us" evidently influenced the wording of Mahākaccāna's statement.

Although this is in itself only a minor error, the same type of conflation recurs in the same way in another three Pāli discourses involving an explanation by Mahākaccāna of a brief statement made by the Buddha.[231] As these instances are found in the collections of medium-length discourses and of numerical discourses, it appears as if an error in oral transmission initiated a tradition of associating Mahākaccana with this type of formulation, rather than being a copyist error. In contrast, in a discourse in the topic-wise collection, where the same pattern of providing a detailed explanation of a brief statement by the Buddha involves instead Ānanda, the relevant passage reports him using the correct formulation "to you."[232]

Whereas variations between "to us" and "to you" can seem negligible, another type of recurrent conflation involves the names of the protagonist(s) in a discourse. An example occurs in the Greater Discourse in the Gosiṅga [Grove] (*Mahāgosiṅgasutta*), in which a range of chief disciples extol qualities that are characteristic of their own personal forte. In this setting, the Pāli version associates Mahāmoggallāna with discussion on the higher teaching (*abhidhamma*).[233] This is unexpected, as the general trend in depicting this disciple is to highlight rather his supernormal powers.[234] Horner (1941, 309) comments that "Moggallāna is chiefly famed for his psychic powers, and there is little reason to suppose him to have had gifts of an *abhidhamma* nature." Several scholars already noted that consultation of the Chinese *Āgama* parallels confirms the impression that some textual error would have occurred.[235] All of the parallels to this Pāli discourse agree in associating Mahāmaudgalyāyana with supernormal powers.[236] Apparently a reference to Mahākaccāna was lost at some point in the transmission of the Pāli version, as a result of which the quality earlier associated with him ended up being instead attributed to Mahāmoggallāna. The resultant inconsistency in the depiction of the latter, compared with the way he is depicted elsewhere, was never ironed out.

6. Loss of Text

The apparent loss of a reference to Mahākaccāna in the Greater Discourse in the Gosiṅga [Grove] leads me over to the general topic of textual loss. Such loss can occur repeatedly even within a single discourse, which appears to have happened in the case of the Discourse on [Progressive] Stages of Taming (*Dantabhūmisutta*). The Pāli discourse and a Chinese

Āgama parallel agree in first describing the gradual taming of a wild elephant, followed by relating different stages of such taming to the gradual training of a Buddhist disciple. In this setting, the going forth of such a disciple corresponds to the elephant being caught and the cultivation of the four establishments of mindfulness (*satipaṭṭhāna/smṛtyupasthāna*) to the elephant being weaned of its forest habits.

Both versions continue by describing how a disciple practices the four establishments of mindfulness free from thought and then cultivates concentration up to the fourth absorption.[237] However, only the Chinese *Āgama* parallel relates these practices to stages of taming the elephant, namely the elephant being first taught to obey orders and then being trained to remain immovable even when placed in a situation closely resembling an actual battle.[238] Earlier, the Pāli version did describe both of these as distinct stages in the taming of an elephant.[239] This makes it fair to assume that at some point in the transmission of the Pāli version the textual portions that related these stages to the gradual training of a disciple were forgotten. Since this happens more than once, it seems likely that this error should be attributed to faulty memory during oral transmission and not to an error occurring in the written medium.

Not only did such an apparent error of memory occur, but the relationship between the process of taming an elephant and the training of a disciple that had been lost in this way was also never reestablished. In particular the stage of the elephant remaining immovable naturally brings to mind the imperturbability that the early discourses regularly associate with the attainment of the fourth absorption. Despite such fairly evident inner connection, the Pāli discourse was passed down from generation to generation without the received text being adjusted by restoring this correlation. Had improvisation or intentional editorial activity been the norm, the obvious relationship between the two types of imperturbability would naturally have led to a reestablishing of the lost connection.

A fairly self-evident instance of textual loss concerns a discourse in the section on tens in the collection of numerical discourses. Besides showing various signs of the occurrence of textual errors, the received discourse no longer has any tenfold item that would justify its inclusion in the section on tens.[240] Parallels extant in Chinese and Tibetan help correct some of the errors in this version,[241] indicating among other things that a treatment of the ten courses of action would have been lost in the course of transmitting the Pāli discourse. This treatment would originally have motivated its inclusion in the section on tens, making it fair to conclude that the loss must have occurred after the discourse had already been allocated to this particular part of the collection of numerical discourses.

Another case involving a substantial loss of text can be seen in the Discourse on Sixfold Purity (*Chabbisodhanasutta*), which describes dimensions of the inner purity of a fully awakened one. Although speaking of six such purities in its title, the Pāli discourse covers only five. These are a fully awakened one's ability to claim freedom from attachment in relation to four ways of verbal expression, the five aggregates, the six elements, the six senses, and freedom from conceit as a result of having cultivated the gradual path of training.[242] In addition to these five, the Chinese *Āgama* parallel reports a fully awakened one's claim to a sixth purity, which concludes as follows:[243]

> In regard to these four nutriments, I attained the knowledge that there is no clinging to anything and that with the destruction of the influxes the mind has been liberated.

The discrepancy between the title of the Pāli version and its content has already been noticed by Pāli commentators. One out of several possible solutions to the problem comes from the "elders who live on the other side of the sea," a reference to reciters from India (as seen from the viewpoint of the Sri Lankan commentators). According to the assessment of these Indian reciters, concordance with the topic announced in the title can be achieved by adding the purity of a fully awakened one in regard to the four nutriments.[244] The Chinese *Āgama* parallel, translated above, confirms this explanation. It seems fair to propose that by the time of reaching Sri Lanka the Pāli discourse had lost such an exposition, which evidently was still known in India. Since at that time writing was not yet in use, this is yet another change that must have happened in the oral medium.

From the perspective of oral transmission, this apparent loss of a whole section of the Pāli discourse is telling, in particular in view of the commentarial gloss on the resultant inconsistency. Although even a substantial part of a discourse can be lost, the present case at the same time also shows the degree to which the reciters were committed to preserving a discourse as they had received it. It would have been easy for them to supply the missing section about the four nutriments on the strength of the discourse's title and the commentarial explanation. There is no conceivable doctrinal reason for not wanting to include an exposition on the four nutriments in this discourse, which could just have been taken from some other discourse that covers this topic. An even easier solution would have been to change the title to "fivefold purity" so as to make it fit with the discourse's content. That no such change was introduced, and the Pāli discourse was instead handed down in full awareness of its present truncated state, points to the intention of the reciters to pass on a discourse the way they had received it. In conjunction with the evidence surveyed above, cases like the present one seriously undermine the credibility of the assumption that intentional intervention can be resorted to as the normative mode for explaining variations.

7. Lack of Homogenization

The evidence presented so far has already brought to light several cases that do not appear to be the result of intentional interventions. Although this much would perhaps already suffice to establish that the assumption of creative individual redactors or editors who intentionally introduce changes here and there is best not taken as the one and only possible explanation, it seems pertinent to pursue further the fact that apparent errors have not been smoothed out subsequently. This can be illustrated with the help of a few Pāli discourse passages that have not been harmonized and even stand in contrast to each other, even though they pertain to the same transmission lineage.

A simple example would be the story of Raṭṭhapāla's going forth, briefly mentioned in the first chapter of my exploration as probably having provided the blueprint for the narrative behind the promulgation of the rule on celibacy in some *Vinayas*. Descriptions of Raṭṭhapāla's going forth occur in a medium-length Pāli discourse and a range of parallels.[245] Even though the Pāli version gives a rather detailed narrative of what happened when Raṭṭhapāla returned to visit his family as a monastic, it does not cover a versified exchange between him and his father that is reported in the Pāli *Vinaya*.[246] The same discourse also reports a series of verses spoken by Raṭṭhapāla to his former wives. These recur in the collection of Verses by Elders (*Theragāthā*), which continues with another verse that could equally well have been included among the verses in the medium-length discourse.[247] Had homogenization been the rule, the discourse on Raṭṭhapāla should have been made to conform with these two instances found in other Pāli collections.

Another and particularly telling example can be observed in two versions of the same discourse, found in two different collections, which differ in the effect the otherwise same instruction had on its protagonist, Kasi Bhāradvāja. In the topic-wise collection he takes refuge as a lay follower, but in the Section of Discourses (*Suttanipāta*) he goes forth and becomes an arahant.[248] Such variations clearly have come into being within the same Theravāda transmission lineage.

A comparable difference can be seen in reports in Pāli discourses of how the non-Buddhist ascetic Acela Kassapa went forth and became an arahant. The first such case is the Discourse on Bakkula, which reports that this happened after hearing about the marvelous qualities of the monastic Bakkula.[249] The Chinese *Āgama* parallel does not give the name of the visitor and, even though he clearly was delighted on hearing about the marvelous qualities of the Buddhist monk, he did not go forth, nor is there any indication that he reached a level of awakening.[250]

Acela Kassapa's going forth recurs in a member of the collection of long discourses, which reports that he went forth after hearing a discourse by the Buddha on asceticism.[251] In this case the Chinese *Āgama* parallel agrees that he went forth.[252] According to both versions, after going forth he became an arahant/arhat.

A Pāli discourse in the topic-wise collection also reports that Acela Kassapa went forth and eventually became an arahant, this time after hearing a different discourse by the Buddha on the topic of what causes pleasure and pain.[253] According to three parallels to this discourse, however, he instead attained stream entry during the discourse, did not go forth, and was soon after killed by a cow.[254]

In another discourse in the same topic-wise collection, Acela Kassapa once more goes forth and eventually becomes an arahant, this time after being inspired by a meeting with a householder.[255] A Chinese *Āgama* parallel reports the same happy outcome, with the difference that it does not provide the proper name of the ascetic who was so inspired by the householder's exposition as to go forth as a Buddhist monastic.[256]

In sum, in the Pāli discourses Acela Kassapa went forth and became an arahant on four distinct occasions. Although in principle the same person could go forth on several occasions, it would not be possible for the same person to become an arahant each time.[257] Nor does it seem particularly probable that four different persons by the same name of Acela Kassapa went forth and became arahants. Judging from the situation in the Chinese *Āgama* parallels, the long discourse in which he gets to hear a teaching from the Buddha about asceticism could have provided the starting point for a proliferation of the depiction of his going forth and eventual attainment of full awakening, which during oral transmission migrated to other contexts. Despite the resultant incongruency, this was never rectified.

Proceeding beyond the early discourses, according to Endo (2012, 41) even the Pāli commentarial tradition shows that homogenization was not the rule, since

> the Sri Lanka *bhāṇaka*s [reciters] had opportunities to homogenize the texts, if they so wished ... the *bhāṇaka*s could have played a role to homogenize the texts before they were committed to writing. Nevertheless, what we find in the Pāli commentaries is contrary to our expectation, and disparities are often seen among the sources ... In other words, the *bhāṇaka*s did not ... homogenize the texts.

Once homogenization is not undertaken in a comprehensive manner and even obvious inconsistencies and errors are left in the text, it becomes fairly clear that insisting on attributing change in principle to intentional editorial activity would not do justice to the actual textual evidence. This holds not only for the idea of intentional intervention by an individual so-called redactor but also for the assumption of an intentionally organized group editorial effort. The actual textual evidence does not support the idea that the particular texts to which we now have access are the final result of a large-scale editorial undertaking aimed at producing a thoroughly uniform body of texts within the parameters of a certain school or tradition. Instead, the extant texts appear to be just random testimonies to one particular instance of oral transmission that happens to have survived, with all the idiosyncrasies and irregularities that result from the intrinsically variegated and complex nature of oral transmission. I will come back to the problem of assuming intentionality to be the normative explanation for variations found between parallel versions of early Buddhist texts in the last chapter of my study (see below p. 183).

8. Oral Recitation and Memory

Explicit expressions of a concern for accurate transmission are voiced in several discourses, thereby providing a perspective that complements the apparent memory errors surveyed above. One instance occurs in the context of a survey of eight states that are particularly helpful to those embarking on the Buddhist path of practice. One of these is being "learned," whose literal sense of "having heard much" reflects the oral dimension of the acquisition of erudition in the ancient setting. According to a version of this quality in a Chinese *Āgama* passage, such learnedness takes the following form:[258]

> One has heard much and widely, keeping and maintaining without loss of memory the profound teaching that is good in the beginning, middle, and end, with truthful meaning and phrasing, being the equipment of the pure life, which on having been heard enters the heart.

Although the relevant Sanskrit fragments unfortunately have not preserved much of this description,[259] the Pāli counterpart proceeds in comparable ways, similarly highlighting the need for such teachings to have been "retained and verbally recited."[260] This draws attention to the basic predicament of an oral setting, where instructions received on a previous occasion only remain accessible to the extent to which they have been stored in memory. Besides storage at the time of reception, repeated verbal recitation is required to guard against loss of memory.

A concern with correct wording emerges from another Pāli discourse and its Chinese *Āgama* parallel, both of which emphasize the importance of group recitation. The Pāli version draws attention to the need for phrasing and meaning to correspond.[261] The Chinese *Dīrghāgama* parallel to this discourse takes up the same issue in more detail, similarly placing an emphasis on the need for accuracy in both meaning and phrasing.[262] Such a function appears to be a continuous element of orality from ancient to modern India, given that, according to Coward (1988, 146), "group listening to check for errors is still an accepted method of verification in rural India today."

An additional perspective on the same matter emerges with several Pāli discourses in the numerical collection, which emphasize that lack of correct memorization leads to a decline of the teachings:[263]

> Monastics master a discourse that has been badly grasped, with badly arranged words and letters. Monastics, with badly arranged words and letters the meaning is also misleading. Monastics, this is the first condition that leads to the decline and disappearance of the good teaching . . .
>
> Those monastics who are of much learning, who have acquired the transmission (*āgama*), who know by heart the teaching, know by heart the discipline, and know by heart the summaries, do not take care to make others recite a discourse; with their passing away, the root [for the transmission] of the discourse is cut off, bereft of protection. Monastics, this is the third condition that leads to the decline and disappearance of the good teaching.

No parallels are extant for the Pāli discourses presenting the above indications. This diminishes the text-historical strength of their testimony to early Buddhist thought. At the same time, however, it does not imply that these passages must be late. The absence of a parallel could simply be due to the vicissitudes of oral transmission.

That the latter option probably fits the present case can be seen by turning to the account of the first communal recitation (*saṅgīti/saṃgīti*), discussed above (pp. 20 and 37). The different *Vinaya*s agree in presenting this communal recitation as motivated by concerns to prevent a decline of the teachings. This was reportedly achieved not only by affirming adherence to the code of rules without change, but also by a consensus on the body of orally transmitted texts, expressed through a group recitation whose execution would require as its basis the same texts. When viewed from this perspective, the Pāli passage translated above can be seen to make explicit what is already to some extent implicit in the way the different *Vinaya*s present the first communal recitation, in that accurate transmission was considered to ensure the continuity of the Buddhist dispensation.

The same need emerges in the Greater Discourse in the Gosiṅga [Grove], already mentioned above. In agreement with its parallels, the discourse reports Ānanda describing what makes someone a learned person. A version of his description in a Chinese *Āgama* passage from a collection of medium-length discourses takes the following form:[264]

> Suppose a monastic is widely trained in learning much and has retained it without loss of memory, having accumulated extensive learning of what is called the teaching that is sublime in the beginning, sublime in the middle, and also sublime in the end, with its meaning and its phrasing, endowed with purity, revealing the pure life. Being in this way widely trained in learning the teaching, having rehearsed it up to a thousand, reflected on it in the mind, and contemplated it with bright vision and deep penetration, the teaching is communicated concisely and aptly, in accordance with what is correct.

Besides reinforcing the importance of avoiding a loss of memory, the passage also brings out the dimension of passing on the teachings to others. The Pāli version and another two parallels extant in Chinese add the specification that such teachings are addressed to the four assemblies,[265] which comprise males and females who could be either monastics or lay disciples. In the ancient setting, these were the types of Buddhist audience to which a particular teaching could be addressed.

Another point of interest is the emphasis in the above passage on the importance of reflecting on and contemplating the teachings, which differs from the attitude among Vedic reciters toward the texts they were transmitting, a topic to which I will return in the next section. The relevance of recitation for purposes related to contemplation can be seen in circumstantial information provided in a Pāli discourse and its two Chinese *Āgama* parallels, according to which at night, just before dawn, a monastic was reciting texts by himself.[266] A woman overheard him and told her child to be quiet, in order to avoid disturbing the recitation. Another Pāli discourse even reports the Buddha doing the same while alone and in seclusion.[267] The content of the recitation is simply a treatment of the six senses from the viewpoint of dependent arising. This shows that the idea could hardly be that the Buddha is rehearsing such a simple teaching. Instead, such instances suggest that recitation of the texts could at times serve as a means of meditatively reflecting on them. In fact, one of the different occasions recognized in the early discourses for the breakthrough to awakening to happen is precisely during recitation.[268] As I already noted in Anālayo (2011b, 859), such instances show that "oral transmission was perceived not only as a means of preserving texts," but also as fulfilling soteriological functions.

Alongside such functions, however, accurate transmission was clearly a central concern. Making others recite word-by-word features in a rule for Buddhist monastics, already taken up in the first chapter (see above p. 12). According to this rule, monastics should not teach recitation in this way to someone who has not received full ordination.[269] Of further interest for appreciating the formulation of this rule is the background narration provided in some *Vinaya*s. One *Vinaya* explicitly refers to the recitation of the Buddha's discourses as what occasioned the rule in question.[270] Another *Vinaya* begins its narration with lay disciples wanting to learn the recitation of discourses and verses.[271] Yet another *Vinaya* is even more specific, as here the event leading to the promulgation of this rule involved teaching the word-by-word recitation of the Chapter on Going Beyond (*Pārāyanavagga*).[272] As noted by Wynne (2004, 109):[273]

> This evidence suggests that Sutta portions of the early Buddhist literature were learnt verbatim among the ordained . . . although the passage does not rule out the use of improvisational methods, we have important evidence showing that the basic literary training in early Buddhism consisted of word for word repetition, and that some portion of the Suttapiṭaka was transmitted in this manner.

In fact, as succinctly noted by Allon (2021, 113), "had improvisation been the norm . . . we would surely see far greater differences than we do see."

9. The Limitations of Memory

Nevertheless, there is a substantial difference between the Vedic and Buddhist oral traditions, a topic I already took up at the end of the previous chapter (p. 65). Whereas for the Vedic reciters correct wording was of crucial importance, for their early Buddhist counterparts the content of the text to be transmitted was central. Carpenter (1992, 73–74) explains, regarding this characteristic of the Vedic oral tradition:

> The enigma of the Veda, at least for a Western audience, is that the "informative efficiency" of its transmission can often be reduced to nil without this transmission losing its authority or justification . . . Even today young boys devote years to memorizing the Veda word for word without the slightest knowledge of—or apparently, interest in—what these words mean . . . The transmission of the Veda from generation to generation is an

> integral part of the transmission of the legitimate Brahmanical social order and its importance in this regard is unaffected by the question of whether or not the texts transmitted are "meaningful."

In contrast, from an early Buddhist perspective, those who learn the Buddha's teachings without endeavoring to understand them are considered fools.[274] In the words of Lopez (1995, 37),

> the śrotriyas [of the Brahminical tradition] were concerned with the precise preservation of the sounds of the Vedas while the śrāvakas [of the Buddhist tradition] were concerned with the preservation of the meaning of the Buddha's word in the vernacular.

Thus, besides the problem that a substantial number of Buddhist monastics involved in the transmission of the texts would not have gone through the type of mnemonic training of Vedic reciters, the emphasis on understanding the teachings given by the Buddha and his disciples would have further hampered accuracy in recall.

In addition to these, the very nature of memory could offer further help to explain the situation. According to research in cognitive psychology, textual memory does not work in a way comparable to a tape recorder or a copy machine, faithfully producing an exact replica of the words originally read or heard.[275] Memory, far from being merely reproductive, is rather of an active and constructive nature. Already the pioneer in research on memory, Bartlett (1932, 204–5 and 207), explained:

> The first notion to get rid of is that memory is primarily or literally reduplicative, or reproductive . . . if we consider evidence rather than presupposition, remembering appears to be far more decisively an affair of construction, rather than one of mere reproduction . . . when a subject is being asked to remember, very often the first thing that emerges is something of the nature of [an] attitude. The recall is then a construction, made

> largely on the basis of this attitude, and its general effect is that of a justification of the attitude.

In sum, "remembering is not the re-excitation of innumerable fixed, lifeless and fragmentary traces. It is an imaginative reconstruction . . . [and] is thus hardly ever really exact" (213). In other words, at the time of trying to recall, the mind constructs the information anew. It is this act of constructing or reconstructing that will determine the way the information is being remembered.

For example, in an experiment subjects were given the task of remembering the description of a house from either the perspective of a prospective burglar or a prospective buyer of the house.[276] After a first recall, some subjects were asked to shift perspective (e.g., "buyer" instead of "burglar") and consequently were able to recall details they had earlier been unable to remember, whereas a control group that did not change perspective did not show a similar increase in their ability to recall additional details on the second occasion. This shows that the attitude during information retrieval influences what will be remembered.

Alterations of the perceived data can occur not only when trying to recall something that took place in the past, but already at the time when something is heard or read that is to be memorized; information is not simply taken in. Instead, the information is stored in the mind together with inferences made by the reader or listener. The drawing of inferences is in fact a necessary aspect of comprehension; without them, a text will not be understood.

These findings make it all the more understandable why, from the viewpoint of the Vedic reciters, it is a mistake to try to understand the texts that are to be memorized. In this way, the working mechanisms of memory, be it during storage or at the time of retrieval, provide additional background for understanding the substantial number of memory errors that can be detected in Buddhist oral literature through comparative study. In other words, sufficient room needs to be granted to the very limitations of human memory itself.

These limitations are well known among those investigating criminal cases, as eyewitnesses tend to provide substantially different reports of what they actually "observed." Quiroga (2017, 60–62) reports a case that exemplifies this well. A victim of rape had made every effort possible to remember the rapist in order to enable later identification, should occasion permit. When presented with several suspects, after some hesitation the victim identified the rapist. Years later DNA tests, which had not been available when the crime was committed, showed that the rapist was instead another person. Yet, even when confronted again with the innocent prisoner and the true rapist, the victim maintained the earlier identification, unable to recognize the actual culprit. The earlier instance of identification after some hesitation had consolidated an incorrect memory that, from then on, kept overriding the actual memory. Quiroga (2017, 164n15) reports that the victim and the person who had been innocently imprisoned now collaborate to advocate for a change in eyewitness-based conviction.

The case illustrates the degree to which memory can be misleading, and once this has happened, wrong recollection can appear to be remarkably true and accurate from the subject's viewpoint. Applied to the ancient Indian setting, this makes it fairly understandable how a memory lapse by a teacher of recitation could turn into accepted tradition, given that in the oral setting no written proof is available to perform a function comparable to a DNA test in the above case. This leaves the determination of the "correct" version of a text in the hand of the most respected reciter in a particular monastery or transmission lineage, and thereby in the hands of the potential memory shortcomings of that reciter. Once that reciter, perhaps after some hesitation comparable to the rape victim described above, has mistakenly come to the conclusion that a certain error is the correct version of the text, the resultant consolidation of an incorrect memory can result in a remarkable degree of inner certainty. Without external proofs, it will be hard to convince this reciter (and those who respect him as their teacher and guide) that his memory is wrong and that he has made an error.

In sum, it seems to me that the limitations of memory offer a more convincing model for the bulk of variations among parallel versions of early Buddhist texts than intentional change. In contrast, assuming that different errors and variations should just be attributed to intentionally introduced change is somewhat like assuming that all variations between eyewitness accounts must be due to intentional falsehood.

The evidence surveyed in this chapter thereby prevents the wholesale application of Western models of textual production to the case of the early Buddhist oral tradition in the form of assuming that what accounts for change nowadays must have been the same in the past. In her study of an early Mahāyāna text, Nattier (2003a, 52) offers the following pertinent observations:[277]

> What forces lead to the insertion of new material into an existing religious text? Or to put it another way, what is the motive of the interpolator who seeks to add his (or, at least theoretically, her) own ideas to an already authoritative scripture?
>
> This is surely the most natural way for a western-trained scholar to put the question, but to phrase our inquiry in this way is to smuggle in, at the outset, two assumptions about how interpolation works: first, that an interpolator adds to a text in order to express new and creative ideas; and second, that interpolation is necessarily a conscious act. However, an examination of interpolated passages ... reveals an immense body of evidence to counter these assumptions. Even a brief cataloguing of these passages will make it clear that to assume a "creative individual author" as the driving force behind interpolations in Buddhist scripture is to import a model that is foreign to most of the literary processes that have shaped the production of Indian religious texts.

10. Summary

The in-itself-natural assumption that variations between parallel versions must reflect some form of intentional intervention by so-called editors or redactors needs to be revised in view of the actual textual evidence. Mistakes in sequence and meaningless additions can hardly be considered intentional. The same holds for conflations or evidence for loss of text. The case of the Discourse on Sixfold Purity shows that even a substantial part of a discourse could be lost and, despite clear awareness within the tradition of the resultant inconsistency, the presentation was not corrected in any way. The same holds for other cases that corroborate a marked lack of homogenization.

The evidence available in this way makes it in my view commendable to take seriously the indications given in various discourses regarding a concern for accuracy among those responsible for the early Buddhist oral transmission. Although this of course does not imply that intentional change never happened, it seems to me that to default to this type of explanation does not do justice to the available textual material. I contend that this makes it preferable to keep in mind the natural limitations of memory when evaluating the evident shortcomings of the early Buddhist oral tradition.

IV • Systematization

In this chapter I explore various aspects of the systematization of the early Buddhist oral tradition. Although apparently the outcome of a concern with accurate transmission, some of the elements emerging from such a concern can be seen to develop a life of their own, taking on a constructive dimension that goes well beyond mere consolidation of the textual material.

My exploration begins with the pervasive employment of repetition in the early texts and its complement in abbreviations. Then I explore the principle of concatenation as applied to consecutive discourses in a particular collection, followed by examining the arranging of discourses within a collection from the viewpoint of facilitating their oral transmission. Then I turn to variations in formulas, the giving of a summary and its corresponding detailed expositions, and to a specific dimension of the topic of repetition, namely repetition series.

1. Repetition

A general characteristic of early Buddhist texts is the frequent occurrence of repetitions and the employment of formulas or pericopes. Already Rhys Davids (1881, xxiii) drew attention to these two features of Buddhist texts as aids to memorization:

> firstly, the use of stock phrases, of which the commencement once given, the remainder followed as a matter of course; and secondly, the habit of repeating whole sentences, or even

> paragraphs, which in our modern books would be understood or inferred, instead of being expressed.

One feature of repetition, already mentioned earlier in relation to the principle of waxing syllables (see above p. 13), is the stringing together of lists of synonyms. Another pattern can be observed when a particular topic needs to be covered in both its positive and negative manifestations. It is a standard procedure in such cases that the same passage will be repeated with precisely the same words and formulations used for the positive case, making only the most minimal changes required in order to adjust these to the negative case (or vice versa). The same procedure becomes even more prominent when a series of different perspectives on a particular topic are explored. A treatment of, for example, four different types of persons or modes of acting can use nearly the same text four times in order to achieve its aim. In a detailed study of repetitive features in a long discourse, Allon (1997b, 359) comes to the conclusion that almost 87 percent of the text involves some form or other of repetition. Reat (1996/1998, 17) notes:

> There is a great deal of repetition from one *sūtra* to another, not only in terms of the doctrines expressed, but also in terms of extensive verbatim repetition of much material. This suggests that the *Sutta Piṭaka* is a sincere attempt to record memorized versions of individual sermons.

Although the pervasive occurrence of repetition does indeed seem to reflect an attempt to record memorized texts, the very same pattern can take on a more creative dimension. An example for this occurs in the Discourse on the Worthy Person (*Sappurisasutta*), which in agreement with its parallels surveys various potential occasions for the arousing of conceit. One of these is when someone comes from a high family.[278] The Pāli version stands alone in repeating the same treatment for another three cases concerned similarly with someone's family of origin, which could be a great family, a vastly wealthy family, and an outstandingly wealthy family.[279] These seem to be closely similar in meaning. In contrast, the other topics taken up in the Pāli discourse and in the parallel versions involve significantly different possible reasons for a sense of conceit.[280] It seems fair to assume that the relevant passage in the Pāli version would be the result of a proliferation of synonyms or exemplifications that were subsequently mistaken to involve distinctly separate cases. In this way, a listing of synonyms, ostensibly having the purpose of ensuring that a shared meaning impresses itself on the audience, would have led to the creation of additional treatments of what had come to be considered distinct occasions for the arousing of conceit.

In addition to the regular occurrence of repetition within a single text, the early discourses also make frequent use of "pericopes," formulaic expressions or phrases that depict a recurrent situation or event in the same way.[281] Whether it be descriptions of how someone approaches the Buddha or of how someone attains liberation, pericopes will be employed with a fixed set of phrases and expressions, with only the most minimal changes introduced to adapt these pericopes to the individual occasion. These two features, the repetition of passages within a discourse and the use of pericopes throughout a discourse collection, are responsible for the highly repetitive nature of the early discourses. According to Griffiths (1983, 58), the use of such pericopes can be understood to be

> a direct result of the methods by which sacred material was preserved and handed on in the early Buddhist communities; the demands of mnemonic convenience and pedagogic effectiveness created by the system of private learning and public recitation meant that the units of tradition valued by the communities had to be . . . reduced to an easily memorized standard form.

Yit (2008, 289) reasons that the resultant "basic units for memorization and transmission" offer "a practical and natural way to recite, to remember, to convey and to understand the key points of doctrinal concepts and stories."

At the same time, however, the application of a pericope can occasionally result in inconsistencies. An example that at the same time also illustrates the topic of inconsistent presentations, which I explored in the previous chapter, involves the pericope description of the pleased reaction of a listener after having received a teaching from the Buddha. A case of apparent misapplication can be seen in a Chinese *Āgama* discourse. In agreement with its Pāli counterpart and another version extant in Chinese translation, this discourse reports that, after having received a teaching from the Buddha, a brahmin passed away as a nonreturner.[282] The Chinese *Āgama* discourse in question concludes by explicitly including the (recently deceased) brahmin among those who rejoiced in what the Buddha had said.[283] When the formulaic description of such rejoicing was applied to the end of the discourse, the reciters apparently failed to adjust it to its context. This adjustment appears to have been done in the other two versions, as these only report the rejoicing of the monastics, without any reference to a rejoicing by the deceased brahmin.

Such misapplication of a pericope makes it less probable that this was a formalized unit employed during improvisation or as the building block for the intentional creation of a discourse. During an oral performance involving improvisation or intentional creation, attention will be on the meaning of what is being recited, with the formulas only serving in support of the improvisatory or creative oral performance. The way the formulaic passage is used here, however, reflects a lack of attention paid to meaning; otherwise, the resultant inconsistency would have been noted and avoided.

The same holds for the various memory errors surveyed in the previous chapter as well as for instances, identified by von Simson (1965, 137–38), where the counterpart to a particular term shows close phonetic similarity but has a considerably different meaning.[284] Findings of this type point to an attempt by the reciters to remember precisely, with the result of preserving formal aspects even though the meaning has been lost. The same is also evident from the fact that errors occurring due to excessive attention to outer features of the text continued to be transmitted, rather than stimulating a revision of an incoherent presentation.

The pattern that emerges in this way concords with a general trend of increased memorization ability correlating with decreased comprehension ability. Quiroga (2017, 82) reports a particular case of a person with a remarkable ability to memorize effortlessly. However, although "he could recite long passages by rote and remember them for many years, he was unable to abstract the content of a book enough to apprehend its meaning." The price he had to pay for his outstanding memorization skills was that "he was incapable of understanding the content of what he read." Even having a normal conversation could lead him into difficulties, as he "was sometimes unable to avoid noting and remembering small variations in the tone of the voice of the person speaking to him and thus could not follow what he was being told." The evidence provided by comparative study of the early discourses points to the same pattern, albeit not to such an extreme. The very effort and ability to recite by rote can impair awareness of the lack of congruence of the content.

2. Abbreviation

Due to the repetitive nature of considerable portions of the early Buddhist discourses, these naturally lend themselves to abbreviation. The implementation of abbreviation can help to save time during oral rehearsal and, once transmission has shifted to the written medium, enable economic use of writing material. An example illustrating such abbreviation would be the instructions for mindful contemplation of the six sense spheres:[285]

> A monastic knows the eye, knows forms, knows the fetter that arises dependent on both, knows how an unarisen fetter arises, knows how an arisen fetter is removed, and knows how a removed fetter does not arise in the future.
>
> [A monastic] knows the ear, knows sounds ... knows the nose, knows odors ... knows the tongue, knows flavors ... knows the body, knows tangibles ...
>
> [A monastic] knows the mind, knows mind-objects, knows the fetter that arises dependent on both, knows how an unarisen fetter arises, knows how an arisen fetter is removed, and knows how a removed fetter does not arise in the future.

In this way, the full description of what should be known occurs only on the first and last occasions, allowing for an abbreviation of the intervening four sense spheres. Notably, this does not take abbreviation to its greatest potential extent. Even though the first instance already gives the formula in full, this will still be repeated once more on the last instance, rather than being abbreviated also in this case. This pattern reflects the oral setting, where a final repetition of the full exposition serves to ensure that the meaning to be conveyed is fully taken in even when recitation is done in an abbreviated manner. Such a procedure conforms to a general pattern evident in the early discourses, where a particular introductory statement is followed by a detailed exposition that concludes with a repetition of the initial statement. Giving a teaching in this way, the speaker(s) can make sure that the audience keeps in mind the main topic.

From the viewpoint of oral recitation, there would need to be an agreement among reciters on what is abbreviated and what is recited in full. Later exegesis describes the conflict that can result when reciters have different attitudes in this respect.[286] A reciter of swift understanding will get impatient at another who fills out the abbreviations, thinking that they will never get to the end of the recitation. Conversely, a reciter of less swift understanding can feel deprived of sufficient time to become familiar with a text presented in too abbreviated a manner. The description seems to imply a type of group recitation where one of the two reciters leads and the other has to follow. In such a situation, too much or too little abbreviation can indeed become a matter of concern for those who must follow a reciter of different inclinations.

The employment of abbreviation in a particular passage can be based on a prototype provided within the same text or else can apply across different texts within a collection. The above example pertains to the first type, where the model for executing the abbreviation occurs in the same text, here in the form of describing different types of knowing regarding a fetter arising at a particular sense door. The other type of abbreviation can rely on standard phrases found recurrently in the early discourses or on the employment of lists. As noted by Cox (2004, 2), the "need to memorize the teaching obviously promoted the use of categorizing lists as a mnemonic device."[287]

The present case involves one such list, namely the six sense spheres. In principle, it would have been possible to abbreviate even further by not giving the intervening sense spheres in full. Once the eye and forms are mentioned, a reciter would know that next come the ear and sound, then the nose and odors, etc.

A case study of the employment of abbreviation, as evident in the division on the five aggregates in the topic-wise collection extant in Chinese translation, shows that about 69 percent of the text is given in abbreviated form.[288] In other words, the division in question, which according to the reconstructed order is the first in the whole collection, presents only 31 percent of its textual material in full. These figures include whole discourses being given only in abbreviation. Such procedure is a recurrent feature in several collections of short discourses, topic-wise and numerical, which takes the form of following a particular discourse with the indication that the same exposition should be repeated with some often fairly minor terminological change(s).

This type of pattern involves a proliferation of synonyms, in an apparent attempt to cover a broad range of possible alternatives. In itself, the providing of such a comprehensive coverage could have its origin in an attempt at precise recall, perhaps due to the arising of some uncertainty among reciters as to the "correct" formulation. In order to avoid missing potential nuances underlying such differences, all possible instances could have been recorded, resulting in a series of discourses that are otherwise alike.

An illustrative example is the Discourse on [Living in] a Forest Thicket (*Vanapathasutta*), which describes the conditions under which monastics should either leave or else remain where they are staying.[289] The Pāli version has two parallels that occur consecutively in the same Chinese *Āgama* collection and even share the same title.[290] The differences between the two versions involve only rather minor matters of formulation, of the type that can easily result from the vagaries of oral transmission. It seems probable that the existence of these two separate discourses is the result of different reciters recalling this discourse with some variations, combined with a concern for exact transmission, as otherwise such minor variations could have easily been ignored.

Another example involves two discourses in the topic-wise collection extant in Pāli, both of which report the same instruction given by the Buddha to his attendant Ānanda.[291] The only difference between the two versions concerns their introductory narration, as the Buddha gave the instruction after either being prompted by an inquiry from Ānanda or without such prompting. Only the version that reports an inquiry by Ānanda has a Chinese *Āgama* counterpart.[292] The Pāli collection continues with another two discourses on the same topic but given to unnamed monastics, again with the same difference of the Buddha being either prompted by a corresponding inquiry or not.[293] Each of these two Pāli discourses has a parallel in the same Chinese *Āgama* collection.[294] In this way, three times the same instruction in the Chinese *Āgama* collection contrasts with four times the same instruction in the Pāli collection.

The situation found in the Pāli collection results in presenting Ānanda, who according to the different accounts of the first communal recitation (*saṅgīti/saṃgīti*) was the one to have remembered the Buddha's various discourses and thus clearly was perceived by the reciters as endowed with remarkable mental retention, as needing to be given the same instruction twice. Such a presentation goes against the grain of the perception of his abilities and role intrinsic to the reciter tradition. Nor would it make sense to assume that the idea is that the Buddha had forgotten having already given this teaching to Ānanda. Such an idea would conflict with the depiction of the Buddha in other discourses. Instead, it seems fair to assume that the doubling of references to Ānanda as the recipient of the same instruction would be the result of a transmission error. The fact that the alternatives of being prompted by an inquiry or not are already found in relation to unnamed monastics must have led to the same two alternatives being applied to Ānanda, without noticing the repercussions of the resultant presentation.

This is, in fact, not the only such instance, as another doublet of Pāli discourses reports Ānanda asking the same question on two occasions, with the Buddha giving two nearly identical teachings in reply.[295] The absence of a parallel prevents pursuing this further, but it is probable that in this case as well an accident in transmission resulted in the coexistence of two closely similar discourses. Although such cases would have originated from transmission errors, the resultant alternatives appear to have been preserved due to the overarching concern with precise recall.

3. Concatenation

The principle of concatenation already came up in earlier chapters in relation to the sequence of rules and of inspired utterances (see above pp. 11 and 63). The same basic principle of ordering portions of text in such a way that something mentioned in a previous item recurs in the next item can also be seen at work in the arrangement of a sequence of items in a given discourse and in the order in which discourses are arranged within a collection.

The first aspect can be illustrated with the example of seven ways of settling a litigation, already mentioned in the first chapter of my exploration (see above p. 33). The introductory listing of these seven differs from the order of their exposition in the main body of the relevant Pāli discourse but agrees with the sequence adopted in other Pāli listings of this topic.[296] The resultant departure from what within the Pāli oral tradition appears to be a fairly fixed sequential pattern seems to have resulted from a shifting of the exposition of the fifth way of settling a litigation to stand instead in the second position.[297] This fifth way of settling a litigation shares a fairly long phrase with the first way of settling a litigation, a phrase otherwise not found in the remainder of the discourse.[298] It seems that the principle of concatenation, probably applied instinctively rather than resulting from a deliberate decision, led to a shift of the fifth way of settling a litigation to the second position, thereby achieving an overlap of phrasing with the first way of settling a litigation. The bare listing to some extent follows the same principle, although leading to a different result, as the first three terms in this sequence share a reference to the term *vinaya*.[299] In this way, the same principle would explain the order adopted for such listings as well as the departure from that order in the full exposition.

The relevance of concatenation to the ordering of discourses can be illustrated with the first chapter of the Theravāda collection of medium-length discourses, the *Majjhimanikāya* extant in Pāli.[300] The first and second discourses in this chapter begin their respective treatment by examining the case of an untaught ordinary worldling,[301] and proceed from this to a liberated monastic who has gone beyond the influxes and fetters. This similarity in pattern easily provides a relation between the two discourses. The second discourse instructs how to eradicate the influxes; the topic of eradication recurs at the beginning of the third discourse, which criticizes monastics who do not eradicate those things that their teacher told them to eradicate.[302]

Another aspect of proper conduct highlighted in the third discourse is the need to dwell in seclusion,[303] a topic that forms the central theme of the fourth discourse, which expounds the difficulties of living in seclusion. The interrelation between the two discourses is further strengthened by the circumstance that in the third discourse monastics who practice seclusion function as a shining example, just as in the fourth discourse the Buddha's practice of seclusion functions as a shining example for his disciples.[304]

In the context of examining the difficulties of living in seclusion, the fourth discourse describes the obstructive effect of various bad mental qualities, a theme continued in the fifth discourse by examining various bad mental qualities of a monastic. Several of the bad qualities mentioned in the fourth discourse recur in the same terms in the description of bad monastics given at the conclusion of the fifth discourse.[305]

The fifth discourse examines unworthy wishes of a monastic and highlights the importance of making an effort to overcome them. The sixth discourse takes up the same theme from the complementary perspective of worthy wishes of a monastic, explaining how effort should be directed for such wishes to come to fulfillment. The two treatments have a partial overlap, as both take up the case of a monastic who wishes to obtain food and clothing, etc.[306]

The series of worthy wishes in the sixth discourse leads from going beyond unwholesome states of mind, via the attainment of stream entry, to the gaining of full awakening.[307] The seventh discourse takes up the same topics by first treating a series of unwholesome mental states, then referring to the attainment of stream entry, and finally culminating in the attainment of the destruction of the influxes (which equals full awakening).[308] The seventh discourse also completes the topic of food that was already a theme in the two preceding discourses. The fifth and sixth discourses mention a monastic's wish for food, whereas the seventh discourse indicates that even superior types of food will not be an obstruction for someone who has developed the path.[309]

The seventh and eighth discourses base their respective expositions on what needs to be overcome in order to progress on the path. The relationship between these two discourses is so close in this respect that there is a substantial overlap in their lists of mental defilements.[310] The eighth discourse takes up the transcendence of views, a theme the ninth discourse develops from its complementary perspective by exploring various aspects of right view.[311] This theme is already adumbrated in a reference in the eighth discourse to right view as the way to overcome wrong view.[312]

The treatment in the ninth discourse revolves around various aspects that one should "know" (*pajānāti*) in order to accomplish right view. The need to "know" is also the theme of the tenth discourse, where the same activity is mentioned again and again in descriptions of how to develop the four establishments of mindfulness. Both discourses thereby have in common that they expound how one factor of the noble eightfold path can be developed with the help of various aspects that one should "know."[313]

In this way, the discourses found in the first chapter of the Theravāda collection of medium-length discourses have been arranged in such a way that the principle of concatenation facilitates their recall in the established sequence and thereby enables the carrying out of group recitation.

The same principle of providing a link in memory that connects one discourse with the next can at times result in errors of memory. An example can be seen in the seventh and eighth discourses of the fourth chapter in the Theravāda collection of medium-length discourses, which share a reference to the topic of "liberation by the destruction of craving."[314] In the seventh discourse, a celestial visitor asks the Buddha to give a teaching on this topic with the additional stipulation that the explanation should be "succinct" (*saṅkhitta*).[315] The same reference to "liberation by the destruction of craving" qualified as "succinct" recurs another ten times in the same discourse,[316] in keeping with the fact that the Buddha had indeed given only a rather brief reply. The eighth discourse concludes with the Buddha encouraging the monastics in the audience to keep in mind what he had explained in this discourse on the topic of "liberation by the destruction of craving," which also comes with the qualification of being "succinct."[317] This qualification does not fit the context, as the actual exposition in the eighth discourse is rather lengthy. The Chinese parallel in fact does not employ the qualification "succinct."[318]

It seems that the memory connection created between the two discourses through the shared phrase "liberation by the destruction of craving" has led to an inadvertent transfer of the qualification repeatedly used in the seventh discourse to the eighth discourse, as a result of which the Buddha qualifies a lengthy exposition he has just given as being "succinct." The incoherence created in this way neatly exemplifies a central topic of my exploration in this chapter, in that principles of orality meant to facilitate correct memorization can at times have unforeseen results that are the opposite of what the respective principle was supposed to achieve.

The principle of concatenation in general can be applied in different ways, so that the sequence described above for the discourses in the first chapter of the Theravāda collection of medium-length discourses is just one of many different possibilities of ordering discourses. Such ordering appears to have been a process specific to distinct reciter traditions. The sequence of discourses in the Sarvāstivāda collection of medium-length discourses, extant in Chinese translation, is in fact totally different. The two collections have only four chapters in common, and these occur at different places in each respective collection.[319] The contents of these four chapters also differ, as one such chapter only has two discourse parallels,[320] two chapters only four,[321] and only one chapter has nine discourses shared by the two collections. Even in this case, however, the sequence differs, as can be seen from the survey below of the discourse parallels in this chapter. Arranged in the sequence in which these are found in the Theravāda collection (MN 132 to 140), the nine Sarvāstivāda parallels are

167, 165, 166, 170, 171, 163, 164, 169, 162.

The variation in sequence evident in this way show that, even in the case of the one chapter in the two collections that contains by far the highest number of parallels, these do not occur in the same sequence. The arrangement of the medium-length discourses is clearly the outcome of developments specific to each of the two reciter traditions. Even not considering differences in content, already the substantially different arrangement of discourses shows that members of the two reciter traditions would not have been able to perform group recitation together even for a single chapter, let alone for the whole of their respective collections of medium-length discourses.

4. The Structure of the Pāli Medium-Length Collection

As already briefly mentioned when introducing the four discourse collections (see above p. 42), the Theravāda collection of medium-length discourses groups its texts into three main divisions. From the viewpoint of oral transmission, these three divisions are of further interest, as they appear to reflect the need for portioning off textual material to enable reciters to opt for memorizing only a part, as opposed to the entirety, of the collection.

According to Theravāda exegesis, these three divisions were to be learned by a prospective reciter one after the other in succession. Reciters would at first memorize the first division of fifty discourses. When this was accomplished, they would turn to the middle division of fifty discourses. When these had been successfully committed to memory, they would learn the final division of fifty-two discourses.[322] Another relevant indication is that someone wanting to become a reciter of this collection needs to memorize at least the first set of fifty.[323] From this it would follow that the first set of fifty is the minimum that needs to be learned, to which the middle and the final fifty could then be added to become a fully accomplished reciter of the collection. Although these descriptions are only found in commentarial texts, they may reflect ancient patterns among reciters.

Understood in this way, a reciter of lesser talent for memorization would only learn the first fifty discourses. Closer inspection shows that the discourses in this first division take up the most essential themes required for a monastic's training and practice. Learning the first fifty would thus provide a reciter with expositions on the most foundational matters. A reciter with greater abilities could then continue and learn also the second fifty. Having learned two sets of fifty would presumably enable such a reciter to take up preaching on a broader scale. For such a purpose, the five chapters assembled in the second fifty would be particularly apt, as they collect discourses under the chapter headings of being addressed to householders, monastics, wanderers, kings, and brahmins. These five groups are the main audiences that a reciter would encounter when preaching on a broader scale, so that learning this second set of fifty would provide a selection of discourses related to each of these groups, as occasion demands.

A reciter who trains further, in the sense of memorizing all of the discourses in the collection, would also be versed in the more detailed descriptions of meditation practice and related topics provided in several of the discourses collected in the final division. This would enable such a reciter not only to be a preacher in general, but also to act as a teacher for more advanced disciples and fellow monastics, guiding them in their practice.

In this way, the division adopted in the Pāli collection of medium-length discourses appears to suit the exigencies of oral transmission, where reciters of differing degrees of ability need to be provided with a foundational set of discourses, be offered the option of adding more material for teaching a wider audience through the second fifty, and alternatively be able to memorize the entire collection.

5. The Sequence of Long Discourses

A similar pattern appears to hold also for the tripartite division of the collections of long discourses. According to Theravāda exegesis, the Great Chapter (*Mahāvagga*) is the minimum that needs to be memorized from the Pāli collection of long discourses.[324] This contains the Great Discourse on the [Buddha's] Final Nirvana (*Mahāparinibbānasutta*) and a discourse providing detailed information on six former Buddhas.[325]

In the case of the Mūlasarvāstivāda collection of long discourses, extant in a fragmentary Sanskrit manuscript, these two discourses form part of the "Section on Six Discourses" (*Ṣaṭsūtrakanipāta*), which acquired such importance that at times it was transmitted on its own.[326] The same two discourses stand right at the beginning of the Dharmaguptaka collection of long discourses extant in Chinese translation. By endowing the Buddha with six predecessors and depicting in detail his final days, these discourses must have been of increasing appeal in the period following his demise.

At the same time, however, the actual order of discourses in the three collections differs substantially, which can best be illustrated with the help of a survey of those twenty Theravāda discourses that have counterparts in the two parallel collections. The first line of the table presents the Pāli discourses by number, the second line their Dharmaguptaka counterparts, and the third line the corresponding discourses in the Mūlasarvāstivāda collection.[327]

1	2	3	4	5	8	9	11	12	13	14	16	18	19	20	24	28	29	33	34
21	27	20	22	23	25	28	24	29	26	1	2	4	3	19	15	18	17	9	10
47	44	35	33	34	46	36	29	28	45	5	6	13	14	24	9	16	15	3	1

The overall impression conveyed by this survey is one of substantial diversity in the arranging of the discourses. At the same time, however, the processes leading to this diversity can at times be seen as involving similar patterns. This can be exemplified with the first discourse in the Theravāda collection, the Discourse on Brahmā's Net, whose counterparts occur as the twenty-first discourse in the Dharmaguptaka collection and the last (forty-seventh) discourse in the Mūlasarvāstivāda collection.[328] In all three cases, the discourse is part of a division on the topic of morality. This division brings together a range of discourses that share an account of the gradual path (see above p. 39).

In the case of the Theravāda division on morality, the description of morality in the Discourse on Brahmā's Net is longer than the one given in the subsequent discourses' expositions of the gradual path.[329] It would seem natural to begin a collection of discourses on the topic of morality with the one that has the longest exposition of this topic. On this reasoning, the Discourse on Brahmā's Net should indeed occur before other Pāli discourses that have an account of the gradual path.

The exposition on morality in the Mūlasarvāstivāda version of the Discourse on Brahmā's Net has a rather short description of morality, much shorter than its parallels and also considerably less than the coverage given to this topic in another Mūlasarvāstivāda version of the gradual path.[330] On applying the same reasoning as above, it would follow that the Mūlasarvāstivāda version of the Discourse on Brahmā's Net should indeed be found at the end of the section on morality, after the different discourses with an account of the gradual path.

In the case of the Dharmaguptaka collection, the sections on morality in its version of the Discourse on Brahmā's Net is of about the same length as the gradual path account.[331] Since the gradual path account is of more importance, as it is repeated in several other subsequent discourses, it seems again natural that its full execution stands at the head of the division on morality, with the counterpart to the Discourse on Brahmā's Net only coming after that.

Combining the above with the fact that the division on morality is the first division in the Theravāda collection but the third in the other two, the substantially different placing of this discourse might reflect similar processes of organization.[332]

Regarding the different placing of the division on morality, this can be explored by returning to the suggestion in the Theravāda exegetical tradition that the Great Chapter should be memorized first. If this section had from the outset of the formation of the collection been considered the first to be committed to memory, it would have been more natural for it to stand in the first position, as it does in the other two collections. Since this is not the case, perhaps the present order in the Pāli collection of long discourses may reflect a time when the expositions on morality were considered to be the material that reciters should learn first of all. These expositions on morality would in fact provide a reciter with basic instructions similar in kind to several of the discourses found in the first section of the Pāli collection of medium-length discourse.

With the passage of time, however, it could reasonably be expected that the inspiration provided by discourses that provide detailed information on the six former Buddhas or record the last travel of the present Buddha and his passing away acquired increasing importance. After the death of the Buddha, with the increase of disciples who never had a chance to meet the master in person, or even meet someone who had been in his living presence, there would have been an increasing demand for such information in order to foster inspiration and strengthen faith. In such a situation, it would quite probably become preferable for a neophyte reciter of the collection of long discourse to take up first the chapter that contains such inspirational material. If there should indeed have been such a shift of interest, it did not lead to a shifting of the respective division to the first position within the Pāli collection, comparable to its position in the other two collections, but only found reflection in the commentarial recommendation.

Whatever may be the final word on this last suggestion, the above considerations show how keeping in mind the requirements of systematization during oral transmission can provide a perspective on what otherwise may seem rather puzzling differences between the three collections of long discourses.

6. Structural Aspects of the Collections of Short Discourses

As a basic rule, short discourses can find a placing either in the topic-wise collections or else in those arranged numerically. In the latter case, it seems that at an earlier stage the idea may have been just to go from Ones to Tens; the Elevens being included only subsequently.[333] Needless to say, this suggestion does not imply that the section of Elevens as a whole must invariably be later than the rest of the collection.[334] It only means that the present state of the numerical collections is quite probably the result of a gradual process of growth. The idea that an earlier version of the collection of numerically arranged discourses was influenced by the idea of counting from one to ten would correspond to the number of discourses often used elsewhere in different collections for comprising a chapter.

Some degree of gradual evolution can be seen right away with the first chapter among the Ones in the Pāli collection, whose placing in this section relies on a recurrent highlight on "single" (*eka*) things that can obsess the mind. These are the experience of another person through any of the five senses, with the other person being either a male or a female.[335] Taken together, the exposition covers ten such single things that can obsess the mind. Given that the Pāli tradition reckons this exposition to be a "chapter," the presentation amounts to ten distinct discourses: five discourses for a male, taking up each of the senses on its own, and then five discourses for a female, again for each sense. The parallel in the numerical Chinese *Āgama* collection presents a similar analysis in the form of just two discourses, one of which takes up the case of a female and the other that of a male.[336]

As a record of an actual teaching, the impression created by the Pāli version is not particularly compelling, as it would imply that a series of individual instructions on just a single sense door were given, and that moreover such instructions were given at separate times for the case of a female and for the case of a male. At the same time, however, it also needs to be kept in mind that in oral transmission the line between one and ten "discourses" would have been fairly fluid and the decision to reckon this exposition as a chapter in its own right may only have been taken at a relatively late time, perhaps when transitioning to the written medium.[337] In fact, the exposition in the first chapter among the Ones in the Pāli collection is not problematic in itself. Only the form in which it is now found is curious, giving the impression that the notion of a section on Ones, originally meant as a reference point for collecting discourses, has in turn had an impact on the form the discourse(s) eventually acquired. I will come back to this example in the last chapter of my exploration.

Another example for the influence apparently exerted by an already existing strategy of collecting discourses under a particular number occurs among the Elevens. The relevant discourse seems to have achieved its position by adding up two topics covered in its presentation: the five faculties and the six recollections.[338] In this way, a presentation that could perhaps more naturally have been placed either under the Fives or under the Sixes, has instead found inclusion among the Elevens, perhaps as a way to increase the material allocated to this division, as expositions which feature the actual number eleven occur less often than those that feature fives or sixes.

Parallels to this discourse in the Chinese *Āgama*s are instead found among the topic-wise collections, which provide a similar transition from five to six topics.[339] According to the reconstructed order of the nearly completely preserved collection of topic-wise discourses, the text in question was included in a topic-wise division (*saṃyutta/saṃyukta*) under the name of Mahānāma to whom, according to all versions, the Buddha gave this teaching. The Pāli collection of topic-wise discourses does not have a division dedicated to Mahānāma, hence the discourse in question was rather accommodated in the numerical collection. The present case thereby conveniently illustrates the existence of some potential overlap between the two strategies for assembling short discourses.

7. Delimiting the Four Discourse Collections

The possibility of arranging discourses in different ways can also be demonstrated with the example of whole chapters. One such case is a set of ten discourses among the Threes of the Pāli collection of numerically arranged discourses, reflecting the fact that these discourses tackle the topic of the "three" higher trainings. The reciters of the corresponding Chinese *Āgama* tradition instead opted for giving prominence to the shared topic of "training" instead of the number three, hence the parallels are found in the topic-wise collection.[340]

Another example is the first chapter in the Chinese *Āgama* collection of medium-length discourses, which assembles expositions that share the number seven, a fact reflected in its title being the Chapter on Seven Dharmas.[341] Most of the Pāli parallels to this chapter occur among the Sevens of the *Aṅguttaranikāya*.[342] In this case, even though both traditions agree in placing emphasis on the number seven, the set of discourses still ended up in different collections due to divergent evaluations of their length. Whereas the reciters of the Pāli tradition reckoned these discourses to be short and hence allocated them to the numerically assembled short discourses, the reciters of the *Āgama* collection instead treated these discourses as being of medium length. The same pattern recurs in another example, where the later part of the fourth chapter in the same Chinese *Āgama* collection of medium-length discourses assembles discourses that for the most part have their counterparts among the Eights of the *Aṅguttaranikāya*.[343]

Conversely, the last chapter of the Pāli collection of medium-length discourses assembles discourses that share a concern with the six sense spheres, a concern explicitly recognized in its title as the Chapter on the Six Sense Spheres (*Saḷāyatanavagga*). The Chinese *Āgama* parallels are found in the topic-wise collection.[344] In this case, the Pāli reciters considered to be of medium length what their *Āgama* brethren instead treated as short discourses to be allocated to the topic-wise collection.

The rationale behind such different distribution or moving of discourses and even chapters from one collection to another would be to ensure that reciters of each collection had a good coverage of various aspects of the teachings, which at times could have motivated some reciter traditions to allocate material differently.

In the Pāli tradition, the division into four discourse collections eventually led to differences of opinion and understanding among their respective reciters.[345] Mori (1990, 127) notes that the reciters "who were originally responsible for the memorization and transmission of particular Nikāyas or scriptures became gradually the exponents of views and opinions concerning the interpretation of the teaching embodied in them." Endo (2003b, 4) adds that during an initial period the reciters "were expected to keep in memory only the canonical texts . . . but after the commentaries began to be composed, their function changed to include both the canonical text and their commentaries." Due to the resultant increasing specialization, some "among those responsible for the preservation and transmission of the texts and their commentaries . . . tenaciously adhered to their own traditions" (33). Although such tendencies are only attested for the Pāli tradition, of which all discourse collections and the respective commentaries are fully preserved, it can safely be assumed that similar processes would also have impacted other reciter traditions.

The overall picture that suggests itself from the above exploration is that discourses were allocated to one of the four collections in accordance with preferences within a particular transmission lineage. Differing allocations would have been motivated by the wish to ensure that each collection remains sufficiently attractive to be of appeal among prospective reciters, combined with the need of avoiding that any of the four collections becomes unrepresentative of the teachings as a whole, in order to prevent fostering the arising of factionalism and one-sided views among its reciters.

8. Variations of Formulas

Of interest for an appreciation of the early Buddhist oral tradition is also the expectation, mentioned above, that reciters of a particular collection eventually had to memorize the respective commentaries as well, once these had come into existence and become established. This implies a substantial increase of the textual material to be memorized, which in turn would make it considerably more challenging to learn more than one discourse collection.

In other words, the increasing specialization envisaged above would have encouraged the arising of divergences between the discourse collections, simply because fewer reciters would have memorized them all, diminishing the possibility of "corrections." The two reports of the same teaching to Kasi Bhāradvāja leading to substantially different outcomes, mentioned in the previous chapter (see p. 89), are a case in point. The indication in the topic-wise collection that he took refuge as a lay follower differs from the record in the Section of Discourses, according to which he went forth and became an arahant. It seems probable that such differences arose at a time when only few reciters had memorized both of these collections.

In fact, the allocation to a particular collection can be seen to have impacted formulaic descriptions employed in its discourses. This can best be illustrated with additional cases where an otherwise identical Pāli discourse is found in more than one collection. One example is a visit paid by a minister called Vassakāra, who had been sent by King Ajātasattu to inquire about a certain matter from the Buddha.[346] A report of this visit can be found in the Pāli collections of long discourses and of numerical discourses, given below one after the other:[347]

> Vassakāra . . . assented to [the order given to him] by Ajātasattu Vedehiputta, King of Magadha, got state carriages ready, mounted a state carriage, left Rājagaha in the state carriages, and went toward Mount Vulture Peak. After going by carriage as far as the ground was passable for carriages, he descended from the carriage and approached the Blessed One just on foot.

> Vassakāra . . . assented to [the order given to him] by Ajātasattu Vedehiputta, King of Magadha, and approached the Blessed One.

Whereas the first version, taken from the collections of long discourses, describes in detail how Vassakāra got ready, drove by chariot, and then proceeded on foot, the second version does not mention his mode of arrival at all and just reports that he approached the Buddha. As far as the meaning is concerned, the difference is negligible. The lack of explicit reference to carriages in the second version does not intend to convey that Vassakāra went all the way on foot. Instead, it simply reflects the choice of the reciters to present his approach with less details.

The textual portions in question occur in the narrative parts of the respective discourses and thereby share a more fluid nature with the promulgation narratives for monastic rules and the background stories to verses and inspired utterances, surveyed in previous chapters. As noted by Williams (1970, 167), the "oral transmission of teaching is generally more conservative than that of narrative material." Nevertheless, from the viewpoint of these two extracts being reports of the same event found in the same reciter tradition, the differences are remarkable.

A similar pattern can be seen in relation to a visit paid by Māra to the Buddha, after the Buddha's attendant Ānanda had departed.[348] Below are two different versions of his approach, found in the Pāli collections of long and numerical discourses:[349]

> Then, not long after the venerable Ānanda had left, Māra the Bad One approached the Blessed One. Having approached, he

> stood to one side. Standing to one side, Māra the Bad One said this to the Blessed One . . .

> Then, not long after the venerable Ānanda had left, Māra the Bad One said this to the Blessed One . . .

The second version from the collection of numerical discourses no longer reports that Māra approached the Buddha. As in the previous case, the differences that emerge do not affect the meaning. The very circumstance that Māra speaks to the Buddha makes it clear that there must have been some form of approach, even when this is not explicitly mentioned. The same holds for his taking the standing posture. Although only mentioned in the first version, it is a standard feature in the early discourses that celestial beings remain standing when speaking to the Buddha.[350] Hence, the celestial Māra's standing posture can safely be assumed to be implicit in the report in the collection of numerical discourses, even though this is not explicitly mentioned.

Another relevant case is the formulaic description of what happens after the Buddha has finished taking his meal at the host's home. The otherwise same episode takes the following form in a discourse of medium length and a report of the same in the *Vinaya*.[351]

> When the Blessed One had eaten and had removed his hand from the bowl, [the host] took a certain low seat and sat to one side.

> When the Blessed One had eaten and had removed his hand from the bowl, [the host] sat to one side.

The second version, taken from the *Vinaya* account, is certainly not meant to imply that the host did not take a low seat and was therefore behaving less respectfully. The difference is simply a reflection of the degree to which the respective reciter traditions decided to provide details. The present case shows that such variations occur not only among reciter traditions of the different discourse collections, but also can involve those who were passing on *Vinaya* narratives pertaining to the same Theravāda transmission lineage. The general pattern that emerges, as already noted by Norman (1997, 51), gives the impression that

> once the texts had been distributed among groups to preserve and hand them on to their successors, the precise methods of stereotyping which were employed, in an attempt to make remembering easier, were not necessarily the same for each set of *bhāṇaka*s [reciters].

The same type of variation in formulas can also be observed with regularity in comparative studies of discourses transmitted by different reciter traditions. By way of example, the collection of medium-length discourses extant in Chinese translation regularly describes that a monastic would fan the Buddha, that visitors ask for permission before posing a question, and that they depart by circumambulating him three times. The first two descriptions are found only rarely in the respective Pāli counterparts, which also differ by mentioning only a single circumambulation undertaken by departing visitors.[352] Such variations go beyond expressions of respect toward the Buddha, as the two medium-length collections also differ in the frequency with which they mention the sitting mat, a standard requisite of a monastic. Although Minh Chau (1964/1991, 29) took this to point to an actual difference in usage, the lack of corroborating evidence makes it more probable that this is just another variation in formulaic descriptions.[353]

For evaluating such narratives that frame the actual teaching, findings by von Simson (1977) regarding formulas describing how someone approaches another for a discussion, found in Sarvāstivāda discourses extant in Sanskrit, are of interest. Although these show a recurrent tendency to adopt a new formulation for such descriptions, the older form is kept when the description occurs in direct speech, such as when the Buddha reports how someone approached him.[354] This difference points to an attempt by the reciters to maintain a higher degree of fidelity in the transmission of textual portions perceived as being part of the source text, compared to textual material perceived as being part of the narrative frame and thus stemming from previous generations of reciters, rather than being considered the word of the Buddha (or of his chief disciples).

This ties in with an observation made in the previous chapter regarding the explicit permission to supplement the name of a location at which a discourse took place, should this information have been forgotten (see p. 70). The mention of the location occurs in the introductory sentence, which goes back to an explanation provided by the first generations of reciters of the discourse. For this reason, it is naturally perceived as more amenable to later adjustments than the content of the actual teaching.

9. Summary and Exposition

As briefly mentioned above, the employment of abbreviation follows a basic feature evident in the early discourses of announcing a particular topic in a summary manner, followed by providing a detailed analysis, and then concluding with a repetition of the initial summary statement as a way of rounding off the overall presentation. Some discourses explicitly draw attention to this pattern by way of the Buddha announcing that he is about to give a summary statement and a more detailed exposition. Such announcements reflect a clear awareness of this mode of procedure, which would have naturally commended itself in an oral setting. Without recourse to anything else but memory, it makes eminent sense to announce the main topic in brief and repeat it again after it has been covered in detail.

In line with some of the other modes of systematization surveyed in this chapter, such explicit drawing of attention to the combination of a summary with its detailed exposition can take on a life of its own, in the sense of being applied in a way that no longer fits the actual content of the discourse in question. This can be seen in the Discourse on a Summary and an Analysis (*Uddesavibhaṅgasutta*), which begins with the Buddha announcing that he will teach a summary and an analysis.[355] Contrary to this announcement, the discourse reports the Buddha giving only a brief statement and then retiring, without providing the promised analysis of that statement. This then motivates the members of the audience to approach Mahākaccāna and ask him to explain the matter to them.

A Chinese *Āgama* parallel reports the same denouement of events, differing in so far as here the Buddha had just announced that he would give a teaching on the Dharma, without any reference to a summary and an analysis.[356] Due to lacking such a reference, in the Chinese *Āgama* version the Buddha's departure, after giving only a statement in brief, does not create any inconsistency.

A similar pattern can be seen in the case of the Discourse by Mahākaccāna [on the Verses] on an Auspicious Night (*Mahākaccānabhaddekarattasutta*). According to the introductory narration, a monastic had asked the Buddha to teach the summary and the analysis of a set of verses on how to spend time in an auspicious manner.[357] Even though the Buddha agrees to this request, he only recites the verses, which in this case would be the summary statement, and then retires without providing any analysis of their implications. This again motivates the monastics in the audience to approach Mahākaccāna in order to receive an analysis of the verses.

In this case, when requesting of the Buddha a summary and an analysis, the monastic in question had simply repeated a formulation used by a celestial being whom he had just met previously. In the Pāli version, this celestial being had asked the monastic if he knew the summary and analysis of the verses in question.[358] The parallel versions to this Pāli discourses do not have such a reference to a summary and an analysis.[359]

The Discourse by Mahākaccāna [on the Verses] on an Auspicious Night occurs in a chapter of the collection of medium-length discourses that begins with a discourse on this set of verses, in which the Buddha announces a summary and an analysis followed by indeed providing both.[360] Apparently the precedent set in this way found application to subsequent discourses in the same chapter in a somewhat automatic manner, without sufficient attention being paid to the context.

Such somewhat mindless application would have been encouraged by the fact that the entire chapter is called the Chapter on Analysis (*Vibhaṅgavagga*). The title reflects the providing of an analytical explanation as a prominent characteristic of most discourses assembled in this way. This characteristic appears to have given a strong sense of cohesion to these discourses, as most of the members of this chapter have their counterparts in a single chapter on the same topic in the Chinese *Āgama* parallel.[361] As mentioned above (see p. 112), this is the only chapter in the two collections to share such a substantial number of discourses.

In view of the detailed analyses being a characteristic feature of the discourses in this chapter, combined with the precedent of announcing this aspect explicitly in its first discourse, it becomes quite understandable that at times such explicit references to giving an analysis of a summary statement made their way into a context where they are out of place, such as in the two cases examined above. Besides again providing evidence for change that could hardly be intentional, this shows a creative dimension of systematization, in the sense that the grouping together of discourses that share a particular feature can in turn have an impact on the form of these discourses.

10. Repetition Series

The two principles of repetition and abbreviation, discussed above, can combine in the form of indicating that the same discourse should be repeated with at times some quite minor terminological change(s). References to such repetition series, found regularly at the end of short discourses, have a particularly strong effect in terms of an increase of textual material.

An example is the so-called Ganges repetition series in the Pāli collection of topic-wise assembled discourses. According to this repetition series, the undertaking of a particular practice makes the mind slant toward Nirvana just as the river Ganges slants to the east. Based on this model, the repetition series then works through the same material again, with the difference that the reference to the river Ganges should be replaced by referring to other rivers in India that similarly slant to the east.[362] The full set can then be repeated once more with the difference that, instead of slanting to the east, the same rivers slant to the ocean.[363]

This repetition series can in turn be combined with other repetition series, thereby multiplying the increase of discourses. Executing such repetition series in various ways can result in quite different overall counts of discourses. In fact, the indications on how these repetition series should be combined with each other are not necessarily straightforward and can result in some uncertainty. Given the actual textual volume that would result from working through all variations of the repetition series found in the first division in the Great Chapter of the Pāli collection of topic-wise discourses, for example, an oral performance would be rather time consuming, making it doubtful that the entire series was regularly recited in full.

At the same time, however, the actual form taken by these repetition series does not give the impression of being haphazard. As noted by Wynne (2004, 107),

> the numerous *peyyāla* [abbreviation] sections usually come after one preliminary Sutta which spells out word for word the pattern which is to be understood for the Suttas that follow. This hardly allows for free improvisation.

Although Gethin (2020a, 146) sees an "intrinsic open-endedness" in the method leading to such repetition series, the way these are formulated does give the impression of being intended to provide precise indications as to how they are to be executed, even though it may not always be clear to us how this should exactly be done. An intrinsic open-endedness of the type that invites an improvisatory form of oral performance could reasonably be expected to look more like certain previous-birth stories extant in fragmentary narrative texts, which can give just keywords or brief phrases that seem to call for supplementation. Commenting on a Sanskrit collection of such previous-birth stories from Bairam-Ali in Turkmenistan, Karashima and Vorobyova-Desyatovskaya (2015, 148) reason:

> It is quite probable that a master of storytelling wrote (or ordered to write) this manuscript for his successor or disciple to transmit the contents of the stories. For him or for his pupils, those stories were completely well known and the writer did not feel the necessity of writing them down in full.

In the case of previous-birth stories extant in British Library Kharoṣṭhī manuscripts, Lenz (2003, 86–87) comments that, whereas the usual procedure of abbreviation is to "refer to specific fixed textual units," in this type of text the abbreviation "formulae seem to call upon their readers to fill in omitted text according to their prior knowledge of Buddhist story literature, rather than to merely recite text by rote."[364] For example, the beginning of one such previous-birth story announces what appears to be the title and then indicates that the text should be expanded (Lenz 2010, 54), presumably by supplying the setting of the narrative, followed by what appear to be keywords reflecting the onset of the actual tale:

> The Ājīvika Avadāna. Expansion (*should be made) thus. (*An) ājīvika . . . the king's palace.

The features evident in this way point indeed to an improvisatory type of oral performance, based on selected keywords or phrases as basic orientation points. This is quite different from the repetition formulas used regularly in the early discourses, which call for the supplementation of precisely formulated textual units found in full in a previous part of the same textual collection.

11. Systematization and Orality

The impact of the types of systematization surveyed above on the early Buddhist oral tradition appears to have been an ongoing process. In fact, according to Ong (1982/1996, 34–36),

> In a primar[il]y oral culture, to solve effectively the problem of retaining and retrieving carefully articulated thought, you have to do your thinking in mnemonic patterns, shaped for ready oral recurrence. Your thoughts must come into being in heavily rhythmic, balanced patterns, in repetitions or antitheses, in alliterations and assonances, in epithetic and other formulary expressions . . .

> In an oral culture, to think through something in non-formulaic, non-patterned, non-mnemonic terms, even if it were possible, would be a waste of time, for such thought, once worked through, could never be recovered with any effectiveness, as it could be with the aid of writing . . .
>
> Heavy patterning and communal fixed formulas in oral cultures serve some of the purposes of writing in chirographic cultures, but in doing so they of course determine the kind of thinking that can be done, the way experience is intellectually organized. In an oral culture, experience is intellectualized mnemonically.

From this viewpoint, it would seem reasonable to assume that some degree of formalization or systematization was probably characteristic of the early Buddhist oral tradition from its very beginnings.[365] An example supporting early formalization would be the specific opening, transition, and closing formulas used in the *Itivuttaka* and its parallels, mentioned above (see p. 55).

The need to make sure that the audience keeps in mind the main points made in an oral presentation is in fact still evident in contemporary times, making it commendable to start a speech by briefly stating what will be covered and repeating this brief summary once the speech comes to its conclusion. This is precisely the pattern already mentioned, where a discourse begins by announcing a topic in a summary manner, then expounds it in detail, and finally concludes by repeating the earlier initial announcement. Rather than reflecting only a subsequent adjustment to facilitate its oral transmission, this particular feature can safely be assumed to have been an integral part of the text in question from the outset. The same may also hold for repetition in general. Levman (2020, 136) reasons:

> In modern times some might consider a lot of this repetition gratuitous; but it is hard to put ourselves in the position of a society where the primary form of communication was not through written materials and mass media, but through con-

versation and dialogue. Here repetition would be more of a necessary part of communication.

A relevance already at the time of actual teaching probably applies also to the basic principle of listing synonyms. The function of ensuring that a particular idea impresses itself on the audience would have been required right from the outset of the delivery of a particular teaching, although the length to which these sometimes go may often be the result of later expansion.

Even the ordering of listings of synonyms according to the principle of waxing syllables could have already been an early feature. Norman (1997, 53) illustrates the application of this principle with an example from English language usage which, although based on a different principle, aptly conveys the sense that such ordering need not invariably be something that is done intentionally and in full awareness of what it involves. The example concerns a big red armchair; speaking instead of a "red big armchair" somehow feels not quite correct. "The order is fixed for us in a pattern by something we do not know about and do not have to worry about. It is, so to speak, automatic." In keeping with this example, the ordering of synonyms according to the principle of waxing syllables could well have happened in a comparable way with ancient Indian speakers.

With some degree of systematization probably being already part of the verbal expressions of a particular text from the outset, and other aspects of formalization gradually being added to that, the fluidity and complexity of orality becomes quite apparent. The formal aspects taken by this oral tradition appear to have been influenced by an attempt at improving accuracy of recall. In fact, the early Buddhist discourses reflect the use of mnemonic aids to a greater extent than Vedic texts,[366] pointing to a need of the Buddhist reciters to boost their ability to recall with precision in a way not required by their Vedic counterparts. At the same time, however, as evident in the examples surveyed in this chapter, strategies and modes of systematization apparently originating from attempts to boost precise recall appear to have soon taken on a dynamic of their own, thereby becoming in themselves sources for change.

12. Summary

The early Buddhist texts reflect the requirements of oral transmission in a range of interrelated ways. These requirements can be seen to have influenced the allocation of discourses to a collection as well as their sequential position within it. A pervasive characteristic of the discourses themselves is textual repetition, taking the form of listings of synonyms for a particular term, the employment of formulaic descriptions and stereotyped lists, as well as affording occasions for the implementation of abbreviations. The systematization evident in this way appears to have been the result of a gradual process, with some such elements quite probably being employed from the outset. The gradual development of some aspects of systematization, originally quite probably intended to provide an element of stability, can in the course of time itself become a source for further developments and turn into a cause of change.

V. Additions and Innovations

The more creative or dynamic dimensions of the early Buddhist oral tradition are the central theme of the present chapter. I begin with a tendency of abbreviations and lists to take on a life of their own and become considerably more productive than their original purpose would have suggested. Another source for substantial textual expansion appears to be the providing of a commentary on a source text during oral recitation. I survey several examples for this tendency, some of which can reflect rather significant developments in Buddhist thought, and discuss the notion of discourse parallelism in relation to the assumption that there has been an initial instance of delivering a certain teaching (the "original"). In the final part of this chapter I explore the problem of accurate source monitoring as a factor that would have contributed to blurring what in the early period of transmission was probably already a not clearly defined boundary between commentary and source text.

1. Creative Dimensions of Abbreviation

The tendency of features of systematization, discussed in the previous chapters, to assume a creative dimension can be illustrated with an extreme case in the use of abbreviation, found in a Chinese *Āgama* discourse of medium length that has no parallel.[367] The discourse combines an abbreviated account of the gradual path with a list of practices that mainly incorporate the standard list of thirty-seven qualities pertinent to awakening (*bodhipakkhiyā dhammā, bodhipākṣika-dharmāḥ*), which are in turn combined with a series of synonyms for overcoming ignorance. Once the resultant combination has been worked through once, the discourse shifts from ignorance as the first link in the standard account of dependent arising to each of the ensuing links.

Executing in full the material presented in abbreviation would result in a discourse more than twice as long as the entire *Āgama* collection (which takes several days to recite).[368] In other words, it can safely be assumed that this discourse was never recited in full and instead came into existence in its present abbreviated form.

Although providing a remarkable illustration of the extent to which abbreviation can turn into proliferation, content-wise the discourse stays well within the compass of early Buddhist thought. In other words, the building blocks for this discourse are simply taken from other discourses, an in-itself-natural tendency in oral transmission.[369] Thus, even this case, where abbreviation has run riot and become an exercise in its own right rather than actually abbreviating a text that earlier existed in full, the material itself does not involve any doctrinal innovation.

A comparable creative dimension can be observed in relation to repetition series, which can even have an impact on the structure of a discourse collection. An example in case is the Division on Absorption (SN 53) in the Pāli collection of topic-wise assembled discourses. This basically combines the standard description of the four absorptions with various repetition series.[370] The first discourse in this division is at the same time the first instance of the Ganges repetition series, discussed in the previous chapter (see above p. 127). This case is particularly noteworthy, as it not only lacks a counterpart in other extant reciter traditions, but also has the same title (*Jhānasaṃyutta*) as another Division on Absorption (SN 34) found in the same Pāli collection, which does have a Chinese *Āgama* counterpart.[371] From the viewpoint of oral transmission, the creation of two divisions with the same title is unexpected, because in order to facilitate allocating discourses and keeping divisions in sequence, different titles would be an obvious choice. This makes it probable that the creation of a second division with the same title took place at a time when the requirements of memorization were no longer of central importance.

Comparing the two divisions on the same topic, the one that has a counterpart in another tradition describes various abilities required in order to deepen concentration. In contrast, the other division on this topic, found only in the Pāli tradition, merely applies repetition series found already in previous divisions to the standard description of the four absorptions. Although this combination just recycles material already found elsewhere, the result of this procedure introduces a distinctly new perspective: it conveys the position that the mere cultivation of absorption makes the mind slant toward Nirvana. This stands in contrast to recurrent indications in other discourses that absorption attainment in itself fails to lead to Nirvana.[372]

The creation of a second Division on Absorption can best be understood when considered within its contextual setting in the Great Chapter, which concerns various aspects of the path. Most of the topics covered here correspond to a list found recurrently in the early discourses, already briefly mentioned above, which presents the "qualities pertinent to awakening."

The standard listing of qualities pertinent to awakening has in some reciter traditions been expanded by adding the four absorptions.[373] Although Pāli versions of this list have not taken this step, the formation of an additional Division on Absorption, placed in the Great Chapter after those topics that correspond to the qualities pertinent to awakening, follows a similar pattern. As a result of that placing, however, the repetition series found in previous divisions can also come to be applied to the description of the four absorptions. In an oral setting, the application of an item found in several previous instances to the next instance can happen even quite accidentally. It does not take much to repeat once more what has been repeated several times earlier when reciting through the Great Chapter. The net result of the proposed development, however, introduces a significant doctrinal position and thereby probably goes well beyond the original intent. By including the absorptions under the topic of the path, it now presents absorption attainment as in itself the path by making the mind slant to Nirvana.

The present case shows how the formation of a scaffolding for assembling discourses can, in combination with the principle of abbreviation, assume a role that goes beyond just organizing existing textual material. In this way features, which appear to have arisen to ensure an accurate repetition of passages, can acquire a life of their own and become quite creative. Perhaps it is only natural that formal principles, once they have come into existence in the course of oral transmission, have an impact on how texts are remembered and transmitted. This would not be surprising in view of the nature of human memory. As explained by Rosenberg (1987, 81) in a study of the complexity of oral tradition in general, memory is "not a reduplicative process, for instance, but a procedure of creative reconstruction."

2. Remembering Lists

Another source for textual expansion can take the form of remembering the wrong list at the wrong time. As noted by von Hinüber (1996/1997, 31), "pieces of texts known by heart may intrude into almost any context once there is a corresponding key word." Ways in which the associative dimension of memory can have such results can be seen in the case of the Greater Discourse to Sakuludāyin (*Mahāsakuludāyisutta*), which in agreement with its Chinese *Āgama* parallel describes five qualities of the Buddha. Four of these qualities are his virtue, his knowledge and vision, his wisdom, and his teaching of the four noble truths. The fifth quality in the Chinese *Āgama* version is the Buddha's teaching of the higher knowledges of recollection of past lives and the destruction of the influxes.[374] The counterpart to what amounts to just two lines in the Chinese *Āgama* version (in the Taishō edition) are over eleven pages in the Pāli text (of the PTS edition), which report the Buddha teaching in detail the following items:[375]

- the four establishments of mindfulness,
- the four right efforts,
- the four bases of success,
- the five faculties,
- the five powers,
- the seven factors of awakening,
- the noble eightfold path,
- the eight liberations,
- the eight spheres of transcendence,
- the ten spheres of totality,

- the four absorptions,
- insight into the nature of body and consciousness,
- production of a mind-made body,[376]
- supernormal powers,
- the divine ear,
- telepathic knowledge of the minds of others,
- recollection of past lives,
- the divine eye,
- the destruction of the influxes.

This long exposition contrasts with the much shorter coverage given to the other four qualities of the Buddha in the same Pāli discourse, which taken together amount to less than two pages (in the PTS edition).[377] The perspective afforded by the Chinese *Āgama* parallel makes it reasonable to assume that a textual expansion has taken place, leading to an assembling of various aspects of teachings found elsewhere among the discourses and considered to be important by the reciters.

Closer inspection shows that the first part of this listing follows an ascending numerical order, beginning with the standard list of thirty-seven "qualities pertinent to awakening." Items in the later part of the list, however, appear in a sequence also found in the standard exposition of the gradual path in the collection of long discourses.[378] This gives the impression that two independent listings have been combined in the present instance.

The apparent combination results in some internal inconsistencies, as the Pāli discourse follows each item in its list with the indication that this had led many disciples to reach the consummation and perfection of direct knowledge, an expression the commentary understands to intend the attainment of full awakening.[379] Elsewhere the early discourses do not attribute such a potential to any of the items in this list beginning with the spheres of totality (*kasiṇāyatana/kṛtsnāyatana*) up to the divine eye. This supports the impression of a conflation, resulting in the application of a formulaic statement of awakening potential to practices that, in early Buddhist thought in general, are not considered to have such a potential on their own.

As a result of the apparent textual expansion, the Greater Discourse to Sakuludāyin has become a rather long discourse that could have received a more suitable placing among the collection of long discourses rather than being in the collection of discourses of medium length, where it is now found. This makes it probable that the suggested textual expansion would have taken place when this Pāli discourse had already been allocated to its present collection. At the same time, the recurrent statement after each item makes it clear that this is not just a case of an additional manuscript leaf being accidentally added. In other words, the most probably scenario is that this apparent addition happened during the period of oral transmission of the collection of medium-length discourses.

Another example can be found in the Lesser Discourse on the Simile of the Heartwood (*Cūḷasāropamasutta*). The main point made in the Pāli discourse and its Chinese *Āgama* parallel is to highlight that various types of achievements should not lead to conceit and be mistaken for the final goal.[380] The Pāli version continues after the achievement of knowledge and vision by listing various states that are considered still superior and more sublime, namely the four absorptions, the four immaterial spheres, and the attainment of the cessation of perception and feeling.[381] None of these are mentioned in the Chinese *Āgama* parallel. Although the Pāli discourse introduces each of these as superior to the previously mentioned knowledge and vision, from a doctrinal viewpoint such a qualification would not apply to the absorptions or the immaterial spheres. Moreover, at an earlier point the same discourse had already mentioned accomplishment in concentration.[382] It would be difficult to imagine an accomplishment in concentration apart from the four absorptions (and the immaterial spheres). Yet, the first part of the present passage proposes that the first absorption is superior to knowledge and vision, even though such knowledge and vision had just before been qualified as superior to accomplishment in concentration.

The Pāli commentary explains that the four absorptions and immaterial spheres are here listed as superior to knowledge and vision since they serve as the path to the attainment of the cessation of perception and feeling.[383] The explanation does not solve the issue, as it fails to explain why each absorption is individually qualified as a superior state. At the same time, however, the commentarial explanation points to what probably led to the present state of affairs: an intrusion of a standard list in a context where it was not required. Since elsewhere progress through the four absorptions and four immaterial spheres is shown to lead to the attainment of the cessation of perception and feeling, this apparently led to their intrusion in the present context, which in turn resulted in each of them being presented as superior to what the discourse had already mentioned previously.

Another example for the apparent intrusion of a list is the Discourse on Purification of Alms Food (*Piṇḍapātapārisuddhisutta*). The title aptly conveys the main theme of the discourse, which is how a monastic should act so as to purify the food offerings received from lay supporters. The Chinese *Āgama* parallel indicates that this can take place by closely examining if anything seen while begging for alms has caused the arising of sensual desire, craving, and attachment.[384] If that happened, a strong effort should be made to overcome this unwholesome mental condition. In addition to taking up the possible arising of unwholesome reactions to sense experience, the Pāli version covers a whole range of other topics:[385]

- overcoming the five types of sensual pleasure,
- overcoming the five hindrances,
- understanding the five aggregates of clinging,
- developing the four establishments of mindfulness,
- developing the four right efforts,
- developing the four bases of success,
- developing the five faculties,
- developing the five powers,
- developing the seven factors of awakening,
- developing the noble eightfold path,
- developing tranquility and insight,
- realizing knowledge and liberation.

The net result of this presentation is that a monastic would have to become highly accomplished in order to do justice to this whole range of stipulations. In contrast, the brief and straightforward indication given in the Chinese *Āgama* version offers quite an adequate exposition of how a monastic should act in order to become a pure recipient of alms food. Such purification can already take place at levels of development that fall short of awakening and that have not yet fully mastered the whole range of practices mentioned in the Pāli version. It seems fair to propose that an expansion has taken place in the latter, leading among other things to an integration of the list of the thirty-seven qualities pertinent to awakening.

3. Substantial Additions

In the two cases surveyed above, taken from the Greater Discourse to Sakuludāyin and the Discourse on Purification of Alms Food, the apparent textual expansion goes beyond merely adding a list on its own. Instead, each item of the lists in question comes embedded in a portion of text that integrates the item into the overall presentation. This goes to show that the process leading to the present situation in these two Pāli discourses involves considerably more than just the addition of a list and must be reflecting a complex process taking place in the oral medium. Other instances of addition confirm this tendency; in fact, at times even new discourses can come into being based on the evident fascination exerted by lists.[386]

One example for textual expansion occurs in the Greater Discourse on the Establishments of Mindfulness (*Mahāsatipaṭṭhānasutta*), found in the collection of long discourses. This discourse differs from the Discourse on the Establishments of Mindfulness (*Satipaṭṭhānasutta*), a medium-length discourse, in the degree of detail accorded to the last topic taken up for contemplation in both versions: the four noble truths. The shorter of the two discourses simply enjoins that one should know, as it really is, "this is *dukkha*," "this is the arising of *dukkha*," "this is the cessation of *dukkha*," and "this is the path leading to the cessation of *dukkha*."[387] The same statement forms the beginning of the relevant part in the long-discourse version, followed by a detailed explanation of its implications. In this way, what (in the PTS editions) are four lines of text in the medium-length discourse become nearly ten pages in the long discourse, which employs a considerable amount of abbreviation and thus would be much longer if it were expanded in full.[388]

In the case of the second noble truth, the more detailed exposition relies on stipulating various conditions for the arising of craving (the third truth repeats the same exposition for the corresponding cessation of craving). The resultant detailed exposition works through the following topics:

- a sense organ,
- its sense object,
- the corresponding consciousness,
- the corresponding contact,
- the corresponding feeling tone,
- the corresponding perception,
- the corresponding volition,
- the corresponding craving,
- the corresponding thought,
- the corresponding pondering.

Particularly noteworthy is the inclusion of craving in the above list. The relevant exposition takes the following form:[389]

> In the world, craving for forms . . . in the world, craving for sounds . . . in the world, craving for odors . . . in the world, craving for tastes . . . in the world, craving for tangibles . . . in the world, craving for mental objects is of a pleasing nature and of an agreeable nature; when arising, it is there that this craving arises; when establishing itself, it is there that it establishes itself.

In this way, the passage indicates that craving can serve as a condition for the arising of craving. The implications of this proposition are far from self-evident and it would not be easy to envisage a form of mindfulness practice that could do justice to this instruction. In other words, the presentation seems to be the result of adopting a list that has not been sufficiently adjusted to its new context.

The list begins with the standard analysis of sense experience into organ, object, and consciousness. Another standard presentation considers the convergence of these three to be contact. The reference to consciousness then finds a complement in mentioning the other three mental aggregates of feeling tone, perception, and volition (the last as a counterpart to the fourth aggregate of formations). The reference to volition naturally leads over to craving. Although the building up of the list until the mention of craving follows an inner logic, this no longer does justice to the context, resulting in the somewhat pointless proposition that craving arises from craving.[390]

The commentarial nature of the additional material found in the Greater Discourse on the Establishments of Mindfulness has already been noted by various scholars.[391] The starting point would have been the short statement on the four noble truths, shared by the two Pāli versions. At some point during transmission, the elaborations and explanations that perhaps accompanied an oral exposition of this short statement appear to have become part of the discourse itself, leading to the version now found in the collection of long discourses.

The present case illustrates a process of considerable relevance for appreciating the dynamics behind the formation and transmission of the early discourses, namely the possibility that explanations originally given in the form of a commentary could in the course of time become part of the text on which they comment.

The addition of commentarial material could itself have been part of a gradual process of textual expansion. This possibility can be explored with the example of the section on morality in the Discourse on Brahmā's Net. As briefly mentioned above (see p. 115), the Theravāda and Dharmaguptaka versions of this discourse have a rather long exposition on this topic, whereas the Mūlasarvāstivāda versions are quite brief. Closer inspection makes it probable that the longer expositions are based on expanding the brief exposition common to the parallels. In fact, the Pāli version divides its presentation into a shorter, a medium-length, and a long exposition on morality.[392] The medium-length exposition works in more detail through some topics already broached in the short treatment, and its way of proceeding in this respect is similar to a Pāli commentary on a comparable short exposition on morality in a different Pāli discourse.[393] The apparent integration of such a commentary into the Discourse on Brahmā's Net does not appear to have been the final word on the matter, as the tendency of textual expansion eventually led to an additional long exposition on the topic of morality. This goes to show that the processes under discussion here are best visualized as ongoing rather than as a onetime event.

4. The Providing of a Commentary

The providing of a commentary alongside the recitation of a particular text is a feature that can safely be assumed to have been of continuous and pervasive relevance for the giving of oral teachings. Nance (2012, 78) summarizes the responsibility of a teacher of Dharma in the following way:

> On the one hand, figures of pedagogical authority (preachers, teachers, and commentators) were presumed to bear responsibility for preserving the words of Buddhas; in the service of disseminating the teaching, these words were to be memorized and recited or transcribed accurately. On the other hand, these figures were presumed to bear responsibility for interpreting that which they had memorized. They did not simply recite the words of their predecessors, but also offered interpretations of those words to various audiences. To understand traditional Buddhist pedagogy requires that we keep these two responsibilities simultaneously in view.

The two intertwined responsibilities that emerge in this way would have been of relevance since the beginning stages of the early Buddhist oral tradition. The form in which the discourses have come down already involves the addition of some degree of commentary to contextualize the actual teaching: an introductory statement that informs the audience of the location at which the discourse was believed to have been given and a concluding statement reporting the (usually delighted) reaction of the audience. The standard introductory phrase of the type "at one time the Blessed One was dwelling at" such-and-such a place and its concluding counterpart in the report that the members of the audience "delighted in the words of the Blessed One" could obviously not intend to be recording something believed to have been spoken at the time when the actual teaching was given.[394] This is thus a rather early commentary, probably added when the discourse in question was repeated to others. Such textual elements are similar in kind to the promulgation narratives of monastic rules and the stories that purport to record the circumstances under which a particular verse or inspired utterance was spoken, surveyed in previous chapters (see above pp. 26 and 59).

Notably, although a reference to the Buddha's whereabouts is in itself obviously an addition made by the reciters, in doing so they would have simply followed a precedent set according to the early discourses by the Buddha himself. This can be seen in discourses in which he is shown to report to others an encounter he had on another occasion, as such reports tend to begin with him indicating where he was staying at that time.[395]

In addition to the standard introductory and concluding phrases, at times the reciters also voice their opinion. An example occurs in relation to a teaching given by the Buddha's chief disciple Sāriputta/Śāriputra to a brahmin on his deathbed, leading the latter to rebirth in heaven. The reciters of the Pāli version apparently considered it worth explicitly highlighting that the brahmin could have been led beyond a heavenly rebirth; their description of Sāriputta's departure from the brahmin's side notes that he had established the brahmin in an inferior celestial world and left, even though there was still more to be done.[396]

Whereas in this instance only the Pāli reciters openly give vent to their opinion, another discourse in the same collection shows both reciter traditions expressing an explicit evaluation, which in this case is praise rather than criticism. The main protagonist of the discourse is an arahant/arhat monastic who, in a discussion with a visitor, lists his own outstanding qualities or types of conduct. In both versions this takes the form of alternating between the reported speech of the speaker and the reciters repeating the same quality with an additional indication that this is a marvelous quality of this monastic. These additional indications take the following form in the Pāli and Chinese versions:[397]

> This we also remember as a wonderful and marvelous quality of the venerable Bakkula.

> This we reckon as a marvelous quality of the venerable Vatkula.

The net effect of this reciter's remark is that the highlight placed on each quality, by repeating what had already been described by the speaker himself, is additionally endowed with the status of being a marvel. As briefly mentioned in an earlier chapter, internal evidence situates this discourse several decades after the Buddha's decease (see above p. 43). A closer inspection of the actual qualities, moreover, shows that these reflect a shift in the conception of an arahant/arhat by way of placing an increasing emphasis on austere external conduct.[398]

In this way, the addition of the above reciters' remarks appears to be motivated by the wish to promote the more austere arahant/arhat ideal depicted in this discourse.[399] This particular example can be taken to illustrate a general pattern of continuous negotiation, in line with the demands of a particular situation when giving a teaching, between the actual text and corresponding explanations given by the reciter(s).

For a commentarial explanation in general to fulfill its purpose, it would have to be given soon after the term or passage in question had been recited.[400] In an oral setting, where the members of the audience need not necessarily have been trained in memorization skills, it would not work particularly well to recite a longer text in its entirety at first and only then offer comments on some of its aspects. Instead, the most convenient way of proceeding in a general teaching situation would be to intersperse the recital of a particular text with comments and explanations that serve to facilitate an understanding or contextualization of the part of the teaching that has just been heard. The proposed combination of a more fixed type of text with more fluid explanations or comments can be seen to have antecedents in ancient Indian recitation practices. Based on ideas originally expressed by Oldenberg (1883),

Alsdorf (1963/1974, 36) discusses a comparable pattern in relation to dialogic Vedic hymns (*ākhyāna*), which can take the following form:

> The stanzas, which are alone canonical, are introduced by and interspersed with explanative prose passages expressly regarded as a mere commentary and betraying their later origin by not unfrequently being at variance with, or even flatly contradicting, the verses . . . only the verses, consisting mainly of dialogues or monologues, final summaries or other highlights of the story, were fixed, while the prose potions were, at least originally, supplied by every narrator in his own words.

It seems fair to propose that the narratives accompanying monastic rules, verses, or inspired utterances follow the basic pattern set by this precedent. However, in the case of the discourses, a precise distinction between what the reciters considered canonical and what they saw as comments or explanations provided by previous generations of reciters is not necessarily self-evident. In fact, several discourses present themselves as explanations given by chief disciples of some statement attributed to the Buddha. A standard procedure then takes the form of members of the audience repeating this explanation in front of the Buddha. The latter's approval tends to take the form of indicating that he would have explained the matter in the same way, hence the exposition should be committed to memory. Malalasekera (1928/1994, 88–89) explains:

> Sometimes it happened that accounts of . . . discussions were duly reported to the Teacher, and some of them were approved by him . . . the utterances of the disciples that won such approbation . . . formed the nucleus of the commentaries. . . . It sometimes happened that for a proper understanding of the text explanations of a commentarial nature were quite essential; and in such cases the commentary was naturally incorporated into the text and formed part of the text itself.

In this way, as noted by Goonesekera (1967, 336), "the earliest beginnings of exegetical literature can be traced to the canon itself." This basic pattern is not confined to the early discourses and the *Vinaya*. The same procedure can be seen to have informed the development of early Abhidharma literature (Anālayo 2014c, 79–89) and appears to be also found in Buddhist texts of a more narrative orientation, evident in a tendency to combine passages phrased in an old style, similar to the discourses, with textual material in a new style, more akin in form and content to the commentaries.[401]

In sum, during the long period of oral transmission, the giving of a "commentary" need not have been confined to the material that is now extant in written form and explicitly designated as such. Instead, the situation is probably best envisaged as an ongoing and ever-changing process of negotiation between a particular text and the target audience, with the boundary between that text and the ensuing negotiations not as clearly determined as these have become when eventually shifting to the written medium.[402]

5. Evidence for the Incorporation of a Commentary

The above suggestion can find corroboration in a number of instances where notions found in the commentarial texts of one transmission lineage manifest in the corresponding source text of another transmission lineage. The material for a study of such instances is limited by the circumstance that a complete set of commentaries is only extant in Pāli. For this reason, the instances taken up here involve similarities between Theravāda exegetical texts and discourses from other reciter traditions. As the Greater Discourse on the Establishments of Mindfulness already shows, however, the Pāli tradition is certainly not immune to being affected by the same pattern of integrating commentarial material.

One example concerns an instruction in a Pāli discourse to contemplate that "this is empty of a self and what belongs to a self."[403] The Chinese *Āgama* parallel presents the same contemplation in this way:[404]

> this world is empty, empty of a self and what belongs to a self, empty of being permanent, empty of being everlasting, empty of existing continuously, and empty of being unchanging.

In this way, in addition to being empty of a self, the Chinese parallel stresses in various complementary ways that the world is also empty of permanence. Although impermanence is a pervasive concern of the early discourses in various reciter lineages, the idea of presenting this topic as a form of emptiness does not seem to be attested among Pāli discourses and instead only appears in later works of the same tradition.[405]

Another instance similarly related to insight meditation concerns an instruction on avoiding clinging or attachment to what is experienced through the senses.[406] A Chinese *Āgama* parallel offers the following additional instruction:[407]

> At the time of the arising of the eye, when it arises one also does not know from where it comes, at the time of the cessation of the eye, when it ceases one also does not know where it goes.

A counterpart to this type of description can be found only in Pāli exegesis, which similarly indicates that the sense spheres do not come from anywhere before they arise and do not go anywhere after they cease.[408]

Another example is a reference to the "world" in the context of the famous dictum that the world and the path to its end are to be found within this fathom-long body.[409] According to one of the Chinese *Āgama* parallels, the path to the end of the world is the noble eightfold path.[410] The Pāli commentary similarly explains that the path to the end of the world corresponds to the fourth noble truth of the path.[411]

One more example is the proclamation in a Pāli discourse that the advice given by the Buddha is "supreme among things of today."[412] The corresponding passage in two parallels extant in Chinese declares that the Buddha's teaching is able to subdue or control non-Buddhist wanderers or practitioners.[413] A related idea can be found in the corresponding Pāli commentary, which glosses the expression "things of today" as a referent to the six non-Buddhist teachers.[414]

In addition to occurring in doctrinal contexts, the same tendency can also be seen at work in narrative portions of a discourse. This can be illustrated with the example of the introductory narration in the Discourse on Brahmā's Net, which reports that the Buddha had become aware of the fact that a group of monastics was having a discussion. The Pāli version simply mentions that the Buddha joined the group and asked them what they had been talking about.[415] Quite probably in order to defend the idea that the Buddha was omniscient and hence did not need to ask such a question, the commentary explains that he already knew what they had been discussing and only asked to get the conversation started.[416] The same idea can be found reflected in a Chinese *Āgama* parallel, in which case the discourse itself indicates that the Buddha inquired from the monastics "knowingly."[417]

Another example similarly involving the introductory narration occurs in a Pāli discourse and its two Chinese *Āgama* parallels. The Pāli version proceeds as follows:[418]

> The venerable Kassapagotta, who at that time had gone for the day's [meditative] abiding, gave an exhortation to a certain hunter.

The two Chinese *Āgama* parallels, given below one after the other, provide additional information on the hunter:[419]

> There was hunter named Chizhi, who set up a trap for deer not far away from Daśabalakāśyapa. Out of empathy, at that time Daśabalakāśyapa taught that hunter the Dharma.

> There was a certain hunter called Lianjia who set up a trap for deer not far away from the venerable. At that time, the venerable had pity for the hunter and taught him the Dharma.

The more detailed introductory narrations in the two Chinese parallels agree that the protagonist was hunting for deer. This concords with the Pāli commentary, which glosses the reference to a hunter in the Pāli discourse as referring to a deer hunter.[420]

Variations related to the introductory narration of a discourse can at times involve a substantial amount of text. The Discourse on Minor Defilements (*Upakkilesasutta*) begins with a brief report of how the Buddha attempted to stop a quarrel that had broken out among some monastics.[421] According to the Chinese *Āgama* parallels, for this purpose the Buddha related a long story of the past that illustrates forgiveness.[422] The Theravāda *Vinaya* agrees with this report, as it also records the Buddha delivering this tale from the past to the quarreling monastics.[423]

The Lesser Discourse with an Analysis of Karma (*Cūḷakammavibhaṅgasutta*) begins with a young brahmin approaching the Buddha.[424] Several parallels provide additional background to this meeting, relating how on a previous encounter the Buddha had been barked at by the dog living in this brahmin's household.[425] Such a narration is also found in the Pāli commentary.[426]

The Discourse with an Analysis of Elements (*Dhātuvibhaṅgasutta*) and several of its parallels begin with an encounter between the Buddha and a particular monastic.[427] A parallel extant in Chinese precedes this encounter by relating what had inspired this particular monastic to go forth.[428] The Pāli commentary does the same.[429] Commenting on this case, Nattier (2008, 165n6) reasons that this "demonstrates that material classified as a commentary in one tradition (e.g., that represented by Buddhaghosa) could be incorporated into a sūtra itself in another textual lineage."

The apparent lack of a clearly defined boundary between prose texts of different provenance, stored in the memories of the reciters, concords with the role assumed by a commentary in the ancient Indian setting in general. As pointed out by Cutler (1992, 549),

> in traditional Indian culture a literary composition is rarely if ever appreciated as a self-contained 'text in itself.' To the contrary, texts are almost always embedded in contexts—for instance, as oral performance before an audience, as a component of a hereditary body of knowledge, as an accompaniment to ritual—that either explicitly or implicitly contain elements of commentary.

According to Deutsch (1988, 170), the role of commentaries are seen in the Indian setting in the following manner:

> The exegetical material expands, refines, [and] modifies arguments and ideas, and presents new ones, usually with increasing precision (oftentimes, somewhat unfortunately, in terms of multiplication of distinctions reminiscent of scholasticism), seeking to bring greater systematic coherence to its body of ideas. The philosopher-commentator, in other words, seeks to remain faithful to his authoritative sources, but in his own creative terms.

This makes it hardly surprising if during oral transmission material of a commentarial type should have gradually managed to become part of the text on which it comments.

6. The Implications of Parallelism

The selected examples surveyed above to exemplify the apparent intrusion of commentarial material into the source text do not involve matters of substantial doctrinal import. This is not invariably the case, however, and in what follows I will take up two examples that are of considerable significance. Given that the providing of a commentary can at times reflect substantially later thought, identifying commentarial additions can be particularly helpful for reconstructing early stages in the development of Buddhist thought and practice. Before turning to two examples for this potential of comparative study, however, by way of providing a background I briefly need to examine the notion of parallelism,[430] a notion that has come up repeatedly in the preceding pages and whose basic taxonomy I already explored in the second chapter (see above p. 47).

The implications of identifying parallels can be exemplified with the first regulation mentioned in the different codes of rules for monks, taken up in the first chapter of my study. This concerns the case of a fully ordained monastic who, without having renounced his monastic status, intentionally engages in sexual intercourse with a human being or an animal.[431] The different codes of rules show closely similar formulation of this regulation. This makes it hardly reasonable to envisage that each version came into existence independently from the others. In order to ascertain this possibility beyond my subjective assessment, I consulted a professional statistician. According to his assessment, the possibility of seven (or more) fairly similar parallel versions of this rule coming into existence independently of each other is so low as to be statistically negligible.[432] Given that this already applies when the first rule is considered on its own, what to say of the whole code of rules? It seems fair to assume that the various versions of this text, which despite several differences are overall quite similar, go back to a shared precedent.

The statistical impossibility of assuming that the various codes of rules came into existence independently of each other helps to place into perspective a tendency to overstate the in-itself-correct assessment that an original version can no longer be recovered. This can take the form of assuming an absolute open-endedness, as if there had never been a beginning point.[433] This is not the case.

The situation can be illustrated with the same case of the first rule for monks. Despite some significant variations, studied above (see p. 27), the *Vinaya* accounts agree that the rule on celibacy was promulgated by the Buddha after a monk had engaged in sex with his former wife in order to ensure an heir to the family. The historicity of this breach of celibacy can no longer be verified, though it seems reasonable to assume that some sexual intercourse happened. Nor can it be proven beyond doubt that the rule was indeed promulgated by the Buddha himself, although this appears to be a reasonable scenario. What is certain, however, is that at some point someone must have said something to make celibacy binding on Buddhist monks. Whoever that was and whatever form this statement took, it provided the starting point for centuries of oral transmission leading to the parallel versions of the regulation that are now extant.

Turning to the discourses, just as parallel rules purport to record the same promulgation by the Buddha on a particular issue, in the same way parallel discourses can be identified based on the assessment that they appear to be recording the same teaching given by the Buddha (or one of his disciples) on a particular occasion. Chief criteria here are that the form and content of the teaching itself are reasonably similar, as a lack of concern about precision regarding the location and audience, prevalent in the ancient Indian setting, can easily lead to variations in the introduction to a discourse regarding where the teaching was given and to whom.

The nature of oral tradition is such that the quest to reconstruct the "original" or "Ur-version" of a particular rule or discourse is a futile endeavor, a topic I will explore in more detail at the outset of the next chapter (see below p. 167). In relation to Buddhist oral texts in general, Salomon (2018, 57) reasons that

> most scholars have abandoned the quest for a single "original" version of the canon as a wild-goose chase. For even if there ever were, in theory, a single original form of the canon, or at least of a group of individual texts as the Buddha himself uttered them two and a half millennia ago, there is no hope of finding it intact.

This is indeed the case. A proper appreciation of the situation points to the need of avoiding any tendency toward reification of a supposedly pure original. This has been highlighted by Silk (2013/2015, 207), who illustrates the complexity of orality by proposing that

> it is entirely plausible, if not overwhelmingly likely, that the Buddha, preaching far and wide, presented 'the same' sermon more than once, but in different terms, and perhaps organized somewhat differently. There is absolutely nothing Post-Modern about this scenario, which should be acceptable even to the most conservative and hide-bound traditionalist. But let us think for a brief moment about the implications of this scenario. If we do not want to accept that Ānanda actually memorized every utterance of the Buddha, and that somehow these versions erased all other 'records' of the Buddha's preaching (as perhaps the traditional accounts of the First Council would imply), then it seems entirely acceptable that the utterances of the Buddha, even if remembered by

> (some) members of his audiences verbatim, nevertheless circulated from the very beginning in *multiform*. It would simply be impossible to take a single presentation of a teaching of the Buddha—a single instance of a sermon delivered at a unique time and place—and then consider that other teachings around the same topic, other instances of preaching on the same subject, given by the Buddha himself elsewhere, constitute mere variants or recensions of that arbitrarily privileged 'original' sermon.

Such privileging should indeed be set aside, and the complexity of orality needs to be recognized, where texts exist in multiform rather than as a single unit. However, this does not mean that there was never a starting point in the first place. That is, what makes the search for an "Ur-version" or "original" meaningless is not that a starting point never existed.[434] Taking such a position would make it difficult to explain how the extant versions came into being. In the example provided in the above quote, a particular speaker could hardly be giving different sermons on the same topic at the same time. Instead, one of these must have been the earliest instance of delivering this particular teaching. That is, idea of a sermon being given "more than once" has its reference point in the idea that it was given "once." The assumption of some such starting point is required for the phrase "more than once" to make sense.

Pointing to such temporal precedence does not carry any value implications; in fact, it is quite possible that later sermons present the same topic in a better form due to reflecting more experience in teaching. But the existence of several iterations of a particular teaching by the same speaker does not efface the fact that there must have been a first instance of giving this teaching. In other words, the point of refraining from a search for an "Ur-version" or "original" is because a starting point can no longer be convincingly reconstructed. Neither the first nor the subsequent sermons in the above scenario can be retrieved in their original form, that is, in the way they were given orally. I take the occasion to quote myself (Anālayo 2016h, 26):

> The wish to avoid the quest for an ur-text need not lead us to the opposite stance of disregarding that there have been pre-versions to the text we have in hand. Such an opposite stance can easily lead to ignoring historical layers in the development of a particular text, thereby potentially also ignoring the multiplicity of conditions, cross-fertilizations, and other dynamics that have influenced the oral transmission of what we now access in the form of a written testimony of a particular instance of this complex process. Once the indeed unwarranted valorisation of anything early as intrinsically superior to later "degenerations" has been left behind, the historical dimension as such offers an important tool for contextualization that should not be too easily dismissed.

An illustration of the situation could perhaps be the example of the fruits on a bush or tree. The seed from which the bush or tree sprung no longer survives and there is no way to reconstruct its precise individual shape and color. Nevertheless, that seed did at some time in the past exist, and since an apple tree will not grow from a mango seed, the seed planted in the past must have been of the same type as the fruit now found on the bush or tree. Although searching for the original seed that eventually led to the present fruit is indeed meaningless, as the very growth of the bush or tree implies that this seed has been transformed and no longer exists, at the same time it is meaningful to consider the fruits on the bush or tree as the outcome of the seed planted in the past.

7. A Key Element for the Bodhisattva Path

Based on the above considerations regarding the notion of discourse parallelism as providing a background for comparative studies, I now turn to a description that seems to be of considerable relevance to subsequent developments in Buddhist thought and practice. This is a list of specific bodily marks with which, according to the texts, the Buddha had been endowed. Closer study shows that the conception of these marks appears to reflect a process of cross-fertilization between textual descriptions and depictions of the Buddha in ancient Indian art (Anālayo 2017a, 51–63).

One out of several examples is the physical form of the Buddha's head, which originally appears to have been qualified as being well rounded, comparable to a turban. In ancient Indian art, however, a custom of portraying divine beings and revered teachers with long hair, worn in a topknot, was apparently also applied to depictions of the Buddha (even though the texts clearly convey the impression that he was shaven headed). In the course of time, such depictions in turn seem to have influenced textual accounts, which describe the Buddha's head as endowed with a protuberance of sorts. The evolution taking place in this way can best be illustrated by translating descriptions of the Buddha's head in three parallel discourses, beginning with the Pāli version:[435]

> His head is [shaped like] a turban.
>
> He has on the crown of his head a fleshy topknot that is round and in proportion.
>
> He has on the crown of his head a fleshy topknot which shines with light, keeping in check that of the sun and cutting off that of the moon.

This example can serve as a welcome reminder that the transmission of the texts did not happen in a vacuum and for this reason is probably best envisaged as a constant process of negotiation between a range of developments in the ancient Indian setting and the recitation of the texts. In this constant process of negotiation, the texts are not just on the passively receiving end but can at times offer significant input in their own right.

A case in point is the Discourse on the Marks (*Lakkhaṇasutta*), which in agreement with its Chinese *Āgama* parallel sets out by listing the altogether thirty-two physical marks believed to have been possessed by the Buddha. The Pāli version's list culminates in his turban-shaped head, which the Chinese *Āgama* parallel instead describes by referring to a fleshy topknot, similar to the second of the three versions translated above (these two discourses belong to the same transmission lineage). The Pāli Discourse on the Marks and its parallel continue after the list of marks by indicating that one endowed with them is destined to become a ruler over the whole world or, should he decide to go forth, a fully awakened one.[436] Whereas the Chinese *Āgama* version proceeds with the standard conclusion to a discourse, the Pāli version continues with a lengthy exposition on these thirty-two marks that is unique among the early discourses. This exposition takes off from the following reasoning:[437]

> As to a great person, monastics, seers who are outsiders also bear in mind these thirty-two marks of a great person, yet they do not know: "By the doing of this deed one gains this mark."

The above statement serves to introduce the presentation of a distinctly Buddhist perspective on these marks, which otherwise feature in the early discourses as a predominantly Brahminical lore.[438] This perspective concerns their karmic conditionality. It establishes a relationship between certain deeds done by the future Buddha in a past life and his present possession of a particular mark.[439] In the case of the mark of having a head shaped like a turban, the relevant prose passage proceeds in this way:[440]

> Having formerly been a human, he was a leader among the multitude in wholesome states, foremost among the multitude in good bodily conduct, good verbal conduct, good mental conduct, in openhanded generosity, in maintenance of virtue, in keeping the observance day, in being reverential toward the mother and reverential toward the father, reverential toward recluses and reverential toward brahmins, in being respectful toward the head of the clan, and in various other very wholesome activities . . . passing away from there and coming to this present condition he gains this mark of a great person: His head is [shaped like] a turban.

Elsewhere the discourses indicate that the wearing of a particular turban was one of the royal insignia of a head-anointed king.[441] This would explain the relationship drawn in the above passage, where leadership in wholesome conduct leads to acquiring the mark of having a turban-like head, which serves as a physical expression of the leadership status of its owner.

In the context of an oral recitation of the marks, such a distinctly Buddhist perspective could easily have come into existence as a comment by a reciter, by way of explaining to the audience in what way Buddhist knowledge of these marks is superior to its Brahminical antecedents. The appeal of such an explanation, due to a gradually increasing interest in these marks, would in turn have encouraged providing additional details, until a prolonged exposition had come into existence that eventually became part of the discourse itself, similar to the exposition on the four noble truths in the Greater Discourse on the Establishments of Mindfulness.

What endows this suggested development with considerable significance is the circumstance that this is the only known instance among the early discourses testifying to the idea that particular deeds done in the past are required in order to become a Buddha. Although the explicitly stated purpose of the Discourse on the Marks is just to place the marks within the pervasive early Buddhist interest in karma and conditionality, the net result of this type of presentation, also reflected in other texts,[442] can safely be assumed to have provided a crucial element for the gradual arising of the bodhisattva ideal.

In terms of my preceding discussion of parallelism as a basis for comparative study, the suggested conclusion does in no way intend to posit the Chinese parallel as an Ur-version of any kind. Its description of the Buddha's head as having a fleshy topknot shows that this text also underwent development. The precise form of the common starting point of the two parallels can no longer be ascertained, beyond proposing that it would probably have given a list of the Buddha's physical marks. But what form this list took remains open to question. Perhaps one day in the future a fragment of a version of this discourse will be discovered that has a shorter list of the marks, without any reference to the head, for example, giving the impression that even the standard Pāli reference to the head being shaped like a turban is already a later development. Who knows? There is no way for us to be completely sure about any part of the Chinese or Pāli discourse being an exact reflection of the original.

Nevertheless, some starting point in the past must have provided the seed out of which the two extant versions grew in the course of oral transmission. Therefore, it is possible to establish a relative chronology by identifying what are probably later additions. Helpful tools for identifying later developments are contextualization of features unique to one of the two versions within the early texts in general and, whenever possible, relating these to relevant archeological findings as well as to the overall historical development of Buddhist thought. In the present case, such apparently later developments are evident in the conception of the Buddha's head as having a protuberance of sorts and the idea that his performing certain deeds in the past caused his present acquisition of the physical requirements for becoming a Buddha.

The latter of the two is of additional significance, as it shows that apparent beginnings of ideas central to the Mahāyāna traditions can with considerable certainty be attributed to developments taking place within the orbit of early Buddhist thought. The situation with the numerical collection extant in Chinese is different, as here already existing Mahāyāna thought has impacted several of its discourses.[443] But the Discourse on the Marks clearly shows an influence in the opposite direction, whose starting point, as noted by Zysk (2016, 168), is "the specific aim of incorporating the central, pan-Indian doctrine of *karman* and rebirth into the system of human marks." As a result of the apparent developments triggered by such concerns, however, a crucial contribution to the evolution of the bodhisattva ideal can be identified. This is not to take the position that the beginnings of Mahāyāna can be traced to this particular Pāli discourse. Instead, the point is only that the Discourse on the Marks testifies to a significant development. As highlighted by Skilling (2008, 68), it is in particular this discourse's establishing a "relation between the deeds of the Bodhisattva and the resultant marks of the Buddha that is essential to developed Buddhology."

8. An Abhidharma Treatment

The Greater Discourse on the Establishments of Mindfulness and the Discourse on the Marks are both long discourses, which due to their length are obvious places to look for substantial additions. At the same time, however, the tendency for such additions is not confined to members of the collections of long discourses. An example found in a text of medium length is the Discourse on the Great Forty (*Mahācattārīsaka-sutta*),[444] which sets out on the topic of right concentration, the last factor of the noble eightfold path.

The three parallel versions agree in highlighting that concentration becomes right if it is endowed with the other seven factors of the path. A minor difference is that a version extant in Tibetan just speaks of "right concentration," whereas the Pāli and Chinese *Āgama* versions additionally qualify such right concentration to be "noble."[445] This difference is in line with a general tendency in the early discourses to employ this qualification increasingly.[446]

The three versions agree in highlighting the central role of right view, the first factor of the eightfold path, as a precursor to the other path factors. The parallels show how right view operates in collaboration with right effort and right mindfulness in order to establish path factors like right intention, right speech, right action, and right livelihood. In each case, right view stands for the discernment of whether a particular path factor is right or wrong, right effort represents the mental exertion to emerge from what is wrong and stay within the realm of what is right, and right mindfulness performs the function of monitoring it all.

The Chinese and Tibetan versions proceed beyond right livelihood by providing definitions of right effort, right mindfulness, and right concentration (the Chinese version stands alone in also defining right liberation and right knowledge). The definitions of the items covered in these two versions differ substantially from each other; they also no longer continue the mode of presentation adopted for earlier path factors, whose overall point was to show their interrelation and to contrast right and wrong manifestations of each path factor. In particular, a definition of right concentration is out of place, given that this had already been given right at the outset as the basic theme of the discourse. The definition given there, according to which right concentration requires the collaboration of the other path factors, is shared by the three parallels, whereas the definitions given later in the Chinese and Tibetan versions differ from this and from each other.[447] It seems fairly evident that an expansion has taken place along the lines of completing a list without sufficient attention paid to the context.

Although the Pāli version does not proceed beyond right livelihood, it testifies to another mode of expanding the presentation. This takes place by providing an additional distinction of right path factors into mundane and supramundane types, thereby proceeding beyond the contrast between right and wrong path factors that is shared by the parallels. The supramundane description relates the right path factors to the mind free of influxes (*anāsavacitta*) of one who is endowed with and cultivating the noble path.[448]

Some of the terms employed in this context are distinctly late and otherwise only found in Abhidharma texts.[449] In the same vein, the reference to cultivating the noble path is based on the idea of the path as understood in later tradition, where it stands for the moment when one of the four stages of awakening is attained. In contrast, the notion of the path in other early discourses is not confined to a single moment but can comprise even extended periods of cultivation and practice.[450] It is against the background of the momentary conception of the path that the supramundane right path factors are related to being free of influxes. This qualification of being without influxes does not apply to arahants/arhats for the remainder of their lives, once they have attained full awakening, which is the sense carried by the eradication of the influxes in other early discourses. Instead, it qualifies only the actual moment of awakening, which can be any of the four levels of awakening, not necessarily the highest one. In this way, the present passage reflects a crucial shift in perspective that is characteristic of Abhidharma thought and is not attested in this way in other Pāli discourses.

In terms of my discussion of parallelism, once again the proposed conclusion does not involve an attempt to arrive at an Ur-version. All three extant versions show clear signs of later expansion. The seed that provided the starting point for these three lines of development is beyond reach and it would be futile to speculate about its precise form. Yet, dismissing the quest for a reconstruction of the original version of the Discourse on the Great Forty does not make it impossible to identify later developments in each version. Such identification can provide a helpful tool for a better understanding of the evolution of early Abhidharma thought.

The importance of cultivating the eightfold path and in particular right concentration is of course a topic that naturally calls for attention. From this viewpoint, an elaboration of the present discourse in various ways is hardly surprising, be this by completing what the reciters presumably perceived as an incomplete list, as apparently happened in the Chinese and Tibetan versions, or by providing a supramundane perspective, as attested in the Pāli version. Such a supramundane perspective could in principle have arisen as an additional explanation given alongside oral recitation of the source text, similar to providing a karmic perspective on the marks of a Buddha. Such an explanation would then have become part of the discourse itself at some point during its transmission.

A minor difference is that in the Discourse on the Marks the commentarial exposition has been appended at the end of what appears to have been the source text, whereas in the Discourse on the Great Forty what would have started as a commentary has been added to the exposition of each path factor. Both modalities can be understood to reflect the circumstances of oral delivery: The list of marks will be given first in toto as a summary statement that can then be followed by a detailed exposition. Since the exposition mentions each mark again, the members of the audience need not be able to keep the whole list in mind in order to follow the exposition. The same procedure would not work well for the considerably more complex exposition of the path factors in the Discourse on the Great Forty, which would have made it preferable to add a comment each time the description of a particular path factor has just been recited. In this way, fascinating testimonies to significant developments in Buddhist thought may have developed quite naturally out of the dynamics of oral recitation and the requirement to negotiate, through the providing of a commentary, between the root text and the perceived needs of the audience.

Needless to say, the above is not meant to posit the Discourse on the Great Forty as the sole source for this development, just as the Discourse on the Marks need not be the only source for the arising of the notion of the path to Buddhahood. But both passages are testimonies to this development, comparable to fossils of an archaeopteryx or similar *avialae*. Finding such fossils enables us to reconstruct the gradual evolution of birds, even though the individual animals whose remains have been found need not have been the first to develop the ability to fly. In the same way, parallel versions of a discourse can be considered to be comparable to fossils in that they can enable us to understand stages in the development of Buddhist thought by distinguishing between earlier and later elements.[451]

Such distinction need not be taken to carry any value judgment; in fact, in both of the cases discussed above the identification of a later development provides an intriguing window on developments in Buddhist thought. For this reason, the classification of a particular textual part as "late" can at times reflect the most interesting and captivating finding that emerges from a comparative study.

The Abhidharma type of thought evident in the Discourse on the Great Forty can also be seen in two discourses in the topic-wise collection extant in Chinese.[452] This confirms that the Pāli version, discussed above, exemplifies a more general tendency. According to Hirakawa (1993/1998, 127), "the Buddha's disciples were analyzing his teachings with methods similar to those employed later in *abhidharma*. These early analyses were often incorporated into *sūtras*." Skilling (2012, 429) reasons:

> when possible, *ṣūtra* composition . . . kept pace with scholastic trends of the Abhidharma philosophers. Can we envisage a stage when the Abhidharma as a self-conscious enterprise had not yet arisen or gained canonical status? At this stage—the beginnings of Abhidharmic systematization—the natural

format for reformulated material was that of the *sūtra*, and the natural place was the *Sūtrapiṭaka*—where else to place it?

9. The Problem of Accurate Source Monitoring

A recurrent topic in my exploration in the preceding pages has been the coexistence of two basic types of text side by side or even interspersed with each other, one of which is of a more fixed type whereas the other shows clear signs of being considerably more fluid. This can take the form of the monastic rules in contrast to stories reporting their promulgation, or else verses and inspired utterances in contrast to the narratives recording the circumstance of their delivery.

The same appears to apply to portions of discourses, even though these are not as easily distinguished from each other as is the case of rules, verses, and inspired utterances in contrast to their accompanying prose narrations. In the three main cases surveyed in this chapter, the role of the more fixed text taken by the rules or verses/inspired utterances would correspond to the bare statement of the four noble truths, the list of the Buddha's marks, and the basic definitions of the first factors of the path. Each of these appears to have afforded an occasion for additional explanations during oral teaching, leading to the detailed exposition in the respective Pāli discourses of the four noble truths, the providing of a karmic perspective on the marks, and the depiction of supramundane manifestations of several path factors.

Given the lack of a self-evident difference between prose portion of the more fixed type and explanations and comments that are similarly in prose, the possibility of the latter becoming absorbed by the former can easily be envisaged. Warder (1961, 52) notes that, during the first period of transmission, there was "no clear line of demarcation between the Canonical traditions and the Commentarial extensions of them. The Commentaries grew up round the Canon from a very ancient period."

In relation to such apparent lack of clear demarcation between commentary and source text, research on memory can offer a helpful perspective. Goff and Roediger (1998, 28) showed that "imagining actions led subjects to remember that they had actually performed the actions when in fact they had not." This "effect increased with the number of imaginings, as did subjects' confidence about their erroneous responses."

This already in itself disconcerting finding about the reliability of human memory can be complemented by recent research on errors in source monitoring and the related topic of false memories, in the sense that additional information presented after a particular event results in a memory of having experienced something that never happened or else happened in quite a different way.[453] A typical procedure for researching such false memories is to request participants to memorize a list of words that are semantically related, for example "bed, rest, awake, tired, dream." Subsequently, participants are asked to decide if certain words were found in the original list. A false memory occurs when the word "sleep" is mistakenly identified as a member of the earlier list. The error occurred due to a failure to realize that the source of the idea "sleep" was one's own internal associations on reading a list of words related to this topic, rather than being something found explicitly in the actual list of words.

The same basic problem of a lack of accurate source monitoring would help explain the apparent intrusion of commentarial material into the actual text. Even though particular reciters would have been fully aware of being themselves the source of a new way of explanation, once these explanations are passed on to the next generations of reciters, such awareness will inevitably wane. Over successive instances of such transmission, if a comment once made effectively helps improve the oral delivery of a particular message, it becomes itself gradually more firmly established and thereby acquires a more fixed nature, bringing this explanation successively closer to the text on which it comments. In such a situation, it would not be surprising if eventually these two types of text merge in the way evident in the examples surveyed above.

10. Summary

The dynamics of orality are such that even the employment of abbreviation, whose pervasive occurrence in the early texts was quite probably motivated by attempts to facilitate their transmission, can in the course of time acquire a creative function. The same holds for lists, which from being simply a means to structure an oral presentation can evolve and take on a life of their own, by way of intruding in various contexts and thereby leading to textual expansions.

Another important factor with comparable repercussions appears to have been the providing of a commentary alongside a particular teaching. Due to the challenges of keeping a clear dividing line between these two types of prose text in an oral setting, combined with the problem of accurate source monitoring as a feature of human memory, major innovations may have had their humble beginnings as a commentary during oral teaching that eventually made it into the texts themselves.

VI. Implications of Orality

In this last chapter of my exploration, I survey what I believe to be chief implications and consequences of giving due recognition to the oral nature of the early Buddhist texts. I begin with a critical examination of the quest for an original, followed by an equally critical assessment of attempts to reconstruct a pre-canonical Buddhism or to take a definite stance on the "word of the Buddha." Then I propose, as a chief requirement for a proper study of the early Buddhist texts, a comprehensive coverage of all extant versions. In addition, there is a pressing need to be willing to step out of perspectives informed by Western thought and experience of dealing with written texts, subject to intentional change, in order to assess oral material from ancient India on its own terms. In the final part of the present chapter, I attempt a sketch of the dynamics of early Buddhist orality.

1. In Quest of the Original

The problematic nature of a search for the Ur-text, in the sense of attempting to reconstruct the original that stands at the outset of textual developments transmitted orally over centuries, can best be illustrated with a recent study that, alongside several problems, also offers intriguing insights into aspects of the numerical collections. Kuan and Bucknell (2019, 141) introduce their study by announcing, as a chief result of their research, the count of genuine discourses in the Pāli numerical collection. The attempt to determine such a number relies on the idea that at a particular point in time there was a clearly definable original version of this collection, which can be reconstructed. The authors' regular use of the expressions "pseudo-suttas" or "putative suttas" to refer to what in their view are later developments, and the qualification of such instances as "artificial" and "arbitrary," reflects an evaluation based on the underlying notion of a deviation from an authentic original made up of "genuine" discourses. Yet, it is difficult to determine when this original would have existed.

Let it be accepted for the time being, just for the sake of reasoning this case through, that the traditional account of the first communal recitation is correct in that soon after the Buddha's demise the collection of numerical discourses was formed. Presumably until that time, the textual material that came to make up this collection was being transmitted in a less structured manner and, due to the continuous teaching activity of the Buddha and his disciples, kept growing through the addition of new texts. To assume that a collection with a definite number of discourses came into being at least at the time of the first communal recitation, however, stands in contrast to evidence that the discourse collections did not achieve their finalized form at that time (see above p. 43). In the case of the Pāli collection of numerical discourses, of particular relevance is a discourse in this collection that has King Muṇḍa of Magadha as its protagonist.[454] Since this king was apparently the great-grandson of King Ajātasattu,[455] whose reign coincided with the later part of the Buddha's life, this discourse will have to be placed at quite some time after the Buddha's demise and could for this reason not have been included in the first communal recitation (or been part of an earlier collection predating the first *saṅgīti/saṃgīti*). At the same time, however, this discourse does not exhibit the features that Kuan and Bucknell (2019) rely on for designating a text as not authentic.

If this is to be considered a genuine discourse, then the original version of the numerical collection, with its supposedly correct count of discourses, can no longer be allocated to the first communal recitation. If authenticity is instead applied to the time when this discourse became part of the collection, then what qualification should be used for whatever happened before that occasion? Should the textual material transmitted up to that point be considered artificial or genuine? If it is considered genuine, then that means that the category of authenticity can accommodate various changes happening during oral transmission, leaving no real basis for not applying it similarly to changes happening after that time.

If it is instead considered artificial, in order to reserve authenticity for exactly the form the collection had at that short moment of time when the discourse featuring King Muṇḍa became part of the collection and before any other change happened within it, then artificiality becomes an overarching characteristic of the collection during nearly the entire span of its existence. In this way, the above considerations would hopefully reveal that the assumption underlying the quest for the original count of discourses in the numerical collection imposes a notion of a closed canon that does not do justice to the reality of oral transmission.

This is not to deny that at some point in time the Pāli collection of numerical discourses would have come to a closure, in the sense of no longer admitting the addition of new discourses. For the Pāli discourse collections in general, the available evidence suggests that this may hold for the Aśokan period; in that roughly at that time the incorporation of substantially new material into the four collections would have come to an end.[456] Now, again just for the sake of reasoning this case through, let it be assumed that the discourse to King Muṇḍa was the last to enter the Pāli collection of numerical discourses. Yet, it does not follow that the collection acquired a fixed number of discourses even at that time. The survey of the nature of oral transmission and textual memory in the preceding pages makes it fair to assume that there would have been occasions for change to affect the overall count of the collection. Even a simple error by either forgetting to execute a repetition series in one place or else accidentally adding one in another place would result in a substantial alteration of the number of discourses. In view of the natural vagaries of oral transmission, should the definite version of the collection then rather be attributed to its writing down? This is also not really a solution, as it would imply that any unauthentic discourse could only have come into existence after that. Moreover, the written form does not necessarily result in a definite count of discourses. The different Pāli editions of the collection in question, although concurring in main content, differ in their counts of discourses.

In sum, an attempt to reason the case through leads me to a failure to find a Pāli numerical collection with a definite and fixed count of discourse that can be considered the true original, whose contents can then be contrasted to "pseudo-suttas" or "putative suttas."

The idea of attempting to gain access to the true original is not only unwarranted for oral literature; it can even have detrimental repercussions on research.[457] This can be illustrated with the example of the first case taken up for study by Kuan and Bucknell (2019, 143), a text I discussed briefly at an earlier point (see above p. 117) as showing the impact of the notion of Ones on the material assembled under that heading. To recapitulate briefly, the Pāli and Chinese *Āgama* parallels highlight a set of "single" things that obsess the mind, which are the experience through any of the five senses of another person who could be either a male or a female. What in the Chinese *Āgama* version takes the form of two discourses, one for each sex, the Pāli collection presents as a chapter of ten discourses, due to being subdivided into distinct units for each of the senses. Despite some variations, however, the two extant texts appear to be parallel versions of the same basic exposition.[458]

Kuan and Bucknell (2019, 160) consider the present case, together with other texts found in common among the Ones of the two extant discourse collections, as "artificial," as according to their assessment each of the relevant texts "has earned its place in the Ones through having been subdivided."[459] In support of their conclusion, Kuan and Bucknell (2019, 143) argue that the text under discussion, expounding various single things that obsess the mind, has been excerpted from another Pāli discourse found elsewhere in the numerical collection and has then been artificially subdivided so as to fit under the Ones.

That other Pāli discourse concerns a case of incest between a mother and her son, a context in which the exposition corresponding to the set of discourses among the Ones is only a part of the whole discourse. Moreover, the assessment by the authors that the one "incorporates almost verbatim" material from the other, only adding more detail, is not quite accurate; the formulations employed by the two Pāli texts (in relation to each sense door) vary substantially.[460] Given that both texts occur in the same collection, a circumstance which tends to diminish variations, it seems highly improbable that the text under discussion from the Ones was excerpted from the discourse reporting the instance of incest. Yet, this is what Kuan and Bucknell (2019, 144) propose, as according to them the Pāli discourse under discussion was "lifted out of its context, divided into five sections, and then duplicated by switching 'man' and 'woman,' to yield a set of ten pseudo-suttas" that could then be allocated to the Ones.

The proposed reasoning also overlooks the fact that, if the present case were to be reduced to a single discourse, by removing the supposed artificiality of it being subdivided into two or ten discourses, it would still have a right to be among the Ones by dint of its presentation of a series of ten "single" things. Both versions clearly employ the term "single," or more literally "one," in their exposition. In other words, the placement among the Ones is not the result of subdivision.

In fact, it is precisely the qualification "one" that can help to explain the present shape of both versions in question. The Pāli version applies the term "one" to each of the five senses, which through being multiplied by the two sexes results in an overall count of ten occurrences of the term "one."[461] The Chinese *Āgama* discourse, however, applies the term "one" to the set of five senses as a whole, which through being multiplied by the two sexes results in an overall count of two occurrences of the term "one."[462] This explains why the Pāli text came to be seen as covering ten distinct topics and its Chinese *Āgama* counterpart as covering two, namely because of the number of times they refer to "one," the key term responsible for their allocation among the Ones in both numerical collections.

Another point worth consideration is that, in the case of the Pāli version, the standard introductory phrase describing the Buddha's whereabouts and his addressing a monastic audience occurs only once at the outset. It follows that the Pāli text itself could still be read as a single discourse with a teaching in ten sections. Adopting such a reading would only contrast with a textual remark, found after the discourse has come to an end, which identifies the foregoing as a "chapter." The situation is thus considerably less dramatic than assumed by Kuan and Bucknell (2019) and there appears to be no need to view it in terms of a genuine discourse arbitrarily transformed into artificial ones, given that neither the content nor the location is problematic. The only problem, if it is indeed one, is the decision taken at some point in the history of the numerical collection to consider this discourse to be a chapter.

In sum, the indeed not particularly meaningful idea of having the same exposition as a distinct teaching for each sense can be seen as an outcome of the natural vagaries of transmission, in the present case in particular occurring during the structuring of a collection of discourses. Such occurrences do not really deserve being qualified as arbitrary any more than other aspects of the same oral tradition. In view of the constantly changing nature of textual material during oral transmission, there is no sound basis for positing an authentic original that then enables deeming other texts as artificial.

In the hope that with the above example I have sufficiently illustrated the need to forgo the quest for an Ur-text, I would like to emphasize that the research by Kuan and Bucknell (2019) is itself a welcome addition to the field, as they bring to light some intriguing features of the numerical collections. However, a faulty methodological premise has unfortunately led to unconvincing conclusions and even outright errors, quite probably due to the distorting impact of the quest for the true original.

2. Pre-canonical Buddhism

A topic that relates to the futile search for an original is the attempt to reconstruct a so-called pre-canonical Buddhism, in the sense of employing a few selected sources to construe a supposedly very early stage of Buddhist thought that substantially differs from what the bulk of the early discourses convey. The term "pre-canonical Buddhism" corresponds to the title of an article by Schayer (1935), whose arguments can serve as an example for the type of approach taken at that time in the history of research on Buddhism. The chief assumption is that "texts representing ideas and doctrines contradictory to the generally admitted canonical viewpoint are survivals of older, precanonical Buddhism" (124).

One example for this approach is the assertion that "consciousness in early Buddhism was an eternal, indestructible Element," which Schayer (1935, 130) bases on the argument that "there are in Pali sources traces of a doctrine in which *vijñāna* [consciousness] is treated as a relatively stable element which transmigrates."[463] The suggestion appears to correspond to a fairly widespread misunderstanding of Buddhist thought, namely the assumption that the Buddhist notion of rebirth implies an eternal entity that transmigrates.[464]

The only early discourse mentioned in this discussion by Schayer (1935) is part of an acknowledgment by the author of evidence contrary to his suggestion,[465] whereas a simile supposedly supporting his assessment stems from a later work of Theravāda exegesis.[466] With all due recognition to the fact that the author writes at a time when the different types of Buddhist texts and their historical evolution was not as clear as it has become in the meantime, the reasoning as such puts things on their head, as to argue for a pre-canonical Buddhist position the supportive evidence should be from the early texts.

A similar pattern can be seen when Schayer (1935, 128) questions "whether we should really believe that '*sabbaṃ aniccam*', the thesis of universal, general impermanence, is a peculiarity of Buddhism from its very beginning." The only argument provided in support of this position relies on lists found in Abhidharma texts. This is hardly evidence for concluding that "in precanonical Buddhism, impermanence concerned only the elements of *rūpa*," that is, of material form. This conclusion comes with a reference to some tenets held by later Buddhist schools as evidence that "the *dharma-dhātu* as opposed to the *rūpa-dhātu*, denoted a permanent, eternal reality," this being another supposedly pre-canonical teaching. As above, the proposed line of reasoning is the opposite of what would be required to establish some form of pre-canonical Buddhism.

In a subsequent article, Schayer (1937, 15) repeats the same argument: "The fact that *sabbam aniccaṃ* is not known to the earliest Buddhism can no longer be overlooked by Buddhologists." Yet, the exact formulation "all is impermanent" (*sabbaṃ aniccaṃ*) is found in a Pāli discourse, for example, explained to refer to the impermanent nature of the six sense organs, their objects, and the corresponding types of consciousness, etc.[467] This Pāli discourse has a counterpart in a Chinese *Āgama* discourse that makes precisely the same affirmation.[468] In addition to this precise match, the idea that all things are impermanent is pervasively attested in the early discourses.

Keeping in mind the time when the above article was written, it is perhaps less surprising that testimonies to the centrality of the doctrine of impermanence in early Buddhist thought have been overlooked. At the same time, however, since the author's suggestions continue to be influential among some Buddhist scholars, it does seem necessary to point out their shortcomings.

Regarding the standard list of four levels of awakening, Schayer (1937, 16) argues that "the original climax was closed by the third item, viz., by the *anāgamin* [sic, nonreturner], the fourth stage of an *arhant* being obviously a later addition."[469] No supportive evidence from the early texts is provided. Contrary to the proposed assessment, the actual evidence from the early discourses much rather shows all four levels of progress to full awakening to be an integral part of the early Buddhist teachings.[470]

The patterns already evident thus far become even more apparent with another argument provided by Schayer (1935, 125) in support of his approach. This concerns an indication that a person consists of six elements, which "cannot be reconciled with the official theories of the Abhidharma." Needless to say, a position in contrast to Abhidharma theories is not uncommon for the early discourses, but this does not make such a position become pre-canonical.

Although perhaps understandable given the time when the author was writing, it remains problematic if no relevant evidence is adduced at all. In the present case, the author just mentions the Discourse on the Six Elements, without providing any reference at all.[471] An attempt to argue similarly for the reconstruction of a pre-canonical Buddhism by Keith (1936, 5) then mentions the same discourse title, offering a reference to a relevant passage in an exegetical work. This reference does not mention the title of the discourse, and none of the extant versions of this discourse, nor an actual quote from this discourse in the same exegetical work, has exactly the title mentioned by Schayer (1935),[472] leaving me with the impression that he perhaps invented it.

The same problem continues with a defense of Schayer (1935) by Regamey (1957, 53), who asserts that in this discourse consciousness is endowed with the quality of being eternal.[473] The relevant discourse versions, which are the type of texts to be consulted in an attempt to reconstruct a pre-canonical Buddhism, have no qualification at all of consciousness as eternal. The same holds for the assertion by Lindtner (1997,

110), another author writing in defense of Schayer (1935), that in the canonical sources "we hear of the Six Elements (*dhātu*) that seem to form an exception to the otherwise universal law of change." Note that here all six elements, and not just consciousness, are exempted from impermanence. This gives me the impression that a lack of concern for referencing (and consulting) the actual textual sources led from an imaginary title to arguments based on imagination rather than on actual evidence.

The agenda behind the positing of a pre-canonical Buddhism can best be appraised by consulting a summary provided by Pye (2019, 23), apparently another scholar in favor of the validity of the proposed approach: "In a nutshell, the approach under consideration suggests that certain features typical of the Mahayana are likely to have been present in early Buddhism and were not later accretions."

This makes it difficult to avoid the impression that the promotion of a pre-canonical Buddhism could be related to a strategy employed by Mahāyāna polemics. An example is the promotion by Nanjio (1886, xiii), who had studied under Max Müller, of the idea that the first teaching delivered by the Buddha after his awakening was the *Buddhāvataṃsaka* (a text reflecting a mature stage of Mahāyāna thought and cosmology). The present case appears to be in line with the same pattern of attempting to endorse a basic fundamentalist claim made by certain followers of the Mahāyāna, asserting that their teachings go back to the historical Buddha.[474] Such an agenda would help explain the lack of scholarly rigor. It seems as if the inner conviction can become so strong that the actual textual evidence no longer merits full consultation and for this reason also does not need to be referenced.[475]

At the same time, however, it needs to be acknowledged that Schayer (1935) was correct in pointing to Pāli references to the luminous mind or consciousness as precedents for significant developments in later Buddhist thought.[476] However, comparative study of these passages enables a more nuanced assessment (Anālayo 2017d). Rather than being testimonies to a pre-canonical Buddhism, the relevant passages appear to be in line with recurrent instances of textual development and change surveyed in the previous chapters of this book.

3. The "Word of the Buddha"

The impossibility of reconstructing the original from material that has been orally transmitted over centuries also affects the idea that it is possible to be certain what exactly the historical Buddha said. The limitations of orality do not imply that nothing at all can be said about such matters. A whole range of later developments of Buddhist thought can with certainty be identified as such, making it possible to come to the definite conclusion that these cannot be attributed to the historical Buddha. This holds for the *Buddhāvataṃsaka*, for example.

Beyond the merely negative, central early Buddhist teachings, such as dependent arising, not self, the four (noble) truths, among others, stand out in the ancient Indian context for their novelty.[477] At the same time, however, since the extant early discourses do not enable the reconstruction of an original version, the exact words of the Buddha on such topics remain beyond reach. It is no longer possible to establish with certitude that a particular saying was indeed made in exactly this way by the Buddha. For this reason, to my mind Sujato and Brahmali (2014, 179) overstate the situation when they assert:

> We know when the Buddha lived, where he lived, who he associated with, how he lived, and what he taught. We know these things with greater certainty than for almost any other historical figure from a comparable period. And we know this because of the EBTs [early Buddhist texts].

Comparative study of these early Buddhist texts does not support the assessment by the authors that "the changes are in almost all cases details of editing and arrangement, not of doctrine or substance" (12). Take the example of the two discourses discussed in the previous chapter: the Discourse on the Marks and the Discourse on the Great Forty. Each indubitably reflects a substantial doctrinal innovation. Nevertheless, later generations of reciters would have been passing on these Pāli discourses in the assumption that they were transmitting the word of the Buddha. Although in both cases parallel versions transmitted by other reciter lineages enable an identification of later layers in these two Pāli discourses, even material common to the parallels may be late; it could just be that comparative study is not able to furnish evidence for that.

A case illustrating this possibility would be the Discourse on [the Buddha's] Wonderful and Marvelous Qualities (*Acchariyabbhutadhammasutta*) and its Chinese *Āgama* parallel, which have the Buddha's attendant Ānanda as their speaker. The two versions differ substantially in their description of extraordinary qualities of the Buddha, and some of the qualities found in only one version point to important and innovative developments.[478] They agree, however, in stating that the Buddha was born without being in any way sullied by the birth process and right away was able to walk, taking seven steps.[479] Both discourses conclude with the Buddha adding yet another extraordinary quality of his, thereby implicitly approving the listing of qualities given by Ānanda. In fact, in both versions Ānanda introduces each quality by stating that he heard about it, which implies that the ultimate source of these descriptions was the Buddha himself.

My point here is not to enforce a literal reading on such descriptions and then set these in contrast to what we know about the physical condition of a recently born infant. The image of being unsullied by birth is a literary trope that serves to throw into relief the purity of the one just born and needs to be appreciated for its literary qualities rather than being taken as a description of biological facts. In fact, a *Vinaya* text goes further by describing that a celestial king decided to have the mother's womb cleaned up before conception, so as to make it ready for receiving the future Buddha.[480] Another *Vinaya* texts explicitly tackles the question of why the infant took exactly the auspicious number of seven steps, rather than six or eight.[481] As noted by Karetzky (1992, 16), precisely because "no child can immediately walk or talk, let alone make proclamations at birth, it is by these acts that the Buddha's prodigious nature, even as an infant, is revealed."

As a result, however, as pointed out by Gaffney (1996, 84), "in texts like *Acchariyabbhutadhamma-sutta* of the *Majjhima-nikāya*, the description of his [the Buddha's] birth is full of what might almost be called docetic tendencies." The central question here is whether such incipient docetic tendencies should be reckoned as "the word of the Buddha." Comparative study does not provide clear-cut evidence for considering these descriptions to be later additions and hence not deserving of inclusion in this category.

To provide yet another example, take the case of the report in a Pāli discourse and one of its two Chinese *Āgama* parallels that the Buddha gave a detailed prediction of the advent of the future Buddha Maitreya.[482] The other Chinese *Āgama* parallel does not mention the future Buddha at all.[483] A close study, based on the important indication that emerges in this way, enables drawing the conclusion that the whole prediction is probably the result of a later development.[484]

This finding carries considerable significance, given the role of Maitreya in later times, as evidenced in texts and art.[485] Even the author of the most influential work of Theravāda exegesis, Buddhaghosa, is on record for aspiring to be reborn at the time of Maitreya.[486] There can hardly be any doubt that the story of Maitreya's advent was perceived as the word of the Buddha by later generations. It is only through comparative study and access to this other Chinese *Āgama* parallel that a different perspective emerges.

As mentioned in a previous chapter, the four Chinese *Āgama*s were transmitted by different reciter lineages or schools. A complete discourse collection is only extant from the Theravāda tradition. Due to this situation, absence of a parallel to a Pāli discourse can at times simply be the result of the differing distribution of discourses over the four main collections in various transmission lineages. It follows that the ability to access the Chinese *Āgama* discourse that does not report the advent of Maitreya is a fortunate accident of the vicissitudes of transmission. Otherwise, there would be no firm evidence for questioning the prediction of Maitreya as the word of the Buddha. This goes to show that the very nature of the textual sources makes the knowledge that can be derived from them necessarily somewhat haphazard, something that always remains open to revision if some other relevant version should be discovered.

Some uncertainty remains even in the case of teachings like dependent arising, not self, and the four noble truths. Was the profundity of dependent arising indeed a factor motivating the recently awakened Buddha's hesitation to teach at all?[487] A Chinese *Āgama* parallel to the relevant Pāli discourse does not have the entire hesitation episode, making it at least possible that this could be a later addition.[488] In what way did the Buddha disclose his successful awakening to Upaka, who could have been his first convert? The report that Upaka remained unconvinced strengthens the claim that this passage may well report something that indeed happened, simply because a failure of the recently awakened Buddha to convert his first potential disciple would hardly have been invented later. Yet, what precisely the Buddha said to evoke such a reaction remains open to uncertainty.[489]

The more successful teaching given by the Buddha to his five former companions takes the four noble truths as its main theme. Yet, did the Buddha actually use the qualification "noble" or even explicitly employ the term "truth" when giving this teaching?[490] It is also not entirely clear in what way he subsequently taught the doctrine of not self to the same group of five, given that recently published Gāndhārī fragments have preserved a record of the Buddha's second sermon that lacks a substantial portion of the text found in other versions.[491] This leaves open the possibility that the received Pāli version has been expanded.

The uncertainty that emerges in this way pertains not only to the first teachings of the Buddha but extends all the way to his last words. It seems probable that these last words were in some way on the theme of impermanence, but what exact form these took can no longer be determined.[492]

In sum, it needs to be acknowledged that actual words spoken in ancient India more than two millennia ago are beyond reach. What can be accessed now are textual descriptions of what centuries later, at the end point of a prolonged period of textual transmission of the early Buddhist scriptural corpus, were believed to have been the teachings of the Buddha.

At the same time, however, it is these descriptions that have made him a source of lasting inspiration for Buddhists ancient and modern. Their historical-critical study makes it possible to discern layers in the development of such descriptions and thereby understand the growth of Buddhist thought and practice. In the end, this is perhaps even more historically significant than a quest for certainty about the actual words of the person who must have lived in ancient India. As explained by de Jong (1993, 21):

> It is not in the first place the fact that these texts were transmitted for centuries before being written down that makes them very unreliable witnesses to historical events. It is their very nature as oral texts which makes it impossible to use them as material for a historical study . . . but they give us much information about the teachings of early Buddhism.

Although it seems to me that Sujato and Brahmali (2014) overstate the certainty of knowledge that can be derived from the available textual material, they do have a point in warning against excessive skepticism. An example in case is the position argued by Drewes (2017, 1 and 19), according to whom "no basis for treating the Buddha as a historical figure has yet been identified" and that "we do not have grounds for speaking of a historical Buddha at all," hence he may as well be regarded as a mythical figure comparable to Kṛṣṇa. This exaggerated claim has met with deserved criticism by Levman (2019), von Hinüber (2019a), and Wynne (2019).[493]

It seems to me best to adopt a middle-ground position between affirming certainty about what the historical Buddha exactly did or taught and dismissing his existence. The same applies in general for the early Buddhist oral tradition: although it is at present no longer possible to recover the original version of any teaching, it does not follow that such an original version never existed.

4. Comprehensive Coverage

The above considerations would hopefully have confirmed that it is not a promising venue of research to attempt to reconstruct the original constitution of a discourse collection, to construe a pre-canonical Buddhism, or to take a definite stance on the word of the Buddha. What the extant textual sources do allow is a better understanding of stages in the formation and development of Buddhist thought and practice.

Putting to full use the potential of comparative study in this respect requires a comprehensive survey of the extant sources, at least when the aim is to reconstruct "early Buddhism." This is certainly not to deny the validity of, for instance, studying a single *Vinaya* tradition as a legal system in its own. Similarly, the Pāli discourses can indeed be meaningfully studied on their own from the viewpoint of their reception in Theravāda exegesis or from a philological perspective, for example. The point here is only that, in order to arrive at sound conclusions regarding "early Buddhism," research needs to go beyond the confines of a single tradition and take into account all relevant textual material. For *Vinaya* texts, this requirement has fortunately by now been clearly recognized. For example, Clarke (2009, 38) reasons:

> If, then, we are interested in providing a balanced and nuanced picture of Indian monastic Buddhism, it seems certain that we will need to take the evidence provided by all extant monastic codes seriously, and this in turn will mean that the *Vinaya*s other than the Pāli will warrant much more attention.

Clarke (2014, 166) adds that a single *Vinaya* "cannot be accepted as representative of Indian Buddhist monasticisms without first fully examining the other five monastic law codes; we must marshal all available evidence." As succinctly formulated by Kieffer-Pülz (2014, 61–62),

> we have to be aware that there is not just one *Vinaya*, but several, and they stem from distinct schools, from different time periods, from different regions, and were adapted to their environments to different degrees . . . General statements on the basis of only one *Vinaya* should belong to the past.

Although the same need should be similarly obvious for the early discourses, this does not always appear to have found full acceptance. For example, in reply to criticism raised by me of precisely such a failure to take into consideration parallel versions (Anālayo 2008c, 114 and 122), von Hinüber (2015, 198) argues,[494]

> concentration on the Theravāda tradition is neither a "methodological problem" (p. 114) nor a "methodological shortcoming" (p. 122), but a methodological necessity. Only the oldest

> levels of the Buddhist tradition we can reach might occasionally tell something about the very early history of Buddhism.

Granted that this statement is formulated in the context of a debate, as it is made by a leading scholar in the field whose work has considerable impact worldwide, it calls for a comment. If the proposed reasoning were to be accepted, it would result in identifying the Theravāda textual tradition as representing in principle the oldest levels of the Buddhist tradition. Such a position would be difficult to uphold in view of the ample evidence for later change in Pāli discourses that emerges from comparative study (Anālayo 2016g).

A basic principle of scientific procedure is that first all relevant data needs to be gathered and only after that has the time come for interpretation. Admittedly, a problem in gathering all relevant data in the case of studying the early discourses is a dearth of reliable translations of the relevant Chinese and Tibetan sources.[495] This unfortunately restricts the range of those able to carry out research. Nevertheless, this does not change the basic principle of needing to consult all versions of a particular discourse in order to draw conclusions on early Buddhist thought or history.

Although the potential of a full coverage of parallels must have already become fairly evident in the selected examples presented in the preceding pages, one additional example may help to buttress the same point. The example occurs in the context of a debate on the class superiority of brahmins. Some Pāli editions report that King Pasenadi who, like the Buddha, was a member of the warrior class, thought that the Buddha was superior to him in matters of birth; this is the reading followed by leading translators of this passage into English and German.[496] Non-Pāli parallels instead indicate that he did *not* have such a consideration, which fits the context much better, as they were both members of the same class.[497] The corresponding reading is also found in the Burmese edition.[498] Thus, in this instance the parallels help decide which variant reading to adopt. This is not the only case where a Chinese discourse parallel can be of help for adopting the appropriate Pāli variant and thereby correcting the reading followed by leading translators.[499] In view of such potential, is it really meaningful to consider it a methodological necessity that non-Pāli sources are not taken into account?

To quote the words of de Jong (1968, 15): "no student of Buddhism, even if he is interested only in Indian Buddhism, can neglect the enormous corpus of Chinese translations." This is certainly not to deny that for research on early philological developments the texts preserved in Pāli offer a resource superior to parallels translated into languages like Chinese or Tibetan. However, philology is not the only relevant perspective. In addition to form, the content of a text is at least of similar relevance. Many examples surveyed in the course of my present study would have shown that the content of the Pāli discourses was subject to change just as much as that of the parallel versions.

The same basic requirement can be illustrated with the example of a detailed study of the Buddha's biography by Bareau (1963). Although employing a range of relevant material extant in Chinese, he intentionally set aside important Mūlasarvāstivāda sources.[500] In view of this unfortunate decision, it is hardly surprising that conclusions arrived at in this way turn out to be in need of revision, as becomes evident with a more comprehensive survey of the relevant sources.[501] The same fate can safely be expected for any study of early Buddhism that intentionally relies only on part of the relevant source material.

A proper appreciation of early Buddhist thought requires a systematic reading of *all* extant versions, by way of evaluating any passage against the background of its parallels and based on a clear appreciation of the oral nature of these texts. Due to their prolonged oral transmission, the possibility of errors must be taken into account, the occurrence of which can at times be identified with the help of a comparative study of the extant parallel versions.

5. Intentional Change

Besides the need to consider all parallels, the nature of the texts and their transmission requires full recognition. This holds in particular for a tendency to opt too easily for intentionality as the reason for change, which can occur even with scholars who are very well familiar with oral features of the texts. For example, Allon (2021) tends to consider variations between parallels as largely resulting from intentional redactorial activity despite having earlier conducted stimulating research on oral features of Pāli discourse material (Allon 1997b). As mentioned previously (see above p. 70), some changes do indeed appear to have been intentional. But the textual evidence surveyed above makes it in my view advisable not to take intentionality as the main lens through which to understand the early Buddhist oral tradition, as to do so risks overlooking the potential impact of other influences, in particular the shortcomings of memory.

The possibility of unintentional change as such is in fact clearly acknowledged by Allon (2021, 50):

> In a purely oral context, unintentional changes may result from the limitations of memory and the way memory works and the social background and mnemotechnical skills of members of the Buddhist community . . . Examples of unintentional changes are of a word being replaced by a similarly sounding word; words or phrases being accidentally omitted; words or phrases triggering the inclusion of a stock phrase or description found associated with that word or phrase in other texts transmitted by the community; changes in the order of items being listed or in the order of verses due to lack of adequate guides to maintaining a particular order; differences in the names of people and places; commentarial glosses being included in the root text.

Given this acknowledgment, it seems to me that the difference in evaluation between the approaches advocated by the two of us is mainly a matter of emphasis, in that I would relegate intentionality to a relatively minor role.

An example for what I would consider a case of too easily opting for the model of intentionality involves a reference in the Sanskrit fragment version of the Great Discourse on the [Buddha's] Final Nirvana (*Mahāparinirvāṇasūtra*), according to which the Buddha employed the supernormal ability of the divine ear for hearing a conversation taking place within earshot; the Pāli version does not have such a reference.[502] Although Allon (2021, 66) acknowledges that this "could have occurred through unintentional means, by common association alone," according to his assessment "it is more likely to be another instance of intentional change." Since taking such a position calls for some explanation of why such a change was implemented on purpose, he proposes that this was "perhaps motivated by the desire to emphasize the qualities of the Buddha." Such a motivation is indeed evident in many texts, where this usually takes the form of eulogizing his superior qualities. The same does not seem to be relevant in the present instance, however, as it is hardly complimentary to portray the Buddha as requiring supernormal abilities for accomplishing something that anyone with normal hearing abilities can do just as well. This makes it in my view considerably more probable that the present instance results from an unintentional error during transmission.

The need of granting sufficient room for the potential impact of human memory on oral transmission can also be seen in the assessment by Allon (2021, 41) of a tendency for similar textual items to occur together and thereby form a pair: "the phenomenon of sutras and other textual units being arranged in pairs indicates that an enormous amount of culling and modification of discourses must have occurred when these collections were created." This statement seems to envisage the process required to form such pairs as part of a large enterprise of intentional editorial activity.

Yet, as Bartlett (1932, 197) explained in his ground-breaking study of human memory, the various memory traces of an individual "are in fact bound to be related one to another, and this gives to recall its inevitably associative character." In other words, the basic operational mechanism of memory is through forming associations, making it only natural that memories of similar textual units come to be closely related to each other, facilitating in turn their joint recall. In other words, a more parsimonious explanation of the phenomenon of pairs of textual units can be found by taking into account the working mechanism of human memory, obviating any need of postulating an enormous amount of intentional modification.

The assumption of rather complex processes of standardization and arrangement as being responsible for the texts in their present form and arrangement can also be seen in the following statement (Allon 2021, 43):

> The creation of textual units such as sutras which involved multiple and complex decisions regarding language, genre, structure, length, diction, style, standardization, and the creation of collections of such units that clearly involved selecting, culling, and even proliferating textual units, must have been an enormous group undertaking that involved considerable investment of time and effort, as would have been the process of getting the results ratified by the community, to say nothing of its subsequent transmission.

It would be difficult to find actual evidence for the carrying out of such an ongoing "enormous group undertaking that involved considerable investment of time and effort." Had this indeed been the case, which would imply making such activities a central and continuous occupation of the early Buddhist reciters, one could reasonably expect for this to be recorded in some way.

Of course, this is just an argument from silence.[503] However, it receives support from the evidence provided by the texts themselves, whose irregularities do not support the idea that they were "ratified by the community." This proposal, if I understand it correctly, seems to involve the assumption that the versions now extant reflect the latest update representative of the consensus on the specific form of a particular text in a certain Buddhist school or reciter tradition. Instead, however, it seems much rather that the extant versions are just one out of a multitude of variants in oral circulation at the same time, becoming what we now have access to simply due to happening to be the ones that were put down in writing in a form that has been preserved over the many intervening centuries.

Many of the apparent problems caused by the notion of "school affiliation" relate to this issue, namely the conjecture that particular textual collections should be reflecting a process of intentional edition (and subsequent ratification) by the members of the respective school. From this perspective, it becomes difficult to understand the variations that occur quite naturally in orality. Needless to say, these manifest alongside the equally natural occurrence of rectification of errors through group recitation, reinforcing the patterns of similarity found among texts belonging to a particular school or reciter tradition. But such patterns of similarity never inhibit completely the continuous emergence of variations, which is an integral part of the very mechanics of the type of oral transmission under discussion here.

In fact, variations can be found even within the texts of the Theravāda tradition, which could hardly be reflecting the influence of different school affiliations and their respective editorial committees (Anālayo 2017e, 58–63). The same holds for variations between two manuscript testimonies to the Gāndhārī *Dharmapada*.[504] Mūlasarvāstivāda texts similarly give the impression that variation was the norm rather than a thorough homogenization based on an intentionally undertaken processes of redaction and ratification. As noted by Clarke (2015, 73), the actual textual evidence points to "the existence of multiple Mūlasarvāstivāda *Vinayas*." In the same vein, in relation to Mūlasarvāstivāda discourse material, Dhammadinnā (2020, 482) argues for

> a model of multiplicity of versions for the discourse transmission that is not dissimilar to what is emerging in recent scholarship in the case of the Sarvāstivāda and Mūlasarvāstivāda *Vinayas*. This may be read as a reflection of textual transmission among fragmented and spread-out textual communities which nevertheless coalesce under a unifying denominational and ideological umbrella.

It seems to me that, unless we avoid defaulting to the assumption of intentional change, implemented by so-called redactors and subsequently ratified by editorial committees, it will remain difficult to understand evidence for what, from the viewpoint of orality, appear to be just natural fluctuations.

Now, the pervasive tendency to see intentional intervention behind any variation is quite understandable, as it reflects the modes of textual production with which we all are so well familiar. Yet, when it comes to oral literature it misses much of the picture.

The tendency to give a prominent role to intentional modes of textual production is particularly understandable when working with manuscript fragments. Having direct access to a written text produced somewhere between one to two millennia ago can easily give us the impression that basically the same processes must have been at work in ancient and contemporary times, mainly differing in the material used for writing. The sense of commonality that emerges quite naturally in this way can then result in a tendency not to give full recognition to the fact that, in the case of the early discourses at least, the manuscript tradition is a record of what came into existence orally and for centuries was transmitted entirely by oral means.

It seems to me that intentional intervention is only a part (and I contend a minor part) out of a broad range of different influences that have impacted the formation of the early Buddhist discourses. Taking it to be the norm fails to do justice to the multifaceted complexity of the material.

6. A Shift of Perspective

As the above exploration would have shown, a proper understanding of the early Buddhist texts calls for a fundamental shift of perspective away from the all-too-well-known world of written texts to allow for the implications of orality to emerge. Admittedly, this is quite a challenge. As noted by Rosenberg (1987, 73), "'Oral Tradition' . . . the very concept, the comprehension of such a mode of life, is alien to literates."

Comparable to the need to avoid thinking in terms of "councils" by "sects" that undergo separate "schisms," discussed above (see p. 18), there is a need to recognize that those responsible for the formation and transmission of the early Buddhist texts were not "editors" or "redactors." The usage of such terms predestines thinking to move along the lines of the familiar world of written textual production and to default to the myth of intentional change as the norm. In order to encourage a better appreciation of the complexity of early Buddhist orality, I think it would be preferable to speak of "reciters." The term "reciter" is well attested in inscriptions,[505] making it the most appropriate choice for coming to terms with the texts by taking into account their historical, cultural, and social setting as well as, above all, their oral nature.

The difficulties of stepping out of the world of written textual production has impacted a range of scholars, which can be illustrated with a few examples. In the context of a comparative study of the two collections of medium-length discourses, Minh Chau (1964/1991, 75) reasons that differences between parallel versions must be "due either to the compilers' choice or to the characteristics of the schools they represented." In other words, he sees variations as invariably being the outcome of intentional intervention, which could be motivated either by individual preferences or by school affiliation.

Closer inspection based on extending the range of comparison to relevant parallels and indications beyond the two collections of medium-length discourses, in line with the above-mentioned need for a comprehensive coverage, shows several of the conclusions that are based on this premise to be unconvincing or even simply wrong (Anālayo 2008a). This does not diminish the importance of the groundbreaking contribution made by Minh Chau (1964/1991). In fact, at the time he concluded his research nearly sixty years ago, there was hardly any awareness of the significance of oral transmission for understanding Indian Buddhist texts. It does mean, however, that several of his conclusions need revision due to being based on an inappropriate premise.

A related problem is the suggestion that similarities between parallel versions should be viewed as the outcome of later leveling. A particularly influential articulation of this position can be found in Schopen (1985), which on detailed inspection turns out to be baseless (see Wynne 2005 and Anālayo 2012c). The problem here is not just that the arguments proposed fail to hold up under closer scrutiny, but that the idea as such again opts for a simplistic explanation of what actual research shows to be far too complex to be reduced to a mono-dimensional view. The type of evidence surveyed in the previous chapter reflects a range of inconsistencies that are incompatible with such a model. Had homogenizing of the textual material indeed been a central factor, it would have eliminated such inconsistencies. For this reason, the idea that later leveling can be adopted as the main explanation for similarities between parallel versions fails to do justice to the testimony provided by the actual sources.

Although the proposal by Schopen (1985) was formulated at a time when there was hardly a good knowledge of the complexity of orality in Buddhist textuality, the adoption of simplistic explanations is still evident, for example, in the model for understanding the early discourses proposed by Shulman (2019 and 2021c). The main idea, presented under the heading of a "play of formulas," is that formulaic descriptions (or pericopes) are the main building blocks of discourses, the remainder of the relevant texts being secondary to the chief dynamics of creatively combining such formulas in different ways. Although at first sight such a model is not without its attraction, the proposal fails to do justice to the actual textual evidence (Anālayo 2021g). The very first examples given by Shulman (2019) already show that the relevant formulas are secondary elements in the respective discourses, rather than being its primary building blocks (Anālayo 2021f). In fact, formulas are just one aspect in the rich repertoire of early Buddhist orality, and for this reason need to be considered alongside the various other aspects surveyed in the previous chapters.

Even more problematic is the author's proposal that discourses from different transmission lineages that report the same event should no longer be considered parallels; instead, the sharing of formulas should be the criterion for identifying parallels, even if the remainder of the text is quite different. This involves a serious misunderstanding of the methodology of identifying discourse parallels (Anālayo 2021g), resulting in the taking of a position that no longer has a basis in the source material.

Except for the last suggestion, however, the other proposals surveyed above all have a kernel of truth. School affiliation did occasionally have an impact on the oral transmission, leveling did play a minor role, and formulas did at times take on a life of their own. But all of these are just aspects, and often rather minor ones, out of a broad range of different influences that have shaped the early Buddhist oral tradition. A proper appreciation of the oral nature of the early discourses requires considering all its different facets in conjunction, rather than focusing on only one of them. Most important of all, it necessitates leaving room for the possibility of unintentional change. In fact, many of the instances of change that can be identified appear to have their source in the various limitations that inhere in human memory. As already mentioned, a proper understanding of orality can benefit greatly from taking fully into account these limitations. Quiroga (2017, 17) describes the situation as follows:

> We remember almost nothing. The idea that we remember a great deal of the subtleties and details of our experiences, as if we are playing back a movie, is nothing more than an illusion, a construct of the brain. And this is perhaps the greatest secret in the study of memory: the astounding truth that, starting from very little information, the brain creates a reality and a past that makes us who we are, despite the fact that this past, this collection of memories, is extremely slippery; despite the fact that the mere act of bringing a memory to our consciousness inevitably changes it.

Given the degree to which, as human beings, we all rely on our remembrances to make sense of who we are and what we do, it is certainly challenging to acknowledge the remarkable unreliability of human memory. This may be an additional factor obstructing a full recognition of the impact of the limitations of human memory on the early Buddhist oral transmission. It is perhaps only natural to default to the reassuring assumption that changes must be the outcome of intentional redactorial activity, bringing an element of familiarity to an otherwise often perplexing terrain, rather than questioning the reliability of human memory in general, and thereby inevitably also of our own.

Yet, it is precisely these limitations of human recall that explain variations in the accounts given by eyewitnesses who often quite sincerely try to report what they believe to have seen. The same also explains variations in the transmission of the early Buddhist texts. This is not to exclude completely the possibility of falsehood by eyewitnesses or intentional changes by reciters. But such cases are more appropriately seen as exceptions rather than as the general rule.

Even the impact of school affiliation can at times manifest in a somewhat accidental manner. This can be seen in a Chinese *Āgama* discourse, transmitted by Sarvāstivāda reciters, which differs from its Pāli parallel in applying the qualification "really existing" to each of the sense organs of the past.[506] This qualification can safely be taken to reflect the influence of the school affiliation of this discourse collection. A later treatise uses precisely the same expression in its treatment of the tenet, characteristic of the Sarvāstivāda school, that the past and the future really exist.[507] However, the discourse in question does not apply the qualification of the sense organs as "really existing" to present and future times.[508] In other words, although the use of this qualification for past times appears to reflect the influence of thought characteristic of the school affiliation of the reciters who transmitted this particular collection, the same is not applied consistently. Had its application been the outcome of intentional editing, the same qualification should have been similarly applied to sense organs in future and present times.

Besides the need to step out of invariably suspecting sectarian or individual agendas, an attempt to understand the early Buddhist oral tradition requires taking into consideration its antecedents in the Vedic oral tradition. As pointed out by Gombrich (1990, 23), "the Buddhist canon has left us more clues that it is modelled on Vedic literature than has been generally recognized." Taking into consideration patterns of orality already in existence in the same geographical and cultural setting is certainly preferable to reliance on a model based on the performance of epic material by Yugoslavian bards, as suggested by Cousins (1983). At the time of writing this article, nearly forty years ago, his suggestion was an understandable attempt to come to appreciate the oral dimensions of the early texts, and in that sense it has certainly fulfilled its purpose in stimulating further reflections and research. In the meantime, however, with the steady increase of knowledge on early Buddhist orality, to insist on continuing to rely on the same outdated model is not a promising avenue of research.[509] It needs to be recognized that the oral performance of an epic in a Western cultural setting, based on improvising and recreating a story with the aim of entertaining an audience in a bar, differs substantially from the oral transmission of texts performed for purposes of conversion and spiritual inspiration in the ancient Indian religious setting.[510] It would be a mistake to take conclusions drawn from Western epic material as a self-evident standard when evaluating material that is not epic and is situated in a substantially different performance context.[511] Allon (1997a, 42) explains:

> Many factors can influence the character of an oral literature and its method of composition and transmission: the nature of the information being relayed; the attitude towards this material and the extent to which accuracy is required; the character of the performers or composers, their status in society, the type of training they have undergone and the circumstances under which they perform; the nature of the audience and its expectations and therefore its demands on the performer or performers; the medium used (verse or prose) and whether the performance requires musical accompaniment. The Buddhist and Yugoslav-Homeric traditions differ in virtually all of these factors.

The evidence listed earlier in this book to provide a contrast to the idea of intentional change (see above p. 69) equally provides a contrast to the assumption of improvisation as the central modality of the early Buddhist oral transmission. Errors that result from a lack of attention paid to the meaning conveyed by the passage or expression in question provide evidence that counters models based on improvisation, where attention will naturally be on the meaning. In addition, sound and metrical similarities, together with memorization aids like the principle of waxing syllables, concord with explicit indications in the discourses that convey an emphasis on accurate recall.[512] As the preceding pages have amply documented, such an emphasis is of course only one in a whole range of influences and concerns, which have impacted the early Buddhist oral tradition. Nevertheless, this feature confirms that an improvisatory model of textual production fails to explain the situation adequately.

As already mentioned in an earlier chapter (see above p. 128), fragments of certain previous-birth stories convey a good idea of how the Buddhist reciters presented summaries of material for purposes of improvisation. Although of course not all extant collections of previous-birth stories take this form, the relevant Kharoṣṭhī specimen can conveniently be contrasted to early discourses similarly extant in Kharoṣṭhī manuscripts. It seems reasonable to interpret the resultant contrast between bare listings of keywords in the case of previous-birth stories and fully formulated text in early discourses as reflecting different modalities of recitation, namely a more improvisatory approach in contrast to material meant to be recited by rote.

A way of trying to salvage the idea that the early discourses result from improvisation could seem to be the assumption that, by the time of the development reflected in the Kharoṣṭhī manuscripts, the discourses had already become fixed, after having gone through an early period of free improvisation. Such an assumption would be a natural result of thinking in terms of the well-known world of written texts, where a period of change is indeed followed by stability. However, this model is not readily applicable to the early Buddhist oral tradition, as the evidence surveyed in previous chapters shows change to have been a continuous element and not something characteristic of its early stages only. This makes it commendable to shift from the certainty of the written word to the uncertainty of thinking in terms of orality and develop a model that is able to explain the continuous manifestation of change during the centuries of oral transmission. In the remainder of this chapter, I present a modest attempt at formulating a starting point for developing such a model.

7. Dynamics of Orality

In what follows, I proceed beyond the actual textual evidence that has been the mainstay of my exploration thus far. As an alternative to visualizing the situation based on familiar modes of textual production, I attempt to sketch what, within the confines of my ignorance, I consider to be central dynamics of oral transmission that would have impacted the way the texts have been formed and transmitted. What follows is meant simply as a quite subjective reflection of my current and necessarily limited level of understanding. Hopefully, it offers at least a humble starting point for further explorations that will rectify and improve on my ideas.

In an attempt to navigate the proposed shift of perspective from the well-known world of scriptural production to ancient Indian orality, it can be helpful to recognize that in the purely oral stage there are no texts as self-existing entities that could be accessed freely at any time. In short, there is no library of sorts, be it printed or digital. The written texts now extant are in a way like fossils compared to the animal when it was still alive. Of course, a lot can still be known by studying a fossil, but it needs to be kept in mind that there is also quite a lot that the fossil can no longer reveal about the living animal.

An oral text only comes fully into existence at the time of its oral performance. At that time, it is something very lively and active, as the setting and the behavior, intonation, etc., of the reciter makes for a multidimensional experience compared to a written text. But all that comes to an end as soon as the oral performance is over. Moreover, at the time of being recited, only the presently recited portion comes fully alive, being immediately replaced by the next portion. Unless the previous portion has been promptly memorized, it is irretrievably lost. In view of this situation, it can perhaps be helpful to think not in terms of "texts" but rather in terms of "textual memories."

An oral performance is based on the textual memory of the reciters. Considering the textual memories of a particular recitation lineage together, perhaps it would be possible to speak of a field of textual potentiality. For the purpose of exploration, I suggest imagining this field of textual potentiality as a three-dimensional web of interrelated causes and conditions that is continuously evolving and therefore in a state of constant change.

The authority of an individual reciter depends on the claim to accuracy, on the establishing and confirming of the belief that what is now being recited is an accurate reflection of words held to have been spoken originally by the Buddha and his disciples. This claim naturally leads to a concern with precise transmission, which in the three-dimensional web of textual potentiality forms a strong causal influence, resulting in centers of gravity. These centers of gravity, in the sense of being points of relative stability, are constantly being reinforced by group recitation.

Besides the claim to accuracy, however, the reciter's appeal also rests on the ability to address the audience in a meaningful way, considering "where" the performance is situated (geographically and culturally), "who" is there in the audience, and "what" topic seems most appropriate. This requires negotiation, in the sense of the choice of a particular textual memory and often by way of providing a commentary, which I suggest visualizing as being situated more in the periphery of the gravitational centers of the three-dimensional web of textual potentiality. At the outer fringes of this periphery are commentaries that manifest once and then disappear, either because they were too specific to the individual situation or else because they were not particularly successful in addressing the needs of the audience. Other commentaries, however, will be reused by the same and eventually by other reciters, and thus will gradually move closer to the centers of the gravitational field. This holds in particular for commentaries on some recurrent topic, such as a common doctrinal item. Since the relevance of such a commentary goes beyond the particular text in relation to which it arose, it can be reused in oral performances of other texts, as long as these involve the same doctrinal item. In this way, such a commentary gradually acquires a life of its own and gains increasing independence.

In addition to the providing of a commentary, other causal influences on this three-dimensional web are various tools of oral transmission and memorization in the form of repetitions, formulas, lists, abbreviations, etc., which the evidence surveyed in the preceding pages has shown to have a creative dimension of their own. Besides serving to stabilize the centers of gravity, the very same tools are intrinsically also factors of change and thereby contribute to the continuous evolution of the three-dimensional web.

Negotiation between a particular textual memory and the requirements of oral performance must have been ongoing. Textual memories that gradually become no longer relevant to actual teaching can still be carried along in the three-dimensional web of textual potentiality by dint of group recitation. In other words, what goes out of fashion need not go out of use. It can simply stagnate, in the sense that no new negotiations take place around it. The textual memory becomes thereby actually more stable, although never entirely so, as even with repeated group recitation the potential for textual loss or alteration can never be completely avoided.

Textual memories that are still relevant and attractive, however, continue as centers of explanatory activity. The proposed visualization of a three-dimensional web can be employed to make the important point that, in the oral setting, the difference between "source text" and "commentary" is only one of degree; the borderline between the two is porous. Gradually parts of the commentary become so well established that they coalesce with the gravitational center; in other words, they become part of the teaching on which they commented. Some such material acquires a force of its own, due to its attraction and meaningfulness to the audiences, to the extent that it eventually forms a gravitational center of its own. This could still involve the incorporation of bits and pieces of the textual memory that originally was at the gravitational center, but eventually even this can be dispensed with and the commentary becomes the center itself.

This type of development is clearly visible in the evolution of Abhidharma. Perhaps the same also applies for early Mahāyāna, in that the main ideas that eventually inform the Mahāyāna traditions could be visualized as gradually emerging gravitational centers in this three-dimensional web of textual potentiality. It is their coming together to form a matrix of ideas that would make for the "beginnings" of Mahāyāna, comparable to the "beginnings" of Abhidharma.

School affiliation is relevant to the extent to which it reflects distinct reciter traditions and thus distinct fields of textual potentiality. Because reciting the same material together is a matter of communal harmony, group recitation naturally tends to keep reciter traditions relatively separate, although of course not completely sealed off from each other. If the monastics at a particular monastery are reciting a code of rules that differs from the one a visiting monastic is familiar with (and hence from the visitor's subjective perspective appearing to be "wrong"), such a visitor will naturally try to avoid spending the observance day at that monastery. The same holds for reciters, who can hardly be performing together as a group if their textual memories differ in wording, in arrangement, etc. As a result, distinct lineages or fields of textual potentiality establish themselves.

In this way, differences that naturally manifest during oral transmission will either be smoothed out during group recitation or will contribute to the gradual formation of distinct transmission lineages that eventually no longer perform group recitation together. Due to the most basic act of group recitation being the recital of the code of rules, such transmission lineages tend to overlap with school affiliation, although with sufficient geographical separation different lineages can also emerge among members of a single school. In fact, the very nature of orality makes it inevitable that minor differences continuously manifest within the textual corpus of any reciter tradition.

When reciters move into new territory, more negotiation is needed and so the gravitational centers of textual potentiality can be shrunken into easily handled extracts, anthologies, to be expanded again later. The transmission to Gandhāra, Central Asia, and China must have required a considerable amount of negotiation and for this reason inevitably became particularly fertile and dynamic. The transition to Sri Lanka would have required comparatively less negotiation, as Sri Lanka was not as culturally distinct from India as Gandhāra, Central Asia, and China. Less need for negotiation naturally results in more stability of the textual memories.

The probably rather challenging situation of adjusting the teachings to audiences far removed from India would not have been of much appeal to senior reciters who were highly skilled and well established in their respective monastic communities. Such reciters would have had good reasons to stay in India and continue teaching their pupils in order to ensure the transmission of their textual memories to the next generation. This makes it less probable, although of course not impossible, that they would be willing to face the risk of traveling to distant lands. Taking such a risk would seem more probable for junior reciters who had not yet acquired the fame of being highly skilled in memorization and had not yet attracted large numbers of pupils who wish to study with them, or else senior reciters who have been unsuccessful in establishing themselves and garnering a substantial following of disciples. If the above reasoning allows the assumption that the majority of those who went to Gandhāra, for example, were not necessarily those most highly skilled in memorization, an increasing reliance on writing in support of textual transmission would be a natural result.

Overall, the proposed model for understanding the early Buddhist oral tradition emphasizes a combination of tendencies to change with tendencies to stabilization, resulting in a continuously evolving body of textual memories whose actualization in the context of oral performances eventually resulted in the written fossils to which we still have access today.

8. Summary

The nature of oral transmission is such that, even though its contents must go back to a starting point when someone said something, what precisely happened at that uncertain time in the past can no longer be reconstructed. It follows that the quest for the true original or the authentic Ur-version is misguided. Similarly misguided is the attempt to construe a pre-canonical Buddhism that differs substantially from the teachings common to the different versions of the early discourses, an endeavor which appears to be influenced by the polemic move of attempting to authenticate later teachings by attributing them to the historical Buddha.

Although it is reasonable to consider the Buddha to have been a historical person, his actual words can no longer be determined with certainty. A much higher degree of certainty is possible when identifying later developments. In addition, key teachings of early Buddhism that substantially depart from the thought known to have been in circulation in the ancient Indian setting can plausibly be attributed to the Buddha, even though the details remain uncertain.

A proper appreciation of the early Buddhist discourses requires above all a coverage of all relevant sources in as comprehensive a manner as possible. This is a basic requirement of proper scientific work, in that all data should be collected first and only then has the time come for interpretation.

Another and probably equally important requirement is a willingness to step out of the well-known world of written textual production and take seriously the fact that oral material has come into existence in substantially different ways. This enables going beyond the limitations of imposing our own world view and experience on a different time and culture.

Conclusion

The present study will hopefully have brought home the remarkable complexity of the early Buddhist oral tradition. At the same time, however, what at first sight may appear just erratic, on closer study and through familiarity with the working mechanisms of orality can be seen to follow its own rules and patterns. Recognizing these substantially enhances our ability to understand this type of material and to interpret as well as contextualize variations between parallel versions of a particular text.

The fortnightly recitation of the monastic code of rules requires a fixed text to be memorized, whose oral performance could hardly have been a matter of improvisation. Nor does its function throughout Buddhist monastic history make it reasonable to assume that the contents of the rules were open to intentional change. Nevertheless, the extant versions of the code of rules show variations, in line with the natural fluctuations to be expected of orally transmitted material. Given the absence of written records to determine the "correct" reading, if the leader of the ceremonial performance of the code of rules is a highly respected senior, chances are that a slip of memory will not be corrected by others, which in turn can result in a change of the code of rules committed to memory by the students of this teacher and thereby impacting the next generation of reciters. From this perspective, the fortnightly recitation of the monastic code of rules as a model for the functioning of early Buddhist oral transmission can be seen to exemplify at the same time patterns ensuring accurate recall as well as the potential for variations to occur.

The need to inculcate proper monastic behavior can rely on narratives purporting to record the circumstances under which a rule was promulgated. These narratives were evidently not considered fixed in a manner comparable to the rules, leaving room for improvements of a particular tale to enhance its function in a teaching context. Variations between such narratives in different transmission lineages can serve as indicators for the teaching concerns of the reciters.

The above points to two complementary modalities of oral transmission, where a core text of a more fixed type is embedded in a more fluid narrative purporting to record the circumstances under which the core text in question was spoken. Similar patterns can be discerned in textual collections of verses and the respective prose narrations as well as in relation to the discourses.

The evidence presented in the preceding pages counters the assumption that variations between parallel versions of a text must invariably reflect some form of intentional intervention. Mistakes in sequence and meaningless additions, together with substantial textual loss, point much rather to the limitations of textual memory as crucial for understanding the nature of early Buddhist orality. The indications given in various discourses regarding a concern for accuracy among those responsible for the early Buddhist oral transmission need to be appreciated in light of the following two influences: the lack of systematic training of the Buddhist reciters in a way comparable to their Vedic predecessors and an emphasis on understanding the meaning of the transmitted texts as opposed to rote memorization of the material without contextual understanding. Both of these aspects tend to interfere with precise memorization.

In an apparent attempt to deal with the resulting difficulties, the Buddhist reciters relied on various modes of systematization, such as textual repetition, listings of synonyms for a particular term, the employment of formulaic descriptions, stereotyped lists, and abbreviations. Such systematization appears to have been an ongoing process, with some elements quite probably being used from the outset. The textual evidence shows how several of these elements, although originally quite probably intended to provide an element of stability for the purpose of memorization, in the course of time became more creative and thereby productive of change and new developments.

Another important contribution to textual expansion and change appears to have its origin in the providing of a commentary alongside the source text in a teaching situation. The lack of a clear dividing line between these two types of text, memorized by successive generations of reciters, combined with the problem of accurate source monitoring as a potential failure of human memory, appear to have resulted in the gradual integration of new ideas and perspectives into the source text. Comparative study of the early discourses enables discerning instances of the integration of such commentarial explanations. Due to a tendency to reflect later thought, such instances are of particular interest, as they enable reconstructing in more detail historical developments during an early period in the development of Buddhist thought and practice.

Although comparative study of parallel texts from different reciter lineages has a remarkable potential to shed light on the evolution of early Buddhism, it is impossible for it to yield access to the original or Ur-text. The nature of oral transmission is such that, even though the parallel versions now extant must have had a common starting point in the past, this initial oral expression is forever beyond reach. The actual words spoken by the Buddha can no longer be determined with certainty. What can definitely be determined are later developments, whose identification requires a comprehensive coverage of all relevant sources.

By way of concluding on a more personal note: An attempt to carry out such comparative study, within the limits of my abilities, stands in the background of many of my other publications, including an examination of a feature shared by different Buddhist traditions, comprising the Theravāda, Mahāyāna, and secular Buddhist traditions (Anālayo 2021e). This is the polemic move of pretending to be the sole authentic representative of the Buddha's words. For exposing the lack of a sound foundation for such claims, I relied precisely on comparative study of the early discourses. Such comparative study can help to dismantle the claims made on behalf of this type of Buddhist textual fundamentalism, showing what kind of teachings can definitely not be attributed to the Buddha. At the same time, comparative study also undermines the alternative of propounding an early Buddhist fundamentalism, due to the inability to reconstruct the precise and authentic original of the Buddha's words. All such claims collapse in the face of the very means that have preserved the teachings at all: centuries of oral transmission.

Abbreviations

AN	*Aṅguttaranikāya*
B^e	Burmese edition
CBETA	Chinese Buddhist Electronic Text Association
C^e	Ceylonese edition
C	Cone edition
D	Derge edition
DĀ	*Dīrghāgama* (T 1)
Dhp	*Dhammapada*
Dhs	*Dhammasaṅgaṇī*
DN	*Dīghanikāya*
EĀ	*Ekottarikāgama* (T 125)
EĀ^2	partial *Ekottarikāgama* (T 150A)
G	Golden Tanjur edition
It	*Itivuttaka*
It-a	*Itivuttakaṭṭhakathā*
MĀ	*Madhyamāgama* (T 26)
MN	*Majjhimanikāya*
Mp	*Manorathapūraṇī*
N	Narthang edition
Nidd I	*Mahāniddesa*
Nidd II	*Cullaniddesa*
P	Peking edition
Paṭis	*Paṭisambhidāmagga*
Pj	*Paramatthajotikā*
Ps	*Papañcasūdanī*
PTS	Pali Text Society
SĀ	*Saṃyuktāgama* (T 99)

SĀ^{2}	partial *Saṃyuktāgama* (T 100)
SĀ^{3}	partial *Saṃyuktāgama* (T 101)
S^{e}	Siamese edition
SHT	Sanskrithandschriften aus den Turfanfunden
SN	*Saṃyuttanikāya*
Sn	*Suttanipāta*
Sp	*Samantapāsādikā*
Spk	*Sāratthappakāsinī*
Sv	*Sumaṅgalavilāsinī*
T	Taishō edition (CBETA)
Th	*Theragāthā*
Ud	*Udāna*
Ud-a	*Udānaṭṭhakathā*
Up	*Abhidharmakośopāyikāṭīkā*
Vibh	*Vibhaṅga*
Vin	*Vinaya*
Vism	*Visuddhimagga*

Notes

1 Anālayo 2011b. I take the occasion to note some typographical errors: p. 95, last line of main text, before "their Chinese parallels" add "one of"; p. 137n185, line 12, before "Sāriputta" add "by"; p. 152n30, line 5, for "1980a" read "1944/1981" (already corrected in the pdf version); p. 178n174, line 3, delete one of the two instances of "the" (already corrected in the pdf version); pp. 210 and 212, tables 4.3 and 4.4, for "EĀ 24.8" read "EĀ 37.3" (already corrected in the pdf version); p. 211n43, lines 1 and 3, in relation to both references to T 154.16, for "T I" read "T III" (already corrected in the pdf version); p. 237, line 13, for "to be able" read "not be able"; p. 257, line 3, for "not" read "also" (already corrected in the pdf version); p. 320n53, line 1, for "and" read ", which"; p. 362, last sentence of MN 65 study, for "They" read "The two parallels"; pp. 395–99, the references to "T 1428" in the footnotes 37, 40, 44, 46, 48, 50, and 51, as well as in table 8.2, need to be corrected to "T 1482"; p. 466n134, line 2, delete "and" (already corrected in the pdf version); p. 602, last line of main text, for "lover" read "lower"; p. 612 n141, line 3, for "men- tion ed" read "mentioned"; p. 615, line 14, before "perception of imperturbability" add "the"; pp. 677–78, tables 12.8 and 12.9, for "MĀ 187" read "MĀ 81" (already corrected in the pdf version); p. 731, line 6, for "seem" read "seems"; p. 781n122, line 1, before "D" replace the opening bracket with a semicolon; p. 785n140, for "On *atammayata*" read "On *atammayatā*"; p. 788n152, line 17, delete "indicates"; and p. 802n220, line 1, for "462c10a" read "462c10" (already corrected in the pdf version).

2 MN 108 at MN III 10,8: *atthi kho, brāhmaṇa, tena bhagavatā jānatā passatā arahatā sammāsambuddhena bhikkhūnaṃ sikkhāpadaṃ paññattaṃ, pātimokkhaṃ uddiṭṭhaṃ. te mayaṃ tadahuposathe yāvatikā ekaṃ gāmakkhettaṃ upanissāya viharāma te sabbe ekajjhaṃ sannipatāma; sannipatitvā yassa taṃ pavattati* (S^e: *vattati*) *taṃ ajjhesāma. tasmiṃ ce bhaññamāne hoti bhikkhussa āpatti hoti vītikkamo, taṃ mayaṃ yathādhammaṃ yathānusiṭṭhaṃ kāremā ti.*

3 MĀ 145 at T 1.26.654b24: 我等若依村邑遊行, 十五日說從解脫時, 集坐一處. 若有比丘知法者, 我等請彼比丘為我等說法. 若彼眾清淨者, 我等一切歡喜奉行彼比丘所說. 若彼眾不清淨者, 隨法所說, 我等教作是. The translation "one" (as a qualification of "place") is based on adopting an emendation in the CBETA edition; the original speaks of "two," which is clearly an error.

4 Dharmaguptaka *Vinaya*, T 22.1428.818b1, Mahīśāsaka *Vinaya*, T 22.1421.121c29, Mahāsāṅghika *Vinaya*, T 22.1425.447c28 (here the monastic in question has not participated and others report this to the Buddha, who then summons him to his presence), Mūlasarvāstivāda *Vinaya*, Hu-von Hinüber 1994, 306,7, Sarvāstivāda *Vinaya*, T 23.1435.158a22, and Theravāda *Vinaya*, Vin I 105,14. The importance accorded to

such participation can also be seen in MN 77 at MN II 8,28 and its parallel MĀ 207 at T 1.26.783a16, which refer to disciples who live in seclusion except for coming to the fortnightly recitation of the code of rules.

5 For a critical reply to other aspects of the position taken by McGovern 2019 see Anālayo 2020b: 2719–23.

6 AN 3.83 at AN I 230,17: *sādhikaṃ . . . diyaḍḍhasikkhāpadasataṃ*. The parallel SĀ 829 at T 2.99.212c11, on the other hand, speaks of over two hundred and fifty rules, 過二百五十戒; a mention of a version of this discourse preserved in a Sanskrit fragment *uddāna* can be found in Pischel 1904, 1139. The same formulation recurs in AN 3.85 at AN I 231,18, AN 3.86 at AN I 232,33, and AN 3.87 at AN I 234,11, whose parallels in the same *Saṃyuktāgama* collection have instead the reference to over two hundred and fifty rules; see SĀ 819 and SĀ 821 at T 2.99.210b14 and 210c14 (SĀ 820 abbreviates). For discussions of the significance of the reference to over one hundred and fifty rules see, e.g., Dutt 1924/1996, 75, Law 1933, 21, Bhagvat 1939, 64, Pachow 1955, 8, Misra 1972, 33, Dhirasekera 1982/2007, 145, von Hinüber 1998, 258, and Ñāṇatusita 2014, xxxi.

7 The commentary, Mp II 346,30, explains that this count reflects the number of rules that had been promulgated at that time (i.e., the time of the delivery of this discourse), *tasmiṃ samaya paññattasikkhāpadān' eva sandhāy' etaṃ vuttaṃ*.

8 Dharmaguptaka *Vinaya*, T 22.1428.686b15: 若二, 若三說戒中坐, Mahāsāṅghika *Vinaya*, T 22.1425.396a6: 若二, 若三說波羅提木叉中坐, Mahīśāsaka *Vinaya*, T 22.1421.63a1: 已再三說戒中坐, Mūlasarvāstivāda *Vinaya*, T 23.1442.894a1: 若二, 若三同作長淨, Sarvāstivāda *Vinaya*, T 23.1435.127a8: 先曾再三聞說此戒, Theravāda *Vinaya*, Vin IV 144,27: *nisinnapubbaṃ iminā bhikkhunā dvattikkhattuṃ* (S^{e}: *dvittikkhattuṃ*) *pātimokkhe uddissamāne*.

9 According to Wynne 2020, however, the recital of the code of rules would have only been instituted at a time close to the second *saṅgīti*. Although it is not possible to examine fully his somewhat complex argument within the limits of a note, a few points can nevertheless be made. The proposed timing is based on the relatively infrequent occurrence of references to the location Verañjā among the early discourses, leading to the assumption that the *Verañjakaṇḍa*, and with it the *Suttavibhaṅga*, belong "to the early missionary community of Verañjā/Mathurā, established by the time of the Second Council" (183). However, the fact that a particular location is not mentioned frequently does not suffice for drawing such a conclusion. Two relevant occurrences are AN 8.11 at AN IV 172,17 and AN 8.19 at AN IV 197,20, where in the former case the parallels MĀ 157 at T 1.26.679b6 and T 1.75.882a23 agree in mentioning Verañjā, as is the case for one of two parallels in the latter case, MĀ 35 at T 1.26.475c18. Another parallel, EĀ 42.4 at T 1.125.752c24, instead mentions Sāvatthī. The last could be in line with the stipulation in the Mahāsāṅghika *Vinaya* that, in case the location of a particular discourse has been forgotten, it should just be allocated to one of the major places where the Buddha used to stay; see T 22.1425.497a7 and below note 189. Besides the need to keep in mind the attitude toward the mentioning of a location that emerges from this regulation, any particular instance of such a reference is best evaluated based on a comparative study of the parallel versions. The fact of infrequent mention as such could simply be reflecting that the Buddha was believed to have stayed only rarely in that location (according to several sources surveyed in Mochizuki 1940, 37, the Buddha was believed to have spent the twelfth rainy season

after his awakening in the area of Verañjā). In sum, the suggested relationship to the second *saṅgīti* is unconvincing.

Another argument relates to the observation in Anālayo 2011b, 718 of a "relatively minor difference" (meant in terms of the amount of text this involves), where a reference to scrupulously following the code of rules in three Pāli discourses has counterparts in *Madhyamāgama* discourses in general references to moral purity. Wynne 2020, 188–89 considers this to imply that the reference to the code of rules, found in the Pāli versions, is a later addition. This does not necessarily follow, as it is also possible that the presentation in the *Madhyamāgama* is later. In fact, elsewhere the *Madhyamāgama* repeatedly refers to "the recitation of the code of rules," 說從解脫, at the time of the observance day, which shows that this discourse collection recognizes such recitation to have taken place well before the second *saṅgīti*.

Wynne 2020, 189 furthermore argues that there are "only three Suttas which actually refer to the *Pātimokkha* recitation on the Uposatha day. One of these is set after the Buddha's death (MN 108), the narrative in another is completely fictitious (Ud 45), and the other (Ud 48) concerns the schismatic machinations of Devadatta, probably not a part of the earliest Buddhist tradition." The first case, which is the one taken up at the outset of the present chapter based on a translation of the Pāli version and its Chinese parallel, is indeed set shortly after the Buddha's death, but this would still conflict with the proposal that the recitation of the code of rules was only introduced at a time close to the second *saṅgīti*. The second case (more precisely Ud 5.5 at Ud 51,18), reports that the Buddha did not recite the code of rules because an impure monk was in the assembly. The same narrative recurs in AN 8.20 at AN IV 204,20 and a broad range of parallels; for a comparative study see Anālayo 2016e. There is no self-evident reason for judging this particular text to be "completely fictitious" any more or any less than other early discourses. In view of its range of parallels, this episode needs to be considered as a testimony to early Buddhism. It also makes it understandable why the discourses refer only rarely to such recital, simply because unless something extraordinary happened, the recitation of the code of rules as such did not occasion the delivery of a teaching that could then have been included in the discourse collections. The third case (Ud 5.7 at Ud 60,14) regarding Devadatta is not relevant, as it does not explicitly mention the code of rules. Other discourses that also reflect the recital of the code of rules would be, for example, AN 3.83, AN 3.85, AN 3.86, and AN 3.87, together with their parallels SĀ 819, SĀ 820 (abbreviated), SĀ 821, and SĀ 829 (mentioned above in note 6). These also show that it need not be considered to be problematic if the received code of rules no longer takes the form of a verbatim record of what the Buddha was believed to have originally said (Wynne 2020, 192), as the idea seems to be that, after the Buddha had withdrawn from leading the recitation of the code of rules, he nevertheless continued promulgating rules that were gradually added to the code of rules until it eventually reached its present form.

In sum, the few points made here, which do not exhaustively cover all the proposed arguments (and all the criticism that could be raised in reply), should hopefully suffice for the time being to show that the position taken by Wynne 2020 is unconvincing.

10 Dharmaguptaka version, T 22.1429.1015b23: 若自知有犯者即應自懺悔, 不犯者默然, Kāśyapīya version, T 24.1460.659c13: 若有犯者當發露, 無犯者默然, Mahāsāṅghika-Lokottaravāda version, Tatia 1975, 6,6: *yasya vo siyāpattiḥ so 'viṣkarotu,*

asantīye āpattīye tūṣṇīṃ bhavitavyaṃ, Mahāsāṅghika version, T 22.1426.549b16: 有罪者應發露, 無罪者默然, Mahīśāsaka version, T 22.1422a.194c29: 若有罪應發露, 無罪者嘿然 (see also T 22.1422b.200c11), Mūlasarvāstivāda version, Banerjee 1977, 12,4: *yasya syāt āpattiḥ tena āviṣkartavyā, āpattyāṃ asatyāṃ tūṣṇīṃ bhavitavyam*, Sarvāstivāda version, von Simson 2000, 161,4: *yasya vaḥ syāt saty āpattiḥ sāviṣkartavyā, asatyām āpattau tūṣṇīṃ bhavitavyaṃ*, Theravāda version, Pruitt and Norman 2001, 4,14: *yassa siyā āpatti so āvikareyya, asantiyā āpattiyā tuṇhī bhavitabbaṃ*.

11 As already noted by Bhagvat 1939, 120, in this way "the chances of confession during the Uposatha service were lessened" (which in turn would have naturally lessened the probability of corrections of the recital); see also, e.g., Dhirasekera 1982/2007, 196, Dutt 1924/1996, 84, and Oberlies 1997, 179n53.

12 The absence of a definite testimony to the "correct" version helps in evaluating the following suggestion by Allon 2021, 92: "Even in a situation where the monastic community was inclined to follow the highly revered senior monk's altered recitation of the monastic rules out of respect and inability to challenge the alteration, there must have been an awareness by the community of the difference and tacit agreement on their part to adopt the modified version. It is also hard to believe that the lead reciter, who performed the recitation of the *Pātimokkha/Prātimokṣa* precisely because of his command of it, would not at some point have become aware that his recitation differed from his previous one, for example, when another monk led the recitation using the original wording or, in a period when manuscripts were in use, when he consulted a manuscript of it. Again, the adoption of a version with altered wording may have been possible in a single monastery, but individual monasteries rarely sat in isolation. They were closely connected with monasteries of the same *nikāya* in their region or in neighbouring ones, and no doubt beyond that also, which would inevitably lead to [a] difference being noted and either adopted or rejected."

The envisaged process of correction must indeed have occurred frequently. Nevertheless, given the fluidity that is so intrinsic to orality, some variations can escape being corrected. In particular during the period before manuscripts came into use, it would have been difficult to establish the "correct" version against a lapse made by the respected reciter who, precisely when a change is an unintentional result of a memory error, stands less chances of later realizing what happened. Since errors usually arise as minor variations, there is considerable room for a minor variation to bypass correction (keeping in mind that the other monastics present during the recitation are not necessary experts in the memorization of the code of rules) and become the version that from then onward will be perceived as the correct one. Once variations are noticed between the version recited at one monastery and the one recited at another, there would again be no fixed standard for deciding which of the two is the "correct" one. In sum, the indubitable fact that change took place does not automatically imply that the monastics "were willing to change the wording" of the rules, as assumed by Allon 2021, 111. Such a conclusion risks underestimating the emic perception of the rules as well as the potential impact of memory errors and the inherent fluidity of oral transmission.

13 On concatenation in the Avesta, for example, see Schwartz 2002.

14 For examples in the numerical discourse collections see Allon 2001, 18–22, and in the *Saṅgītisutta* and its parallels Anālayo 2014c, 34–36.

15 The examples presented here have already been noted by von Hinüber 1999, 20; on the same principle see also Pruitt and Norman 2001, xl–xli and Allon 2021, 34–35.

16 Pruitt and Norman 2001, 46,13: *yo pana bhikkhu anupasampannaṃ padaso dhammaṃ vāceyya . . . yo pana bhikkhu anupasampannena uttaridirattatirattaṃ sahaseyyaṃ kappeyya . . . yo pana bhikkhu mātugāmena sahaseyyaṃ kappeyya . . . yo pana bhikkhu mātugāmassa uttarichappañcavācāhi dhammaṃ deseyya, aññatra viññunā purisaviggahena.*

17 Vin I 188,22; C^e^ and S^e^ add *purisakathaṃ* after *itthikathaṃ*.

18 See also Allon 1997b, 196–98.

19 Caland 1931, 59 refers to Pāṇini 2.2.34 as showing an explicit recognition of the application of the principle of waxing syllables to *dvanda* compounds and then provides a series of examples where, due to following the law of waxing syllables, the compound members come in a sequence that is the opposite of their natural order.

20 Mahāsāṅghika *Vinaya*, T 22.1425.450b22. The other *Vinaya*s present an alternative that is still shorter, with only the introductory motion being recited: Dharmaguptaka *Vinaya*, T 22.1428.823a29, Mahīśāsaka *Vinaya*, T 22.1421.122a22, Mūlasarvāstivāda *Vinaya*, Hu-von Hinüber 1994, 344,13, Sarvāstivāda *Vinaya*, T 23.1435.159b1, and Theravāda *Vinaya*, Vin I 112,11. From the viewpoint of the function of the recitation to provide an occasion for the admission of transgressions, the Mahāsāṅghika *Vinaya* offers a more compelling version of this type of allowance, rather than including an option that does not involve the recital of the actual rules at all.

21 On the consequence of incurring a breach of a *pārājika* rule see Anālayo 2016e and 2019e.

22 On the Indic forms of this term see Nolot 1987 and Ñāṇatusita 2014, cx–cxvi.

23 The Dharmaguptaka and Theravāda *Vinaya*s indicate that the shorter recitals are meant for times when some obstruction to the full recital has arisen, with a listing of eight obstructions given in T 22.1428.823a3 and a listing of ten obstructions in Vin I 112,36.

24 Allon 2021, 92 unfortunately misunderstands my position when assuming that I take such changes to be necessarily "due to the blurring of boundaries between the root or source text and commentary." Although such blurring was indeed the main topic of the article by me that has led to this impression, my reference to the code of rules in Anālayo 2020b, 2719 was only meant to provide a "particularly good example for the complexity of the situation." This forms part of my argument that defaulting to the assumption of improvisation or intentional change does not adequately capture the complexity of orality, evident in the fact that these two models for understanding the early Buddhist oral tradition are not readily applicable to the case of the recital of the code of rules. A better characterization of my position can be found previously in Allon 2021, 91, in that I see variations to be in general "due to errors of memory," which, in addition to the possibility of an "intrusion of commentarial material into the root text," can also occur due to "other unintentional factors."

25 On the relationship between Mūlasarvāstivāda and Sarvāstivāda, in particular from the viewpoint of the oral transmission of *Āgama* texts, see Anālayo 2020d.

26 On the term Theravāda and the appropriateness of its usage see Anālayo 2013d.

27 See also Anālayo 2021e, 62–63.

28 See, e.g., Mukherjee 1966, Lamotte 1970, Bareau 1991, Ray 1994, 162–73, Deeg 1999, Jing 2009, Borgland 2018, and Li 2019.

29 Dharmaguptaka version, T 22.1429.1022b11, Kāśyapīya version, T 24.1460.665a19, Mahāsāṅghika-Lokottaravāda version, Tatia 1975, 36,2, Mahāsāṅghika version, T 22.1426.555b20, Mahīśāsaka version, T 22.1422a.199c19 (see also T 22.1422b.206a5), Mūlasarvāstivāda version, Schmidt 1989, 92,9, Sarvāstivāda version, von Simson 2000, 258,9, and Theravāda version, Pruitt and Norman 2001, 110,9.

30 The Theravāda *Vinaya*, Vin I 135,5, explicitly prohibits individual monastics from going from a community with which they are in communion (*saṃvāsa*) to one with which they are not in communion (*nānāsaṃvāsa*) on the observance day (which practically speaking prohibits being in the same place with them) when the recital of the code of rules is going to be performed (except if there is some obstruction that forces them to do so). For a more detailed discussion of the improbability of legal acts carried out together by monastics ordained in different *Vinaya* traditions see Anālayo 2020d, 399–400.

31 The *Dīpavaṃsa*, Oldenberg 1879, 37,26: *sattarasa bhinnavādā eko vādo abhinnako*; see also Anālayo 2013d, 218.

32 For a more detailed discussion see Anālayo 2020d, 392–93.

33 Dharmaguptaka *Vinaya*, T 22.1428.966b18, (perhaps) Haimavata *Vinaya*, T 24.1463.817c17, Mahāsāṅghika *Vinaya*, T 22.1425.490a25, Mahīśāsaka *Vinaya*, T 22.1421.190b24, Mūlasarvāstivāda *Vinaya*, T 24.1451.401a19, Sarvāstivāda *Vinaya*, T 23.1435.445c29, Theravāda *Vinaya*, Vin II 284,26; see also, e.g., Suzuki 1904, Franke 1908, Przyluski 1926, Finot 1932, Obermiller 1932, Frauwallner 1952, 242–43, Waldschmidt 1954/1967, Bareau 1955a, 1–30, Dhirasekera 1957, Ch'en 1958, Prebish 1974, 240–46, de La Vallée Poussin 1976, 2–29, Durt 1980, Anuruddha, Fung, and Siu 2008, 3–80, Mettanando 2008, Kumar 2010, and Anālayo 2015d. The same episode is also found in discourse literature: DN 16 at DN II 162,29, Waldschmidt 1951, 422,6, DĀ 2 at T 1.1.28c14, T 1.5.173c27, T 1.6.189b25, and T 1.7.206c20.

34 DN 16 at DN II 77,3 (see also AN 7.21 at AN IV 21,18), Waldschmidt 1951, 120,20, DĀ 2 at T 1.1.11b29, and MĀ 142 at T 1.26.649b16, which precede this injunction with another such principle that throws into relief the importance of communal harmony for preventing decline.

35 Dharmaguptaka *Vinaya*, T 22.1428.968c23: 得受金銀, (perhaps) Haimavata *Vinaya*, T 24.1463.819b10: 金銀七寶得自手捉, Mahāsāṅghika *Vinaya*, T 22.1425.493b3: 可布施僧財物 (here this is the only unallowable activity mentioned, whereas the other versions list another nine unallowable activities), Mahīśāsaka *Vinaya*: T 22.1421.192b3: 受畜金銀錢淨, Mūlasarvāstivāda *Vinaya*, T 24.1451.412a10: 金寶淨法, Sarvāstivāda *Vinaya*, T 23.1435.450b6: 金銀寶物淨, Theravāda *Vinaya*, Vin II 294,7: *kappati jātarūparajataṃ*.

36 See Vajirañāṇavarorasa 1973/2009, 13 and Ṭhānissaro 1994/2013, 195 (commenting on *nissaggiya pācittiya* 1). On the reinterpretation of the *sugata* measurement that led to a lengthening of robes see also Schlingloff 1963, 543–45.

37 Quoted in Seeger 2006/2008, 158n11.

38 See in more detail Anālayo 2018a.

39 As pointed out by de Jong 1974/1979, 241, "la récitation de textes religieux jouissait d'un prestige sacré qui faisait défaut aux textes écrits."

40 T 51.2085.864b17: 而北天竺諸國，皆師師口傳無本可寫，"in North-Indian

countries all was transmitted orally from teacher to teacher and no written texts could be copied."

41 Bechert 1992, 53 reports that "oral tradition continued to exist side by side with written scriptures for many centuries."

42 Most *Vinaya*s just mention the whole group of six monks (*chabbaggiya bhikkhū*/六群比丘/六眾苾芻), except for the Dharmaguptaka *Vinaya*, T 22.1428.686a19, which refers to a single unnamed member of the group of six, and the Sarvāstivāda *Vinaya*, T 23.1435.126c18, which refers to 闡那比丘, who is included as the fourth member in the listing of the individuals that make up the group of six in the Sarvāstivāda **Vinayavibhāṣā* (see next note).

43 The Sarvāstivāda **Vinayavibhāṣā*, T 23.1440.525c29 (on which see Funayama 2006, 44–46) offers the following definition: 六群比丘者: 一難途, 二跋難陀, 三迦留陀夷, 四闡那, 五馬宿, 六滿宿. A listing of the members of the group of six monks in a Pāli commentary, Ps III 186,21, presents the matter in this way: *paṇḍuko lohitako mettiyo bhummajako assaji punabbasuko ti hi ime cha janā chabbaggiyā nāma*. The two lists agree on only two members: 馬宿/Assaji and 滿宿/Punabbasuka.

44 This holds for the Dharmaguptaka *Vinaya*, T 22.1428.638c21, the Mūlasarvāstivāda *Vinaya*, T 23.1442.771c8, and the Theravāda *Vinaya*, Vin IV 14,17. In contrast, the protagonist(s) are an administrative monastic (營事比丘, on which see Silk 2008, 39–73) in the Mahāsāṅghika *Vinaya*, T 22.1425.336c5, unnamed monastics in the Mahīśāsaka *Vinaya*, T 22.1421.39c12, and monastics from the region of 阿羅毘 in the Sarvāstivāda *Vinaya*, T 23.1435.71a6.

45 The Theravāda *Vinaya*, Vin IV 85,21, explicitly refers to the group of six.

46 The Mahāsāṅghika *Vinaya*, T 22.1425.359b21, and the Sarvāstivāda *Vinaya*, T 23.1435.95a22, have no reference to the group of six. The Dharmaguptaka *Vinaya*, T 22.1428.662b8, the Mahīśāsaka *Vinaya*, T 22.1421.54a10, and the Mūlasarvāstivāda *Vinaya*, T 23.1442.824b7, have named monks as their protagonists, where it remains uncertain whether these were reckoned to be members of the group of six in these three traditions.

47 The group of six are mentioned explicitly in the Mahīśāsaka *Vinaya*, T 22.1421.70a9, and the Theravāda *Vinaya*, Vin IV 164,14. The Sarvāstivāda *Vinaya*, T 23.1435.123a21, mentions by name monks that would fall within the Sarvāstivāda definition of this group. The Dharmaguptaka *Vinaya*, T 22.1428.662b10, and the Mūlasarvāstivāda *Vinaya*, T 23.1442.864b9, mention monks by name, hence the position in these two *Vinaya*s depends on whether these are reckoned members of the group of six. The Mahāsāṅghika *Vinaya*, T 22.1425.389a2, refers to forest-dwelling monks.

48 Paṇḍita 2017 argues for considering the group of six to be historical persons; for a critical reply see Anālayo 2021f, 1–4. On an interesting aspect of their role in *Vinaya* literature see also Schopen 2004, 176–78.

49 For a more detailed comparative study see Anālayo 2012a. This article requires a correction: In Anālayo 2012a, 406 I speak of Sudinna in the Theravāda *Vinaya* account being "not recognized by his parents when he approaches his own home, but only by a female slave working in the household." Although Vin III 15,31 does report the recognition by the female slave when Sudinna approaches his own home, at this juncture it does not mention the parents.

50 Dharmaguptaka *Vinaya*, T 22.1428.569c28, Mahāsāṅghika *Vinaya*, T 22.1425.229a17

(where the monk in question is called Yasa, whereas in the other versions his name is Sudinna), and Sarvāstivāda *Vinaya*, T 23.1435.1a9.

51 Mahīśāsaka *Vinaya*, T 22.1421.2b16, and Theravāda *Vinaya*, Vin III 11,34.

52 According to Vin III 13,21, he kept up his hunger strike until he had missed seven meals, *satta pi bhattāni na bhuñji*, whereas T 22.1421.2c16 reports that he went on hunger strike for altogether six days, 絕湌六日.

53 The Mūlasarvāstivāda *Vinaya*, T 23.1442.628a14 (for a translation of the Tibetan counterpart see Martini 2012b), has incorporated only some aspects of this tale; see in more detail Anālayo 2012a: 408–14.

54 For a comparative study see Anālayo 2011b, 451–66.

55 This has already been suggested by Lupton 1894, 771: "I should consider that [the tale of] Sudinna . . . evolved as the correlative of [the tale of] Raṭṭhapāla, in order to illustrate certain precepts of the *Vinaya*." According to von Hinüber 1976, 36–37, a Pāli verb form found in the Sudinna account is probably earlier than its counterpart in the Raṭṭhapāla story. However, a change of the verb form could in principle also have occurred during the period of oral transmission of the *Majjhimanikāya* after the Raṭṭhapāla story had already served as the basis for the *Vinaya* account.

The assumption that the Sudinna tale results from a borrowing of narrative elements from the Raṭṭhapāla tale would find support from the fact that the listing of eminent monks in AN 1.14.2 at AN I 24,18 reckons Raṭṭhapāla as foremost for going forth out of faith. Since the *Vinaya* account of Sudinna depicts him with the same degree of faithful motivation, the listing of eminent disciples seems to be reflecting a time when the story of Raṭṭhapāla's going forth was still considered unique to him and had not yet been applied to the Sudinna tale.

56 Notably, a brief reference to the circumstances believed to have led to the promulgation of this rule can be found in the actual code of rules of the Mahāsāṅghika-Lokottaravāda tradition, Tatia 1975, 6,23, see also T 22.1426.549c8. This brief reference comes after the rule in question, a pattern adopted for all four *pārājikas*. This means that the promulgation story, albeit in a very abbreviated form, would come up every fortnight for recital in this particular tradition.

57 A comparative study of the narrations related to the second rule can be found in Bagchi 1945; for a study of the Theravāda version of this rule see Huxley 1999 and Kieffer-Pülz 2012.

58 For a more detailed comparative study see Anālayo 2014e.

59 Dharmaguptaka *Vinaya*, T 22.1428.575c11, Mahāsānghika *Vinaya*, T 22.1425.254b21 (in this version, the instruction occurs after an assisted suicide motivated by illness has already occurred; similar to the other versions, however, the Buddha's instruction then leads to further suicides motivated by disgust with the body), Mahīśāsaka *Vinaya*, T 22.1421.7a27, Mūlasarvāstivāda *Vinaya*, T 23.1442.659c21 (see also T 23.1443.923b15), Sarvāstivāda *Vinaya*, T 23.1435.7b21, and Theravāda *Vinaya*, Vin III 68,3.

60 SN 54.9 at SN V 320,9 and SĀ 809 at T 2.99.207b22.

61 An example for this epithet is AN 6.10 at AN III 285,5: *anuttaro purisadammasārathi*. The rendering of this epithet in the two parallels, SĀ 931 at T 2.99.237c23 and SĀ² 156 at T 2.100.432c11, reads instead: "a supreme person, a tamer of humans," 無上士, 調御丈夫. Nattier 2003b, 227 explains that this type of error is based on splitting the Indic counterpart to the compound *purisadammasārathi*, resulting in mistaking

its latter part *dammasārathi* to be a second epithet in its own right; see also Endo 1997/2002, 180.

62 Mahāsāṅghika *Vinaya*, T 22.1425.254b25: 乃至六十人. This is followed by reporting at T 22.1425.254c3 that it took him a fortnight to kill those sixty men, which implies that this is the overall count of casualties. Mūlasarvāstivāda *Vinaya*, T 23.1442.660a13: 乃至六十苾芻. This is followed by indicating at T 23.1442.660a21 that this refers to the total number of monks killed. Sarvāstivāda *Vinaya*, T 23.1435.7c14: 乃至六十.

63 Dharmaguptaka *Vinaya*, T 22.1428.576a13: 日殺 ... 乃至六十人, Mahīśāsaka *Vinaya*, T 22.1421.7b20: 於一日中殺...乃至六十, Theravāda *Vinaya*, Vin III 69,23: *saṭṭhiṃ pi bhikkhū ekāhena jīvitā voropesi* (which is preceded by listing lower numbers).

64 According to the Pāli commentary, Sp II 401,21, altogether five hundred monks were killed, *pañca bhikkhusatāni jīvitā voropesi*.

65 Dharmaguptaka *Vinaya*, T 22.1428.576a14: 時彼園中死屍狼藉, 臭處不淨, 狀如塚間.

66 The mass suicide of monks is a particularly telling example of the type of textual evidence overlooked by Shulman 2021c, 17, 118, and 226 when proposing that "this is the heart of the literary project of the *Nikāya*s—to depict the magnificent Buddha," in fact, the "early discourses . . . are, quite sincerely, visualizations of the Buddha," in that these "texts are about the Buddha, and they are designed to provide idealized, moving pictures of him." As pointed out by Allon 2021, 118, "it is too limiting to maintain that this is the central project of early Buddhist texts. Early Buddhist texts do much more than visualize the Buddha." The evidence provided by the early discourses (in contrast to some later texts) indeed gives the impression that the main emphasis is on the teachings, compared to which the visualization of an idealized picture of the Buddha emerges as a considerably less significant concern; see also Anālayo 2021d, 595–96.

67 For a detailed comparative study see Anālayo 2016c and for replies to criticism Anālayo 2019g, 51–67.

68 For a comparative study of this discourse see Anālayo 2012b and 2013a.

69 The different settings have inevitably also led to distinct introductory formulas employed at the outset: SN 54.9 at SN V 320,8: *ekaṃ samayaṃ* as against Vin III 68,2: *tena samayena*.

70 Vin III 68,6 adds *ādissa ādissa asubhasamāpattiyā vaṇṇaṃ bhāsati* to the description, common to the two versions, according to which the Buddha *anekapariyāyena asubhakathaṃ katheti asubhāya vaṇṇaṃ bhāsati asubhabhāvanāya vaṇṇaṃ bhāsati*. The additional formulation involves a reference to "the attainment of the lack of attractiveness," *asubhasamāpatti*, an expression that in Pāli discourse and *Vinaya* literature seems to be peculiar to this particular episode.

71 Vin III 68,17. Minor variations occur already before this simile, such as a lack of the introductory phrase *atha kho te* when reporting the repercussions of the Buddha's instruction on the monks, the choice of *sakena kāyena* instead of *iminā kāyena* to refer to the monks' attitude toward their own bodies, and the description of their reaction just as *aṭṭiyanti* (C^e: *aṭṭīyanti*) *harāyanti jigucchanti* instead of *aṭṭiyamānā* (C^e: *aṭṭīyamānā*) *harāyamānā jigucchamānā satthahārakam pariyesanti*.

72 Frauwallner 1956, 46 reasons that the "story of the death of the Buddha and the account of the two earliest councils formed originally one single narrative. This narrative . . . belonged to the *Vinaya* already in its earliest form recognizable to us." Shulman 2021c, 90 considers this proposal to be "rather unlikely. The MPS [DN 16] reads

not as a unity but as an assembly of Buddhist texts." This seems to misunderstand the proposal, which does not intend positing DN 16 as a unit that in its present form was transposed from the *Vinaya* to the *Dīghanikāya*. Instead, the idea of such a narrative appears to have originated as part of the *Vinaya* project of constructing a history of the Buddha's dispensation. This would have been a process of assembling textual pieces already in the *Vinaya* setting, and the same process of textual accumulation could have still continued once the text had been shifted to the *Dīghanikāya*. In support of his assessment, however, Shulman 2021c, 90 (and note 21) refers to Norman 1983, 37 as supposedly being "suspicious" of such a proposal. Following up this reference brings to light an expression of agreement rather than suspicion, namely the reasoning that DN 16 "fits together so closely with the story, related in the Cullavagga of the Vinaya-piṭaka, of the first council held immediately after his death, that it seems clear that both stories are based upon what was originally one connected narrative," with a footnote appended to this reasoning then referencing Frauwallner 1956, 46.

73 DN 16 at DN II 154,17 and Vin II 290,9.

74 Waldschmidt 1951, 284,17, DĀ 2 at T 1.1.26a19, T 1.5.168c13, T 1.6.184b12, T 1.7.204c4, and EĀ 42.3 at T 2.125.751c7.

75 MN 22 at MN I 130,2 and Vin II 25,11 and again Vin IV 133,33; von Hinüber 1999, 70 considers the present case to be one of several instances where material originated as part of a discourse and then was integrated into the *Vinaya*.

76 MĀ 200 at T 1.26.763b3 and the following *Vinayas*: Dharmaguptaka, T 22.1428.682a9, Mahāsāṅghika, T 22.1425.367a3, Mahīśāsaka, T 22.1421.56c12, Mūlasarvāstivāda, T 23.1442.840b21 (see also Yamagiwa 2001, 86,7), and Sarvāstivāda, T 23.1435.106a3.

77 MN 104 at MN II 247,6 (see also DN 33 at DN III 254,11, AN 7.80 at AN IV 144,4, and Vin IV 207,3), MĀ 196 at T 1.26.754a21, and T 1.85.905c4. Occurrences in the codes of rules are found in the Dharmaguptaka version, T 22.1429.1022a22, the Kāśyapīya version, T 24.1460.665a3, the Mahāsāṅghika-Lokottaravāda version, Tatia 1975, 35,1, the Mahāsāṅghika version, T 22.1426.555a25, the Mahīśāsaka version, T 22.1422a.199c5 (see also T 22.1422b.205c19), the Mūlasarvāstivāda version, Banerjee 1977, 54,1, the Sarvāstivāda version, von Simson 2000, 256,1, and the Theravāda version, Pruitt and Norman 2001, 108,5.

The study by Sasaki 2020 of the seven ways of settling a litigation in MN 104 is unfortunately not reliable. For example, the author's assumption that "the *Sāmagāmasutta* emphasizes only procedures for resolving disputes about the Way or the course of practice" (11–12) stands in direct contrast to the description of *sativinaya* in MN 104 at MN II 247,29, which concerns a monastic being reproved for a grave offense (*gāruka āpatti*), explained to be a *pārājika* or one bordering on *pārājika*. This is not just about "disputes about the Way or the course of practice." The same passage also counters the proposal that the "*Sāmagāmasutta* was composed by someone who criticized the mundane and detailed rules of the *Vinaya*. The compiler's principle was as follows: Rules such as those in the *Vinaya* are trivial and unimportant" (12). One would be at a loss to understand the coverage given to ways of settling a litigation like the one just mentioned if the exposition in the *Sāmagāmasutta* were indeed to spring from an attitude that *Vinaya* rules are unimportant. Another problem is the assessment that the *Sāmagāmasutta*'s presentation of *sativinaya* is "obviously mistaken" as "the procedure presented in [the] *Sāmagāmasutta*, which omits the most important element, namely, approval through *ñatticatutthakamma*, cannot be effective in resolving a conflict" (29), in contrast to the full description of the procedure in Vin IV 80,1. Yet, given the context of providing just a survey of the seven ways of settling a litigation, it is natural that the *Sāmagāmasutta* does not give all the details that can be found in the *Vinaya* account of an actual instance of how *sativinaya* should be implemented to clear Dabba Mallaputta of a false accusation. Although lack of space prevents me from clarifying other misunderstandings in Sasaki 2020, the above should suffice to show that his conclusions are unconvincing and in need of revision.

78 AN 2.17 at AN I 98,9 and EĀ 46.1 at T 2.125.775c8. Ten reasons for the promulgation of rules are listed in the following *Vinaya*s: Dharmaguptaka, T 22.1428.570c3, Mahāsāṅghika, T 22.1425.228c24, Mahīśāsaka, T 22.1421.3b29, Mūlasarvāstivāda, T 23.1442.629b21, Sarvāstivāda, T 23.1435.1c15, and Theravāda, Vin III 21,17.

79 As already documented by Schlingloff 1963, 551, promulgation narratives were not fixed in the way this holds for the rules: "Wir werden also zu dem Schluß gedrängt, daß die Erzählungen . . . noch nicht in dem Maße wörtlich fixiert waren, wie der durch die Liturgie festgelegte Wortlaut der Ordenssatzung."

80 MN 93 at MN II 147,10 refers to a sixteen-year-old brahmin who had acquired mastery of the three Vedas. One of its parallels, T 1.71.876c10, also records his age to have been fifteen or sixteen (the reference is cryptic and would literally refer to "156"). Another parallel, MĀ 151 at T 1.26.663c8 (which refers to his ability in terms of his knowledge of the *four* Vedas), does not specify his age.

81 According to von Hinüber 1989, 68, monastics learning the Buddhist texts would begin at its earliest when being seven years older than their Brahminical counterparts, a decisive difference that must have impacted the quality of their transmission: "Der Unterricht in den heiligen Texten der Buddhisten konnte demnach frühestens im Lebensalter von fünfzehn Jahren beginnen, einem geradezu fortgeschrittenen Alter im Vergleich mit der brahmanischen Tradition. Entscheidende sieben Jahre, in denen sich die Texte leichter in das Gedächtnis einprägen, gingen den Buddhisten verloren, was auf die Qualität der Überlieferung kaum ohne Folgen geblieben sein wird."

82 The presence of a substantial percentage of brahmins among Buddhist monastics suggests itself from the surveys in Sarao 1989, 93–139, Chakravarti 1996, 198–220, and Nakamura 2000, 360–62.

83 Vin II 287,27 speaks of five such *nikāya*s, which additionally includes the *Khuddakanikāya*.

84 The former occurs in Aśoka's Rock Edict XII, Bloch 1950, 123,29, Girnār: *bahusrutā ca assu kallaṇagama ca*, Kalsı: *bahuṣṣuta cā kayyānāgā ca*, Ṣāhbāzgarhī: *bahuśruta ca kalaṇagama ca*, Mānsehrā: *bahuśruta ca kayaṇagama ca*. An inscription from Nāgārjunakoṇḍa (no. 6, 12) in turn refers to *dīgha-majhima-nikāyadharena*; see Tsukamoto 1996, 316. Tournier 2014, 25n95 comments that this provides "epigraphical evidence that at least the Aparamahāvinaseliyas also called the divisions of their *Sūtrapiṭaka nikāya*." Inscriptions from Bhārhut (no. 186) and Sāñcī (no. 228) refer to reciters of the five *nikāyas*; see Tsukamoto 1996, 599 and 756.

85 See also Anālayo 2016a.

86 Dharmaguptaka *Vinaya*, T 22.1428.968b15, Mahīśāsaka *Vinaya*, T 22.1421.191a18, Mūlasarvāstivāda *Vinaya*, T 24.1451.407a3, Sarvāstivāda *Vinaya*, T 23.1435.448b13, Theravāda *Vinaya*, Vin II 287,15.

87 Von Hinüber 2008, 26 speaks of a "deeply rooted dissent" evident in the portrayal of

these two disciples in the narrative of the first communal recitation; see also Anālayo 2015d.

88 Mahāsāṅghika *Vinaya*, T 22.1425.491b26: 若使我集者, 如法者隨喜, 不如法者應遮; 若不相應應遮, 勿見尊重而不遮.

89 (Perhaps) Haimavata *Vinaya*, T 24.1463.818a14, according to which the other participants explained to Mahākassapa/Mahākāśyapa that the presence of Ānanda was required so that they could ask him in case something had been forgotten: 所廢忘處應當問之.

90 For studies of the gradual path account see, e.g., Franke 1917, 50–80, Eimer 1976, 26–34, Bucknell 1984, Meisig 1987, 35–80, Crangle 1994, 149–52, Manné 1995, Ramers 1996, Freiberger 2000, 71–86, Yit 2004, Melzer 2006, 12–24, Anālayo 2016d, and Gethin 2020b (on which see also Anālayo 2021a, 30–36).

91 See especially the ground-breaking work by Hartmann 2004.

92 The *Dīrghāgama* collection occurs in the Taishō edition as no. 1; individually translated long discourses as nos. 2 to 25.

93 See in more detail Anālayo 2014f, 35–44.

94 This suggestion is found in the Sarvāstivāda **Vinayavibhāṣā*, T 23.1440.504a1.

95 Sv I 15,2.

96 See in more detail Anālayo 2017e.

97 See in more detail Anālayo 2019a and 2020d.

98 The count is based on a revision of the parallels identified by Akanuma 1929/1990; see Anālayo 2007b.

99 The *Madhyamāgama* collection occurs in the Taishō edition as no. 26; individually translated medium-length discourses as nos. 27 to 98.

100 See the surveys in Chung and Fukita 2011 and Allon and Silverlock 2017.

101 MN 124 at MN III 125,6: *asīti me, āvuso, vassāni pabbājitassā ti* and MĀ 34 at T 1.26.475a21: 我於此正法, 律中學道已來八十年.

102 In recognition of this, the Pāli commentary, Ps IV 197,2, indicates that this discourse was included at the second *saṅgīti*: *idaṃ pana suttaṃ dutiyasaṅgahe saṅgahītaṃ*.

103 For other relevant indications in the early discourses see Anālayo 2011b, 557 and 865n47.

104 T 23.1440.503c28.

105 Sv I 15,5.

106 Sv I 15,8.

107 T 23.1440.503c29.

108 See in more detail Gethin 2007.

109 On Baoyun's translation activities see Lettere 2020.

110 See in more detail Glass 2010. Critical replies to the suggestion by Karashima 2020, 741–47 that the manuscript brought by Faxian rather served as the original underlying Taishō no. 100 can be found in Bingenheimer 2020, 826–31 and Su 2020, 871–76; see also Anālayo 2020d, 415–17.

111 This different text is now found in the collection as SĀ 604 and SĀ 640/641; see Anesaki 1908, 70.

112 The nearly complete *Saṃyuktāgama* collection occurs in the Taishō edition as no. 99 and the partial collections as nos. 100 and 101 (on the former see especially Bingenheimer 2011 and on the latter Harrison 2002); individually translated topic-wise discourses occur as nos. 102 to 124.

113 See the survey in Chung 2008 and the editions in Glass 2007; for a survey of Gāndhārī fragment parallels to early discourses in general see Falk and Strauch 2014, 62–63.

114 This is the *Abhidharmakośopāyikāṭīkā*, D 4094 or P 5595; for a survey of discourse parallels in this work see Honjō 1984. The *Abhidharmakośopāyikāṭīkā* is currently being edited, studied, and translated by Bhikkhunī Dhammadinnā.

115 Some of these discourses form a group under the title of being *Mahāsūtras*; see Skilling 1994 and 1997b.

116 See Skilling 1997a, 96.

117 The *Ekottarikāgama* collection occurs in the Taishō edition as no. 125; individually translated numerical discourses in Taishō nos. 126 to 149. The anthology occurs as no. 150A, on which see in more detail Harrison 1997.

118 These have been edited by Tripāṭhī 1995 and Jantrasrisalai, Lenz, Qian, and Salomon 2016.

119 See Anālayo 2012b, 28–29. It is not entirely clear to me if Kuan and Bucknell 2019, 156 intend to argue against such a conclusion by pointing out that some well-represented doctrinal sets are also found in the *Aṅguttaranikāya*. However, the proposed conclusion does not require that only rarely mentioned doctrinal sets were included in the numerical collections. Instead, the point is only that once particular doctrinal sets had been included in the topic-wise collections, they had already found an allocation and were for this reason no longer in need of being placed among the numerical collections. In other words, the two collections of short discourses are best viewed as complementary. Discourses that cover a particular doctrinal theme tend to involve some number as well, hence they could in principle be allocated to either of these two collections.

120 T 23.1440.503c27.

121 Sv I 15,11.

122 On Mahāyāna thought evident in the collection see Anālayo 2013c, on the interpolation of material from another text Anālayo 2013e, and on evidence for a reworking of the collection by merging material from different discourses Anālayo 2014/2015 and 2015c.

123 A Mahāsāṅghika affiliation, besides being according to Mayeda 1985, 102–3 an opinion often proposed by Japanese scholars (whose research I am unfortunately unable to consult, due to my ignorance of Japanese), has been argued by Pāsādika 2010, and Kuan 2012, 2013a, 2013b, and 2013c; see also Anālayo 2013e, 14–19. For an assessment of the finding by Hiraoka 2013 of narrative affinities between the *Ekottarikagama* collection and Sarvāstivāda texts see Anālayo 2016b, 211–14. For a reply to Palumbo 2013 regarding the same supposition of a Sarvāstivāda affiliation see Kuan 2017, 447. In fact, as rightly stated by Harrison 2002, 19, "T.125, the *Zengyi ahan jing* 增壹阿含經, is probably Mahāsāṃghika (whatever it is, it can hardly be Sarvāstivādin)," *pace* Silk 2015, 17.

124 For a critical reply to the suggestion by Shulman 2021a, 4n14 that "comparison with other extant versions of the early discourses may reveal interesting insights, but should not be thought to bring us closer to the historical realities of early Buddhism . . . Thus, we could read Chinese versions of Suttas in order to understand ideals of masculinity in early Chinese Buddhism"; see Anālayo 2021c.

125 See in more detail Anālayo 2007d.

126 MN 55 at MN I 368,17.

127 See the survey in Hartmann 2004, 127 and the *uddāna* in Hartmann 2002, 138. According to the identification in Bechert and Wille 2004, 439, fragment SHT VI 1525 V1 to R2, Bechert and Wille 1989, 174, also belongs to a version of this discourse.

128 This puts into perspective the proposal by Minh Chau 1964/1991, 31 that "the dropping from all the Chinese *Āgama*s of the Pāli sutta *N*° 55, *Jīvakasutta*, in which the Buddha was reported to allow the monks to take three kinds of meat, confirms the Sarv[āstivāda]'s attitude against meat-eating"; see also Schmithausen 2020, 37n176.

129 See the survey in Anālayo 2011b, 339n147.

130 MN 58 at MN I 392,9.

131 Hoernle fragment Or. 15009/100, Hirabayashi 2009, 167 (identified by Hartmann and Wille 1992, 28), and the 大智度論, T 25.1509.321b15 to 321b25.

132 This is the *Saṅgītiparyāya*, T 26.1536.396a7: 如世尊為持倶胝牛戒布剌拏說: 圓滿當知. The name of the protagonist is 圓滿, introduced as an observer of the cow conduct, 牛戒, which clearly corresponds to MN 57 at MN I 387,10: *puṇṇo . . . govatiko* (S^e: *govattiko*).

133 This position has been taken by von Hinüber 1994a; on the notion that the first three limbs served as an early principle for arranging texts see Choong 2020, with a critical reply in Travagnin and Anālayo 2020, 983–97.

134 Nyanatiloka 1952/1988, 193 comments that the *aṅga* system "is a classification according to literary styles, and not according to given texts." Similarly, Dutt 1957, 89 holds that the list of *aṅga*s "rests on an analysis of different forms of composition found in the canon," and Jayawickrama 1959, 11 asserts that "it is a mere description of the literary types." According to Kalupahana 1965, 616, it "does not refer to nine different groups of literature, but to nine types of composition," a position also taken by Lamotte 1980, 2282. Norman 1983, 16 reasons that "it is probable that the list of nine *aṅga*s did not originally refer to specific works in the canon, but was a description of various types of text." Klaus 2010, 518 points out that the texts do not present the *aṅga*s as an attempt at ordering the texts, but rather as attempts at classification or just enumeration. Cousins 2013, 106 comments that "there is no indication anywhere that any of this has anything to do with an arrangement of the canonical literature in some kind of earlier recension." Skilling 2017, 293n55 concludes that "the *Aṅga*s are not actual collections of texts"; see also Anālayo 2016a.

135 AN 6.51 at AN III 361,15: *bhikkhu dhammaṃ pariyāpuṇāti: suttaṃ geyyaṃ veyyākaraṇaṃ gāthaṃ udānaṃ itivuttakaṃ jātakaṃ abbhutadhammaṃ vedallaṃ.* (B^e: *so) yathāsutaṃ yathāpariyattaṃ dhammaṃ vitthārena paresaṃ deseti, yathāsutaṃ yathāpariyattaṃ dhammaṃ vitthārena paresaṃ vāceti, yathāsutaṃ yathāpariyattaṃ dhammaṃ vitthārena sajjhāyaṃ karoti, yathāsutaṃ yathāpariyattaṃ dhammaṃ cetasā anuvitakketi anuvicāreti manasānupekkhati. yasmiṃ āvāse therā bhikkhū viharanti bahussutā āgatāgamā dhammadharā vinayadharā mātikādharā tasmiṃ āvāse vassaṃ upeti. te kālena kālaṃ upasaṅkamitvā paripucchati paripañhati: idaṃ, bhante, kathaṃ; imassa kv' attho ti?* No parallel to this discourse appears to be known. Here and elsewhere, my employment of plural "they" in translations is motivated by concerns of gender-sensitive writing; the original is clearly in the singular.

136 On *geyya* see Jayawickrama 1959, 12.

137 On *veyyākaraṇa* see Travagnin and Anālayo 2020, 987–89.

138 According to Rhys Davids and Stede 1921/1993, 281, the term *jātaka* can literally be understood to convey the sense "belonging to, connected with what happened" (*jāta* + *ka*). In the course of time, however, various fables and fairy tales from the past appear to have evolved into accounts of the past lives of the Buddha; see Anālayo 2010a, 55–71, 2015b, and 2016h.

139 Examples among Pāli discourses would be MN 43 and MN 44, as both carry *vedalla* in their title.

140 Parallels to occurrences of the nine *aṅga*s in Pāli discourses usually present lists that cover an additional set of three, resulting in listings of twelve textual limbs; see, e.g., Nattier 2004. However, a listing of nine *aṅga*s can also be found, for example, in the Chinese counterpart to the *Itivuttaka*, T 17.764.684a3: 契經, 應頌, 記別, 伽他, 自說, 本事, 本生, 方廣, 未曾有法.

141 Anālayo 2016a, 30.

142 Skilling 2009, 64 already noted that "there was no standardization of titles."

143 MN 59 at MN I 400,25: *Bahuvedanīyasutta*, SN 36.19 at SN IV 223,11: *Pañcakaṅga-sutta*.

144 MN 26 at MN I 175,12: *Ariyapariyesanāsutta* (Bᵉ and Sᵉ: *Pāsarāsisutta*), MN 61 at MN I 420,25: *Ambalaṭṭhikārāhulovādasutta* (Sᵉ: *Cūḷarāhulovādasutta*), MN 149 at MN III 290,24: *Mahāsaḷāyatanikasutta* (Sᵉ: *Saḷāyatanavibhaṅgasutta*); for more examples and a discussion see Anālayo 2010e, 52–54.

145 An example would be MN 115 at MN III 67,30 and its parallels MĀ 181 at T 1.26.724c1, T 17.776.713c27, T 26.1537.502c16, D 297 *sha* 301a7 or P 963 *lu* 330a8, and Up 1032 at D 4094 *ju* 33b2 or P 5595 *tu* 36b5. Alongside some variations in the actual titles listed, the parallels clearly agree in listing several alternatives.

146 On this apparent shift, which must have happened at a time when the requirements of oral memorization were no longer prominent, and its possible reasons see Anālayo 2016a: 17–18.

147 On disparate conceptions of the *Khuddakanikāya* see, e.g., Lamotte 1957, 345, Norman 1983, 9, Abeynayake 1984, 33–46, Collins 1990, 108n11, von Hinüber 1996/1997, 42–43, Baba 2005, and Freiberger 2011, 218.

148 Dhp 60 to Dhp 75, Dhp 76 to Dhp 89, and Dhp 90 to Dhp 99.

149 See Roth 1980 or Cone 1989 for the former and Brough 1962/2001, Lenz 2003, and Falk 2011, 16–19 for the latter. A convenient juxtaposition of the parallel versions can be found in Ānandajoti 2020.

150 Taishō nos. 210 and 211. On the former see Dhammajoti 1995 and on the latter Willemen 1999.

151 T 4.211.575b19.

152 See in more detail Appleton 2011.

153 It-a 29,10.

154 In the case of the early discourses, the reference to "at one time" in this standard formula does not seem to qualify the preceding "thus have I heard" and instead would relate to the location mentioned right afterward; see Anālayo 2014a, 41–45 and below note 395.

155 It 1.1 at It 1,4: *vuttaṃ h' etaṃ bhagavatā, vuttam arahatā ti me sutaṃ*.

156 Demoto 2016, 127: *uktam idaṃ bhagavatoktam arhatā iti me śrutam* (or in an abbreviated manner: *uktam idam śrutaṃ*) and T 17.765.662b15: 吾從世尊聞如是語. Whereas the Sanskrit version ranges from Ones to Eights, the Chinese version only

proceeds from Ones to Threes. As the Threes lack summary verses, Watanabe 1906, 45 reasons that the text could be defective. The titles also differ: Pāli *Itivuttaka*, Sanskrit *Itivṛttaka*, and Chinese 本事經.

157 It 1.1 at It 1,8: *etam attham bhagavā avoca; tatth' etaṃ iti vuccati.*

158 Demoto 2016, 127: *etam artham ucyate* and T 17.765.662b20: 爾時, 世尊重攝此義而說頌曰.

159 It 1.1 at It 1,16: *ayam pi attho vutto bhagavatā iti me sutan ti* and Demoto 2016, 127: *ayam api śrutam* (or *ayam apy artha ukto*). The Chinese parallel comes without a conclusion, similar to the case of many of the short discourses collected in the *Saṃyuttanikāya* and the *Aṅguttaranikāya*. A parallel to the *Itivuttaka*'s standard conclusion occurs once in the *Udāna* at the end of its first chapter, Ud 1.10 at Ud 9,9: *ayam pi udāno vutto bhagavatā iti me sutan ti* (not in S^e^).

160 Demoto 2016, 129 suggests that an expansion of the Sanskrit *Itivṛttaka* appears to have taken place based on incorporating discourses from an *Ekottarika* collection.

161 The commentaries are the *Mahāniddesa* and the *Cullaniddesa*, Nidd I and Nidd II.

162 Instances surveyed here are restricted to explicit references in Pāli discourses that recur in at least one of the parallel versions.

163 SN 22.3 at SN III 9,18: *vuttam idaṃ, bhante, bhagavatā aṭṭhakavaggiye* (E^e^: *aṭṭhakavaggike*) *māgaṇḍiyapañhe* and SĀ 551 at T 2.99.144b3: 如世尊義品答摩揵提所問偈. The reference is to Sn 844; see also T 4.198.180b23.

164 Ud 5.6 at Ud 59,23: *soḷasa aṭṭhakavaggikāni sabbān' eva sarena abhaṇi* (C^e^: *abhaṇī*); see also Vin I 196,36 and for a detailed study of the different *Vinaya* versions, together with a survey of other references to these two chapters, Lévi 1915.

165 Sn 976 to 1149.

166 AN 6.61 at AN III 399,20: *vuttam idaṃ, āvuso, bhagavatā pārāyane metteyyapañhe* and SĀ 1164 at T 2.99.310b22: 世尊說波羅延低舍彌德勒所問. The reference is to Sn 1042.

167 AN 3.32a at AN I 133,6: *idañ* (Ce: *idaṃ*) *ca pana me taṃ, ānanda, sandhāya bhāsitaṃ pārāyane* (C^e^: *pārāyaṇe*) *puṇṇakapañhe* and AN 3.32b at AN I 134,8: *idañ* (C^e^: *idaṃ*) *ca pana me taṃ, sāriputta, sandhāya bhāsitaṃ pārāyane* (C^e^: *pārāyaṇe*) *udayapañhe*; with their counterparts in SĀ 982 at T 2.99.255c9: 我於此有餘說, 答波羅延富隣尼迦所問 and SĀ 983 at T 2.99.256a9: 我於此有餘說, 答波羅延憂陀耶所問 (on the swapping of verses between these two and the situation in SĀ^3^ 8 see Harrison 2002, 9–10); see also SHT V 1375aV1, Sander and Waldschmidt 1985, 246. The references concern Sn 1048 and Sn 1106 to Sn 1107.

168 SN 22.4 at SN III 13,5: *vuttam idaṃ, bhante, bhagavatā sakkapañhe*, with a parallel in SĀ 552 at T 2.99.144c24: 如世尊於界隔山天帝釋石窟說言 (the reference is to DN 21 at DN II 283,9 with parallels in DĀ 14 at T 1.1.64c2, T 1.15.249b9, MĀ 134 at T 1.26.637a9, T 4.203.477c8, see also Waldschmidt 1932, 91–93, SHT V 1422R4, Sander and Waldschmidt 1985, 253). AN 10.26 at AN V 46,19: *vuttam idaṃ, bhante, bhagavatā kumāripañhesu* (S^e^: *kumārīpañhesu*) and SĀ 549 at T 2.99.143a9: 如世尊所說, 答僧耆多童女所問, 如世尊說僧耆多童女所問偈 (the reference is to SN 4.25 at SN I 126,14, with parallels to the reply given to Māra's daughter Craving in SĀ 1092 at T 2.99.287a25 and SĀ^2^ 31 at T 2.100.383c21).

169 SN 41.5 at SN IV 292,24: *yaṃ* (C^e^ and S^e^: *yan*) *taṃ bhagavatā vuttaṃ* and SĀ 566 at T 2.99.149b25: 世尊說此偈 (the reference is to Ud 7.5 at Ud 76,26; see also SHT XI 5262Vb, Wille 2012, 287).

170 Hoernle 1916 and Falk 2011, 13–15 (with more relevant Gāndhārī material being at present under preparation by Mark Allon and Stefan Baums; see also Salomon 2020, 179).

171 T 4.198.174b8, titled 義足經, which would correspond to *arthapadasūtra* in Sanskrit (the addition of *sūtra*/經 to a title is a recurrent feature of Chinese translations, often serving as a marker of canonical status and for this reason not necessarily rendering an Indic original).

172 Note that the reference in SN 22.3 speaks of the *Māgaṇḍiyapañhe*, rather than the *Māgandiyasutta*.

173 Sn 835: *disvāna taṇhaṃ aratiṃ ragañ ca* (S^{e}: *aratiñ ca ragaṃ*), *nāhosi chando api methunasmiṃ; kim ev' idaṃ muttakarīsapuṇṇaṃ, pādā pi naṃ samphusituṃ na icche* and T 4.198.180b5: 我本見邪三女, 尚不欲著邪婬. 今奈何抱屎尿, 以足觸尚不可.

174 Pj II 551,1, commenting on Sn 862 to Sn 877; for a study of this trope in a range of texts see Skilling 2020a.

175 T 4.198.181b12.

176 T 4.198.181a21.

177 As already noted by Barua 1928, 214, this is particularly evident from the fact that this introductory set of verses, the *Vatthugāthā* (Sn 976 to Sn 1031), are not covered in the *Cullaniddesa*, giving the impression that they would become part of the collection only after the canonical commentary had come to a closure. Jayawickrama 1948, 243–49 offers several arguments in support of considering the *Vatthugāthā* to be several centuries later than the remainder of the *Pārāyanavagga*.

178 Sanskrit: Bernhard 1965 (on which see Schmithausen 1970), followed by Nakatani 1987 and various fragments published in the series *Sanskrithandschriften aus den Turfanfunden* and *British Library Sanskrit Fragments*. Tibetan: Beckh 1911 and Zongtse 1990; see also Balk 1984 for Prajñāvarman's commentary on the collection. Chinese: T 4.213.777a8, see Willemen 1978. Tocharian and Uighur fragments: Sieg and Siegling 1931, Lévi 1933, 41–56, von Gabain 1954, 23–24 and 38–44, and Thomas 1971 and 1979. Parts of another commentary, the *Udānālaṃkāra* attributed to Dharmasoma, have been preserved in Tocharian fragments; see Lévi 1933, 72–77 and Sieg and Siegling 1933 and 1949. The contents of these collections show considerable overlap with the *Dharmapada* collections.

179 This is the 出曜經, T 4.212.609c21.

180 Anālayo 2009a. The assessment by Shulman 2021c, 24n56 of patterns of concatenation that emerge from a close inspection of prose narratives in the *Udāna* as springing from literary concerns fails to do justice to the needs of the reciters to rely on aids in memorization. This can be seen particularly well in the similar employment of concatenation among different verses, resulting in a sequence in which the preceding verse shares some term with the ensuing one, even though in their present position such verses can be at a considerable distance from each other due to a prose narration placed between them. This hardly reflects just literary concerns and much rather points to such verses being at first transmitted without prose and at that time related to each other through concatenation.

In the case of the early discourses in general, literary concerns can only have their impact within the parameters of oral transmission, which in turn depends for its continuity entirely on memory. For this reason, it fails to make sense to promote explanations based on literary concerns at the expense of ignoring the basic requirements of oral transmission. As already pointed out by Allon 2021, 117, the tendency by Shulman 2021c to dismiss the mnemonic functions of formulas in favor of their literary and poetic qualities "is to confuse the wording of the formula with the formula status of that wording. It is certainly the case that the wording that constitutes some formulas has poetic and aesthetic aspects . . . functioning to emphasize the qualities of the Buddha, showing that he is the superior being and the one most worthy of respect, making his teaching appealing, making the ideas and practices of rivals unappealing, and so on, with the wording of other categories of formulas doing other jobs. However, that wording, whether it be short or long, whether it constitutes a fraction of the sutra or large sections of it, becomes a formula and is recognized as a formula through its repetitive use" in the context of facilitating memorization and not because it performs a particular literary function.

In fact, a problem with overstressing the literary function is that it does not really explain the repetitive nature of the texts. Allon 2021, 117 reasons: "The question is, why choose highly structured and standardized, that is, formulaic, wording to give a compelling perception of the Buddha and his message? Or more broadly, why use the same wording time and again to depict a given quality, attainment, practice, thought, concept, action, event, or the like? Why not use innovative and poetically rich wording that differed on each telling, each text, each description being unique, the diversity and richness adding to the appeal of the text and the perception of the Buddha and his teaching?" In other words, the very repetitive nature of the early Buddhist texts implies that literary concerns were not the sole or even primary motivation, instead of which mnemonic requirements must have been responsible for the frequent employment of formulas.

181 Winternitz 1920/1968, 67 sees the prose sections as later additions by commentators. Similarly, Lamotte 1968, 465 considers the introductory narration to be often later than the inspired utterance. Norman 1983, 61 notes that "some of the *suttas* have either been adapted, or even invented, to provide an occasion for the utterance." In sum, in the words of Abeynayake 1984, 66, "the stories that occur in the *Udāna* are not as early as the stanzas."

182 Ud 7.9 at Ud 79,5: *kiṃ kayirā udapānena, āpā ce sabbadā siyuṃ? taṇhāya mūlato chetvā, kissa pariyesanaṃ care ti?*

183 T 4.212.707c20.

184 See in more detail Anālayo 2009a.

185 The extracts occur at Ud 21,12+14: *bhikkhuno . . . ṭhitassa* and Ud 24,17: *na vedhati* (S^e: *vedhatī*) *sa bhikkhu*. Ud 24,16+17: *maddito kāmakaṇṭako . . . sukhadukkhesu na vedhati* (S^e: *vedhatī*) *sa bhikkhu* and Ud 27,17+18: *jito kāmakaṇṭako . . . sukhadukkhesu na vedhati* (S^e: *vedhatī*) *sa bhikkhu*. Ud 27,18: *pabbato viya so ṭhito* and Ud 27,29+30: *yathā pi pabbato selo . . . pabbato va*. Ud 27,29: *acalo suppatiṭṭhito* and Ud 28,7: *sati kāyagatā upaṭṭhitā*.

186 Caillies, Denhièr, and Kintsch 2002.

187 Silk 2020, 29 sees an anachronism in a supposed reference in the Pāli commentarial tradition to Ānanda's status as an arahant/arhat at the time when he was hearing the Buddha's teachings. The impression that the highest level of awakening was attributed to him already at that time appears to rest on a Pāli passage whose different versions only state that he was asserting his status as a disciple, Sv I 31,3 = Ps I 7,12 = Spk I 9,5

= Mp I 10,13 = Pj I 103,26 = Ud-a 18,3 = It-a I 28,24: *sāvakattaṃ paṭijānanto*, which Silk 2020, 27 translates as "asserting his status as an Arhat" (Masefield 1994/2001, 35 just has: "claiming sāvaka-status"). Here, the term *sāvaka* conveys just the sense of a "disciple" and does not on its own imply the reaching of a level of awakening.

188 Examples involving *Majjhimanikāya* discourses have already been covered in Anālayo 2011b, consultation of which would enable placing the extracts presented here in the context of a comparative survey of the entire discourse in question.

189 T 22.1425.497a7 and T 24.1451.328c18, with its Tibetan counterpart and a discussion in Schopen 1997/2004; another occurrence is the introduction to the *Ekottarikāgama*, T 2.125.550b13 (and its commentary, T 25.1507.33b19).

190 MN 142 at MN III 256,6: *bhavissanti kho pan' ānanda, anāgatamaddhānaṃ gotrabhuno kāsāvakaṇṭhā dussīlā pāpadhammā, tesu dussīlesu saṅghaṃ uddissa dānaṃ dassanti. tadā p' ahaṃ, ānanda, saṅghagataṃ dakkhiṇaṃ asaṅkheyyaṃ appameyyaṃ vadāmi. na tv' ev' āhaṃ, ānanda, kenaci* (C[e]: *kenacī*) *pariyāyena saṅghagatāya dakkhiṇāya pāṭipuggalikaṃ dānaṃ* (S[e]: *pāṭipuggalikadānaṃ*) *mahapphalataraṃ vadāmi.*

191 MN 6 at MN I 33,16 and its parallel MĀ 105 at T 1.26.595c23; another parallel, EĀ 37.5, does not cover the topic of the fruitfulness of gifts.

192 MN 39 at MN I 271,16 and its parallel MĀ 182 at T 1.26.724c25 (see also SHT VI 1392V2, Bechert and Wille 1989, 113), in which case another parallel, EĀ 49.8 at T 2.125.801c22, has only a brief reference to the need to maintain morality (the overall presentation in this discourse appears to reflect a loss of text; see Anālayo 2011b, 258). MN 40 at MN I 281,10 and its parallel MĀ 183 at T 1.26.725c24.

193 T 1.84.904a22 proceeds directly from the seven types of offerings to the four purifications of a gift and thus has no indication regarding monastics who are clan members, etc. The relevant Gāndhārī fragments have unfortunately not sufficiently preserved the part corresponding to MN 142 at MN III 256,6, preventing the drawing of conclusions on where this version stands in this respect vis-à-vis the others.

194 Up 4103 at D 4094 *ju* 255a4 or P 5595 *tu* 290b4: *ma 'ongs pa'i dus na sa'i rigs zhes bya ba la mgul pa chos gos* (not in G) *tshal bu thogs pa dag 'byung bar 'gyur te.*

195 MĀ 180 at T 1.26.722b1: 當來時有比丘, 名姓種, 不精進, 著袈裟衣.

196 The reference occurs in the *Maitrismit*, Geng and Klimkeit 1988, 202. The qualification of such future monastics is translated by the authors as "gesetzlos und disziplinlos," lawless and undisciplined (my ignorance of Uighur prevents me from consulting the original).

197 On the term *āsava* and my reasons for rendering it as "influx" see Anālayo 2012e, 80–83.

198 The Pāli listing occurs in MN 2 at MN I 7,10, which has parallels in MĀ 10 at T 1.26.432a10, T 1.31.813b6, EĀ 40.6 at T 2.125.740b1, and Up 2069 at D 4094 *ju* 92b2 or P 5595 *tu* 105b1; see also table 1.2 in Anālayo 2011b, 30.

199 See table 9.1 in Anālayo 2011b, 462. For similar variations in the monastic's reply see table 9.2 in Anālayo 2011b, 464.

200 See table 13.9 in Anālayo 2011b, 744.

201 See tables 12.8 and 13.5 in Anālayo 2011b, 677 and 725; in the former case, the Pāli version continues with another three items that have no counterpart in the parallel.

202 See tables 14.1, 11.2, and 14.2 in Anālayo 2011b, 779, 588, and 784.

203 The first discourse is MN 45 at MN I 305,11, which has a parallel in MĀ 174 at T 1.26.711b21. The second discourse is MN 46 at MN I 310,36, which has parallels in

MĀ 175 at T 1.26.712c13 and T 1.83.902b14; see also table 5.5 in Anālayo 2011b, 287. The same basic exposition occurs in yet another sequence in DN 33 at DN III 229,6, with a parallel in DĀ 9 at T 1.1.50c2 that agrees with the sequence adopted in DN 33, whereas another parallel, T 1.12.229a18, adopts the sequence found also in MN 45. The reconstructed Sanskrit fragment parallel in Stache-Rosen 1968, 115 appears to have suffered from a typographical error, as it has the pleasant way in both respects twice (judging from the German translation, provided alongside the edition, the second way should read *pratyutpannaduḥkham* instead of *pratyutpannasukham*). The presentation in the *Saṅgītiparyāya*, T 26.1536.398c6, corresponds to MĀ 174, MĀ 175, and T 83.

204 MN 19 at MN I 115,20.

205 MĀ 102 at T 1.26.589a26: 斷, 除, 吐. 所以者何? 我見因此故, 必生無量惡不善之法. 猶如春後月, 以種田故, 放牧地則不廣; 牧牛兒放牛野澤. 牛入他田, 牧牛兒即執杖往遮. 所以者何? 牧牛兒知因此故, 必當有罵, 有打, 有縛, 有過失也.

206 MN 19 at MN I 116,36.

207 A similar shift to the wrong position appears to have happened with a set of three similes in relation to the future Buddha's ascetic practices in MN 36 at MN I 240,29, which can be corrected with the help of the Sanskrit fragment parallel; see Anālayo 2011b, 235–37. Since in particular the third simile implies that the undertaking of asceticism is not required for progress to awakening, it makes little sense for the Buddha to report that these similes occurred to him *before* relating his ascetic practices.

The suggestion by Shulman 2019, 125n67 (repeated in Shulman 2021a, 13n71 and 2021c, 217n49) that this incoherent placing should be understood to reflect the polemic intent of the discourse fails to solve the issue, as the similes will achieve such an intent much better if they stand *after* the report of the Buddha's own practice of asceticism; see in more detail Anālayo 2021f, 11–12. As already noted in Ñāṇamoli 1995/2005, 1229n387, it is "puzzling that in the following paragraphs the Bodhisatta is shown engaging in self-mortification *after* he had here come to the conclusion that such practices are useless for the attainment of enlightenment. This dissonant juxtaposition of ideas raises a suspicion that the narrative sequence of the sutta has become jumbled."

208 For a case illustrating the result of such shifting, whereby the whole series loses a considerable part of its evocative power, see Anālayo 2011b, 409–10.

209 MN 100 at MN II 212,24: *kin nu kho, bho gotama, atthi devā ti?*

210 Already Horner 1957/1970, xx commented: "I find the sudden introduction of this question about *devas* rather perplexing"; see also Marasinghe 1974, 127 for a discussion of this issue.

211 The exchange on the existence of *devas* begins in fragment 346v1 of the *Śaṃkarakasūtra*, Zhang 2004, whereas the report of the Buddha's going forth in quest of awakening begins only in fragment 348r3.

212 Ps III 454,1: *māṇavo sammāsambuddho ajānanto va pakāsesī ti saññāya āha.*

213 MN 78 at MN II 25,18: *dasahi kho ahaṃ, thapati, dhammehi samannāgataṃ purisapuggalaṃ paññāpemi* (B[e]: *paññapemi*) *sampannakusalaṃ paramakusalaṃ uttamapattipattaṃ samaṇaṃ ayojjhaṃ*. This is followed by an unrelated discussion of unwholesome conduct.

214 MN 78 at MN II 28,34: *katamehi cāhaṃ* (S[e] without *cāhaṃ*), *thapati, dasahi dhammehi samannāgataṃ purisapuggalaṃ paññāpemi* (B[e]: *paññapemi*) *sampannakusalaṃ*

paramakusalaṃ uttamapattipattaṃ samaṇaṃ ayojjhaṃ? This is followed immediately by a detailed exposition which concludes at MN II 29,10 by repeating the initial statement: *imehi kho ahaṃ, thapati, dasahi dhammehi samannāgataṃ purisapuggalaṃ paññāpemi* (B^e: *paññapemi*) *sampannakusalaṃ paramakusalaṃ uttamapattipattaṃ samaṇaṃ ayojjhaṃ*.

215 MĀ 179 at T 1.721c11: 是謂學見跡成就八支, 漏盡阿羅訶成就十支. 物主, 云何學見跡成就八支? 謂學正見至學正定, 是謂學見跡成就八支. 物主, 云何漏盡阿羅訶成就十支? 謂無學正見至無學正智, 是謂漏盡阿羅訶成就十支. The discussion in MĀ 179 differs insofar as it also covers the eight qualities of one in training, in addition to the ten qualities of a fully awakened one that are taken up in both versions. Nevertheless, it conforms to the standard pattern of proceeding from an initial statement to the corresponding query initiating a detailed exposition, which concludes with a repetition of that initial statement; see in more detail Anālayo 2009c, 167–70.

216 In the case of the first absorption as part of the gradual path account, for example, MN 79 at MN II 38,9 states: *ayam pi kho, udāyi, dhammo uttaritaro ca paṇītataro ca yassa sacchikiriyāhetu bhikkhū mayi brahmacariyaṃ caranti.*

217 MĀ 208 at T 1.26.785c24; see also Anālayo 2005b, 94–95 and 2021a, 32–33.

218 MN 20 at MN I 122,2: *yaṃ vitakkaṃ ākaṅkhissati taṃ vitakkaṃ vitakkessati, yaṃ vitakkaṃ nākaṅkhissati na taṃ vitakkaṃ vitakkessati. acchecchi taṇhaṃ, vāvattayi* (B^e and S^e: *vivattayi*) *saṃyojanaṃ, sammā mānābhisamayā antam akāsi dukkhassā ti*; already discussed in Anālayo 2005a, 8–9. On the employment of "they" for translating what in the original are singular forms see above note 135.

219 MĀ 101 at T 1.26.589a6: 欲念則念, 不[欲]念則不念. 若比丘欲念則念, 不欲念則不念者, 是謂比丘隨意諸念, 自在諸念跡, after which the discourse concludes in the standard way by reporting the delighted reaction of the audience on hearing the Buddha's exposition.

220 MN 2 at MN I 12,3: *acchecchi taṇhaṃ, vāvattayi* (B^e and S^e: *vivattayi*) *saṃyojanaṃ, sammā mānābhisamayā antam akāsi dukkhassā ti.*

221 MĀ 10 at T 1.26.432c26, T 1.31.814b2, EĀ 40.6 at T 2.125.741b10, and Up 2069 at D 4094 *ju* 94b3 or P 5595 *tu* 107b8.

222 MN 9 at MN I 47,22: *so sabbaso rāgānusayaṃ pahāya, paṭighānusayaṃ paṭivinodetvā, asmī ti diṭṭhimānānusayaṃ samūhanitvā, avijjaṃ pahāya vijjaṃ uppādetvā, diṭṭheva dhamme dukkhassantakaro hoti. ettāvatā pi kho, āvuso, ariyasāvako sammādiṭṭhi hoti, ujugatāssa diṭṭhi, dhamme aveccappasādena samannāgato, āgato imaṃ saddhamman ti*; already discussed in Anālayo 2005a, 5–6.

223 Chung and Fukita 2020, 186,17: *<i>yatā aryyaśrāva(kaḥ a)smiṃn dha(r)m(a)v(i)naye dṛṣṭisaṃpannaś ca bhavati ṛjvyā ca dṛṣṭyā samanvāgato bhavat(i buddhe c)ā(vetyaprasādena sa)man(v)āgato bhavati, āgata imaṃ saddharmam u<pa>gata i(ma)ṃ (sa)ddharmam a(v)aiti sa<ddha>rmam ity ucyate*; MĀ 29 at T 1.26.461c8: 是謂比丘成就見, 得正見, 於法得不壞淨, 入正法中; SĀ 344 at T 2.99.94b24: 於此法律正見具足, 直見成就, 於佛不壞淨成就, 來入正法, 得此正法, 悟此正法.

224 MN 77 at MN II 6,1: *appāhāro samaṇo gotamo, appāhāratāya ca vaṇṇavādī ti, iti ce maṃ, udāyi, sāvakā sakkareyyuṃ garukareyyuṃ* (B^e: *garuṃ kareyyuṃ*) *māneyyuṃ pūjeyyuṃ*.

225 MN 77 at MN II 5,32: *bhagavā hi, bhante, appāhāro, appāhāratāya ca vaṇṇavādī.*

226 Sakuludāyin's statement employs the expression "recluse Gautama" in MĀ 207 at T

1.26.782c7: 沙門瞿曇少食, 稱說少食, whereas the reflection by the disciples refers to the Buddha as "our Blessed One," T 1.26.783a6: 我世尊少食, 稱說少食. The present case is at the same time yet another instance of innocent variations in regard to sequence, as MĀ 207 lists the qualities mentioned in MN 77 in the sequence 2, 3, 1, 4, 5; see table 8.4 in Anālayo 2011b, 422. Hence taking little food, the first quality in MN 77, occurs in third position in MĀ 207.

227 See in more detail Anālayo 2011b, 417–21.

228 MN 138 at MN III 225,11 and 228,32: *yaṃ kho no, āvuso, bhagavā saṅkhittena uddesaṃ uddisitvā*.

229 MĀ 164 at T 1.26.696a27: 謂世尊略說此義.

230 MN 138 at MN III 224,8: *idam kho no, āvuso kaccāna, bhagavā saṅkhittena uddesaṃ uddisitvā*. Such a confusion becomes all the more probable since the members of the audience later approach the Buddha to report both their own reasoning and Mahākaccāna's explanation.

231 The first instance is MN 18 at MN I 111,31 and 112,37, which reports Mahākaccāna stating *yaṃ kho no, āvuso, bhagavā saṅkhittena uddesaṃ uddisitvā*, thereby reflecting the formulation used by the monastics when inviting him to expatiate at MN I 110,26: *idam kho no, āvuso kaccāna, bhagavā saṅkhittena uddesaṃ uddisitvā*. The parallels report Mahākaccāna's exposition without a reference to "us" (or "you"); MĀ 115 at T 1.26.604c3: 謂世尊略說此義 and EĀ 40.10 at T 2.125.743b11: 今如來所言 and 743c12: 世尊因此緣略說其義. The second instance is MN 133 at MN III 195,24 and 198,6, where Mahākaccāna again is on record for stating *yaṃ kho no, āvuso, bhagavā saṅkhittena uddesaṃ uddisitvā*, apparently influenced by the formulation used by the monastics at MN III 194,14: *idam kho no, āvuso kaccāna, bhagavā saṅkhittena uddesaṃ uddisitvā*. His statement in the parallel MĀ 165 at T 1.26.698b5 just takes the form 謂世尊略說此教, without any reference to "us" (or "you"). The third instance is AN 10.172 at AN V 257,19 and 258,37 where Mahākaccāna reportedly states: *yaṃ kho no, āvuso, bhagavā saṅkhittena uddesaṃ uddisitvā*, following the earlier statement by the monastics at AN V 255,30: *idam kho no, āvuso kaccāna, bhagavā saṅkhittena uddesaṃ uddisitvā* (no parallel to this discourse appears to be known).

232 SN 35.116 at SN IV 95,18: *yaṃ kho vo, āvuso, bhagavā saṅkhittena uddesaṃ uddisitvā*, even though the formulation used earlier by the monastics at SN IV 94,1 reads: *idam kho no, āvuso ānanda, bhagavā saṅkhittena uddesaṃ uddisitvā* (the parallel SĀ 234 at T 2.99.57a13 just reads: 向者世尊略說法已). However, another instance involving Ānanda, AN 10.115 at AN V 227,17, follows the pattern set by the Mahākaccāna episodes, as he is on record for stating *yaṃ kho no, āvuso, bhagavā saṅkhittena uddesaṃ uddisitvā* (the parallel MĀ 188 at T 1.26.735b9 just reads: 謂世尊略說此義).

233 MN 32 at MN I 214,24; already discussed in the context of a survey of several such variations involving the names of protagonists in Anālayo 2007f, 27–29.

234 This can be seen, for example, in the listing of eminent disciples in AN 1.14 at AN I 23,18, where he features as outstanding for his supernormal abilities, a position also reflected in the parallel EĀ 4.2 at T 2.125.557b6. The same association recurs in the *Divyāvadāna*, Cowell and Neil 1886, 395,9.

235 See, e.g., Anesaki 1901, 899, Minh Chau 1964/1991, 76, and Prasad 1998, 417.

236 SHT V 1346V, Sander and Waldschmidt 1985, 233, MĀ 184 at T 1.26.727c15, EĀ 37.3 at T 2.125.711a18, and T 3.154.81b29.

237 MN 125 at MN III 136,26 fails to mention the first absorption; on the significance of this from the viewpoint of oral transmission see Anālayo 2006a, 17–18.

238 MĀ 198 at T 1.26.758b19 and 758b29.

239 MN 125 at MN III 133,9 and 133,16, corresponding to MĀ 198 at T 1.26.757c29 and 758a4.

240 AN 10.208 at AN V 299,11.

241 See Anālayo 2009b, Martini 2012a, and Dhammadinnā 2014.

242 The exposition of these five begins in MN 112 at MN III 30,8; I already drew attention to the present issue in Anālayo 2005b, 104–5 and 2008b.

243 MĀ 187 at T 1.26.732b18: 此四食得知無所受, 漏盡心解脫.

244 Ps IV 94,23: *parasamuddavāsī therā pana . . . catuhi āhārehi saddhiṃ cha koṭṭhāse vadanti.*

245 See Anālayo 2011b: 451–66.

246 Vin III 148,30, which is absent from the report of their encounter in MN 82 at MN II 62,24 to 63,6, even though this information could easily have been integrated here.

247 MN 82 at MN I 64,25 corresponds to Th 769 to Th 774, whereas Th 775 remains without a counterpart. Th 774 and Th 775 are closely similar, leaving no evident reason why the second of the two could not have been accommodated in MN 82.

248 SN 7.11 at SN I 173,22 and Sn 1.4 at Sn 16,3 (the reference here is to the page, as the relevant indication occurs in a prose section rather than in verse).

249 MN 124 at MN III 127,14.

250 MĀ 34 at T 1.26.475c13 just reports that he rejoiced together with the monastics who were present. Minh Chau 1964/1991, 75 already noted that only the Pāli version reports his going forth and becoming an arahant/arhat.

251 DN 8 at DN I 176,29.

252 DĀ 25 at T 1.1.104c11, which at T 1.1.102c26 introduces him as 倮形梵志姓迦葉, listed in Akanuma 1930/1994, 4 as corresponding to the Pāli name Acela Kassapa and its Sanskrit counterpart Acela Kāśyapa.

253 SN 12.17 at SN II 21,26.

254 SĀ 302 at T 2.99.86b3, T 14.499.768c20, and a Sanskrit fragment in Chung and Fukita 2020, 172,1.

255 SN 41.9 at SN IV 302,9; von Hinüber 1997, 68 already noted this instance and MN 124 as separate occasions reporting the going forth of Acela Kassapa.

256 SĀ 573 at T 2.99.152b24.

257 In fact, Malalasekera 1937/1995, 26 finds it difficult to reconcile the different reports of Acela Kassapa's going forth.

258 DĀ 10 at T 1.1.54c28: 多聞廣博, 守持不忘諸法深奧, 上中下善, 義味誠諦, 梵行具足, 聞已入心 (adopting the sequential variant 誠諦 instead of 諦誠).

259 Mittal 1957, 85.

260 DN 34 at DN III 285,24: *dhātā vacasā paricitā*; see also DN 33 at DN III 267,8, AN 10.17 at AN V 23,22, and AN 10.18 at AN V 26,11, where the same quality occurs as part of ten states of protection.

261 DN 29 at DN III 127,16: *atthena atthaṃ vyañjanena vyañjanaṃ saṅgāyitabbaṃ na vivaditabbaṃ* (S[e]: *vicaritabbaṃ*); the reference is to the qualities pertinent to awakening (*bodhipakkhiyā dhammā*).

262 After describing how to behave if there is a disagreement regarding the meaning or the phrasing (or both), DĀ 17 at T 1.1.74b14 takes up the case of agreement in both

respects, preceded by a recurrent reference to the importance of communal harmony: 如是比丘盡共和合, 勿生諍訟, 同一師受, 同一水乳 . . . 若有比丘說法, 中有比丘作如是言: 彼所說句正, 義正. The reconstructed Sanskrit fragment parallel, 281r8 in DiSimone 2020, 174, has preserved a reference to the need to memorize and recite the teaching.

263 AN 4.160 at AN II 147,19 and 147,28: *bhikkhū duggahitaṃ* (C^e: *duggahītaṃ*) *suttantaṃ pariyāpuṇanti dunnikkhittehi padabyañjanehi. dunnikkhittassa, bhikkhave, padabyañjanassa attho pi dunnayo hoti. ayaṃ, bhikkhave, paṭhamo dhammo saddhammassa sammosāya antaradhānāya saṃvattati . . . ye te bhikkhū bahussutā āgatāgamā dhammadharā vinayadharā mātikādharā, te na sakkaccaṃ suttantaṃ paraṃ vācenti. tesaṃ accayena chinnamūlako suttanto hoti appaṭisaraṇo. ayaṃ, bhikkhave, tatiyo dhammo saddhammassa sammosāya antaradhānāya saṃvattati*; see also, e.g., AN 2.2.10 at AN I 59,1, AN 5.154 at AN III 176,18, AN 5.155 at AN III 177,5, and AN 5.156 at AN III 178,24.

264 MĀ 184 at T 1.26.727a22: 若有比丘廣學多聞, 守持不忘, 積聚博聞所謂法者, 初妙, 中妙, 竟亦妙, 有義, 有文, 具足清淨, 顯現梵行. 如是諸法廣學多聞, 翫習至千, 意所惟觀, 明見深達; 彼所說法簡要捷疾, 與正相應; with parallels in MN 32 at MN I 213,1, EĀ 37.3 at T 2.125.710c17, and T 3.154.81a17.

265 MN 32 at MN I 213,6: *catassannaṃ* (E^e: *catunnaṃ*) *parisānaṃ dhammaṃ deseti*, EĀ 37.3 at T 2.125.710c19: 與四部之眾而為說法, and T 3.154.81a20: 為諸四輩, 講說經典.

266 SN 10.6 at SN I 209,19, SĀ 1321 at T 2.99.362c10, and SĀ^2 320 at T 2.100.480c21. The present and the next example put into perspective the assessment by Shaw 2021, 14 that being "in the company of others is another, completely necessary, aspect of the conditions for oral literature," in that those who hear an oral text "would not have been alone in the way we engage with texts as readers. They would have to have been in the presence of perhaps a lot of people." Although the importance of group activity is indeed prominent in an oral setting, the possibility of reciting a text to oneself needs to be taken into account as well.

267 SN 12.45 at SN II 74,15. For a reply to criticism of my study of this and the previous case in Anālayo 2011b, 857, voiced by Shulman 2021c, 192, see Anālayo 2021g, 6.

268 DN 33 at DN III 241,26, DN 34 at DN III 279,12 (abbreviated), AN 5.26 at AN III 22,14, DĀ 9 at T 1.1.51c10, DĀ 10 at T 1.1.53c22, and SĀ 565 at T 2.99.149a6; see also Collins 1992, 126–27, Anālayo 2009d, and Pāsādika 2017.

269 Dharmaguptaka, T 22.1429.1018b15: 與未受大戒人共誦者, Kāśyapīya, T 24.1460.662b3: 與未受具戒人同誦, Mahāsāṅghika-Lokottaravāda, Tatia 1975, 19,16: *anupasaṃpannaṃ pudgalaṃ padaśo dharmaṃ vāceya*, Mahāsāṅghika, T 22.1426.552a25: 教未受具戒人說句法, Mahīśāsaka, T 22.1422a.197a13: 教未受具戒人經並誦者 (see also T 22.1422b.202c28: 以闡陀偈句教未受具戒人者), Mūlasarvāstivāda, Banerjee 1977, 32,11: *anupasaṃpannāya pudgalāya padaśo dharmaṃ vācayet*, Sarvāstivāda, von Simson 2000, 205,3: *anupasaṃpannena pudgalena sārdhaṃ padaśo dharmaṃ vācayet*, Theravāda, Pruitt and Norman 2001, 46,12: *anupasampannaṃ padaso dhammaṃ vāceyya*. Although not all of these versions explicitly use the expression "word-by-word," it seems reasonable to consider the basic idea of a fixed text to be at least implicit, given that conjoint recitation (共誦/同誦) would require a text whose wording is fixed.

270 Dharmaguptaka *Vinaya*, T 22.1428.638c21: 與諸長者共在講堂誦佛經語.

271 Mahīśāsaka *Vinaya*, T 22.1421.39c11: 學誦經偈.

272 Mahāsāṅghika *Vinaya*, T 22.1425.336c5: 教眾多童子句句說波羅耶那; see also Lévi 1915, 422.

273 In reply to this assessment, Shulman 2021b, 215 argues that this formulation could also be understood to imply "that other ways of preaching to the laity were sanctioned, some of which must have been inspired by texts. This implies that the latter were also used in more diverse ways than through word-by-word recitation." This does not stand in conflict with the position taken by Wynne 2004, who does not present word-by-word recitation as the sole way of employing the texts. The point remains that the instruction implies that texts were memorized in this way, which is an important factor to keep in mind when evaluating the nature of the early Buddhist oral tradition.

274 MN 22 at MN I 133,23 and MĀ 200 at T 1.26.764a12. Lamotte 1949, 346 explains that "le religieux qui se borne à mémoriser les textes sans essayer de les comprendre manque à son devoir."

275 For a survey of the different failings of memory see Schacter 1999.

276 Anderson and Pichert 1978.

277 Allon 2021, 51 comments that her observation "may very well be the case for these instances of interpolation in the *Ugraparipṛcchā*, but this does not cover all instances of change in Buddhist texts, early or otherwise." Note that the reference in Nattier 2003a, 52 to the assumption that "interpolation is necessarily a conscious act" only rules out defaulting to intentionality; it does not imply that all instances of change are necessarily unintentional. Her important assessment does seem to be pertinent not only to the text she has been studying but to the study of Buddhist oral texts in general.

278 MN 113 at MN III 37,15 refers to a "high family," *uccākula*, MĀ 85 at T 1.26.561a26 to a "powerful and wealthy family," 豪貴族, T 1.48.837c29 to a "great family," 大姓, and EĀ 17.9 at T 2.125.585a23 to a "powerful family," 豪族.

279 MN 113 at MN III 38,5 also takes up the "great family," *mahākula*, the "vastly wealthy family," *mahābhogakula*, and the "outstandingly wealthy family," *uḷārabhogakula*. Ps IV 98,18 suggests that the *uccākula* refers only to warriors and nobles, whereas the *mahākula* covers warriors, nobles, and also merchants. Again, the *mahābhogakula* stands for being "endowed with great wealth," but the *uḷārabhogakula* implies being endowed with "outstanding and excellent wealth." The understandable attempt to read a different meaning into the members of these two pairs seems a bit contrived.

280 Anālayo 2011b, 641.

281 For a critical examination of the interpretation advanced by Shulman 2019, 2021b, and 2021c of the function of such formulaic phrases see Allon 2021, 113–18 and Anālayo 2021f, 5–14 and 2021g.

282 MN 91 at MN II 146,8, MĀ 161 at T 1.26.689c23, and T 1.76.886a16.

283 MĀ 161 at T 1.26.690a4: 梵志梵摩及諸比丘，聞佛所說，歡喜奉行. The resultant discrepancy has already been noted by Minh Chau 1964/1991, 207, who points out that MĀ 161 describes the brahmin "rejoicing over the Buddha's speech, when he was reported dead already in the preceding paragraph."

284 Some of the examples for this pattern are: *vivattacchaddo* / *vighuṣṭaśabdo*; *brahmujjugatto* / *bṛhadṛjugātro*; *muducittaṃ* / *muditacittaṃ*; *aññataro* / *ājñātavān*; *sammodi sammodanīyaṃ* / *sammukhaṃ sammodanīṃ*.

285 MN 10 at MN I 61,15: *bhikkhu cakkhuñ ca pajānāti, rūpe ca pajānāti, yañ ca tad ubhayaṃ paṭicca uppajjati saṃyojanaṃ tañ ca pajānāti, yathā ca anuppannassa saṃyojanassa uppādo hoti tañ ca pajānāti, yathā ca uppannassa saṃyojanassa pahānaṃ hoti tañ ca pajānāti, yathā ca pahīnassa saṃyojanassa āyatiṃ anuppādo hoti tañ ca pajānāti. sotañ ca pajānāti, sadde ca pajānāti . . . pe . . . ghānañ ca pajānāti, gandhe ca pajānāti . . . jivhañ ca pajānāti, rase ca pajānāti . . . kāyañ ca pajānāti, phoṭṭhabbe ca pajānāti . . . manañ ca pajānāti, dhamme ca pajānāti, yañ ca tad ubhayaṃ paṭicca uppajjati saṃyojanaṃ tañ ca pajānāti, yathā ca anuppannassa saṃyojanassa uppādo hoti tañ ca pajānāti, yathā ca uppannassa saṃyojanassa pahānaṃ hoti tañ ca pajānāti, yathā ca pahīnassa saṃyojanassa āyatiṃ anuppādo hoti tañ ca pajānāti* (B[e] does not abbreviate). The corresponding instruction in the parallel MĀ 98 at T 1.26.584a14 also employs abbreviation.

286 Vism 351,16: *yathā dvīsu bhikkhūsu bahupeyyālaṃ tantiṃ sajjhāyantesu, tikkhapañño bhikkhu sakiṃ vā dvakkhattuṃ vā peyyālamukhaṃ vitthāretvā, tato paraṃ ubhato koṭivasen' eva sajjhāyaṃ karonto gacchati. tatra nātitikkhapañño evaṃ vattā hoti: kiṃ sajjhāyo nāma esa oṭṭhapariyāhatamattaṃ kātuṃ na deti, evaṃ sajjhāye kariyamāne kadā tanti paguṇā bhavissatī ti? so āgatāgataṃ peyyālamukhaṃ vitthāretvā va sajjhāyaṃ karoti. tam enaṃ itaro evam āha: kiṃ sajjhāyo nām' esa pariyosānaṃ gantuṃ na deti, evaṃ sajjhāye kariyamāne kadā tanti pariyosānaṃ gamissatī ti?*

287 On the relevance of lists for the development of Abhidharma thought see Anālayo 2014c.

288 See Anālayo 2020e; on the topic of abbreviation see also Anālayo 2021a and 2022.

289 MN 17 at MN I 104,17.

290 MĀ 107 and MĀ 108 at T 1.26.596c25 and 597c12, both being entitled "Discourse on the Forest," 林經.

291 SN 54.13–14 at SN V 328,23 and 333,23.

292 SĀ 810 at T 2.99.208a9.

293 SN 54.15–16 at SN V 334,20 and 335,17.

294 SĀ 811–812 at T 2.99.208c10.

295 AN 3.76–77 at AN I 223,12 and 224,7.

296 MN 104 at MN II 247,6; a sequence that recurs in DN 33 at DN III 254,11, AN 7.80 at AN IV 144,4, and Vin IV 207,3, each of which only lists the seven ways without providing a full exposition of their significance (for which see Vin II 93,32). Horner 1959, 33n7 already noted that in the main exposition in MN 104 "the usual order is altered."

297 The actual exposition, beginning in MN 104 at MN II 247,10, adopts the sequence 1, 5, 2, 3, 4, 6, 7 (compared to the introduction, see below note 299). This gives the impression that at some point during oral transmission the exposition of the fifth way of settling a litigation by opinion of the majority (*yebhuyyasikā*) shifted to the second position.

298 MN 104 at MN II 247,13 and MN II 247,22: *sabbeh' eva samaggehi sannipatitabbaṃ. sannipatitvā dhammanetti samanumajjitabbā. dhammanettiṃ samanumajjitvā yathā tattha sameti tathā taṃ adhikaraṇaṃ vūpasametabbaṃ*. The idea of "drawing out the guideline of Dharma" is specific to these two ways of settling a litigation and the two terms expressing this idea, *dhammanetti* and *samanumajjati*, do not seem to occur anywhere else among the Pāli discourses or *Vinaya*.

299 The listing proceeds in this way: *sammukhāvinayo* (1), *sativinayo* (2), *amūḷhavinayo*

(3), *paṭiññāya kāretabbaṃ* or *patiññātakaranaṃ* (4), *yebhuyyasikā* (5), *tassapāpiyyasikā* (6), *tiṇavatthārako* (7).

300 My exposition is based on a survey of such interrelationships by Franke 1914, which covers the discourses MN 1 to MN 76; for similar patterns in the collection of long discourses see Franke 1913b. Due to a lack of awareness of the nature and functioning of oral literature at that early stage in the history of Buddhist studies, the conclusions he drew based on his findings are in need of revision.

301 MN 1 at MN I 1,9 and MN 2 at MN I 7,17, and MN 1 at MN I 5,10 and MN 2 at MN I 12,4; see in more detail Anālayo 2010e.

302 MN 2 at MN I 7,10 and MN 3 at MN I 14,14.

303 MN 3 at MN I 14,2 contrasts disciples who do not follow their teacher's example, and do not practice seclusion, with disciples who follow the example of their teacher by dedicating themselves to seclusion. The topic of seclusion then forms one of the main themes broached at the outset of MN 4 at MN I 16,30.

304 MN 3 at MN I 15,4 and MN 4 at MN I 16,22. The two discourses also have in common a mention of the Buddha's compassion; see MN 3 at MN I 12,15 and MN 4 at MN I 23,35.

305 MN 4 at MN I 19,30 and MN 5 at MN I 32,13 refer to laziness; MN 4 at MN I 20,10 and MN 5 at MN I 32,13 mention lack of concentration; and MN 4 at MN I 20,19 and MN 5 at MN I 32,14 share a reference to lack of wisdom.

306 MN 5 at MN I 29,35 and MN 6 at MN I 33,12.

307 MN 6 at MN I 35,36.

308 MN 7 at MN I 38,32.

309 MN 5 at MN I 30,7, MN 6 at MN I 33,12, and MN 7 at MN I 38,11.

310 MN 7 at MN I 36,29 and MN 8 at MN I 42,35.

311 MN 8 at MN I 40,15 and MN 9 at MN I 46,20.

312 MN 8 at MN I 42,18.

313 MN 9 at MN I 46,30 and MN 10 at MN I 56,16; the reference is only to the first occurrence, as each of the two discourses employs the term *pajānāti* well over a hundred times.

314 Franke 1914, 501 qualifies the occurrence of this expression in the two discourses as an important point of correspondence, "eine wichtige Übereinstimmung."

315 MN 37 at MN I 251,17: *saṅkhittena taṇhāsaṅkhayavimutto*.

316 MN I 252,3, 252,32, 254,9, 254,15, 254,33, 254,36, 255,17, 255,22, 256,2, and 256,6.

317 MN 38 at MN I 270,37: *saṅkhittena taṇhāsaṅkhayavimuttiṃ dhāretha*.

318 MĀ 201 at T 1.26.769c29: 此經稱愛盡解脫; see also Anālayo 2019c, 144–45.

319 See in more detail Anālayo 2010e.

320 This is the chapter on kings, occurring as the ninth chapter in MN and the sixth in MĀ, which share the two discourse parallels MN 81 / MĀ 63 and MN 83 / MĀ 67.

321 These are the chapters on pairs and on brahmins. One of these two occurs as the fourth chapter in MN and the fifteenth in MĀ, which share the four discourse parallels MN 31 / MĀ 185, MN 32 / MĀ 184, MN 39 / MĀ 182, and MN 40 / MĀ 183. The other chapter occurs as the tenth chapter in MN and the twelfth in MĀ, which share the four discourse parallels MN 91 / MĀ 161, MN 93 / MĀ 151, MN 96 / MĀ 150, and MN 99 / MĀ 152.

322 Vism 95,23 *mūlapaṇṇāsaṃ sajjhāyantassa majjhimapaṇṇāsako āgacchati, taṃ sajjhāyantassa uparipaṇṇāsako*.

323 Sp IV 789,14.

324 Sp IV 789,15.

325 DN 16 at DN II 72,1 and DN 14 at DN II 1,1.

326 See in more detail Hartmann 1994.

327 For the latter the identification of parallels follows Hartmann and Wille 2014.

328 See in more detail Anālayo 2015a, 85–89.

329 The exposition on morality in DN 1 ranges from DN I 4,1 to 12,14, comprising over eight pages in the PTS edition, whereas the same topic in DN 2 goes from DN I 63,13 to 69,31, less than seven pages in the same edition. The difference appears to be mainly due to the fact that similar expositions of each aspect of morality are followed by a different concluding statement, where DN 1 keeps highlighting that a worldling might praise the Tathāgata for such conduct, whereas DN 2 just briefly notes that such is the conduct (of a monastic).

330 Weller 1934, 12,6 to 12,30; see also Anālayo 2014a, 47–50. This can be compared to the exposition on morality as part of an account of the gradual path in the *Saṅghabhedavastu*, Gnoli 1978, 232,9 to 240,17, which is substantially longer.

331 DĀ 21 at T I 88c19 to T I 89c18 and DĀ 20 at T I 83c14 to T I 84c13; thus in both versions the exposition on morality corresponds to one page in the Taishō edition.

332 Although my presentation is meant to identify patterns relevant to all three extant collections of long discourses, Shulman 2021c, 59n67 dismisses the suggestion that length of the shared exposition on morality could be relevant to the positioning of the *Brahmajālasutta* and argues that it was instead placed first in the Theravāda *Dīghanikāya* "as a strategic opening, with its unique synthesis of philosophy and worshipping the Buddha." He considers this to be more meaningful than the idea of seeing "the placing of discourses in a collection as resulting from technical consideration regarding their length" (24n56).

The idea of a strategic opening is not applicable to the other two collections of long discourses and therefore does not explain dynamics of discourse allocation common to different lineages of oral transmission. In fact, it even seems doubtful that this idea holds for the Theravāda tradition during the period of the formation of the discourse collections, given that a fairly similar discourse, the *Pañcattayasutta* (MN 102), has not been positioned as a strategic opening in the *vagga* in which it occurs, let alone in the whole *Majjhimanikāya*. Had there been a wish to posit such analyses of views as strategic openings, it could reasonably be expected that the same would have been applied to the *Pañcattayasutta*.

Similarly problematic is a general dismissal by Shulman 2021c, 24n56 of concatenation as a principle in the ordering of collections, on the assumption that "this is not what would make the difference for a reciter's ability to remember . . . the sequence of discourses in the *Vagga*. Rather, the connection stems from literary concerns." It is not clear why literary concerns should have been central for the order of long discourses, where precisely their length makes it more probable that just a single discourse (or even just extracts from it) will be chosen for giving a teaching. Recitation of the whole *vagga* would for this reason be mainly relevant to ritual performances or group recitation for memorization purposes, two contexts where literary concerns are probably less prominent. Moreover, the suggestion of literary concerns as the main, if not only, factor to be taken into account ignores the need for memorization aids that are such a characteristic feature of the early discourse collections. This is evident, for example, in the creation of mnemonic verses, *uddāna*, to facilitate precise recall of all textual items in a *vagga* in their established sequence. Here as well as elsewhere, the in-itself-justified attempt to accord recognition to literal dimensions of the texts should not be done at the expense of ignoring the very means required for their transmission.

333 In the case of the *Aṅguttaranikāya*, this suggests itself from the circumstance that the final section of the Tens contains discourses with twenty, thirty, and forty items: AN 10.211 at AN V 304,10 (twenty), AN 10.212 at AN V 305,10 (thirty), and AN 10.213 at AN V 306,26 (forty), followed by a few more discourses with tens; see also the discussion in Norman 1983, 56 and von Hinüber 1996/1997, 40. On indications relevant to the hypothesis that the same may have been the case for the *Ekottarikāgama* see Anālayo 2013e, 37–38n109. On the unconvincing suggestion by Kuan and Bucknell 2019 that the section on Ones is a later addition see below note 459.

334 Kuan and Bucknell 2019, 155 argue for the possibility of discourses among the Tens being derivative of their counterparts found among the Elevens. This possibility would not contrast with the idea that the section on Elevens is itself a later expansion of the collection, since the prolonged period of oral transmission would leave ample scope for such influence to happen after the collection had evolved to the stage of including a section on Elevens.

335 AN 1.1 at AN I 1,9; see also Kuan and Bucknell 2019, 143.

336 EĀ 9.7 and EĀ 9.8 at T 2.125.563a14 and 563a28.

337 Pande 1957, 235 reasons that in the case of the Ones "the vaggas rather than the suttas constitute its real divisions."

338 AN 11.12 at AN V 329,9, which transitions from the first to the second topic in a way that names the count of both: *pañcasu dhammesu patiṭṭhāya cha dhamme uttariṃ* (Be: *uttari*) *bhāveyyāsi*.

339 SĀ 932 at T 2.99.238b24: 依此五法, 修六念處 and SĀ2 157 at T 2.100.433b27: 恒應修習如是五事, 并六念法.

340 AN 3.81 to 3.90 at AN I 229,1, whose parallels, listed in the order of the Pāli discourses, begin with SĀ 828 (found at T 2.99.212b18), followed by SĀ 827, SĀ 829, SĀ 824, SĀ 821, SĀ 820, SĀ 819, SĀ 817, SĀ 816, and SĀ 830. Kuan and Bucknell 2019, 157 consider it "likely that in the Pali tradition this block of ten sutta, now a vagga of AN, was formerly a *saṃyutta* of SN." It could also be envisaged that a set of discourses in a collection of Threes, which was grouped together as a chapter due to an inner thematic connection, was subsequently shifted to the collection of topic-wise discourses.

341 T 1.26.421a12: 七法品.

342 See the discussion in Bucknell 2017, 89–90.

343 See the discussion in Bucknell 2017, 91–92.

344 See the discussion in Bucknell 2014, 80–82 and the comparative survey in Anālayo 2011b, 1054–55.

345 See, e.g., Adikaram 1946/1994, 27–32, Goonesekera 1968, 689, Norman 1983, 9, and Endo 2003a.

346 See Allon 1997b, 39.

347 DN 16 at DN II 73,4: *vassakāro ... rañño māgadhassa ajātasattussa vedehiputtassa paṭissutvā, bhaddāni bhaddāni yānāni yojāpetvā* (Be and Se *yojetvā*), *bhaddaṃ bhaddaṃ* (second *bhaddaṃ* not in Ce and Ee) *yānaṃ abhiruhitvā, bhaddehi bhaddehi yānehi rājagahamhā niyyāsi yena gijjhakūṭo pabbato tena pāyāsi. yāvatikā yānassa*

bhūmi yānena gantvā, yānā paccorohitvā pattiko 'va yena bhagavā ten' upasaṅkami and AN 7.20 at AN IV 18,4: *vassakāro . . . rañño māgadhassa ajātasattussa vedehiputtassa paṭissutvā* (E[e] and S[e] *paṭissunitvā*), *yena bhagavā tenupasaṅkami.*

348 See Allon 1997b, 62.

349 DN 16 at DN II 104,12 (= Ud 6.1 at Ud 63,13): *atha kho māro pāpimā acirapakkante āyasmante ānande yena bhagavā ten' upasaṅkami; upasaṅkamitvā ekamantaṃ aṭṭhāsi. ekamantaṃ ṭhito kho māro pāpimā bhagavantaṃ etad avoca* and AN 8.70 at AN IV 310,11: *atha kho māro pāpimā acirapakkante āyasmante ānande bhagavantaṃ etad avoca.*

350 According to Wagle 1985, 60, "the standard description mentioned in the text[s] is that the gods on their visits to the Buddha salute him and stand on one side . . . the gods are not referred to as sitting (*nisīdi*) near the Buddha as was the case with humans who normally followed that procedure in the presence of the Buddha"; see also Anālayo 2011b, 248n208.

351 MN 85 at MN II 93,9: *bhagavantaṃ bhuttāviṃ onītapattapāṇiṃ* (C[e]: *oṇītapattapāṇiṃ*) *aññataraṃ nīcaṃ āsanaṃ gahetvā ekamantaṃ nisīdi* and Vin II 128,36: *bhagavantaṃ bhuttāviṃ onītapattapāṇiṃ ekamantaṃ nisīdi.*

352 See Anālayo 2011b, 20–21.

353 See Anālayo 2011b, 20n125.

354 The circumstance that this change has not been applied to instances involving the Buddha's own speech makes it in my view improbable that other instances of such a change express "a form of branding," as suggested by Allon 2021, 104. It is also not clear to me how such branding would have worked. Reciters of one tradition would know what tradition they belong to and thus have no need for any additional marker of identity. There also does not appear to be evidence of competition between reciters belonging to different traditions regarding the learning of their respective textual collections. In the case of the Pāli discourse collections, the Theravāda reciters in Sri Lanka would have had no need to compete with other schools. Given that Theravāda reciters could memorize all four collections, or just one, or just part of one collection, the idea of branding would also not explain differences between the four *Nikāya*s in the use of formulas, etc., which have been studied so well by Allon 1997b. In sum, it seems to me that the idea of "branding" could be an instance of applying a pattern evident in contemporary society to a setting where this does not fit particularly well.

355 MN 138 at MN III 223,5: *uddesavibhaṅgaṃ vo, bhikkhave, desissāmi.*

356 MĀ 164 at T 1.26.694b16: 我當為汝說法.

357 MN 133 at MN III 193,5: *sādhu me, bhante, bhagavā bhaddekarattassa uddesañ ca vibhaṅgañ ca desetū ti.*

358 MN 133 at MN III 192,10: *dhāresi tvaṃ, bhikkhu, bhaddekarattassa uddesañ ca vibhaṅgañ cā ti?*

359 MĀ 165 at T 1.26.696c7: 受持跋地羅帝偈耶?, T 21.1362.881c10: 聞善夜經不?, D 313 *sa* 161b4 or P 979 *shu* 171b1 (also found in D 617 *ba* 56b2 or P 599 *ya* 96b5, and again in D 974 *waṃ* 90a5): *dge slong khyod kyis mtshan mo bzang po'i mdo sde shes sam?*

360 MN 131 at MN III 187,17.

361 This is the 根本分別品.

362 SN 45.91 to SN 45.96 at SN V 38,14; the other rivers are the Yamunā, Acīravatī,

Sarabhū, and Mahī, which are mentioned individually and then once all together, a procedure that results in an overall count of six discourses.

363 SN 45.97 to SN 45.102 at SN V 39,16.

364 See also Lenz 2003, 92–98 for examples of similar patterns in other texts.

365 According to Williams 1970, 166, although some aspects of formalization must have been applied in the course of transmission, "it is possible that the Buddha's teaching methods included repetition and stylized formulae to aid memorization." Levman 2020, 265 remarks that "many of the *suttas* . . . are organized like a musical form, with a euphonic reprise . . . used as a basic formal principle of the teaching. This assists memory, but more importantly induces an impactful reception on the part of the audience, as the sound communicates on an affective level, parallel to and simultaneous with the symbolic meaning of the actual words."

366 See von Hinüber 1994b, 6 and Allon 1997b, 363.

367 MĀ 222 at T 1.26.805c11 to 809a25.

368 Anālayo 2014c, 44–47.

369 As observed by Allon 1997b, 367, "the insertion of another list of, say, 'five good things' in a text containing a parallel list of fives would not be a violation of *buddhavacana*, because the Buddha had in fact spoken of these 'five good things' on another occasion."

370 SN 53.1 to SN 53.54 at SN V 307,5.

371 SN 34.1 to SN 34.55 at SN III 263,20, which has a counterpart in SĀ 883 at T 2.99.222c13. In this case, what is a whole division (*saṃyutta*) in the Pāli version corresponds to a single discourse in its Chinese *Āgama* parallel.

372 See Anālayo 2017c, 109–75, 2019f, 2020a, and 2022b, 189–207. Even the definition of the path factor of right concentration as corresponding to the four absorptions appears to be a later development; see Anālayo 2019b.

373 Anālayo 2020/2022 and 2022b, 149–57.

374 MĀ 207 at T 1.26.783b15.

375 MN 77 at MN II 11,3 to 22,15. In relation to a brief summary of this case in Anālayo 2011b, 885, Shulman 2021c, 154n8 argues that here "we actually find that the well-known formula of the four *satipaṭṭhānas* is inserted, followed by the other categories on the list of the thirty-seven *bodhipakkhiyadhammas*; the relevant formulas are all found at the level of sutta, primarily in the *Mahāvagga* of the SN, so there is no need to refer to the commentary (although this collection could itself be considered a good example of the lack of differentiation between 'discourse' and 'commentary')." If the notion of a commentary can be applied to the *Mahāvagga*, then why not also to the *Mahāsakuludāyisutta*? In both cases, the usage is not meant to relegate the relevant textual parts to the time of the finalization of the Pāli commentaries. Instead, the point is just that certain expositions may have originated in explanations given by the reciters which, in the course of oral transmission, became part of the discourse itself. In other words, the proposal is to envisage "the arising of a more detailed explanation of all the other aspects of the path in the form of a commentary that then made its way into the Pāli discourse" (Anālayo 2011b, 885).

376 The mind-made body appears to be the means believed to enable some feats of levitation, as is particularly evident in AN 8.30 at AN IV 235,21; see in more detail Anālayo 2016f, 16–18. De Notariis 2021, 12 proposes to "read this passage in light of *cātumahābhūtikena kāyena iddhiyā* (S, V, 282), which, similarly,

suggests that the same act of levitation could be performed through the physical and material body. Indeed, there is enough evidence in Buddhist texts to suppose that the *iddhi*s were regarded as real phenomena and not only as mere imaginative and mental acts." In my detailed study in Anālayo 2016f, I noted several instances showing that supernormal feats like levitation were at times regarded as involving the physical body. But that does not apply to AN 8.30, as the relevant Pāli verse and its parallels extant in Chinese and Tibetan speak unmistakably of the mind-made body. SN 51.22 at SN V 282,18 (a Pāli discourse without known parallels) reports the Buddha traveling to the Brahmā world either with his mind-made body or with his physical body. These are alternatives, of which only the one that employs the same terminology as AN 8.30 and its parallels is the relevant one, namely the one by way of the mind-made body. Besides, SN 51.22 is about travel to the Brahmā world, whereas AN 8.30 is about travel on earth. Such considerations prevent reading AN 8.30 in the light of levitation with the physical body described in SN 51.22.

377 MN 77 at MN II 9,14 to 11,2.

378 DN 2 at DN I 73,23 to 84,12; see also Eimer 1976, 53.

379 Ps III 243,4: *abhiññāvosānapāramīpattā ti . . . arahattaṃ pattā.*

380 MN 30 at MN I 200,10: *attān' ukkaṃseti paraṃ vambheti* and EĀ 43.4 at T 1.125.759b15: 自譽, 毀呰他人.

381 MN 30 at MN I 203,25.

382 MN 30 at MN I 201,24: *samādhisampadaṃ ārādheti.*

383 Ps II 234,27: *ime nirodhapādakā, tasmā uttaritarā ti veditabbā.*

384 SĀ 236 at T 2.99.57b15.

385 MN 151 at MN III 295,13 to 297,20.

386 Examples are DĀ 11 at T 1.1.57c2 and DĀ 12 at T 1.1.59b19 as full or partial extracts from the two basic lists that underlie DĀ 10 at T 1.1.52c29, which combines a progression from ones to tens with a list of ten themes; see in more detail Anālayo 2014f.

387 MN 10 at MN I 62,21: *idaṃ dukkhan ti yathābhūtaṃ pajānāti, ayaṃ dukkhasamudayo ti yathābhūtaṃ pajānāti, ayaṃ dukkhanirodho ti yathābhūtaṃ pajānāti, ayaṃ dukkhanirodhagāminī paṭipadā ti yathābhūtaṃ pajānāti.* The two Chinese *Āgama* parallels, MĀ 98 and EĀ 12.1, do not cover the topic of the four truths at all.

388 DN 22 at DN II 304,26 to 313,27.

389 DN 22 at DN II 309,23: *rūpataṇhā loke . . . pe . . . saddataṇhā loke . . . pe . . . gandhataṇhā loke . . . pe . . . rasataṇhā loke . . . pe . . . phoṭṭhabbataṇhā loke . . . pe . . . dhammataṇhā loke piyarūpaṃ sātarūpaṃ, etth' esā taṇhā uppajjamānā uppajjati, ettha nivisamānā nivisati.*

390 For another relatively minor example illustrating the same tendency for redundancy due to apparent expansion of a list see Anālayo 2008b, 268n18. In this case, the passage gives separate references to the states (*dharma*s) to be experienced through a sense and again to the objects of the same sense. The unsuccessful attempt by the commentators to make sense of this presentation shows that the redundancy did not escape notice, which in turn makes it fair to assume that this double mention of the same item in different terms would not be the result of an intentional development.

391 Winternitz 1920/1968, 51 refers to DN 22 as an example for *Dīghanikāya* discourses that give the impression of being enlarged versions of shorter texts, in the present case through the addition of commentarial type of material. Bapat 1926, 11–12 considers

this part of DN 22 to be "an amplified version of an originally small sutta . . . explaining, in a commentarial fashion, the details of the four noble truths." According to Thomas 1927/2003, 252, during the oral transmission of the early discourses "there would also be the danger of unwittingly including discourses or commentaries . . . which were not an original part of the collection. An instance occurs in the case of the *Satipaṭṭhāna-sutta*. It is found both in the *Dīgha* (No. 22) and *Majjhima* (No. 10), but in the former case a long passage of commentary on the Four Truths has been incorporated." Barua 1971/2003, 371 considers DN 22 as resulting from "additions after the style of a commentary." Bodhi 2005, 261 sums up that the passage in question "may have originally been an early commentary incorporated into the discourse." The general pattern of commentary becoming part of the text itself has already been noted by von Simson 1965, 130 in the context of a detailed comparative study of Pāli and Sanskrit discourse material ("zahlreiche Zusätze der Sanskritversion . . . scheinen geradezu aus der fortlaufenden Kommentierung des überlieferten Textes in diesen selbst eingedrungen zu sein").

392 This takes the form of concluding the respective expositions in DN 1 at DN I 5,27, 8,34, and 12,18 with the remarks *cūḷasīlaṃ* (C^c: *cullasīlaṃ*) *niṭṭhitaṃ*, *majjhimasīlaṃ niṭṭhitaṃ*, and *mahāsīlaṃ niṭṭhitaṃ*.

393 Ps II 208,23 (on MN 27 at MN I 180,4) lists the same five seeds not to be harmed that are mentioned in the medium-length section on morality in DN 1 at DN I 5,31 (with the statement in MN 27 corresponding to the smaller section in DN 1 at DN I 5,4); see in more detail Anālayo 2014a, 47–50.

394 As already noted by Przyluski 1926, 346, "dans un *sūtra* commençant par ces mots: 'Ainsi j'ai entendu. Une fois le Buddha demeurait à . . .', le cadre même du récit ne peut avoir été prononcé par le Buddha."

395 Particularly intriguing instances of this tendency are Pāli discourses that recur elsewhere as direct records of what happened, with both modes of presentation being supported by parallels. Three examples for this pattern are: SN 3.18 at SN I 87,20 and its parallels SĀ 1238 at T 2.99.339a23 and SĀ^2 65 at T 2.100.396a18 take the form of the Buddha reporting a teaching he had previously given to Ānanda, whose actual delivery is recorded in SN 45.2 at SN V 2,8 and its parallels SĀ 726 at T 2.99.195b10, SĀ 768 at T 2.99.200c3, and D 300 *sha* 304b7 or P 966 *lu* 334b3. SN 47.43 at SN V 185,4 and its parallel SĀ^3 4 at T 2.101.494a18 take the form of the Buddha reporting a reflection that occurred to him soon after his awakening, the actual occurrence of which is recorded in SN 47.18 at SN V 167,5 and its parallels SĀ 1189 at T 2.99.322a28 and SĀ^2 at T 2.100.410b10. In AN 4.21 at AN II 20,5, a Sanskrit fragment parallel, Skilling, Saerji, and Assavavirulhakarn 2016, 160, and Up 9022 at D 4094 *nyu* 84a4 or P 5595 *thu* 103b2, the Buddha reports another reflection that occurred to him soon after his awakening, the actual occurrence of which is recorded in SN 6.2 at SN I 138,30, SĀ 1188 at T 2.99.321c18, and SĀ^2 101 at T 2.100.410a3 (see also T 4.212.718b26, which takes the form of a report by the Buddha but in this case without specifying the location where he was staying).

Two additional points emerge: One is that the correspondence these discourses establish between the Buddha's self-report in the form *ekam idāham mahārāja/ bhikkhave samayaṃ . . . viharāmi* and the formulation in their counterparts as *ekaṃ samayaṃ bhagavā . . . viharati* confirms my conclusion in Anālayo 2014a, 45 that the standard specification "at one time" at the outset of an early discourse intends the time of the events reported in the main body of the discourse.

The other point is that the final two cases of the Buddha's self-report in SN 47.43 and AN 4.21 are of additional interest, as according to the counterparts in SN 47.18 and SN 6.2 the Buddha was alone and only Brahmā witnessed his reflection. It follows that the existence of these two discourses would anyway have to be attributed to a report given by the Buddha to his monastic disciples at some later time, obviating the need for another discourse that explicitly indicates this fact. The resultant doubling seems to reflect the concern of the reciters to transmit faithfully, rather than feeling free to make intentional changes, as in the present case they could have easily simplified the situation without incurring any real loss of material, thereby diminishing the amount of text to be transmitted.

396 MN 97 at MN II 195,20: *sati uttarikaraṇīye* (C[e]: *uttariṃ*), *hīne brahmaloke patiṭṭhāpetvā, uttāy' āsanā pakkāmi*, which anticipates a statement reportedly made by the Buddha to the same effect on seeing Sāriputta returning. The corresponding description in the parallel MĀ 27 at T 1.26.458b10 does not express a comparable evaluation of Sāriputta's teaching; see also Anālayo 2011b, 570–72.

397 MN 124 at MN III 125,19: *idam pi mayaṃ āyasmato bakkulassa* (B[e]: *bākulassa*) *acchariyaṃ abbhutadhammaṃ* (E[e]: *abbhutaṃ dhammaṃ*) *dhārema* and MĀ 34 at T 1.26.475b6: 是謂尊者薄拘羅未曾有法. The commentary, Ps IV 193,10, reports that *dhammasaṅgāhakattherehi niyametvā ṭhapitāni*, thereby clearly recognizing that these were added by the reciters, rather than being a reaction by the audience witnessing Bakkula's proclamations.

398 See in more detail Anālayo 2007a and 2010d.

399 Viewed from this perspective, the present case can be seen as an early instance for a recurrent pattern where, as noted in Anālayo 2010a, 34n56, the "explicit indication—expressed in these refrain-like statements—to the effect that the respective material is worthwhile memorizing . . . would be in line with a tendency prominent in later times of building into a text protective measures that assure its survival."

400 For a critical reply to the suggestion by Norman 1997, 158–60 (see also von Hinüber 2019b, 92) that commentary and original were transmitted separately see Anālayo 2010b, 13–16 and 2019g, 57–58.

401 Such a combination of two distinct styles has been identified by Oldenberg 1882, 114 in the *Lalitavistara*, by Oldenberg 1912a, 141 in the *Mahāvastu*, by Oldenberg 1912b, 156–57 in the *Divyāvadāna*, and by Oldenberg 1898, 672 in what he refers to as northern Buddhist texts ("nordbuddhistische Texte") in general; von Simson 1985, 81 comments that this pattern is probably of general relevance and would not be limited to the texts examined by Oldenberg.

402 An example reflecting the lack of clear boundaries is the finding by Allon 2021, 86 of an instance where apparently the reciters of "the Sanskrit version converted what was originally a sutra narrator statement into the words of the Buddha."

403 MN 106 at MN II 263,26 (correcting *saññaṃ* to *suññaṃ*, which is an obvious error).

404 MĀ 75 at T 1.26.542c18: 此世空,空於神,神所有,空有常,空有恒,空長存,空不變易; see also de Jong 2000, 177 and Baba 2004. A similar formulation can be found in a Tibetan parallel, Up 4058 at D 4094 *ju* 228b6 or P 5595 *tu* 261a6.

405 See Paṭis I 109,10, Nidd II 279,12, and Vism 654,22.

406 MN 143 at MN III 259,12, with a parallel in SĀ 1032 at T 2.99.269c16.

407 EĀ 51.8 at T 2.125.819c14: 若眼起時,則起亦不知來處.若眼滅時,則滅亦不知去處 (adopting a variant that adds 則起).

408 Vism 484,6.

409 SN 2.26 at SN I 62,19 (= AN 4.45 at AN II 48,31, repeated in AN 4.46); a case already noted by Wen 2006, 18.

410 SĀ 1307 at T 2.99.359b5: 何等為世間滅道跡? 謂八聖道.

411 Spk I 117,28: *paṭipadan ti maggasaccaṃ.*

412 MN 107 at MN III 7,2: *paramajjadhammesu.*

413 MĀ 144 at T 1.26.653c7: 能伏一切外道異學 and T 1.70.876b15: 能攝一切異學.

414 Ps IV 70,18. In relation to a brief survey of this case and the next (see below note 416) in Anālayo 2011b, 883–84, Shulman 2021c, 153n8 argues that "the examples Anālayo brings for the infiltration of commentary into discourses are unconvincing (2011: 883–886); most can be accounted for by acknowledging the texts' flexible character, specifically with regard to the possibility of introducing an accepted formula at appropriate places. In both cases from the *Gaṇakamoggallāna-sutta* and the *Brahmajāla-sutta* (2011: 883–884), a more straightforward explanation would not assume a commentary separate from the texts, but would rather understand the changes in the Chinese texts as natural elaborations within the ideological world of the *Nikāya*s/*Āgama*s. Thus, for the *Gaṇakamoggallāna*, defining the Buddha's teaching as the best among 'the teachings of today' (Anālayo's translation for *paramajjadhammesu*) could easily lend itself to a reference to the teachings of 'heterodox wanderers,' so that the link to the Pāli commentary's mention of the doctrine of the six heretical teachers (*chasattharādhammā* [sic]) does not add much. For the *Brahmajāla*, the mention of the Buddha's supernatural knowledge in one Chinese version need not result from commentary, but may rather supply information one can glean from other, similar scenarios (on this specific case, see Chapter 2, n. 29)."

Besides involving a misunderstanding, as my proposal does not posit commentarial explanations as invariably "separate from the texts" but much rather is based precisely on the lack of a clear defining line between the two during oral transmission, the reference in the *Gaṇakamoggallānasutta* and its parallels is not a formula, as the relevant phrase *paramajjadhammesu* is unique to this discourse (note also that my translation "teachings of today" is meant to render only *ajjadhammesu*, not the whole phrase). Since Shulman 2021c, 171 defines formulas as "units of textual articulation that repeat across texts, and that strictly maintain their form," the suggestion of explaining this case as "the possibility of introducing an accepted formula at appropriate places" does not work.

The reference to "Chapter 2, n. 29" leads me to Shulman 2021c, 48n29, which has no relationship to the *Brahmajālasutta* (a reference related to the introduction to the *Brahmajālasutta* can be found in Shulman 2021c, 22n53, which occurs in his first chapter, but this just mentions my finding without further comments). Thus, it is not clear what the criticism could be. The relevant part of Anālayo 2011b, 884 takes the following position: "While the *Dīgha-nikāya* [version] simply mentions that, when the Buddha joined the monks, he sat down and asked them what they had been talking about, the commentary clarifies that he asked this question even though he knew what their discussion had been about. This is made explicit in the *Dīrgha-āgama* discourse itself, which indicates that the Buddha inquired from the monks 'knowingly.'" In this way, the same type of information is provided in the commentary of one tradition and in the discourse of another, both ostensibly resulting from the perceived need to forestall the impression that the Buddha did not know and had to ask. It is precisely this type of pattern that my presentation intends to highlight. In fact, elsewhere Shulman 2021c, 20n46 offers a similar observation, in that information on a particular park belonging to a queen found in the Pāli commentary (Sv III 832,5) is stated explicitly in the Chinese version (although the reference to the latter seems to have been taken from the unreliable translation by Ichimura 2015, 269 rather than from the Chinese text of DĀ 8 at T 1.1.47a24, which does not mention a queen).

For replies to other criticism by Shulman 2021c, related to the topic of commentarial type of explanations found in discourse versions of some traditions, see also above note 375, below note 444, and Anālayo 2021g, 16–17.

415 DN 1 at DN I 2,23.

416 Sv I 49,18: *jānanto yeva kathāsamuṭṭhāpanatthaṃ bhikkhū pucchi*; see also above note 414.

417 DĀ 21 at T 1.1.88b29: 知而故問.

418 SN 9.3 at SN I 198,22: *tena kho pana samayena āyasmā kassapagotto divāvihāragato aññataraṃ chetaṃ* (C[e]: *cetaṃ*) *ovadati.*

419 SĀ 1339 at T 2.99.369b19: 有獵師名曰尺只, 去十力迦葉不遠張網捕鹿. 爾時十力迦葉為彼獵師哀愍說法 and SĀ[2] 359 at T 2.100.491a27: 有一獵師名連迦, 去尊者不遠施鹿羂撥. 爾時尊者憐愍獵師, 為其說法.

420 Spk I 289,29: *migaluddakaṃ.*

421 MN 128 at MN III 152,25; for a reply to criticism of my study of this discourse by Shulman 2021c, 159 see Anālayo 2021g, 13–16.

422 MĀ 72 at T 1.26.532c16 and EĀ 24.8 at T 2.125.626c5.

423 Vin I 342,3.

424 MN 135 at MN III 202,12.

425 Kudo 2004, 2,13, MĀ 170 at T 1.26.703c24, T 1.78.887b7, T 1.79.888b19, and T 1.81.895c2; see also Rosenberg 1920, 405 for the beginning of a Sogdian version of this story.

426 Ps V 9,12.

427 MN 140 at MN III 238,1, MĀ 162 at T 1.26.690a24, and Up 1041 at D 4094 *ju* 35a2 or P 5595 *tu* 38a5.

428 T 14.511.779a10; see also T 4.211.580c19.

429 Ps V 33,22.

430 Ground-breaking contributions to the identification of discourse parallels are Anesaki 1908 and Akanuma 1929/1990.

431 Dharmaguptaka version, T 22.1429.1015c6, Kāśyapīya version, T 24.1460.659c24, Mahāsāṅghika-Lokottaravāda version, Tatia 1975, 6,19, Mahāsāṅghika version, T 22.1426.549b27, Mahīśāsaka version, T 22.1422a.195a8 (see also T 22.1422b.200c20), Mūlasarvāstivāda version, Banerjee 1977, 14,4, Sarvāstivāda version, von Simson 2000, 163,4, and Theravāda version, Pruitt and Norman 2001, 8,4.

432 The statistician is Oleg Medvedev at the University of Waikato, New Zealand; email 8 October 2020.

433 This appears to be the idea behind the suggestion by Shulman 2019, 130n71 that the early Buddhist oral tradition should be understood to follow the pattern of a rhizome, in the sense that "texts, or pieces of texts, branch off in diverse ways, in a

way that resembles crab grass, rather than conforming to the standard picture of a text as a tree with a logical sequence of development." Although the image of a rhizome is evocative in the context of the modern globalized world with its complex interrelations, it does not reflect the nature of the early Buddhist texts adequately. In a subsequent publication, Shulman 2021c, 173 additionally presents the example of a banyan tree as an alternative image to exemplify the nature of the early Buddhist oral tradition. This would indeed be a more fitting illustration, since a banyan tree grows from a seed but then develops aerial prop roots that grow into trunks, which often can no longer be distinguished from the trunk that grew from the seed. On this understanding, the image of a banyan tree would grant the existence of a starting point in the past but at the same time make it clear that this can no longer be identified.

However, in spite of the appropriate choice of the banyan tree imagery, in the same publication Shulman 2021c, 151 criticizes my work for involving the assumption "that there was an original version to each discourse, which may have evolved over time, but can ultimately be traced back to a specific historical incident of teaching. This means that a discourse is a clearly defined analytical unit, and that there is a slippery equation between concrete events of teaching and the discourses we find today." The suggestion that there must have been some starting point in the past does not entail any assertion about the precise form this took, which need not have been "a clearly defined analytical unit." The proposal of a causal continuity between a concrete event of teaching and the discourse we find today is similar to the proposal that there is a causal continuity between the seed of a banyan and the trunk(s) that grew from it, which is hardly a slippery equation.

The same basic misunderstanding appears to be also evident in a reference by Shulman 2021a, 13n69 to "the attempt for the one true original text pursued by scholars like Anālayo." My work throughout involves discerning earlier and later textual layers without any attempt to arrive at the original. For a critical reply to other aspects of the presentation in Shulman 2021a and 2021c see Anālayo 2021c and 2021g.

434 This appears to be the position taken by Silk 2021, 152, made in the context of a discussion of Indian Mahāyāna *sūtra* literature, who criticizes the assumption that there must have been an earliest composition standing in the background of the different versions now extant: "But it is not an error in that we simply cannot access the 'original' text, which is perhaps now lost but nevertheless existed. It is an error because the very nature of the genre does not permit the existence of such a kernel or core composition."

435 MN 91 at MN II 137,9: *uṇhīsasīso* (Se: *uṇhisasīso*), MĀ 161 at T 1.26.686c12: 頂有肉髻, 團圓相稱, and T 1.76.884a9: 頂有肉髻, 光明煒煒, 過日, 絕月 (adopting the variant 煒煒 instead of 煌煌).

436 DN 30 at DN III 145,4 and MĀ 59 at T 1.26.494a26.

437 DN 30 at DN III 145,17: *imāni kho* (Ee adds *te*), *bhikkhave, dvattiṃsa mahāpurisassa* (Ee has the opposite order *mahāpurisassa dvattiṃsa*) *mahāpurisalakkhaṇāni bāhirakā pi isayo dhārenti, no ca kho te jānanti: imassa kammassa katattā* (Be: *kaṭattā*; Se adds *pe*) *idaṃ* (Ce and Se: *imaṃ*) *lakkhaṇaṃ paṭilabhatī ti*.

438 See in more detail Anālayo 2017a, 63–68; the opposite position taken by Shulman 2021c, 185n91 ignores my detailed discussion of the topic and is also not fully in line with his own assessment that "the doctrine of the thirty-two marks . . . corresponds

to a key Brahmanic assumption regarding the embodiment of spiritual status" (186). Shulman 2021c, 185n92 also considers my comparative study of MN 91 in Anālayo 2011b, 528 to involve a "subtle attempt to interpret the marks as less metaphysically pregnant, reading the texts to imply an effort is needed to verify them. This interpretation is contestable since the expertise needed is not one of keen vision but of knowing the texts." The proposed reasoning overlooks my discussion in note 44 (pp. 535–36) of the same comparative study, in which I survey various instances showing that the early discourses did not present the Buddha as someone easily recognizable by others (see in more detail Anālayo 2017a, 57–61). Such descriptions convey the impression that, from the viewpoint of the reciters, "the Buddha did not have longer hair than other monks or even any other physical mark of a type that would have made it easy for others to recognize him immediately." Moreover, in note 7 (p. 528) of the same study I note references to the ability to recognize the thirty-two marks, which give the impression that mastery of this lore made one become a brahmin of high repute. In the ancient oral setting, mere knowledge of a list of thirty-two items would hardly have sufficed for acquiring such repute. In fact, such knowledge is referred to as *mahāpurisalakkhaṇesu anavayo* (e.g. MN 91 at MN II 133,16), "being an expert in the marks of a great person" (in a different context in AN 5.135 at AN III 152,30, *anavaya* occurs on a par with *sikkhita*, "trained," to describe accomplishment of a warrior king in various skills such as riding an elephant, archery, etc.; in fact, Shulman 2021c, 180 translates *anavaya*, used in MN 91 in relation to the marks of a great person, as "expert"). According to the commentary, Ps III 363,1, the lore of the thirty-two marks was set forth in 12,000 works. Setting aside the hyperbolic number of works, this commentarial gloss nevertheless concords with the impression conveyed by the discourses that mastering the lore of the thirty-two marks was a demanding task. For these reasons I suggested that "the original conception of these marks would probably have intended nuances, perceptible only to a keen observer who was trained in the art of detecting them, not abnormal physical marks that are so plainly evident that one cannot fail to notice them" (528).

439 See in more detail Anālayo 2017a, 103–27.

440 DN 30 at DN III 169,3: *pubbe manussabhūto samāno bahujanapubbaṅgamo ahosi kusalesu dhammesu bahujanapāmokkho* (Cᵉ: *bahujanānaṃ pāmokkho*) *kāyasucarite vacīsucarite manosucarite dānasaṃvibhāge sīlasamādāne uposathupavāse* (Sᵉ: *uposathūpavāse*) *matteyyatāya* (Eᵉ: *metteyyatāya*) *petteyyatāya sāmaññatāya brahmaññatāya kule jeṭṭhāpacāyitāya aññataraññataresu ca adhikusalesu dhammesu . . . so tato cuto itthattaṃ āgato samāno imaṃ mahāpurisalakkhaṇaṃ paṭilabhati: uṇhīsasīso hoti.* After describing the two destinies of someone who has the marks, the discourse repeats key aspects of the above prose passage in verse form, on the late nature of which see Warder 1967, 94 and Sv III 922,33.

441 An example is MN 89 at MN II 119,27 and its parallel MĀ 213 at T 1.26.795c13.

442 For example, Conze 1964, 226 comments on a particular section in the *Pañcaviṃśatisāhasrikā Prajñāpāramitā* that it "shows many similarities with the *Lakkhaṇasuttanta* of *Dīgha Nikāya*." For other relevant texts see Anālayo 2017a, 112n23 and 125–26.

443 Anālayo 2013c.

444 For a more detailed discussion see Anālayo 2010c, and 2014c, 129–36. Based on consulting a brief summary of this case in Anālayo 2011b, 885–86, Shulman 2021c,

154n8 argues that "the reference to an aspect of the path that is 'beyond the world' (*lokuttara*) could indeed be influenced by 'commentary,' but there is little left of the 'discourse' without it—the discourse itself is already an act of commentary, allowed within the flexible reality of text formation." The reference to a "flexible reality of text formation" appears to intend his theory that formulas were the primary building blocks out of which discourses were created. Yet, the exposition in the *Mahācattarīsakasutta* presents an analysis of the collaboration of the path factors that is unique to its exposition and not found elsewhere. This would therefore not fall under his definition of a formula, which stands for "units of textual articulation that repeat across texts, and that strictly maintain their form" (171).

Moreover, my brief summary comes with a footnote reference in Anālayo 2011b, 885n130 to the relevant part of my full study of this case on p. 660, where I explain: "According to the preamble found in all versions of the discourse, the main intent of the present exposition was to show the supportive function of the other seven path-factors for right concentration ... This intent of the exposition would not require a supramundane description of the path-factors." Consultation of my full study, found in the same publication, could have clarified the situation, something that could also have been achieved by consulting the discourse. Either way of following up would have shown that the situation is the opposite of the proposition that "there is little left of the 'discourse'" apart from the description of the supramundane path factors. Without this description, the main teaching conveyed by the *Mahācattarīsakasutta* is still intact and able to perform its function, as confirmed by its parallels, which achieve the same without bringing in any supramundane path factors.

445 Up 6080 at D 4094 *nyu* 44a2 or P 5595 *thu* 83b1: *yang dag pa'i ting nge 'dzin*, compared to MN 117 at MN III 71,16: *ariyo sammāsamādhi* and MĀ 189 at T 1.26.735c4: 聖正定.

446 For the case of the four "noble" truths see Anālayo 2006b and for other examples 2019b.

447 MĀ 189 at T 1.26.736b16 lists the four absorptions: 離欲, 離惡不善之法, 至得第四禪成就遊, whereas Up 6080 at D 4094 *nyu* 46b1 or P 5595 *thu* 86a5 gives a list of synonyms for concentration: *sems* (not in C and D; G, N, and P add *can*) *gnas pa dang, rab tu gnas pa dang, mngon par gnas pa dang, rang bzhin du gnas pa dang, mi g.yeng ba dang, yang dag par sdud pa dang, zhi gnas dang, ting nge 'dzin dang, sems rtse gcig pa ste*.

448 For the case of right intention, for example, MN 117 at MN III 73,13 reads: *ariyacittassa anāsavacittassa ariyamaggasamaṅgino ariyamaggaṃ bhāvayato takko vitakko saṅkappo appanā vyappanā cetaso abhiniropanā vacīsaṅkhāro* (E^e^: *vacāsaṃkhāro*).

449 The terms *appanā*, *vyappanā*, and *cetaso abhiniropanā*, found in the definition listed in the previous note, do not seem to recur at all in other discourses. The same terms feature in a definition of right intention in Dhs 63,21 and Vibh 106,28 (to be supplemented from Vibh 86,8). Notably, in the *Vibhaṅga* this is the definition of right intention according to the methodology of the Abhidharma, the *abhidhammabhājaniya*, which is preceded by covering the same topic from the viewpoint of the discourses, the *suttabhājaniya*. This confirms that this mode of definition carries a distinct Abhidharmic flavor.

450 See Anālayo 2012e, 77–78.

451 It seems to me that the two case studies presented here put into perspective an

assessment of the potential of comparing early discourse parallels by Gethin 2020b, 67 as follows: "The danger in such contexts is that scholarly judgements about what is earlier and later amount to little more than intuitions and preferences." His note 1 gives the impression that his study is particularly aimed at offering a contribution to the ongoing discussion on the path to awakening, mentioning the publications by La Vallée Poussin 1936/1937, Griffiths 1981, Schmithausen 1981, Cousins 1984, Vetter 1988, Bronkhorst 1993/2000, Zafiropulo 1993, and Wynne 2007. Nevertheless, the way the above statement is formulated reads as if it puts into question the potential of comparative studies in general, hence I feel a need to address it at least briefly.

Gethin 2020b, 66 supports his assessment with the example of his comparative study of the scheme of the path to awakening in MN 101 and MN 26 in the light of their respective parallels MĀ 19 and MĀ 204. In my own study of the first of these two cases (Anālayo 2011b, 589), I just mention the differences between MN 101 and MĀ 19, without drawing any conclusion as to what may be earlier or later. This often happens in comparative studies, in that it may seem best for differences to be simply acknowledged, although in the present case I could have followed the reasonable suggestion by Gombrich 1994, 1087 that the gradual path account in the Pāli version is probably "an irrelevant insertion of a stock passage." Turning to the second case, in Anālayo 2011b, 187 I drew attention to the possibility that the part of MN 26, which is without support from its parallel MĀ 204, could have been influenced by the same presentation found in the preceding discourse MN 25, in which case the passage in question fits the context better and receives support from its parallel MĀ 178. This suggestion is based on a feature attested elsewhere for the early discourses where, during the prolonged period of oral transmission, a particular text can influence another text that occurs in the same collection. I contend that the formulation of such a hypothesis on historical stages in textual development, in particular as long as it does not involve a quest for the original, is not just a matter of personal intuitions or preferences.

Gethin 2020b, 66 considers the possibility of various considerations influencing change, reasoning that "how such considerations relate to relative chronology is not straightforward: the literary and aesthetic do not necessarily coincide with the didactic and doctrinal, and either might override the other." Whatever may be the motivation, any change must have happened at some point in time, earlier or later. Envisaging different possible influences on the oral transmission does not prevent discerning between earlier and later elements in the resultant texts. In fact, immediately after the statement quoted at the outset of the present note, Gethin 2020b, 67 cautions: "This is, of course, not to deny that it is impossible (sic) to make any scholarly judgements about relative chronology." The intended sense of his caution would be "not to deny that it is *possible*." Note 135, appended to this statement, approvingly refers to Cousins 2018 who shows that in early Pāli texts the terms *thūpa* and *cetiya* convey more a sense of a "mound" and something "sacred," respectively, and only gradually come to stand for an actual *stūpa* in later Pāli texts. Once the possibility of discerning historical layers is granted for a close study of Pāli texts, such as the one provided by Cousins 2018, the same possibility needs to be granted in principle for comparative studies that involve non-Pāli texts.

452 SĀ 785 at T 2.99.203a19 and SĀ 789 at T 2.99.204c14; see in more detail Anālayo 2010c, 72–81.

453 For a survey of relevant research see Anālayo 2020b, 2721–22.

454 AN 5.50 at AN III 57,21.

455 *Mahāvaṃsa* 4.2, Geiger 1958, 21,5; see also Malalasekera 1938/1998, 641.

456 For a detailed discussion see Anālayo 2012c.

457 The present discussion only takes up selected problems from the presentation by Kuan and Bucknell 2019 and does not intend to offer an exhaustive survey of what appear to me to be unconvincing conclusions.

458 AN 1.1 at AN I 1,9 and EĀ 9.7–8 at T 2.125.563a14 have been recognized as parallels by Akanuma 1929/1990, 267.

459 The full reasoning in Kuan and Bucknell 2019, 160 takes the following form: "the number of suttas shared in common between the Ones of EĀ and the Ones of AN is nine . . . every one of those nine has earned its place in the Ones through having been subdivided. The coexistence of these two features (shared subdividing technique and shared content) in the Ones of EĀ and AN cannot reasonably be interpreted as indicating that they were already features of the ancestral EĀ/AN—for two reasons. First, the artificiality of the subdividing technique indicates that it is a late development. Second, no corresponding Book of Ones exists in $EĀ^2$, a fact that correlates well with the artificiality of the Ones in AN and the corresponding part of EĀ. It is likely, therefore, that the observed resemblances between the Ones of AN and EĀ are due to borrowing at some time after the two traditions had separated . . . The evidence indicates, therefore, that the ancestral AN/EĀ/$EĀ^2$ had nipātas running from the Twos to the Elevens."

The argument regarding $EĀ^2$ or T 150A concerns a text which in its reconstructed form contains forty-four short discourses arranged numerically (for the remarkable way in which this reconstruction has been achieved see Harrison 1997). This collection, which lacks discourses not only from the Ones but also from the Sixes, Sevens, Tens, and Elevens, appears to be an anthology. As noted by Allon 2021, 39, "the lack of sutras from the Ones in T 150a may very well have been due to it being an anthology, thus discrediting it as evidence."

Kuan and Bucknell 2019, 156 additionally reason that, as the collection "has only two suttas identifiable as belonging to nipātas above the Fives, one sutta for the Eights and one for the Nines, it appears that the second half of the text has been lost, with the exception of fragments containing just these two isolated suttas." It would be quite surprising if fragmentary remains should have succeeded in preserving two discourses completely intact but at the same time have completely lost without any trace anything else from the second half of the collection. Moreover, the suggested scenario would imply that the supposedly completely preserved first half of the collection had only forty-two short discourses. This is hardly a reasonable count for the first half of an entire *Ekottarikāgama*.

Given the early date of the translation, it is much more convincing to assume that an anthology was either created or translated for the purpose of propagating Buddhist thought at this early time in its history in China. This would also fit the title assigned to the collection as 雜經四十四篇, translated by Harrison 1997, 262 as "*Sūtra* Miscellany in 44 Sections." The title fits an anthology better than a full *Ekottarikāgama*, even if only partially preserved. In fact, just the possibility that the coverage of this text may reflect the choice of the compiler(s) already prevents drawing conclusions regarding the nature of divisions found in the complete numerical collections that are not reflected in EĀ² or T 150A.

The case of AN 1.1 and EĀ 9.7–8 exemplifies a recurrent mode of giving a teaching that involves "one" quality or item, resulting in sufficient material for the coming into existence of a section on Ones. When considered together with related modes of presentation, such as, for example, the listing of outstanding disciples (which of course are also single in regard to being foremost in a particular respect), there seems to be no need to consider the Ones as necessarily later (more "artificial") than the other sections in the numerical collections.

460 AN 1.1 at AN I 1,10 reads: *yaṃ evaṃ purisassa cittaṃ pariyādāya tiṭṭhati*, whereas AN 5.55 at AN III 68,9 reads: *evaṃ rajanīyaṃ evaṃ kamanīyaṃ evaṃ madanīyaṃ evaṃ bandhanīyaṃ evaṃ mucchanīyaṃ evaṃ antarāyakaraṃ anuttarassa yogakkhemassa adhigamāya*, followed by indicating *sattā rattā giddhā gadhitā* (Cᵉ: *gathitā*, occurring before *giddhā*) *mucchitā ajjhopannā* (Bᵉ: *ajjhosannā*), *te dīgharattaṃ socanti*, none of which is found in AN 1.1 (just as the idea of *cittaṃ pariyādāya tiṭṭhati* does not occur in AN 5.55).

461 AN 1.1 at AN I 1,9: *ekarūpam pi . . . ekasaddam pi . . . ekagandham pi . . . ekarasam pi . . . ekaphoṭṭhabbam pi*, a series first applied to the case of a female and then to that of a male.

462 EĀ 9.7 at T 2.125.563a14: 一法 and EĀ 9.8 at T 2.125.563a29: 一法.

463 Another argument by Schayer 1935, 127 is that "the extension of the term *dharma* to all elements . . . is an innovation of later scholastics," in contrast to the position supposedly taken by "precanonical Buddhism which actually divided the world into two opposite categories of *rūpa* and *dharma*." Yet, an instance of the famous dictum that "all dharmas are not self" explicitly refers to the five aggregates and thereby clearly comprises both the material and the immaterial; see SN 22.90 at SN III 132,26 and its parallel SĀ 262 at T 2.99.66b14.

464 For a more detailed discussion see Anālayo 2018b, 9–17.

465 The relevant quote occurs in SN 12.61 at SN II 94,21, which has parallels in Sanskrit fragments, Chung and Fukita 2020, 113,13, and Hoernle fragment Or. 15009/166v3, Melzer 2009, 209, as well as in SĀ 289 at T 2.99.81c11.

466 Schayer 1935, 131 mentions the simile of a person who "swings over a ditch by means of a rope hanging from a tree" and in a footnote gives reference to "Visuddhimagga p. 554, where this simile is interpreted in accordance with the theory of momentariness." Yet, for his argument to work, a simile found in a canonical work would be required.

467 SN 35.43 at SN IV 28,18.

468 SĀ 196 at T 2.99.50a25: 一切無常.

469 The reasoning by Schayer 1937, 16 that "the *ārūpya-dhātu* seems to correspond to the *anāgamin*" [sic] is a misunderstanding; these are two distinct concepts and the gaining of rebirth in the former does not require having reached any level of awakening. Problematic is also the idea that "descriptions of *mokṣa* in oldest records as *acyuta-pada, dhruva*, etc. . . . show clearly that deliverance was still conceived of by early Buddhism as a reaching of some 'immovable' place, excluding the possibility of returning, and not as a 'transcending' beyond the world; in other words as reaching of the *anāgamin*-state [sic], and not of the *arhant*-state." The Pāli phrase *accuta-pada* appears to occur only in the *Niddesa*s (e.g., Nidd I 343,6); the only relevant references to *dhuva* in a positive sense (as in most instances *dhuva* is rather being

rejected) seem to be SN 43.20 at SN IV 370,1, which has no counterpart in the parallel SĀ 890 at T 2.99.224b7, and It 43 at It 37,20, which does not appear to have a parallel in T 765 (the survey in Watanabe 1906, 46 suggests a relation to the twenty-fourth discourse in the section on the Twos, inspection of which does not give the impression that this is a case of parallelism).

470 See Anālayo 2021b for a critical examination of various theories proposed by scholars on the supposed lateness of one or the other of these four levels of realization. One of these scholars is Horner 1934, who instead argues for the earliness of the arahant/arhat but understood by her as involving a continuity of existence beyond death, combined with the assumption that *saṃsāra* was originally regarded by the earliest Buddhists in a positive light. This shows that proposing interpretations that do not reflect the textual sources particularly well was not unusual at that stage in the history of Buddhist studies.

471 Schayer 1935, 125 just indicates that in "various sources (Pali, Sanscrit, Tibetan and Chinese) we find the quotation of the Ṣaddhātu-Sūtra" (sic).

472 The discussion of the "Ṣaḍdhātusūtra" in Keith 1936, 5 comes with references to the "*Visuddhimagga*, pp 487f," just related to its stance on the topic in general (the relevant passage does not take the form of a discourse quotation) and the "*Abhidharmakośa*, I, 49ff," intending the volume and page of the translation by de La Vallée Poussin 1923/1971, which corresponds to *Abhidharmakośabhāṣya* I.28, Pradhan 1967, 18,9: *ṣaḍ dhātavaḥ uktāḥ*. In his note 2, de La Vallée Poussin 1923/1971, 49 relates this reference to MN 140. Versions of the passage under discussion occur in MN 140 at MN III 239,17, MĀ 162 at T 1.26.690b27, T 14.511.780a11, and Up 1041 at D 4094 *ju* 36a1 or P 5595 *tu* 39a5. The respective titles speak of "an analysis of the elements" (*dhātuvibhaṅga*), "an analysis of the six elements" (分別六界), "the five wishes of King Bimbisāra" (蓱沙王五願), and "a full analysis of the six elements" (*khams drug rab tu rnam par 'byed pa*). The discourse titles that do refer to the "elements" invariably combine this with a reference to their "analysis," so that none of the extant versions has a title that just mentions the "six elements," this being the title given by Schayer 1935, 125.

The same holds for a citation of the title of a Tibetan version of this discourse, quoted by Skilling 1997b, 34 as *khams drug gi rnam par dbye ba*, which also refers to an "analysis of the six elements." The actual discourse quotation in the *Abhidharmakośabhāṣya* I. 35, Pradhan 1967, 24,10, reading *ṣaḍdhātur ayaṃ bhikṣo puruṣa iti*, mentions the *Garbhāvakrānti[sūtra]* as its source; see also the *Abhidharmakośavyākhyā*, Wogihara 1932, 67,1. Yet another title can be found in the *Śikṣāsamuccaya*, Bendall 1902, 244,11: *tathā pitṛputrasamāgame darśitam, ṣaḍdhātur ayaṃ mahārāja puruṣaḥ ṣatsparśāyatanaḥ* (note the reference to the "Great King"). None of these quotations corresponds to the title given by Schayer 1935, 125.

473 Regamey 1957, 53: "le Ṣaḍdhātusūtra . . . dans ce texte, le *vijñāna*, énuméré à côté des éléments impermanents, est le seul à posséder la qualité d' éternité."

474 See Anālayo 2021e.

475 The type of reasoning involved can perhaps be exemplified with an argument advanced in support of the supposed antiquity of "Mahâyâna-sûtras" by Fujishima 1889, 54–55: "si ces derniers n'avaient pas existé auparavant, d'où les aurait-on tirés?"

476 The relevant Pāli passages are DN 9 at DN I 223,12, MN 49 at MN I 329,30, and AN 1.6.1–2 at AN I 10,10. Regarding the former two, Schayer 1935, 131 comments:

"*nirvāṇa* is described as absorption of four sensuous elements together with all distinctions and discriminations in the infinite consciousness, radiant on all sides." This does not do justice to the actual Pāli text, in line with an approach evident elsewhere of not giving appropriate attention to the actual textual evidence.

477 According to Lamotte 1958, 708, for example, "pour apprécier le bouddhisme primitif, le seul témoignage—ou indice—valable dont nous disposions est l'accord foncier entre *Nikāya* d'une part et *Āgama* de l'autre. Ce témoignage ou cet indice a plus de poids que des hypothèses savantes échafaudées à vingt-cinq siècles de distance." Bareau 1974, 280 reasons that "le Bouddhisme vécu et prêché par le Buddha et ses premiers disciples est donc bien, dans ses grandes lignes tout au moins, celui que nous trouvons décrit et enseigné dans les textes canoniques antiques qui nous sont parvenue en sanskrit, en pāli ou en traduction chinoise."

478 See Anālayo 2010a, 28–46 and 84–92; in relation to the latter discussion also Anālayo 2013b, 181–85.

479 MN 123 at MN III 122,33 and 123,19, with their counterparts in MĀ 32 at T 1.26.470b3+29.

480 *Saṅghabhedavastu*, Gnoli 1977, 40,4; for a Jain counterpart to this motif see Roth 1983, 182.

481 *Mahāvastu*, Marciniak 2020, 29,13 (= Senart 1890, 21,1); on the *Vinaya* nature of this text see Tournier 2012.

482 DN 26 at DN III 76,1 and DĀ 6 at T 1.1.41c29.

483 MĀ 70 at T 1.26.524b29.

484 See Anālayo 2010a, 95–113 and 2014d.

485 For the latter see, e.g., Huntington 1984, Inchang 1992, Filigenzi 1999, and Behrendt 2014.

486 Vism 713,6; see also Anālayo 2021e, 79.

487 MN 26 at MN I 167,34.

488 See Anālayo 2011a.

489 A comparison of the different extant versions in Anālayo 2011b, 183–84 enables proposing a general pattern of the exchange with Upaka, but it does not seem possible to take matters further. A reply to criticism of my study of this episode by von Hinüber 2019, 247n40 and Shulman 2021c, 212n39 can be found in Anālayo 2020f 33n9 and 2021g, 19–20 respectively.

490 See Norman 1984 and Anālayo 2006b, and for a comparative study of the first sermon Anālayo 2012b and 2013a.

491 See Allon 2020.

492 See Anālayo 2014b, 4–8.

493 For minor corrections to Levman 2019, 40–42 and von Hinüber 2019a, 253–55 see Anālayo 2019d, 92–95 and 2020f, 21–25 respectively. To these it could be added that Drewes 2017, 16 also overstates his case when asserting that "it is not clear that the tradition itself envisioned the Buddha as an actual person" and that the early discourses, "such as the *sutta*s of the Pali canon, say hardly anything about the Buddha's life, and identify him in only vague terms." The supposed vagueness, in the sense of an absence of references to his personal name, reflects a general feature of modes of address and is not specific to the case of the Buddha. For example, the Pāli *Vinaya* reports that Ānanda did not dare to pronounce Mahākassapa's name; see Vin I 92,37. This is not an instance of vagueness and does not imply that Mahākassapa is not envisioned as

an actual person. Instead, it reflects modes of address in use in the early texts. Another example is the Buddha's chief disciple Sāriputta, whom the discourses also do not refer to by his name Upatissa. Again, this does not imply that the texts do not consider him to be an actual person. Although the position taken by Drewes 2017, 16 is thus clearly unconvincing, at the same time it does serve to highlight the overall concern of the early textual sources with what the Buddha taught rather than with what he did as an individual, which concords with the assessment in note 66 above.

494 The starting point for the discussion is von Hinüber 2008; for further contributions see von Hinüber 2019b and Anālayo 2019g, 51–61.

495 The first complete Chinese *Āgama* translation published in English is the rendering by Ichimura 2015, 2016, and 2018 of the collection of long discourses (T 1). Unfortunately, this translation is highly unreliable. Besides a failure to consult relevant scholarship, combined with misunderstandings of the Chinese, the author tends to interpolate personal ideas (often mistaken) without marking these off as something that is not found in the original. As a result, someone unable to consult the Chinese original could be misled into a variety of erroneous conclusions; see in more detail Anālayo 2020c.

An English translation of the Chinese *Āgama* collection of medium-length discourses (T 26) has been completed, the first two volumes of which have been published in Bingenheimer, Anālayo, and Bucknell 2013 and Anālayo and Bucknell 2020. Although, due to being the only one in the editorial team without formal training in Sinology, my role was not to ensure the accuracy of the English translation, my involvement in the project nevertheless makes me feel confident that this translation will be a reliable reference for those unable to consult the Chinese original. Aside from small errors of the type that invariably happen when a text is translated for the first time, the translation of T 26 will not be marred by major misunderstandings and unmarked interpolations comparable to the case of the translation of T 1.

496 DN 27 at DN III 84,3: *nanu sujāto samaṇo gotamo, dujjāto 'ham asmi*; a reading found also in C^e and S^e and adopted by the translators Neumann 1912/2004, 478, Franke 1913a, 276, Rhys Davids and Rhys Davids 1921, 80, and Walshe 1987, 409.

497 DĀ 5 at T 1.1.37b23, T 1.10.218a20, MĀ 154 at T 1.26.674b8, Up 3104 at D 4094 *ju* 192a5 or P 5595 *tu* 219b1.

498 B^e reads: *na naṃ sujāto samaṇo gotamo, dujjāto 'ham asmi*.

499 For another case see Anālayo 2011b, 508n323 (also discussed in 2007e, 173n15 and 2016g, 51), in which case the less appropriate reading has been followed by Neumann 1896/1995, 672, Chalmers 1927, 60, and Horner 1957/1970, 298, as a result of which the ensuing passage in the Pāli discourse fails to make sense.

500 In a survey of the sources employed for this work, Bareau 1963, 9 states: "Nous avons aussi laissée de côté, après les avoir minutieusement étudiés cependant, deux importants ouvrages, le *Vinayapiṭaka* des Mūlasarvāstivādin et le *Catuṣpariṣatsūtra*," on the assumption that these "appartiennent clairement à une phase postérieure de l'évolution de la légende du Buddha." Closer inspection of his research gives the impression that these texts were not "minutieusement étudiés," as the information they offer provides important perspectives not taken into consideration in Bareau 1963. In fact, alongside later elements, these sources also contain much of relevance that appears to be quite early.

501 Anālayo 2012b, 31–33; see also Anālayo 2013a, 13–14.

502 A reference to the divine ear occurs also in the parallels T 1.6.187b15 and T 1.7.203c13 but not in the parallels DĀ 2 at T 1.1.25a14 and T 1.5.171c15.

503 Allon 2021, 112 makes a similar and in my view pertinent argument from silence regarding the unconvincing proposal that the early Buddhist oral tradition relied predominantly on improvisation based on fixed formulas, pointing out in reply that "we have no evidence of this, no handbook of formulas, no mention of monks learning formulas."

504 After surveying various such differences, Lenz 2003, 23 succinctly formulates the puzzling nature of his results in the query: "But why do the Dhp-G^{L} [Gāndhārī London *Dharmapada*] and the Dhp-G^{k} [Gāndhārī Khotan *Dharmapada*], which are apparently versions of essentially the same text, differ so widely in their presentation of individual verses?"

505 Early inscriptional references to a *bhāṇaka* has been found on the Bhilsa Topes, Sāñcī, Lüders 1973, 59 (no. 602), on Bhārhut pillar and rail inscriptions, p. 72 (no. 738), p. 75 (no. 762), p. 76 (no. 773), p. 79 (no. 789), p. 80 (no. 804), p. 84 (no. 833), and on Kārlā pillar inscriptions, p. 117 (nos. 1094 and 1095); for an Amarāvatī reference to a *saṃyuktakabhanaka* see Sivaramamurti 1942/1956, 279. Early Sri Lankan inscriptions refer to different *majhima-baṇakas*, Paranavitana 1970, 26 (no. 330), p. 53 (no. 708) and p. 66 (no. 852), as well as to a *śayutaka-baṇaka*, p. 50 (no. 666), an *eka-utirika-baṇaka*, p. 32 (no. 407), and also to a *sutata-pāḷi-bāṇaka*, p. 97 (no. 1202).

506 MĀ 165 at T 1.26.697c20: 實有; see in more detail Anālayo 2008d.

507 T 27.1545.393a24: 實有過去未來; see also Bareau 1955b, 137 and Cox 1995, 136–37, with further references in her notes, and a study of the impact of this notion in discourses extant in Tibetan by Dhammadinnā 2019, 8–14.

508 For the sense organs related to the present and the future, MĀ 165 at T 1.26.698a15+21 just employs 有, without 實.

509 An example is the attempt by McGovern 2019 to revive the proposal originally made by Cousins 1983; for critical replies see Anālayo 2020b: 2719–23 and Allon 2021, 109–13.

510 The difference could perhaps also be appreciated by comparing these two short videos: "The Tradition of Vedic Chanting," https://www.youtube.com/watch?v=qP-casmn0cRU, and "The Singer of Tales—Albert Lord—Kino—Avdo Mededovic," https://www.youtube.com/watch?v=jtx9w5U44Q4 (already noted in Shaw 2021, 254–55).

511 The problem of applying the findings by Parry and Lord to the early Buddhist case is therefore not merely one of using research done on verse for texts that are predominantly in prose, *pace* Cousins 2013, 99–100.

512 See the survey in Anālayo 2007c and for a study of similar features in Buddhist Sanskrit texts von Simson 1965.

References

Abeynayake, Oliver. 1984. *A Textual and Historical Analysis of the Khuddaka Nikāya*. Colombo: Tisara.

Adikaram, E. W. 1946/1994. *Early History of Buddhism in Ceylon, or "State of Buddhism in Ceylon as Revealed by the Pāli Commentaries of the 5th Century A.D."* Dehiwela, Sri Lanka: Buddhist Cultural Centre.

Akanuma Chizen. 1929/1990. *The Comparative Catalogue of Chinese Āgamas and Pāli Nikāyas*. Delhi: Sri Satguru.

———. 1930/1994. *A Dictionary of Buddhist Proper Names*. Delhi: Sri Satguru.

Allon, Mark. 1997a. "The Oral Composition and Transmission of Early Buddhist Texts." In *Indian Insights: Buddhism, Brahmanism and Bhakti*, edited by Peter Connolly and Sue Hamilton, 39–61. London: Luzac Oriental.

———. 1997b. *Style and Function: A Study of the Dominant Stylistic Features of the Prose Portions of Pāli Canonical Sutta Texts and Their Mnemonic Function*. Tokyo: International Institute for Buddhist Studies of the International College for Advanced Buddhist Studies.

———. 2001. *Three Gāndhārī Ekottarikāgama-Type Sūtras, British Library Kharoṣṭhī Fragments 12 and 14*. Seattle: University of Washington Press.

———. 2018. "The Formation of Canons in the Early Indian Nikāyas or Schools in the Light of the New Gāndhārī Fragment Finds." *Buddhist Studies Review*, 35: 223–42.

———. 2020. "A Gandhari Saṃyukta-āgama Version of the 'Discourse on Not-self' (Pali Anattalakkhaṇa-sutta, Sanskrit *Anātmalakṣaṇa-sūtra)." In *Research on the Saṃyukta-āgama*, edited by Bhikkhunī Dhammadinnā, 201–58. Taipei: Dharma Drum Corporation.

———. 2021. *The Composition and Transmission of Early Buddhist Texts with Specific Reference to Sutras*. Bochum: Projekt Verlag.

Allon, Mark and Blair Silverlock. 2017. "Sūtras in the Senior Kharoṣṭhī Manuscript Collection with Parallels in the Majjhima-nikāya and/or Madhyama-āgama." In *Research on the Madhyama-āgama*, edited by Bhikkhunī Dhammadinnā, 1–54. Taipei: Dharma Drum Publishing Corporation.

Alsdorf, Ludwig. 1963/1974. "The Ākhyāna Theory Reconsidered." In *Ludwig Alsdorf, Kleine Schriften*, edited by Albrecht Wezler, 36–48. Wiesbaden: Franz Steiner.

Anālayo, Bhikkhu. 2005a. "Some Pali Discourses in the Light of Their Chinese Parallels." *Buddhist Studies Review*, 22.1: 1–14.

———. 2005b. "Some Pali Discourses in the Light of Their Chinese Parallels, Part Two." *Buddhist Studies Review*, 22.2: 93–105.

———. 2006a. "The Chinese Version of the Dantabhūmi Sutta." *Buddhist Studies Review*, 23.1: 5–19 (reprinted in 2012d).

———. 2006b. "The Ekottarika-āgama Parallel to the Saccavibhaṅga-sutta and the Four (Noble) Truths." *Buddhist Studies Review*, 23.2: 145–53 (reprinted in 2016b).

———. 2007a. "The Arahant Ideal in Early Buddhism—The Case of Bakkula." *Indian International Journal of Buddhist Studies*, 8: 1–21 (reprinted in 2012d).

———. 2007b. "Comparative Notes on the Madhyama-āgama." *Fuyan Buddhist Studies*, 2: 33–56.

———. 2007c. "Oral Dimensions of Pāli Discourses: Pericopes, Other Mnemonic Techniques, and the Oral Performance Context." *Canadian Journal of Buddhist Studies*, 3: 5–33 (reprinted in 2017b).

———. 2007d. "Reflections on Comparative Āgama Studies." *Chung-Hwa Buddhist Journal*, 21: 3–21.

———. 2007e. "What the Buddha Would Not Do, According to the Bāhitika-sutta and Its Madhyama-āgama Parallel." *Journal of Buddhist Ethics*, 14: 153–79 (reprinted in 2012d).

———. 2007f. "Who Said It? Authorship Disagreements between Pāli and Chinese Discourses." In *Indica et Tibetica 65, Festschrift für Michael Hahn zum 65. Geburtstag von Freunden und Schülern überreicht*, edited by Konrad Klaus and Jens-Uwe Hartmann, 25–38. Wien: Arbeitskreis für tibetische und buddhistische Studien, Universität Wien.

———. 2008a. "The Chinese Madhyama-āgama and the Pāli Majjhima-nikāya: In the Footsteps of Thich Minh Chau." *Indian International Journal of Buddhist Studies*, 9: 1–21.

———. 2008b. "The Sixfold Purity of an Arahant, According to the Chabbisodhana-sutta and Its Parallel." *Journal of Buddhist Ethics*, 15: 241–77 (reprinted in 2012d).

———. 2008c. "Theories on the Foundation of the Nuns' Order—A Critical Evaluation." *Journal of the Centre for Buddhist Studies*, 6: 105–42.

———. 2008d. "The Verses on an Auspicious Night, Explained by Mahākaccāna—A Study and Translation of the Chinese Version." *Canadian Journal of Buddhist Studies*, 4: 5–27 (reprinted in 2012d).

———. 2009a. "The Development of the Pāli Udāna Collection." *Bukkyō Kenkyū*, 37: 39–72.

———. 2009b. "Karma and Liberation: The Karajakāya-sutta (AN 10.208) in the Light of Its Parallels." In *Pāsādikadānaṃ, Festschrift für Bhikkhu Pāsādika*, edited by Martin Straube, Roland Steiner, Jayandra Soni, Michael Hahn, and Mitsuyo Demoto, 1–24. Marburg: Indica et Tibetica (reprinted in 2012d).

———. 2009c. "Qualities of a True Recluse (Samaṇa)—According to the Samaṇamaṇḍikā-sutta and its Madhyama-āgama Parallel." *Journal of the Centre for Buddhist Studies*, 7: 153–84 (reprinted in 2012d).

———. 2009d. "Vimuttāyatana." In *Encyclopaedia of Buddhism, Volume 8*, edited by W. G. Weeraratne, 613–15. Sri Lanka: Department of Buddhist Affairs.

———. 2010a. *The Genesis of the Bodhisattva Ideal*. Hamburg: Hamburg University Press.

———. 2010b. "The Influence of Commentarial Exegesis on the Transmission of Āgama Literature." In *Translating Buddhist Chinese, Problems and Prospects*, edited by Konrad Meisig, 1–20. Wiesbaden: Harrassowitz.

———. 2010c. "The Mahācattārīsaka-sutta in the Light of Its Parallels—Tracing the Beginnings of Abhidharmic Thought." *Journal of the Centre for Buddhist Studies*, 8: 59–93 (reprinted in 2012d).

———. 2010d. "Once Again on Bakkula." *Indian International Journal of Buddhist Studies*, 11: 1–28 (in part reprinted in 2012d).

———. 2010e. "Structural Aspects of the Majjhima-nikāya." *Bukkyō Kenkyū*, 38: 35–70.

———. 2011a. "Brahmā's Invitation: The Ariyapariyesanā-sutta in the Light of Its Madhyama-āgama Parallel." *Journal of the Oxford Centre for Buddhist Studies*, 1: 12–38 (reprinted in 2012d).

———. 2011b. *A Comparative Study of the Majjhima-nikāya*. Taipei: Dharma Drum Publishing Corporation.

———. 2012a. "The Case of Sudinna: On the Function of Vinaya Narrative, Based on a Comparative Study of the Background Narration to the First Pārājika Rule." *Journal of Buddhist Ethics*, 19: 396–438 (reprinted in 2017f).

———. 2012b. "The Chinese Parallels to the Dhammacakkappavattana-sutta (1)." *Journal of the Oxford Centre for Buddhist Studies*, 3: 12–46 (reprinted in 2015e).

———. 2012c. "The Historical Value of the Pāli Discourses." *Indo-Iranian Journal*, 55: 223–53 (reprinted in 2017b).

———. 2012d. *Madhyama-āgama Studies*. Taipei: Dharma Drum Publishing Corporation.

———. 2012e. "Purification in Early Buddhist Discourse and Buddhist Ethics." *Bukkyō Kenkyū*, 40: 67–97 (in part reprinted in 2017f).

———. 2013a. "The Chinese Parallels to the Dhammacakkappavattana-sutta (2)." *Journal of the Oxford Centre for Buddhist Studies*, 5: 9–41 (reprinted in 2016b).

———. 2013b. "The Evolution of the Bodhisattva Concept in Early Buddhist Canonical Literature." In *The Bodhisattva Ideal, Essays on the Emergence of Mahāyāna*, edited by Bhikkhu Ñāṇatusita, 165–208. Kandy: Buddhist Publication Society.

———. 2013c. "Mahāyāna in the Ekottarika-āgama." *Singaporean Journal of Buddhist Studies*, 1: 5–43 (reprinted in 2016b).

———. 2013d. "A Note on the Term Theravāda." *Buddhist Studies Review*, 30.2: 216–35 (reprinted in 2016b).

———. 2013e. "Two Versions of the Mahādeva Tale in the Ekottarika-āgama: A Study in the Development of Taishō 125." In *Research on the*

Ekottarika-āgama (Taishō 125), edited by Bhikkhunī Dhammadinnā, 1–70. Taipei: Dharma Drum Publishing Corporation (reprinted in 2016b).

———. 2014a. "The Brahmajāla and the Early Buddhist Oral Tradition." *Annual Report of the International Research Institute for Advanced Buddhology at Soka University*, 17: 41–59 (reprinted in 2017b).

———. 2014b. "The Buddha's Last Meditation in the Dīrgha-āgama." *Indian International Journal of Buddhist Studies*, 15: 1–43.

———. 2014c. *The Dawn of Abhidharma*. Hamburg: Hamburg University Press.

———. 2014d. "Maitreya and the Wheel-Turning King." *Asian Literature and Translation: A Journal of Religion and Culture*, 2.7: 1–29 (reprinted in 2017b).

———. 2014e. "The Mass Suicide of Monks in Discourse and Vinaya Literature." *Journal of the Oxford Centre for Buddhist Studies*, 7: 11–55 (reprinted in 2017f).

———. 2014f. "Three Chinese Dīrgha-āgama Discourses without Parallels." In *Research on the Dīrgha-āgama*, edited by Bhikkhunī Dhammadinnā, 1–55. Taipei: Dharma Drum Publishing Corporation (reprinted in 2017b).

———. 2014/2015. "Discourse Merger in the Ekottarika-āgama (2): The Parallels to the Kakacūpama-sutta and the Alagaddūpama-sutta." *Journal of Buddhist Studies*, 12: 63–90 (reprinted in 2016b).

———. 2015a. "The Brahmajāla and the Early Buddhist Oral Tradition (2)." *Annual Report of the International Research Institute for Advanced Buddhology at Soka University*, 18: 79–94 (reprinted in 2017b).

———. 2015b. "The Buddha's Past Life as a Princess in the Ekottarika-āgama." *Journal of Buddhist Ethics*, 22: 95–137 (reprinted in 2016b).

———. 2015c. "Discourse Merger in the Ekottarika-āgama (1): The Parallel to the Bhaddāli-sutta and the Latukikopama-sutta, Together with Notes on the Chinese Translation of the Collection." *Singaporean Journal of Buddhist Studies*, 2: 5–35 (reprinted in 2016b).

———. 2015d. "The First Saṅgīti and Theravāda Monasticism." *Sri Lanka International Journal of Buddhist Studies*, 4: 2–17 (reprinted in 2017f).

———. 2015e. *Saṃyukta-āgama Studies.* Taipei: Dharma Drum Publishing Corporation.

———. 2016a. "Āgama and Aṅga in the Early Buddhist Oral Tradition." *Singaporean Journal of Buddhist Studies*, 3: 9–37 (reprinted in 2017b).

———. 2016b. *Ekottarika-āgama Studies.* Taipei: Dharma Drum Publishing Corporation.

———. 2016c. *The Foundation History of the Nuns' Order.* Bochum: Projektverlag.

———. 2016d. "The Gradual Path of Training in the Dīrgha-āgama, From Sense-Restraint to Imperturbability." *Indian International Journal of Buddhist Studies*, 17: 1–24.

———. 2016e. "The Legal Consequences of Pārājika." *Sri Lanka International Journal of Buddhist Studies*, 5: 1–22 (reprinted in 2017f).

———. 2016f. "Levitation in Early Buddhist Discourse." *Journal of the Oxford Centre for Buddhist Studies*, 10: 11–26.

———. 2016g. "Selected Madhyama-āgama Discourse Passages and Their Pāli Parallels." *Dharma Drum Journal of Buddhist Studies*, 19: 1–60.

———. 2016h. "The Vessantara-Jātaka and Mūlasarvāstivāda *Vinaya* Narrative." *Journal of the Oxford Centre for Buddhist Studies*, 11: 11–37.

———. 2017a. *Buddhapada and the Bodhisattva Path.* Bochum: Projektverlag.

———. 2017b. *Dīrgha-āgama Studies.* Taipei: Dharma Drum Publishing Corporation.

———. 2017c. *Early Buddhist Meditation Studies.* Barre, MA: Barre Center for Buddhist Studies.

———. 2017d. "The Luminous Mind in Theravāda and Dharmaguptaka Discourses." *Journal of the Oxford Centre for Buddhist Studies*, 13: 10–51.

———. 2017e. "The 'School Affiliation' of the Madhyama-āgama." In *Research on the Madhyama-āgama*, edited by Bhikkhunī Dhammadinnā, 55–76. Taipei: Dharma Drum Publishing Corporation.

———. 2017f. *Vinaya Studies.* Taipei: Dharma Drum Publishing Corporation.

———. 2018a. "Bhikṣuṇī Ordination." In *Oxford Handbook of Buddhist Ethics*, edited by Daniel Cozort and James Mark Shields, 116–34. Oxford: Oxford University Press.

———. 2018b. *Rebirth in Early Buddhism and Current Research*. Somerville, MA: Wisdom Publications.

———. 2019a. "Comparing the Tibetan and Chinese Parallels to the Cūḷavedalla-sutta." In *Investigating Principles: International Aspects of Buddhist Culture, Essays in Honour of Professor Charles Willemen*, edited by Lalji Shravak and Supriya Rai, 1–36. Hong Kong: The Buddha-Dharma Centre of Hong Kong.

———. 2019b. "Definitions of Right Concentration in Comparative Perspective." *Singaporean Journal of Buddhist Studies*, 5: 9–39.

———. 2019c. "On the Mahātaṇhāsaṅkhaya-sutta." *Indian International Journal of Buddhist Studies*, 20: 143–57.

———. 2019d. *Mindfully Facing Climate Change*. Barre, MA: Barre Center for Buddhist Studies.

———. 2019e. "Pārājika Does Not Necessarily Entail Expulsion." *Annual Report of the International Research Institute for Advanced Buddhology at Soka University*, 22: 3–8.

———. 2019f. "The Role of Mindfulness in the Cultivation of Absorption." *Mindfulness*, 10.11: 2341–51.

———. 2019g. "Women in Early Buddhism." *Journal of Buddhist Studies*, 16: 33–76.

———. 2020a. "A Brief History of Buddhist Absorption." *Mindfulness*, 11.3: 571–86.

———. 2020b. "Early Buddhist Oral Transmission and the Problem of Accurate Source Monitoring." *Mindfulness*, 11.12: 2715–24.

———. 2020c. "Ichimura Shohei: The Canonical Book of the Buddha's Lengthy Discourses." *Indian International Journal of Buddhist Studies*, 21: 159–70.

———. 2020d. "'Mūlasarvāstivādin and Sarvāstivādin': Oral Transmission Lineages of Āgama Texts." In *Research on the Saṃyukta-āgama*, edited by Bhikkhunī Dhammadinnā, 387–426. Taipei: Dharma Drum Corporation.

———. 2020e. "Peyāla in the Skandha-saṃyukta: Contraction and Expansion in Textual Transmission." In *Research on the Saṃyukta-āgama*, edited by Bhikkhunī Dhammadinnā, 53–108. Taipei: Dharma Drum Corporation.

———. 2020f. "The Tevijjavacchagotta-sutta and the Anupada-sutta in Relation to the Emergence of Abhidharma Thought." *Journal of Buddhist Studies*, 17: 21–33.

———. 2020/2022. "The Qualities Pertinent to Awakening: Bringing Mindfulness Home." *Mindfulness*, 13.

———. 2021a. "Abbreviation in the Madhyama-āgama." *Annual Report of the International Research Institute for Advanced Buddhology at Soka University*, 24: 23–38.

———. 2021b. "The Four Levels of Awakening." *Mindfulness*, 12.4: 831–40.

———. 2021c. "Dimensions of the 'Body' in Tranquility Meditation." *Mindfulness*, 12.10: 2388–93.

———. 2021d. "Overcoming Fear by Recollecting the Buddha: His Role in Early Buddhist Texts." *Mindfulness*, 12: 594–603.

———. 2021e. *Superiority Conceit in Buddhist Traditions: A Historical Perspective*. Somerville, MA: Wisdom Publications.

———. 2021f. "Understanding Early Buddhist Oral Narrative." In *Dharmayātrā: Felicitation Volume in Honour of Ven. Tampalawela Dhammaratana*, edited by François Chenet, Mahinda Deegalle, Malini Dias, Xiaoping Dong, Patricia Gaden, Siyan Jin, Godagama Mangala, Bhikkhu Pāsādika, Wei Shan, Siddharth Singh, Bhikkhuni Soun, Bangwei Wang, and François Wang-Toutain, 1–19. Paris: Éditions Nuvis.

———. 2021g. "Visions of the Buddha: A Critical Reply." *Journal of Buddhist Studies*, 18: 1–36.

———. 2022a. "Abbreviation in the Ekottarika-āgama." *Annual Report of the International Research Institute for Advanced Buddhology at Soka University*, 25.

———. 2022b. *Developments in Buddhist Meditation Traditions: The Interplay between Theory and Practice*. Barre, MA: Barre Center for Buddhist Studies.

Anālayo, Bhikkhu and Roderick S. Bucknell. 2020. *The Madhyama Āgama (Middle Length Discourses), Volume 2*. Berkeley: Numata Center for Buddhist Translation and Research.

Ānandajoti, Bhikkhu. 2020. *A Comparative Edition of the Dhammapada*. Published online at https://www.ancient-buddhist-texts.net/

Buddhist-Texts/C3-Comparative-Dhammapada/Comparative-Dhammapada.pdf.

Anderson, Richard C. and James W. Pichert. 1978. "Recall of Previously Unrecallable Information Following a Shift in Perspective." *Journal of Verbal Learning and Verbal Behaviour*, 17.1: 1–12.

Anesaki Masaharu. 1901. "Correspondence: Chinese Āgamas and Pāli Nikāyas." *Journal of the Royal Asiatic Society*, 895–900.

———. 1908. "The Four Buddhist Āgamas in Chinese: A Concordance of Their Parts and of the Corresponding Counterparts in the Pāli Nikāyas." *Transactions of the Asiatic Society of Japan*, 35.3: 1–149.

Anuruddha, Kākkāpalliye, M. M. Y. Fung, and S. K. Siu. 2008. *The First and Second Buddhist Councils: Five Versions: English Translations from Pāli and Chinese*. Hong Kong: Chi Lin Nunnery.

Appleton, Naomi. 2011. "Dhammapada and Dhammapada Commentary: The Story of the Verses." *Religions of South Asia*, 6.2: 245–56.

Baba Norihisa. 2004. "On Expressions Regarding 'Śūnya' or 'Śūnyatā' in the Northern Āgamas and the Pali Commentaries." *Journal of Indian and Buddhist Studies*, 52.2: 946–44.

———. 2005. "On the Order of the Compilation of the Abhidhammapiṭaka and the Khuddakanikāya." *Journal of Indian and Buddhist Studies*, 53.2: 994–91.

Bagchi, Prabodh Chandra. 1945. "The Story of Dhanika, the Potter's Son, as Told in the Different Vinayas." In *B. C. Law Volume, Part 1*, edited by D. R. Bhandarkar, K. A. N. Sastri, B. M. Barua, B. K. Gosh, and P. K. Gode, 419–35. Calcutta: Indian Research Institute.

Balk, Michael. 1984. *Prajñāvarman's Udānavargavivaraṇa: Transliteration of Its Tibetan Version*. Bonn: Indica et Tibetica.

Banerjee, Anukul Chandra. 1977. *Two Buddhist Vinaya Texts in Sanskrit: Prātimokṣa Sūtra and Bhikṣukarmavākya*. Calcutta: World Press.

Bapat, P. V. 1926. "The Different Strata in the Literary Material of the Dīgha Nikāya." *Annals of the Bhandarkar Institute*, 8: 1–16.

———. 1950. "The Arthapada-Sūtra Spoken by the Buddha." *Visva-Bharati Annals*, 3: 1–109.

Bartlett, Frederic C. 1932. *Remembering: A Study in Experimental and Social Psychology*. Cambridge: Cambridge University Press.

Barua, B. M. 1928. "Aṭṭhakavagga and Pārāyanavagga as Two Independent Buddhist Anthologies." In *Proceedings and Transactions of the Fourth Oriental Conference, Allahabad, Volume II*, 211–19. Allahabad: The Indian Press.

Barua, Dipak Kumara. 1971/2003. *An Analytical Study of Four Nikāyas*. Delhi: Munshiram Manoharlal.

Bareau, André. 1955a. *Les premiers conciles bouddhiques*. Paris: Presses Universitaires de France.

———. 1955b. *Les sectes bouddhiques du Petit Véhicule*. Paris: Publications de l'École Française d'Extrême-Orient.

———. 1963. *Recherches sur la biographie du Buddha dans les Sūtrapiṭaka et le Vinayapiṭaka anciens: De la quête de l'éveil à la conversion de Śāriputra et de Maudgalyāyana*. Paris: École Française d'Extrême-Orient.

———. 1974. "Le parinirvāṇa du Buddha et la naissance de la religion bouddhique." *Bulletin de l'École Française d'Extrême Orient*, 61: 275–99.

———. 1991. "Les agissements de Devadatta selon les chapitres relatifs au schisme dans les divers Vinayapiṭaka." *Bulletin de l'École Française d'Extrême Orient*, 78: 87–132.

Bechert, Heinz. 1992. "The Writing Down of the Tripiṭaka in Pāli." *Wiener Zeitschrift für die Kunde Südasiens*, 36: 45–53.

Bechert, Heinz and Klaus Wille. 1989. *Sanskrithandschriften aus den Turfanfunden, Teil 6*. Stuttgart: Franz Steiner.

———. 2004. *Sanskrithandschriften aus den Turfanfunden, Teil 9*. Stuttgart: Franz Steiner.

Beckh, Hermann. 1911. *Udānavarga, Eine Sammlung buddhistischer Sprüche in tibetischer Sprache, Nach dem Kanjur und Tanjur mit Anmerkungen herausgegeben*. Berlin: Reimer.

Behrendt, Kurt A. 2014. "Maitreya and the Past Buddhas: Interactions between Gandhāra and Northern India." In *South Asian Archaeology and Art, Papers from the 20th Conference of the European Association for South Asian Archaeology and Art Held in Vienna from 4th to 9th of July 2010*, edited by Deborah Klimburg-Salter and Linda Lojda, 29–40. Turnhout: Brepols.

Bendall, Cecil. 1902. *Çikshāsamuccaya: A Compendium of Buddhistic Teaching Compiled by Çāntideva, Chiefly from Earlier Mahāyāna-Sūtras*. St. Pétersbourg: Académie Impériale des Sciences.

Bernhard, Franz. 1965. *Udānavarga, Band 1*. Göttingen: Vandenhoeck & Ruprecht.

Bhagvat, Durga N. 1939. *Early Buddhist Jurisprudence (Theravāda Vinaya-Laws)*. Delhi: Cosmo Publications (undated reprint).

Bingenheimer, Marcus. 2011. *Studies in Āgama Literature, With Special Reference to the Shorter Chinese Saṃyuktāgama*. Taiwan: Shin Weng Feng Print Co.

———. 2020. "A Study and Translation of the Yakṣa-saṃyukta in the Shorter Chinese Saṃyukta-āgama." In *Research on the Saṃyukta-āgama*, edited by Bhikkhunī Dhammadinnā, 763–841. Taipei: Dharma Drum Corporation.

Bingenheimer, Marcus, Bhikkhu Anālayo, and Roderick S. Bucknell. 2013. *The Madhyama Āgama (Middle Length Discourses), Volume 1*. Berkeley: Numata Center for Buddhist Translation and Research.

Bloch, Jules. 1950. *Les inscriptions d'Asoka, Traduites et commentées*. Paris: Société d'Édition Les Belles Lettres.

Bodhi, Bhikkhu. 2005. *In the Buddha's Words: An Anthology of Discourses from the Pāli Canon*. Boston: Wisdom Publications.

Borgland, Jens Wilhelm. 2018. "Devadatta and the Extracurricular Ascetic Practices: Some Highlights from the Story of the First Buddhist Schism as Told in the Saṃghabhedavastu of the Mūlasarvāstivāda Vinaya." In *Reading Slowly, A Festschrift for Jens E. Braarvig*, edited by Lutz Edzard, Jens Wilhelm Borgland, and Ute Hüsken, 89–114. Wiesbaden: Harrassowitz.

Boucher, Daniel. 2005. "Review" [of Allon 2001]. *Indo-Iranian Journal*, 48: 289–95.

———. 2008. "Review" [of Glass 2007]. *Bulletin of the Asia Institute*, 18: 189–93.

Bronkhorst, Johannes. 1993/2000. *The Two Traditions of Meditation in Ancient India*. Delhi: Motilal Banarsidass.

———. 2016. *How the Brahmins Won: From Alexander to the Guptas*. Leiden: Brill.

Brough, John. 1962/2001. *The Gāndhārī Dharmapada: Edited with an Introduction and Commentary*. Delhi: Motilal Banarsidass.

Bucknell, Roderick S. 1984. "The Buddhist Path to Liberation: An Analysis of the Listing of Stages." *Journal of the International Association of Buddhist Studies*, 7.2: 7–40.

———. 2014. "The Structure of the Sanskrit Dīrgha-āgama from Gilgit vis-à-vis the Pali Dīgha-nikāya." In *Research on the Dīrgha-āgama*, edited by Bhikkhunī Dhammadinnā, 57–101. Taipei: Dharma Drum Publishing Corporation.

———. 2017. "Ekottarika-Type Material in the Madhyama-āgama." In *Research on the Madhyama-āgama*, edited by Bhikkhunī Dhammadinnā, 77–112. Taipei: Dharma Drum Publishing Corporation.

Caillies, Stéphanie, Guy Denhière, and Walter Kintsch. 2002. "The Effect of Prior Knowledge on Understanding from Text: Evidence from Primed Recognition." *European Journal of Cognitive Psychology*, 14: 267–86.

Caland, W. 1931. "A Rhythmic Law in Language." *Acta Orientalia*, 9: 59–68.

Carpenter, David. 1992. "Ritual and Society: Reflections on the Authority of the Veda in India." *Journal of the American Academy of Religion*, 60.1: 57–77.

Chakravarti, Uma. 1996. *The Social Dimensions of Early Buddhism*. Delhi: Munshiram Manoharlal.

Chalmers, Robert. 1927. *Further Dialogues of the Buddha: Translated from the Pali of the Majjhima Nikāya, Vol. II*. London: Oxford University Press.

Ch'en Kenneth. 1958. "The Mahāparinirvāṇasūtra and the First Council." *Harvard Journal of Asiatic Studies*, 21: 128–33.

Choong Mun-keat. 2020. "Ācāriya Buddhaghosa and Master Yinshun 印順 on the Three-aṅga Structure of Early Buddhist Texts." In *Research on the Saṃyukta-āgama*, edited by Bhikkhunī Dhammadinnā, 883–931. Taipei: Dharma Drum Corporation.

Chung Jin-il. 2008. *A Survey of the Sanskrit Fragments Corresponding to the Chinese Saṃyuktāgama*. Tokyo: Sankibo.

Chung Jin-il and Fukita Takamichi. 2011. *A Survey of the Sanskrit Fragments Corresponding to the Chinese Madhyamāgama: Including References to Sanskrit Parallels, Citations, Numerical Categories of Doctrinal Concepts and Stock Phrases*. Tokyo: Sankibo Press.

———. 2020. *A New Edition of the First 25 Sūtras of the Nidānasaṃyukta*. Tokyo: Sankibo Press.

Clarke, Shayne. 2009. "Monks Who Have Sex: Pārājika Penance in Indian Buddhist Monasticism." *Journal of Indian Philosophy*, 37: 1–43.

———. 2014. *Family Matters in Indian Buddhist Monasticism*. Honolulu: University of Hawai'i Press.

———. 2015. "Vinayas." In *Brill's Encyclopedia of Buddhism, Volume I, Literature and Languages*, edited by Jonathan A. Silk, Oskar von Hinüber, and Vincent Eltschinger, 60–87. Leiden: Brill.

Collins, Steven. 1990. "On the Very Idea of the Pali Canon." *Journal of the Pali Text Society*, 15: 89–126.

———. 1992. "Notes on Some Oral Aspects of Pali Literature." *Indo-Iranian Journal*, 35: 121–35.

Cone, Margaret. 1989. "Patna Dharmapada." *Journal of the Pali Text Society*, 13: 101–217.

Conze, Edward. 1964. "The Buddha's Lakṣaṇas in the Prajñāpāramita." *Journal of the Oriental Institute, Baroda*, 14: 225–29.

Cousins, L. S. 1983. "Pali Oral Literature." In *Buddhist Studies: Ancient and Modern*, edited by Philip Denwood and Alexander Piatigorsky, 1–11. London: Curzon.

———. 1984. "Samatha-yāna and Vipassanā-yāna." In *Buddhist Studies in Honour of Hammalava Saddhātissa*, edited by G. Dhammapāla, Richard Gombrich, and K. R. Norman, 56–68. Nugegoda: University of Jayewardenapura.

———. 2013. "The Early Development of Buddhist Literature and Language in India." *Journal of the Oxford Centre for Buddhist Studies*, 5: 89–135.

———. 2018. "Cetiya and Thūpa: The Textual Sources." In *Relics and Relic Worship in Early Buddhism: India, Afghanistan, Sri Lanka and*

Burma, edited by Janice Stargard and Michael D. Willis, 18–39. London: The British Museum.

Coward, Harold. 1986. "Oral and Written Texts in Buddhism." *The Adyar Library Bulletin*, 50: 299–313.

———. 1988. *Sacred Word and Sacred Text, Scripture in World Religions*. New York: Orbis.

Cowell, E. B. and R. A. Neil. 1886. *The Divyāvadāna: A Collection of Early Buddhist Legends, Now First Edited from the Nepalese Sanskrit Mss. in Cambridge and Paris*. Cambridge: Cambridge University Press.

Cox, Collett. 1995. *Disputed Dharmas: Early Buddhist Theories on Existence: An Annotated Translation of the Section on Factors Dissociated from Thought from Saṅghabhadra's Nyāyānusāra*. Tokyo: International Institute for Buddhist Studies.

———. 2004. "Abhidharma." In *Encyclopedia of Buddhism*, edited by Robert E. Buswell, 1–7. New York: Macmillan.

Crangle, Edward Fitzpatrick. 1994. *The Origin and Development of Early Indian Contemplative Practices*. Wiesbaden: Harrassowitz Verlag.

Cutler, Norman. 1992. "Interpreting Tirukkural: The Role of Commentary in the Creation of a Text." *Journal of the American Oriental Society*, 112.4: 549–66.

Dalai Lama, H. H. 2010. "Human Rights and the Status of Women in Buddhism." In *Dignity and Discipline, Reviving Full Ordination for Buddhist Nuns,* edited by Thea Mohr and Jampa Tsedroen, 253–79. Somerville, MA: Wisdom Publications.

Davidson, Ronald M. 1990/1992. "An Introduction to the Standards of Scriptural Authenticity in Indian Buddhism." In *Chinese Buddhist Apocrypha*, edited by Robert E. Buswell, 291–325. Delhi: Sri Satguru.

Deeg, Max. 1999. "The Saṅgha of Devadatta: Fiction and History of a Heresy in the Buddhist Tradition." *Journal of the International College for Advanced Buddhist Studies*, 2: 183–218.

de La Vallée Poussin, Louis. 1923/1971. *L'Abhidharmakośa de Vasubandhu, Traduction et annotations, Nouvelle édition anastatique présentée par Étienne Lamotte, Tome I*. Bruxelles: Institut Belge des Hautes Études Chinoises.

———. 1936/1937. "Musīla et Nārada: le chemin du nirvāṇa." *Mélanges Chinois et Bouddhiques*, 5: 189–222.

———. 1976. *The Buddhist Councils*. Calcutta: Bagchi.

Demoto Mitsuyo. 2016. "Fragments of the Itivṛttaka." In *Buddhist Manuscripts, Volume IV (Manuscripts in the Schøyen Collection)*, edited by Jens Braarvig, 123–50. Oslo: Hermes.

de Jong, Jan Willem. 1968. *Buddha's Word in China*. Canberra: Australian National University.

———. 1974/1979. "À propos du Nidānasaṃyukta." In *Buddhist Studies (by J. W. de Jong)*, edited by Gregory Schopen, 237–49. Berkeley: Asian Humanities Press.

———. 1993. "The Beginnings of Buddhism." *The Eastern Buddhist*, 26.2: 11–30.

———. 2000. "The Buddha and His Teachings." In *Wisdom, Compassion, and the Search for Understanding: The Buddhist Studies Legacy of Gadjin M. Nagao*, edited by Jonathan A. Silk, 171–81. Honolulu: University of Hawai'i Press.

De Notariis, Bryan. 2021. "Rejoinder to Ven. Anālayo and a Short List of Corrigenda." *Annali di Ca' Foscari, Serie Orientale*, 57: 9–16.

de Silva, Lily. 1990. "Giving in the Pali Canon." In *Dāna: The Practice of Giving*, edited by Bhikkhu Bodhi, 19–38. Kandy: Buddhist Publication Society.

Deutsch, Eliot. 1988. "Knowledge and the Tradition Text in Indian Philosophy." In *Interpreting across Boundaries: New Essays in Comparative Philosophy*, edited by Gerald James Larson and Eliot Deutsch, 165–73. Princeton: Princeton University Press.

Dhammadinnā, Bhikkhunī. 2014. "Semantics of Wholesomeness: Purification of Intention and the Soteriological Function of the Immeasurables (Appamāṇas) in Early Buddhist Thought." In *Buddhist Meditative Traditions: Their Origin and Development*, edited by Chuang Kuo-pin, 51–129. Taipei: Shin Wen Feng Print.

———. 2019. "Co-textuality of Sūtra and Early Abhidharma in the Abhidharmakośopāyikā-ṭīkā's Discourse Quotations." *Journal of Buddhist Studies*, 16: 1–32.

———. 2020. "Highlights from a Comparative Study of the Saṃyukta-āgama Sūtra Quotations in the Abhidharmakośopāyikā-ṭīkā." In *Research on the Saṃyukta-āgama*, edited by Bhikkhunī Dhammadinnā, 481–589. Taipei: Dharma Drum Publishing Corporation.

Dhammajoti, Bhikkhu K. L. 1995. *The Chinese Version of Dharmapada: Translated with Introduction and Annotations*. Sri Lanka: University of Kelaniya, Postgraduate Institute of Pali and Buddhist Studies.

Dhirasekera, Jotiya. 1957. "Buddhaghosa and the Tradition of the First Council." *University of Ceylon Review*, 15.3/4: 167–81.

———. 1982/2007. *Buddhist Monastic Discipline, A Study of Its Origin and Development in Relation to the Sutta and Vinaya Piṭakas*. Dehiwala: Buddhist Cultural Centre.

DiSimone, Charles. 2020. *Faith in the Teacher: The Prāsādika and Prasādanīya Sūtras from the (Mūla-)Sarvāstivāda Dīrghāgama Manuscript, A Synoptic Critical Edition, Translation, and Textual Analysis*. PhD thesis (revised). München: Ludwig-Maximilians-Universität.

Drewes, David. 2017. "The Idea of the Historical Buddha." *Journal of the International Association of Buddhist Studies*, 40: 1–25.

Durt, Hubert. 1980. "Mahalla/Mahallaka et la crise de la Communauté après le parinirvāṇa du Bouddha." In *Indianisme et Bouddhisme, Mélanges offerts à Mgr. Étienne Lamotte*, 79–99. Louvain-la-Neuve: Institut Orientaliste.

Dutt, Sukumar. 1924/1996. *Early Buddhist Monachism*. Delhi: Munshiram Manoharlal.

———. 1957. *The Buddha and Five After-Centuries*. London: Luzac.

Eimer, Helmut. 1976. *Skizzen des Erlösungsweges in buddhistischen Begriffsreihen*. Bonn: Religionswissenschaftliches Seminar der Universität Bonn.

Eltschinger, Vincent. 2020. "Aśvaghoṣa and His Canonical Sources: 4. On the Authority and the Authenticity of the Buddhist Scriptures." In *Archaeologies of the Written: Indian, Tibetan, and Buddhist Studies in Honour of Cristina Scherrer-Schaub*, edited by Vincent Tournier, Vincent Eltschinger, and Marta Sernesi, 127–69. Naples: Unior Press.

Endo Toshiichi. 1997/2002. *Buddha in Theravada Buddhism: A Study of the Concept of Buddha in the Pali Commentaries*. Sri Lanka, Dehiwela: Buddhist Cultural Centre.

———. 2003a. "Selective Tendency in the Buddhist Textual Tradition?" *Journal of the Centre for Buddhist Studies, Sri Lanka*, 1: 55–72 (reprinted in Endo 2013).

———. 2003b. "Views Attributed to Different Bhāṇakā (Reciters) in the Pāli Commentaries." *Buddhist Studies*, 31: 1–42 (reprinted in Endo 2013).

———. 2012. "Transformation of Buddhism in Sri Lanka: Sri Lanka's Contribution to the Buddha-Concept in the Pāli Commentaries." *Journal of the Centre for Buddhist Studies*, 10: 33–48.

———. 2013. *Studies in Pāli Commentarial Literature: Sources, Controversies and Insights*. Hong Kong: Centre of Buddhist Studies, University of Hong Kong.

Falk, Harry. 2011. "The 'Split' Collection of Karoṣṭhī Texts." *Annual Report of the International Research Institute for Advanced Buddhology at Soka University*, 14: 13–23.

Falk, Harry and Ingo Strauch. 2014. "The Bajaur and Split Collections of Kharoṣṭhī Manuscripts within the Context of Buddhist Gāndhārī Literature." In *From Birch Bark to Digital Data: Recent Advances in Buddhist Manuscript Research*, edited by Paul Harrison and Jens-Uwe Hartmann, 51–78. Wien: Verlag der Österreichischen Akademie der Wissenschaften.

Filigenzi, Anna. 1999. *Il Bodhisattva Maitreya nell'arte rupestre dello Swat, Appunti sull'iconografia e sul culto del Buddha Venturo*. Rome: Istituto Italiano per l'Africa e l'Oriente.

Finot, Louis. 1932. "Mahāparinibbānasutta and Cullavagga." *Indian Historical Quarterly*, 8: 241–46.

Franke, R. Otto. 1908. "The Buddhist Councils at Rājagaha and Vesālī, as Alleged in Cullavagga XI., XII." *Journal of the Pali Text Society*, 6: 1–80.

———. 1913a. *Dīghanikāya, Das Buch der langen Texte des buddhistischen Kanons, In Auswahl übersetzt*. Göttingen: Vandenhoeck & Ruprecht.

———. 1913b. "Die Verknüpfung der Dīghanikāya-Suttas untereinander." *Zeitschrift der Deutschen Morgenländischen Gesellschaft*, 67: 409–61.

———. 1914. "Die Zusammenhänge der Majjhimanikāya-suttas." *Zeitschrift der Deutschen Morgenländischen Gesellschaft*, 68: 473–530.

———. 1917. "Die Buddhalehre in ihrer erreichbar-ältesten Gestalt (im Dīghanikāya)." *Zeitschrift der Deutschen Morgenländischen Gesellschaft*, 71: 50–98.

Frauwallner, Erich. 1952. "Die Buddhistischen Konzile." *Zeitschrift der Deutschen Morgenländischen Gesellschaft*, 102: 240–61.

———. 1956. *The Earliest Vinaya and the Beginnings of Buddhist Literature*. Rome: Istituto Italiano per il Medio ed Estremo Oriente.

Freiberger, Oliver. 2000. *Der Orden in der Lehre, Zur religiösen Deutung des Saṅgha im frühen Buddhismus*. Wiesbaden: Harrassowitz.

———. 2011. "Was ist das Kanonische am Pāli-Kanon?" In *Kanonisierung und Kanonbildung in der asiatischen Religionsgeschichte*, edited by Max Deeg, Oliver Freiberger, and Christoph Kleine, 209–32. Wien: Verlag der Österreichischen Akademie der Wissenschaften.

Fujishima Ryauon. 1889. *Le Bouddhisme Japonais, Doctrines et histoire des douze grandes sectes bouddhiques du Japon*. Paris: Maisonneuve et Ch. Leclerc.

Funayama Tōru. 2006. "Masquerading as Translation: Examples of Chinese Lectures by Indian Scholar-monks in the Six Dynasties Period." *Asia Major*, 19.1/2: 39–55.

Gaffney, Sean. 1996. "The Pāli Nidānakathā and Its Tibetan Translation: Its Textual Precursors and Associated Literature." In *The Buddhist Forum, Volume IV, Seminar Papers 1994–1996*, edited by Tadeusz Skorupski, 75–91. London: School of Oriental and African Studies.

Geiger, Wilhelm. 1958. *The Mahāvaṃsa*. London: Pali Text Society.

Geng, Shimin and Hans-Joachim Klimkeit. 1988. *Das Zusammentreffen mit Maitreya, Die ersten fünf Kapitel der Hami-Version der Maitrisimit*. Wiesbaden: Otto Harrassowitz.

Gethin, Rupert. 2007. "What's in a Repetition? On Counting the Suttas of the Saṃyutta-nikāya." *Journal of the Pali Text Society*, 29: 365–87.

———. 2014. "Keeping the Buddha's Rules: The View from the Sūtra Piṭaka." In *Buddhism and Law, An Introduction*, edited by Rebecca Redwood French and Mark A. Nathan, 63–77. New York: Cambridge University Press.

———. 2020a. "Reading Repetitions in the Saṃyutta-nikāya and Early Abhidhamma: From the Mahā-vagga to the Dhammasaṅgani." In *Research on the Saṃyukta-āgama*, edited by Bhikkhunī Dhammadinnā, 109–69. Taipei: Dharma Drum Corporation.

———. 2020b. "Schemes of the Buddhist Path in the Nikāyas and Āgamas." In *Mārga, Paths to Liberation in South Asian Buddhist Traditions*, edited by Cristina Pecchia and Vincent Eltschinger, 5–77. Wien: Österreichische Akademie der Wissenschaften.

Glass, Andrew. 2007. *Four Gāndhārī Saṃyuktāgama Sūtras: Senior Kharoṣṭhī Fragment 5*. Seattle: University of Washington Press.

———. 2010. "Guṇabhadra, Bǎoyún, and the Saṃyuktāgama." *Journal of the International Association of Buddhist Studies*, 31.1/2: 185–203.

Gnoli, Raniero. 1977. *The Gilgit Manuscript of the Saṅghabhedavastu: Being the 17th and Last Section of the Vinaya of the Mūlasarvāstivādin, Part I.* Rome: Istituto Italiano per il Medio ed Estremo Oriente.

———. 1978. *The Gilgit Manuscript of the Saṅghabhedavastu: Being the 17th and Last Section of the Vinaya of the Mūlasarvāstivādin, Part II.* Rome: Istituto Italiano per il Medio ed Estremo Oriente.

Goff, Lyn M. and Henry L. Roediger. 1998. "Imagination Inflation for Action Events: Repeated Imaginings Lead to Illusory Recollections." *Memory & Cognition*, 26.1: 20–33.

Gombrich, Richard F. 1988. *Theravāda Buddhism: A Social History from Ancient Benares to Modern Colombo*. London: Routledge & Kegan Paul.

———. 1990. "How the Mahāyāna Began." *The Buddhist Forum*, 1: 21–30.

———. 1991. "Pātimokkha: Purgative." In *Studies in Buddhism and Culture, In Honour of Professor Dr. Egaku Mayeda on His Sixty-Fifth Birthday*, edited by the Editorial Committee of the Felicitation Volume for Professor Dr. Egaku Mayeda, 31–38. Tokyo: Sankibo Busshorin.

———. 1994. "The Buddha and the Jains: A Reply to Professor Bronkhorst." *Asiatische Studien*, 48: 1069–96.

Goonesekera, Lakshmi R. 1967. "Aṭṭhakathā." In *Encyclopaedia of Buddhism*, edited by G. P. Malalasekera, 2.2: 335–52. Sri Lanka: Department of Buddhist Affairs.

———. 1968. "*Bhāṇaka*." In *Encyclopaedia of Buddhism*, edited by G. P. Malalasekera, 2.4: 688–90. Sri Lanka: Department of Buddhist Affairs.

Griffiths, Paul J. 1981. "Concentration or Insight: The Problematic of Theravāda Buddhist Meditation-Theory." *Journal of the American Academy of Religion*, 49.4: 605–24.

———. 1983. "Buddhist Jhāna: A Form-Critical Study." *Religion*, 13: 55–68.

Harrison, Paul. 1997. "The Ekottarikāgama Translations of An Shigao." In *Bauddhavidyāsudhākaraḥ: Studies in Honour of Heinz Bechert on the Occasion of His 65th Birthday*, edited by Petra Kieffer-Pülz and Jens-Uwe Hartmann, 261–84. Swisstal-Odendorf: Indica et Tibetica.

———. 2002. "Another Addition to the An Shigao Corpus? Preliminary Notes on an Early Chinese Saṃyuktāgama Translation." In *Early Buddhism and Abhidharma Thought: In Honor of Doctor Hajime Sakurabe on His Seventy-Seventh Birthday*, edited by the Sakurabe Ronshu Committee, 1–32. Kyoto: Heirakuji shoten.

Hartmann, Jens-Uwe. 1994. "Der Ṣaṭsūtraka-Abschnitt des in Ostturkestan überlieferten Dīrghāgama." *Zeitschrift der Deutschen Morgenländischen Gesellschaft*, 25.10: 324–34.

———. 2002. "Further Remarks on the New Manuscript of the Dīrghāgama." *Journal of the International College for Advanced Buddhist Studies*, 5: 133–50.

———. 2004. "Contents and Structure of the Dīrghāgama of the (Mūla-) Sarvāstivādins." *Annual Report of the International Research Institute for Advanced Buddhology at Soka University*, 7: 119–37.

Hartmann, Jens-Uwe and Klaus Wille. 1992. "Die nordturkestanischen Sanskrit-Handschriften der Sammlung Hoernle (Funde buddhistischer Sanskrit-Handschriften, II)." In *Sanskrit-Texte aus dem Buddhistischen Kanon: Neuentdeckungen und Neueditionen, Zweite Folge*, 9–63. Göttingen: Vandenhoeck & Ruprecht.

———. 2014. "The Manuscript of the Dīrghāgama and the Private Collection in Virginia." In *From Birch Bark to Digital Data: Recent*

Advances in Buddhist Manuscript Research, edited by Paul Harrison and Jens-Uwe Hartmann, 137–55. Wien: Verlag der Österreichischen Akademie der Wissenschaften.

Hirabayashi Jiro. 2009. "The Sanskrit Fragments Or. 15009/91–100 in the Hoernle Collection." In *Buddhist Manuscripts from Central Asia: The British Library Sanskrit Fragments*, edited by Seishi Karashima and Klaus Wille, 160–68. Tokyo: International Research Institute for Advanced Buddhology, Soka University.

Hirakawa Akira. 1993/1998. *A History of Indian Buddhism: From Śākyamuni to Early Mahāyāna*, translated by P. Groner. Delhi: Motilal Banarsidass.

Hiraoka Satoshi. 2013. "The School Affiliation of the Ekottarika-āgama." In *Research on the Ekottarika-āgama (Taishō 125)*, edited by Bhikkhunī Dhammadinnā, 71–105. Taipei: Dharma Drum Publishing Corporation.

Hoernle, A. F. Rudolf. 1916. "The Sutta Nipāta in a Sanskrit Version from Eastern Turkestan." *Journal of the Royal Asiatic Society*, 709–32.

Honjō Yoshifumi. 1984. *A Table of Āgama Citations in the Abhidharmakośa and the Abhidharmakośopāyikā*. Kyoto.

Horner, I. B. 1934. "The Four Ways and the Four Fruits in Pāli Buddhism." *Indian Historical Quarterly*, 785–96.

———. 1941. "Abhidhamma Abhivinaya (In the First Two Piṭakas of the Pali Canon)." *Indian Historical Quarterly*, 17.3: 291–310.

———. 1957/1970. *The Collection of the Middle Length Sayings (Majjhima-Nikāya), Vol. II, The Middle Fifty Discourses*. London: Pali Text Society.

———. 1959. *The Collection of the Middle Length Sayings (Majjhima-Nikāya), Vol. III, The Final Fifty Discourses (Uparipaṇṇāsa)*. London: Pali Text Society.

Huntington, John C. 1984. "The Iconography and Iconology of Maitreya Images in Gandhara." *Journal of Central Asia*, 7.1: 133–78.

Hu-von Hinüber, Haiyan. 1994. *Das Poṣadhavastu, Vorschriften für die buddhistische Beichtfeier im Vinaya der Mūlasarvāstivādins*. Reinbek: Dr. Inge Wezler Verlag für Orientalistische Fachpublikationen.

Huxley, Andrew. 1999. "Buddhist Case Law on Theft: The Vinītavatthu on the Second pārājika." *Journal of Buddhist Ethics*, 6: 313–30.

Ichimura Shohei. 2015. *The Canonical Book of the Buddha's Lengthy Discourses, Volume I*. Berkeley: Bukkyo Dendo Kyokai America.

———. 2016. *The Canonical Book of the Buddha's Lengthy Discourses, Volume II*. Berkeley: Bukkyo Dendo Kyokai America.

———. 2018. *The Canonical Book of the Buddha's Lengthy Discourses, Volume III*. Berkeley: Bukkyo Dendo Kyokai America.

Inchang Kim. 1992. *The Future Buddha Maitreya: An Iconological Study*. Delhi: D. K. Printworld Ltd.

Jantrasrisalai, Chanida, Timothy Lenz, Lin Qian, and Richard Salomon. 2016. "Fragments of an Ekottarikāgama Manuscript in Gāndhārī." In *Manuscripts in the Schøyen Collection, Buddhist Manuscripts, Volume IV*, edited by J. Braarvig, 1–122, Oslo: Hermes Publishing.

Jayawickrama, N. A. 1948. "A Critical Analysis of the Sutta Nipāta: The Vaggas of the Sutta Nipāta." *University of Ceylon Review*, 6: 229–57.

———. 1959. "Buddhaghosa and the Traditional Classifications of the Pāli Canon." *University of Ceylon Review*, 17.1/2: 1–17.

Jing Yin. 2009. "Devadatta's Personality and the Schism." In *Buddhist and Pali Studies in Honour of the Venerable Professor Kakkapalliye Anuruddha*, edited by K. L. Dhammajoti and Y. Karunadasa, 369–92. Hong Kong: Centre of Buddhist Studies, University of Hong Kong.

Kalupahana, David J. 1965. "Aṅga." In *Encyclopaedia of Buddhism*, edited by G. P. Malalasekera, 1.4: 616–19. Sri Lanka: Department of Buddhist Affairs.

Karashima Seishi. 2020. "The Underlying Languages of the Three Chinese Translations of the Saṃyukta-āgamas (Taishō nos. 99, 100, 101) and Their School Affiliations." In *Research on the Saṃyukta-āgama*, edited by Bhikkhunī Dhammadinnā, 707–61. Taipei: Dharma Drum Corporation.

Karashima Seishi and Margarita I. Vorobyova-Desyatovskaya. 2015. "The Avadāna Anthology from Merv, Turkmenistan." In *The St. Petersburg Sanskrit Fragments (StPSF), Volume 1*, edited by Seishi Karashima and Margarita I. Vorobyova-Desyatovskaya, 145–523. Tokyo: The Institute of Oriental Manuscripts of the Russian Academy of Sciences and the International Research Institute for Advanced Buddhology, Soka University.

Karetzky, Patricia Eichenbaum. 1992. *The Life of the Buddha: Ancient Scriptural and Pictorial Traditions.* Lanham: University Press of America.

Karttunen, Klaus. 1998. "Orality vs. Written Text: Mediaeval Developments in Vedic Ritual Literature." *Electronic Journal of Folklore*, 8: 114–26.

Keith, A. B. 1936. "Pre-canonical Buddhism." *Indian Historical Quarterly*, 12.1: 1–20.

Kieffer-Pülz, Petra. 2007. "Stretching the Vinaya Rules and Getting Away with It." *Journal of the Pali Text Society*, 29: 1–49.

———. 2012. "The Law of Theft: Regulations in the Theravāda Vinaya and the Law Commentaries." *Journal of the Pali Text Society*, 31: 1–54.

———. 2014. "What the Vinayas Can Tell Us about Law." In *Buddhism and Law: An Introduction*, edited by Rebecca Redwood French and Mark A. Nathan, 46–62. New York: Cambridge University Press.

———. 2021. "Notes on the Introductions to the Sanskrit Sarvāstivāda and Mūlasarvāstivāda Prātimokṣasūtras." *Annual Report of the International Research Institute for Advanced Buddhology at Soka University*, 24: 39–51

Killingly, Dermot. 2014. "Svādhyāya: An Ancient Way of Using the Veda." *Religions of South Asia*, 8.1: 109–30.

Klaus, Konrad. 2010. "Zu den buddhistischen literarischen Fachbegriffen sutta und suttanta." In *From Turfan to Ajanta: Festschrift for Dieter Schlingloff on the Occasion of His Eightieth Birthday*, edited by Eli Franco and Monika Zin, 513–26. Lumbini International Research Institute.

Kuan Tse-Fu. 2012. "A Geographical Perspective on Sectarian Affiliations of the Ekottarika Āgama in Chinese Translation (T 125)." *Journal of the Oxford Centre for Buddhist Studies*, 2: 179–208.

———. 2013a. "Legends and Transcendence: Sectarian Affiliations of the Ekottarika Āgama in Chinese Translation." *Journal of the American Oriental Society*, 133.4: 607–34.

———. 2013b: "Mahāyāna Elements and Mahāsāṃghika Traces in the Ekottarika-āgama." In *Research on the Ekottarika-āgama (Taishō 125)*, edited by Bhikkhunī Dhammadinnā, 133–94. Taipei: Dharma Drum Publishing Corporation.

———. 2013c. "The Pavāraṇā Sutta and 'Liberation in Both Ways' as against 'Liberation by Wisdom.'" *Bulletin of the School of Oriental and African Studies*, 1–25.

———. 2017. Review [of Palumbo 2013]. *Journal of the American Oriental Society*, 137.2: 444–48.

Kuan Tse-fu and Roderick S. Bucknell. 2019. "The Structure and Formation of the Aṅguttara Nikāya and the Ekottarika Āgama." *Buddhist Studies Review*, 36.2: 141–66.

Kudo Noriyuki. 2004. *The Karmavibhaṅga: Transliterations and Annotations of the Original Sanskrit Manuscript from Nepal*. Tokyo: Soka University.

Kumar, Ujjwal. 2010. "Truth of the Devil Statement." In *Buddhism, Contemporary Studies, Selected Papers from the 3rd International Conference, Sri Lanka Association of Buddhist Studies (SLABS)*, edited by S. Nanayakkara and R. Bowden, 112–27. Sri Lanka, Pannipitiya: K Line Printing Services.

Lamotte, Étienne. 1949. "La critique d'interprétation dans le Bouddhisme." *Annuaire de l'Institut de Philologie et d'Histoire Orientales et Slaves de l'Université Libre de Bruxelles*, 9: 341–61.

———. 1957. "Khuddakanikāya and Kṣudrakapiṭaka." *East and West*, 7.4: 341–48.

———. 1958. *Histoire du Bouddhisme Indien, Des origines à l'ère Śaka*. Louvain-la-Neuve: Institut Orientaliste.

———. 1968. "Les yakṣa Ajakalāpaka et Bakkula dans les écritures canoniques du Bouddhisme." In *Mélanges d'Indianisme à la mémoire de Louis Renou*, edited by Louis Renou, 445–66. Paris: Éditions de Boccard.

———. 1970. "Le Buddha insulta-t-il Devadatta?" *Bulletin of the School of Oriental and African Studies*, 33: 107–15.

———. 1980. *Le traité de la grande vertu de sagesse de Nāgārjuna (Mahāprajñāpāramitāśāstra), Tome V*. Louvain-la-Neuve: Institut Orientaliste.

Law, Bimala Churn. 1933. *A History of Pāli Literature*. London: Kegan Paul, Trench, Trubner, vol. 1.

Lenz, Timothy. 2003. *A New Version of the Gāndhārī Dharmapada and a Collection of Previous-Birth Stories, British Library Kharoṣṭhī Fragments 16 + 25*. Seattle: University of Washington Press.

———. 2010. *Gandhāran Avadānas, British Library Kharoṣṭhī Fragments 1–3 and 21 and Supplementary Fragments A–C*. Seattle: University of Washington Press.

Lettere, Laura. 2020. "The Missing Translator: A Study of the Biographies of the Monk Baoyun 寶雲 (376?–449)." *Rivista degli Studi Orientali*, 93.1/2: 259–74.

Lévi, Sylvain. 1915. "Sur la récitation primitive des textes bouddhiques." *Journal Asiatique*, 11.5: 401–47.

———. 1933. *Fragments de textes koutchéens, Udānavarga, Udānastotra, Udānalaṃkāra et Karmavibhaṅga, publiés et traduits avec un vocabulaire et une introduction sur le 'Tokharien.'* Paris: Imprimerie Nationale.

Levman, Bryan G. 2019. "The Historical Buddha: Response to Drewes." *Canadian Journal of Buddhist Studies*, 14: 25–56.

———. 2020. *Pāli, the Language: The Medium and Message*. Newcastle upon Tyne: Cambridge Scholars Publishing.

Li Channa. 2019. "Devadatta." In Brill's *Encyclopedia of Buddhism, Volume II: Lives*, edited by Jonathan A. Silk, Richard Bowring, Vincent Eltschinger, and Michael Radich, 141–55. Leiden: Brill.

Lindtner, Christian. 1997. "The Problem of Precanonical Buddhism." *Buddhist Studies Review*, 14.2: 109–39.

Lopez, Donald S. Jr. 1995. "Authority and Orality in the Mahāyāna." *Numen*, 42: 21–47.

Lüders, Heinrich. 1973. *A List of Brahmi Inscriptions, From the Earliest Times to about A.D. 400, with the Exception of Those of Asoka*. Varanasi: Indological Book House.

Lupton, Walter. 1894. "The Raṭṭhapāla Sutta." *Journal of the Royal Asiatic Society*, 769–806.

Malalasekera, G. P. 1928/1994. *The Pāli Literature of Ceylon*. Kandy: Buddhist Publication Society.

———. 1937/1995. *Dictionary of Pāli Proper Names, Vol. I, A–Dh*. Delhi: Munshiram Manoharlal.

———. 1938/1998. *Dictionary of Pāli Proper Names, Vol. II, N–H*. Delhi: Munshiram Manoharlal.

Manné, Joy, 1995. "Case Histories from the Pāli Canon, I: The Sāmaññaphala Sutta, Hypothetical Case History or How to Be Sure to Win a Debate." *Journal of the Pali Text Society*, 21: 1–34.

Marasinghe, M. M. J. 1974. *Gods in Early Buddhism: A Study in their Social and Mythological Milieu as Depicted in the Nikāyas of the Pāli Canon*. Kelaniya: University of Sri Lanka, Vidyalankara Campus Press.

Marciniak, Katarzyna. 2020. *The Mahāvastu: A New Edition, Vol. II*. Tokyo: International Research Institute for Advanced Buddhology, Soka University.

Martini, Giuliana. 2012a. "The 'Discourse on Accumulated Actions' in Śamathadeva's Abhidharmakośopāyikā." *Indian International Journal of Buddhist Studies*, 13: 49–79.

———. 2012b. "The Story of Sudinna in the Tibetan Translation of the Mūlasarvāstivāda Vinaya." *Journal of Buddhist Ethics*, 19: 440–51.

Masefield, Peter. 1994/2001. *The Udāna Commentary (Paramatthadīpanī nāma Udānaṭṭhakathā), Volume I, by Dhammapāla*. Oxford: Pali Text Society.

Mayeda Egaku. 1985. "Japanese Studies on the Schools of the Chinese Āgamas." In *Zur Schulzugehörigkeit von Werken der Hīnayāna-Literatur, Erster Teil*, edited by Heinz Bechert, 94–103. Göttingen: Vandenhoeck & Ruprecht.

McGovern, Nathan. 2019. "Protestant Presuppositions and the Study of the Early Buddhist Oral Tradition." *Journal of the International Association of Buddhist Studies*, 42: 449–91.

Meisig, Konrad. 1987. *Das Śrāmaṇyaphala-Sūtra: Synoptische Übersetzung und Glossar der chinesischen Fassungen verglichen mit dem Sanskrit und Pāli*. Wiesbaden: Otto Harrassowitz.

Melzer, Gudrun. 2006. *Ein Abschnitt aus dem Dīrghāgama*. PhD thesis. München: Ludwig-Maximilians-Universität.

———. 2009. "The Sanskrit Fragments Or. 15009/151–200 in the Hoernle Collection." In *Buddhist Manuscripts from Central Asia: The British Library Sanskrit Fragments*, edited by Seishi Karashima and Klaus Wille, 199–226. Tokyo: International Research Institute for Advanced Buddhology, Soka University.

Mettanando, Laohavanich Mano. 2008. "The First Council and Suppression of the Nuns." *Hsuan Chuang Journal of Buddhist Studies*, 9: 49–120.

Minh Chau, Thich. 1964/1991. *The Chinese Madhyama Āgama and the Pāli Majjhima Nikāya*. Delhi: Motilal Banarsidass.

Misra, G. S. P. 1972. *The Age of Vinaya*. Delhi: Munshiram Manoharlal.

Mittal, Kusum. 1957. *Dogmatische Begriffsreihen im älteren Buddhismus, I, Fragmente des Daśottarasūtra aus zentralasiatischen Sanskrit-Handschriften*. Berlin: Akademie Verlag.

Mochizuki Shinkō. 1940. "The Places of Varṣāvasāna During Forty-five Years of the Buddha's Career after his Enlightenment." *Studies on Buddhism in Japan*, 2: 29–44.

Mohr, Thea and Jampa Tsedroen. 2010. *Dignity and Discipline: Reviving Full Ordination for Buddhist Nuns*. Somerville, MA: Wisdom Publications.

Mori Sodō. 1990. "The Origin and History of the Bhāṇaka Tradition." In *Ānanda: Papers on Buddhism and Indology: A Felicitation Volume Presented to Ānanda Weihena Palliya Guruge on His Sixtieth Birthday*, edited by Y. Karunadasa, 123–29. Colombo: Felicitation Volume Editorial Committee.

Mukherjee, Biswadeb. 1966. *Die Überlieferung von Devadatta dem Widersacher des Buddha in den kanonischen Schriften*. München: Kitzinger.

Nakamura Hajime. 2000. *Gotama Buddha: A Biography Based on the Most Reliable Texts, Volume One*. Tokyo: Kosei Publishing Co.

Nakatani Hideaki. 1987. *Udānavarga de Subaši, Édition critique du manuscrit Sanskrit sur bois provenant de Subaši*. Paris: Collège de France, Institut de Civilisation Indienne.

Nance, Richard F. 2012. *Speaking for Buddhas, Scriptural Commentary in Indian Buddhism*. New York: Columbia University Press.

Ñāṇamoli, Bhikkhu. 1995/2005. *The Middle Length Discourses of the Buddha: A Translation of the Majjhima Nikāya*, edited by Bhikkhu Bodhi. Somerville, MA: Wisdom Publications.

Ñāṇatusita, Bhikkhu. 2014. *Analysis of the Bhikkhu Pātimokkha*. Kandy: Buddhist Publication Society.

Nanjio Bunyiu. 1886. *A Short History of the Twelve Japanese Buddhist Sects: Translated from the Original Japanese*. Tokyo: Bukkyō-sho-ei-yaku-shuppan-sha.

Nattier, Jan. 2003a. *A Few Good Men: The Bodhisattva Path According to The Inquiry of Ugra (Ugraparipṛcchā)*. Honolulu: University of Hawai'i Press.

———. 2003b. "The Ten Epithets of the Buddha in the Translations of Zhi Qian 支謙." *Annual Report of the International Research Institute for Advanced Buddhology at Soka University*, 6: 207–50.

———. 2004. "The Twelve Divisions of Scriptures (十二部經) in the Earliest Chinese Buddhist Translations." *Annual Report of the International Research Institute for Advanced Buddhology at Soka University*, 7: 167–96.

———. 2008. *A Guide to the Earliest Chinese Buddhist Translations: Texts from the Eastern Han 東漢 and Three Kingdoms 三國 Periods*. Tokyo: Soka University.

Neumann, Karl Eugen. 1896/1995. *Die Reden des Buddha, Mittlere Sammlung, Aus dem Pāli-Kanon übersetzt*. Herrnschrot: Beyerlein & Steinschulte.

———. 1912/2004. *Die Reden des Buddha, Längere Sammlung, Aus dem Pāli-Kanon übersetzt*. Herrnschrot: Beyerlein & Steinschulte.

Nolot, Édith. 1987. "Saṃghāvaśeṣa-, saṃghātiśeṣa-, saṃghādisesa-." *Bulletin d'Études Indiennes*, 5: 251–72.

Norman, K. R. 1977. "The Buddha's View of Devas." In *Beiträge zur Indienforschung, Ernst Waldschmidt zum 80. Geburtstag gewidmet*, edited by D. Seyfort Ruegg, Herbert Härtel, and Herbert Hartel, 329–36. Berlin: Museum für Indische Kunst.

———. 1983. *Pāli Literature, Including the Canonical Literature in Prakrit and Sanskrit of all the Hīnayāna Schools of Buddhism*. Wiesbaden: Otto Harrassowitz.

———. 1984. "The Four Noble Truths: A Problem of Pāli Syntax." In *Indological and Buddhist Studies: Volume in Honour of Professor J. W. de Jong on his Sixtieth Birthday*, edited by L. A. Hercus, F. B. J. Kuiper, T. Rajapatirana, and E. R. Skrzypczak, 377–91. Delhi: Sri Satguru.

———. 1997. *A Philological Approach to Buddhism: The Bukkyō Dendō Kyōkai Lectures 1994*. London: School of Oriental and African Studies.

Nyanatiloka Mahāthera. 1952/1988. *Buddhist Dictionary: Manual of Buddhist Terms and Doctrines*. Kandy: Buddhist Publication Society.

Oberlies, Thomas. 1997. "Neuer Wein in alten Schläuchen? Zur Geschichte der buddhistischen Ordensregeln." *Bulletin d'Études Indiennes*, 15: 171–204.

Obermiller, E. 1932. "The Account of the Buddha's Nirvāṇa and the First Councils According to the Vinayakṣudraka." *Indian Historical Quarterly*, 8: 781–84.

Oldenberg, Hermann. 1879. *The Dīpavaṃsa, An Ancient Buddhist Historical Record: Edited and Translated*. London: Williams and Norgate.

———. 1882. "Ueber den Lalitavistara." *Verhandlungen des internationalen Orientalistenkongress*, 5.2: 107–22.

———. 1883. "Das altindische Âkhyâna, mit besondrer Rücksicht auf das Suparṇâkhyâna." *Zeitschrift der Deutschen Morgenländischen Gesellschaft*, 37.1: 54–86.

———. 1898. "Buddhistische Studien." *Zeitschrift der Deutschen Morgenländischen Gesellschaft*, 52: 613–94.

———. 1912a. "Studien zum Mahāvastu." *Nachrichten von der königlichen Gesellschaft der Wissenschaften zu Göttingen, philologisch-historische Klasse aus dem Jahre 1912*, 123–54.

———. 1912b. "Studien zur Geschichte des buddhistischen Kanon." *Nachrichten von der königlichen Gesellschaft der Wissenschaften zu Göttingen, philologisch-historische Klasse aus dem Jahre 1912*, 155–217.

Ong, Walter J. 1982/1996. *Orality and Literacy: The Technologizing of the Word*. London: Routledge.

Pachow, W. 1955. *A Comparative Study of the Prātimokṣa, on the Basis of Its Chinese, Tibetan, Sanskrit and Pali Versions*. Santiniketan: Sino-Indian Cultural Society.

Palumbo, Antonello. 2013. *An Early Chinese Commentary on the Ekottarika-āgama: The Fenbie gongde lun 分別功德論 and the History of the Translation of the Zengyi ahan jing 增一阿含經*. Taipei: Dharma Drum Publishing Corporation.

Pande, Govind Chandra. 1957. *Studies in the Origins of Buddhism*. University of Allahabad, Department of Ancient History, Culture and Archeaology.

Paṇḍita, Ven. 2017. "Who Are the Chabbagiya Monks and Nuns?" *Journal of Buddhist Ethics*, 24: 103–18.

Paranavitana, S. 1970. *Inscriptions of Ceylon, Volume 1, Containing Cave Inscriptions from 3rd Century B.C. to 1st Century A.C. and other Inscriptions in the Early Brāhmī Script*. Colombo: Department of Archeology.

Pāsādika, Bhikkhu. 2010. "Gleanings from the Chinese Ekottarāgama Regarding School Affiliation and Other Topics." In *Translating Buddhist Chinese, Problems and Prospects*, edited by Konrad Meisig, 87–96. Wiesbaden: Harrassowitz.

———. 2017. "Ancient and Modern Interpretations of the Pañcavimuttāyatana." *Journal of the Centre for Buddhist Studies*, 14: 139–47.

Pischel, Richard. 1904. "Neue Bruchstücke des Sanskritkanons der Buddhisten aus Idyuktšari, Chinesisch-Turkestān." *Sitzungsbericht der Königlich Preussischen Akademie der Wissenschaften, Berlin*, 25: 1138–45.

Pradhan, P. 1967. *Abhidharmakośabhāṣya of Vasubandhu*. Patna: Kashi Prasad Jayaswal Research Institute.

Prasad, Mauli Chand. 1998. "Studies in the Origin of the Sarvāstivāda." In *Facets of Indian Culture: Gustav Roth Felicitation Volume: Published on the Occasion of His 82nd Birthday*, edited by C. P. Sinha, 412–19. India, Patna: Bihar Puravid Parishad.

Prebish, Charles S. 1974. "A Review of Scholarship on the Buddhist Councils." *Journal of Asian Studies*, 35.2: 239–54.

Pruitt, William and K. R. Norman. 2001. *The Pātimokkha*. Oxford: Pali Text Society.

Przyluski, Jean. 1926. *Le concile de Rājagṛha, Introduction à l'histoire des canons et des sectes bouddhiques*. Paris: Paul Geuthner.

Pye, Michael 2019. "The Question of Primitive Buddhism in the Closing Works of Stansilaw Schayer." *The Eastern Buddhist*, 48.1: 23–47.

Quiroga, Rodrigo Quian. 2017. *The Forgetting Machine: Memory, Perception, and the "Jennifer Aniston Neuron."* Dallas: BenBella Books.

Ramers, Peter. 1996. *Die 'drei Kapitel über die Sittlichkeit im Śrāmaṇyaphala-Sūtra.' Die Fassungen des Dīghanikāya und Saṃghabhedavastu, verglichen mit dem Tibetischen und Mongolischen*. PhD thesis. Bonn: Rheinische Friedrich-Wilhelms-Universität.

Ray, Reginald A. 1994. *Buddhist Saints in India: A Study in Buddhist Values & Orientations*. New York: Oxford University Press.

Reat, Noble Ross. 1996/1998. "The Historical Buddha and His Teachings." In *Encyclopaedia of Indian Philosophies, Vol. VII: Abhidharma Buddhism to 150 AD*, edited by Karl H. Potter, Robert E. Buswell, Padmanabh S. Jaini, and Noble Ross Reat, 3–57. Delhi: Motilal Banarsidass.

Regamey, Constantin. 1957. "Le problème du bouddhisme primitif et les derniers travaux de Stanislaw Schayer." *Rocznik Orientalisticzny*, 21: 37–58.

Rhys Davids, T. W. 1881. *Buddhist Suttas: Translated from the Pāli*. Oxford: Clarendon Press.

Rhys Davids, T. W. and C. A. F. Rhys Davids. 1921. *Dialogues of the Buddha: Translated from the Pali of the Dîgha Nikâya, Part III*. London: Oxford University Press.

Rhys Davids, T. W. and W. Stede. 1921/1993. *Pali-English Dictionary*. Delhi: Motilal Banarsidass.

Rosenberg, Bruce A. 1987. "The Complexity of Oral Tradition." *Oral Tradition*, 2.1: 73–90.

Rosenberg, Fr. 1920. "Deux fragments sogdien-bouddhiques du Ts'ien-fo-tong de Touen-houang, II: Fragment d'un sūtra." *Izvestiya Rossiyskoy Akademii Nauk*, 399–420.

Roth, Gustav. 1980. "Particular Features of the Language of the Ārya-Mahāsāṃghika-Lokottaravādins and their Importance for Early Buddhist Tradition." In *The Language of the Earliest Buddhist Tradition*, edited by Heinz Bechert, 93–135. Göttingen: Vandenhoeck & Ruprecht.

———. 1983. *Mallī-jñāta, Das achte Kapitel des Nāyādhammakahāo im sechsten Aṅga des Śvetāmbara Jainakanons, herausgegeben, übersetzt und erläutert*. Wiesbaden: Franz Steiner.

Sasaki Shiyuka. 2020. "How Was an Āgama/Nikāya Scripture Composed? The Case of Sāmagāmasutta." *Journal of Indian and Tibetan Studies*, 24: 1–48.

Salomon, Richard. 2008. *Two Gāndhārī Manuscripts of the Songs of Lake Anavatapta (Anavatapta-gāthā), British Library Kharoṣṭhī Fragment 1 and Senior Scroll 14*. Seattle: University of Washington Press.

———. 2011. "An Unwieldy Canon: Observations on Some Distinctive Features of Canon Formation in Buddhism." In *Kanonisierung und Kanonbildung in der asiatischen Religionsgeschichte*, edited by Max Deeg, Oliver Freiberger, and Christoph Kleine, 161–207. Wien: Verlag der Österreichichen Akademie der Wissenschaften.

———. 2018. *The Buddhist Literature of Ancient Gandhāra: An Introduction with Translations*. Somerville, MA: Wisdom Publications.

———. 2020. "Where Are the Gandharan Sūtras? Some Reflections on the Contents of the Gandhari Manuscript Collections." In *Research on the Saṃyukta-āgama*, edited by Bhikkhunī Dhammadinnā, 173–99. Taipei: Dharma Drum Publishing Corporation.

Sander, Lore. 1991. "The Earliest Manuscripts from Central Asia and the Sarvāstivāda Mission." In *Corolla Iranica, Papers in Honour of Prof. Dr. David Neil MacKenzie on the Occasion of His 65th Birthday on April 8th, 1991*, edited by Ronald E. Emmerick and Dieter Weber, 133–50. Frankfurt: Peter Lang.

Sander, Lore and Ernst Waldschmidt. 1985. *Sanskrithandschriften aus den Turfanfunden, Teil 5*. Wiesbaden: Franz Steiner.

Sarao, K. T. S. 1989. *The Origin and Nature of Ancient Indian Buddhism*. Delhi: Eastern Book Linkers.

Schacter, Daniel L. 1999. "The Seven Sins of Memory: Insights from Psychology and Cognitive Neuroscience." *American Psychologist*, 54.3: 182–203.

Scharfe, Hartmut. 2002. *Education in Ancient India*. Leiden: E. J. Brill.

Schayer, Stanislaw. 1935. "Precanonical Buddhism." *Archiv Orientální: Journal of the Czechoslovak Oriental Institute, Prague*, 7: 121–32.

———. 1937. "New Contributions to the Problem of Pre-Hīnayānistic Buddhism." *Polish Bulletin of Oriental Studies*, 1: 8–17.

Schlingloff, Dieter. 1963. "Zur Interpretation des Prātimokṣasūtra." *Zeitschrift der Deutschen Morgenländischen Gesellschaft*, 113: 536–51.

Schmidt, Klaus T. 1989. *Der Schlussteil des prātimokṣasūtra der Sarvāstivādins, Text in Sanskrit und Tocharisch A verglichen mit den Parallelversionen anderer Schulen, auf Grund von Turfan-Handschriften herausgegeben und bearbeitet*. Göttingen: Vandenhoeck & Ruprecht.

Schmithausen, Lambert. 1970. "Zu den Rezensionen des Udānavargaḥ." *Wiener Zeitschrift für die Kunde Südasiens*, 14: 47–124.

———. 1981. "On Some Aspects of Descriptions or Theories of 'Liberating Insight' and 'Enlightenment' in Early Buddhism." In *Studien zum Jainismus und Buddhismus, Gedenkschrift für Ludwig Alsdorf*, edited by Klaus Bruh and Albrecht Wezler, 199–250. Wiesbaden: Franz Steiner.

———. 2020. *Fleischverzehr und Vegetarismus im indischen Buddhismus bis ca. zur Mitte des ersten Jahrtausends n. Chr., Teil 2, Endnoten*. Bochum: Projektverlag.

Schopen, Gregory. 1985. "Two Problems in the History of Indian Buddhism: The Layman/Monk Distinction and the Doctrines of the Transference of Merit." *Studien zur Indologie und Iranistik*, 10: 9–47.

———. 1994. "Ritual Rights and Bones of Contention: More on Monastic Funerals and Relics in the Mūlasarvāstivāda Vinaya." *Journal of Indian Philosophy*, 22: 31–80.

———. 1997/2004. "If You Can't Remember, How to Make It Up: Some Monastic Rules for Redacting Canonical Texts." In *Buddhist Monks and Business Matters, Still More Papers on Monastic Buddhism in India*, edited by Gregory Schopen, 395–407. Honolulu: University of Hawai'i Press.

———. 2004. "On Buddhist Monks and Dreadful Deities: Some Monastic Devices for Updating the Dharma." In *Gedenkschrift J. W. de Jong*, edited by H. W. Bodewitz and Hara Minoru, 161–84. Tokyo: The International Institute for Buddhist Studies.

Schwartz, Martin. 2002. "How Zarathushtra Generated the Gathic Corpus: Inner-textual and Intertextual Composition." *Bulletin of the Asia Institute*, 16: 53–64.

Seeger, Martin. 2006/2008. "The Bhikkhunī-Ordination Controversy in Thailand." *Journal of the International Association of Buddhist Studies*, 29.1: 155–83.

Senart, Émile. 1890. *Le Mahāvastu, Texte sanscrit publié pour la première fois et accompagné d'introductions et d'un commentaire, Tome deuxième*. Paris: Imprimerie Nationale.

Shaw, Sarah. 2021. *The Art of Listening: A Guide to the Early Teachings of Buddhism*. Boulder: Shambhala Publications.

Shulman, Eviatar. 2019. "Looking for Samatha and Vipassanā in the Early Suttas: What, Actually, Are the Texts?" *Indian International Journal of Buddhist Studies*, 20: 95–141.

———. 2021a. "Embodied Transcendence: The Buddha's Body in the Pāli Nikāyas." *Religions*, 12.179: 1–17.

———. 2021b. "Orality and Creativity in the Early Buddhist Discourses." In *The Language of the Sūtras: Essays in Honor of Luis Gómez*, edited by Natalie Gummer, 187–230. Berkeley: Mangalam Press.

———. 2021c. *Visions of the Buddha: Creative Dimensions of Early Buddhist Scripture*. Oxford: Oxford University Press.

Sieg, E. and W. Siegling 1931. "Udānavarga-Uebersetzungen in 'Kucischer Sprache.'" *Bulletin of the School of Oriental Studies*, 6: 483–499.

———. 1933. "Bruchstück eines Udānavarga Kommentars (Udānālaṃkāra?) im Tocharischen." In *Festschrift Moriz Winternitz: 1863—23. Dez.—1933*, edited by Otto Stein and Wilhelm Gambert, 167–73, Leipzig: Otto Harrassowitz.

———. 1949. *Tocharische Sprachreste, Sprache B: Die Udānālaṅkāra-Fragmente*. Göttingen: Vandenhoeck & Ruprecht.

Silk, Jonathan, A. 2008. *Managing Monks: Administrators and Administrative Roles in Indian Buddhist Monasticism*. Oxford: Oxford University Press.

———. 2013/2015. "Establishing / Interpreting / Translating: Is It Just That Easy?" *Journal of the International Association of Buddhist Studies*, 36/37: 205–26.

———. 2015. "Canonicity." In *Brill's Encyclopedia of Buddhism, Volume I, Literature and Languages*, edited by Jonathan A. Silk, Oskar von Hinüber, and Vincent Eltschinger, 5–37. Leiden: Brill.

———. 2020. "A Trust Rooted in Ignorance: Why Ānanda's Lack of Understanding Makes Him a Reliable Witness to the Buddha's Teachings." In *'At the Shores of the Sky,' Asian Studies for Albert Hoffstädt*, edited by Paul W. Kroll and Jonathan A. Silk, 23–37. Leiden: Brill.

———. 2021. "Editing without an Ur-text: Buddhist Sūtras, Rabbinic Text Criticism, and the Open Philology Digital Humanities Project." *Annual Report of the International Research Institute for Advanced Buddhology at Soka University*, 24: 147–63.

Sivaramamurti, C. 1942/1956. *Amaravati Sculptures in the Madras Government Museum*. Madras: Thompson.

Skilling, Peter. 1994. *Mahāsūtras: Great Discourses of the Buddha, Volume I: Texts*. Oxford: Pali Text Society.

———. 1997a. "From bKa' bstan bcos to bKa' 'gyur and bsTan 'gyur." In *Transmission of the Tibetan Canon: Papers Presented at a Panel of the 7th Seminar of the International Association for Tibetan Studies, Graz 1995*, edited by Helmut Eimer, 87–111. Wien: Verlag der Österreichischen Akademie der Wissenschaften.

———. 1997b. *Mahāsūtras: Great Discourses of the Buddha, Volume II*. Oxford: Pali Text Society.

———. 2008. "Narrative, Art, and Ideology: Jātakas from India to Sukhotai." In *Past Lives of the Buddha, Wat Si Chum—Art, Architecture and Inscriptions*, edited by Peter Skilling, 59–104. Bangkok: River Books.

———. 2009. "Redaction, Recitation, and Writing, Transmission of the Buddha's Teaching in India in the Early Period." In *Buddhist Manuscript Cultures, Knowledge, Ritual, and Art*, edited by Stephen C. Berkwitz, Juliane Schober, and Claudia Brown, 53–75. London: Routledge.

———. 2012. "Discourse on the Twenty-Two Faculties' (Translated from Śamathadeva's Upāyikā-ṭīkā)." In *Dharmapravicaya: Aspects of Buddhist Studies, Essays in Honour of N. H. Samtani*, edited by Lalji Shravak and Charles Willemen, 423–58. Delhi: Buddhist World Press.

———. 2017. "The Many Lives of Texts: Pañcatraya and Māyājāla Sūtras." In *Research on the Madhyama-āgama*, edited by Bhikkhunī

Dhammadinnā, 269–326. Taipei: Dharma Drum Publishing Corporation.

———. 2020a. "Conjured Buddhas from the Arthavargīya to Nāgārjuna." In *Archaeologies of the Written: Indian, Tibetan, and Buddhist Studies in Honour of Cristina Scherrer-Schaub*, edited by Vincent Tournier, Vincent Eltschinger, and Marta Sernesi, 709–51. Naples: Unior Press.

———. 2020b. "Discourse on the Relative Value of the Varieties of Knowledge (Vidyāsthānopama-sūtra): A Translation." In *Research on the Saṃyukta-āgama*, edited by Bhikkhunī Dhammadinnā, 327–55. Taipei: Dharma Drum Publishing Corporation.

Skilling, Peter, Saerji, and Prapod Assavavirulhakarn. 2016. "A Possible Sanskrit Parallel to the Pali Uruvelasutta." In *Buddhist Manuscripts, Volume IV (Manuscripts in the Schøyen Collection)*, edited by Jens Braarvig, 159–82. Oslo: Hermes.

Stache-Rosen, Valentina. 1968. *Dogmatische Begriffsreihen im älteren Buddhismus II; Das Saṅgītisūtra und sein Kommentar Saṅgītiparyāya*. Berlin: Akademie Verlag.

Su Ken. 2020. "Notes on the Translation and the Translator of the Shorter Chinese Saṃyukta-āgama." In *Research on the Saṃyukta-āgama*, edited by Bhikkhunī Dhammadinnā, 842–80. Taipei: Dharma Drum Corporation.

Sujato, Bhikkhu and Bhikkhu Brahmali. 2014. *The Authenticity of the Early Buddhist Texts*. Kandy: Buddhist Publication Society.

Suzuki Teitaro. 1904. "The First Buddhist Council." *The Monist*, 14.2: 253–82.

Tatia, N. 1975. *Prātimokṣasūtram of the Lokottaravādamahāsāṅghika School*. Patna: Kashi Prasad Jayaswal Research Institute.

Ṭhānissaro, Bhikkhu. 1994/2013. *The Buddhist Monastic Code I: The Pāṭimokkha Rules Translated & Explained by Ṭhānissaro Bhikkhu (Geoffrey DeGraff), Revised Edition*. California: Metta Forest Monastery.

Thomas, E. J. 1927/2003. *The Life of Buddha as Legend and History*. Delhi: Munshiram Manoharlal.

Thomas, Werner. 1971. *Bilinguale Udānavarga-texte der Sammlung Hoernle*. Wiesbaden: Franz Steiner.

———. 1979. "Nachtrag zur Sanskrit-Udānavarga-Ausgabe." *Kuhns Zeitschrift für vergleichende Sprachforschung*, 93: 242–246.

Tilakaratne, Asaṅga. 2000. "Saṅgīti and Sāmaggī: Communal Recitation and the Unity of the Saṅgha." *Buddhist Studies Review*, 17.2: 175–97.

Tournier, Vincent. 2012. "The Mahāvastu and the Vinayapiṭaka of the Mahāsāṃghika-Lokottaravādins." *Annual Report of the International Research Institute for Advanced Buddhology at Soka University*, 15: 87–104.

———. 2014. "Mahākāśyapa, His Lineage, and the Wish for Buddhahood: Reading Anew the Bodhgayā Inscriptions of Mahānāman." *Indo-Iranian Journal*, 57: 1–60.

Travagnin, Stefania and Bhikkhu Anālayo. 2020. "Assessing the Field of Āgama Studies in Twentieth-Century China, With a Focus on Master Yinshun's 印順 Three-Aṅga Theory." In *Research on the Saṃyukta-āgama*, edited by Bhikkhunī Dhammadinnā, 933–1007. Taipei: Dharma Drum Corporation.

Tripāṭhī, Chandrabhal. 1995. *Ekottarāgama-Fragmente der Gilgit-Handschrift*. Reinbek: Verlag für Orientalistische Fachpublikationen.

Tsukamoto Keisho. 1963. "Mahākāśyapa's Precedence to Ānanda in the Rājagṛha Council." *Journal of Indian and Buddhist Studies*, 11.2: 824–17.

———. 1996. *Indo Bukkyō Himei no Kenkyū* [A Comprehensive Study of the Indian Buddhist Inscriptions], *Vol. 1*. Kyoto: Heirakuji-Shoten.

Vajirañāṇavarorasa, Somdet Phra Mahā Samaṇa Chao Kroma Phrayā. 1973/2009. *The Entrance to the Vinaya, Vinayamukha, Volume Two*. Bangkok: Mahāmakut Rājavidyālaya Press.

Vansina, Jan. 1985. *Oral Tradition as History*. Madison: University of Wisconsin Press.

Vetter, Tilmann. 1988. *The Ideas and Meditative Practices of Early Buddhism*. Leiden: Brill.

von Gabain, Annemarie. 1954. *Türkische Turfan-Texte VIII*. Berlin: Akademie Verlag.

von Hinüber, Oskar. 1976. "Sprachliche Beobachtungen zum Aufbau des Pāli Kanons." *Studien zur Indologie und Iranistik*, 2: 27–40.

———. 1989. *Der Beginn der Schrift und frühe Schriftlichkeit in Indien*. Wiesbaden: Franz Steiner.

———. 1994a. "Die neun aṅgas: Ein früher Versuch zur Einteilung buddhistischer Texte." *Wiener Zeitschrift für die Kunde Süd- und Ostasiens*, 38: 121–35.

———. 1994b. *Untersuchungen zur Mündlichkeit früher mittelindischer Texte der Buddhisten*. Stuttgart: Franz Steiner.

———. 1995. "Buddhist Law according to the Theravāda-vinaya: A Survey of Theory and Practice." *Journal of the International Association of Buddhist Studies*, 18.1: 7–45.

———. 1996/1997. *A Handbook of Pāli Literature*. Delhi: Munshiram Manoharlal.

———. 1997. "Old Age and Old Monks in Pāli Buddhism." In *Aging: Asian Concepts and Experiences, Past and Present*, edited by Susanne Formanek and Sepp Linhart, 65–78. Wien: Österreichische Akademie der Wissenschaften.

———. 1998. "Structure and Origin of the Pātimokkhasutta of the Theravādins." *Acta Orientalia Academiae Scietiarum Hungaricae*, 51.3: 257–65.

———. 1999. *Das Pātimokkhasutta der Theravādin, Seine Gestalt und seine Entstehungsgeschichte, Studien zur Literatur des Theravāda-Buddhismus II*. Stuttgart: Franz Steiner.

———. 2008. "The Foundation of the Bhikkhunīsaṅgha—A Contribution to the Earliest History of Buddhism." *Annual Report of the International Research Institute for Advanced Buddhology at Soka University*, 11: 3–29.

———. 2015. Review [of Mohr and Tsedroen 2010]. *Indo-Iranian Journal*, 58: 194–201.

———. 2019a. "The Buddha as a Historical Person." *Journal of the International Association of Buddhist Studies*, 42: 231–64.

———. 2019b. Review [of Anālayo 2016c]. *Indo-Iranian Journal*, 62: 89–99.

von Simson, Georg. 1965. *Zur Diktion einiger Lehrtexte des buddhistischen Sanskritkanons*. München: J. Kitzinger.

———. 1977. "Zur Phrase yena . . . tenopajagāma / upetya und ihren Varianten im buddhistischen Sanskrit." In *Beiträge zur Indienforschung, Ernst Waldschmidt zum 80. Geburtstag gewidmet*, edited by D. Seyfort Ruegg, Herbert Härtel, and Herbert Hartel, 479–88. Berlin: Museum für Indische Kunst.

———. 1985. "Stil und Schulzugehörigkeit Buddhistischer Sanskrittexte." In *Zur Schulzugehörigkeit von Werken der Hīnayāna-Literatur, Erster Teil*, edited by Heinz Bechert, 76–93. Göttingen: Vandenhoeck & Ruprecht.

———. 2000. *Prātimokṣasūtra der Sarvāstivādins Teil II, Kritische Textausgabe, Übersetzung, Wortindex sowie Nachträge zu Teil I.* Göttingen: Vandenhoeck & Ruprecht.

Wagle, Narenda. 1985. "The Gods in Early Buddhism in Relation to Human Society: An Aspect of Their Function, Hierarchy, and Rank as Depicted in the Nikāya Texts of the Pali Canon." In *New Paths in Buddhist Research*, edited by Anthony Kennedy Warder, 57–80. Durham, NC: Acorn Press.

Waldschmidt, Ernst. 1926. *Bruchstücke des Bhikṣuṇī-Prātimokṣa der Sarvāstivādins, Mit einer Darstellung der Überlieferung des Bhikṣuṇī-Prātimokṣa in den verschiedenen Schulen*. Leipzig: F. A. Brockhaus.

———. 1932. *Bruchstücke buddhistischer Sūtras aus dem zentralasiatischen Sanskritkanon herausgegeben und im Zusammenhang mit ihren Parallelversionen bearbeitet*. Leipzig: F. A. Brockhaus.

———. 1951 (vol. 2). *Das Mahāparinirvāṇasūtra, Text in Sanskrit und Tibetisch, Verglichen mit dem Pāli nebst einer Übersetzung der chinesischen Entsprechung im Vinaya der Mūlasarvāstivādins, Auf Grund von Turfan-Handschriften herausgegeben und bearbeitet*. Berlin: Akademie Verlag.

———. 1954/1967. "Zum ersten buddhistischen Konzil in Rājagṛha." In *Von Ceylon bis Turfan, Schriften zur Geschichte, Literatur, Religion und Kunst des indischen Kulturraums, Festgabe zum 70. Geburtstag am 15. Juli 1967 von Ernst Waldschmidt*, 226–37. Göttingen: Vandenhoeck & Ruprecht.

Walshe, Maurice. 1987. *Thus Have I Heard: The Long Discourses of the Buddha*. London: Wisdom Publications.

Warder, A. K. 1961. "The Pali Canon and Its Commentaries as an Historical Record." In *Historians of India, Pakistan and Ceylon*, edited by C. H. Phillips, 44–56. London: Oxford University Press.

———. 1967. *Pali Metre: A Contribution to the History of Indian Literature*. London: Pali Text Society.

Watanabe K. 1906. "A Chinese Collection of Itivuttakas." *Journal of the Pali Text Society*, 44–49.

Weller, Friedrich. 1934. *Brahmajālasūtra, Tibetischer und mongolischer Text*. Leipzig: Otto Harrassowitz.

Wen Tzung-Kuen. 2006. "巴利註釋書的古層—《雜阿含經》與《相應部註》語句交會的幾個例子." *Fuyan Buddhist Studies*, 1: 1–31.

Wille, Klaus. 2012. *Sanskrithandschriften aus den Turfanfunden, Teil 11*. Stuttgart: Franz Steiner.

Willemen, Charles. 1978. *The Chinese Udānavarga: A Collection of Important Odes of the Law, Fa Chi Yao Sung Ching, Translated and Annotated*. Bruxelles: Institut Belge des Hautes Études Chinoises.

———. 1999. *The Scriptural Text: Verses of the Doctrine, With Parables, Translated from the Chinese of Fa-li and Fa-chü*. Berkeley: Numata Center for Buddhist Translation and Research.

Williams, Raymond B. 1970. "Historical Criticism of a Buddhist Scripture: The Mahāparinibbāna Sutta." *Journal of the American Academy of Religion*, 38.2: 156–67.

Winternitz, Moriz. 1920/1968. *Geschichte der indischen Literatur, Band 2, Die buddhistische Literatur und die heiligen Texte der Jainas*. Stuttgart: K. F. Koehler.

Witanachchi, C. 2006. "Saṅgha." In *Encyclopaedia of Buddhism*, edited by W. G. Weeraratne, 7.4: 699–704. Sri Lanka: Department of Buddhist Affairs.

Wogihara Unrai. 1932. *Sphuṭārthā Abhidharmakośavyākhyā by Yaśomitra, Part I*. Tokyo: The Publishing Association of Abhidharmakośavyākhyā.

Wynne, Alexander. 2004. "The Oral Transmission of Early Buddhist Literature." *Journal of the International Association of Buddhist Studies*, 27.1: 97–127.

———. 2005. "The Historical Authenticity of Early Buddhist Literature: A Critical Evaluation." *Wiener Zeitschrift für die Kunde Südasiens*, 49: 35–70.

———. 2007. *The Origin of Buddhist Meditation*. London: Routledge.

———. 2019. "Did the Buddha Exist?" *Journal of the Oxford Center for Buddhist Studies*, 16: 98–148.

———. 2020. "When the Little Buddhas Are No More: Vinaya Transformations in the Early 4th Century BC." *Journal of the Oxford Center for Buddhist Studies*, 18: 180–205.

Yamagiwa Nobuyuki. 2001. *Das Pāṇḍulohitakavastu, Über die verschiedenen Verfahrensweisen der Bestrafung in der buddhistischen Gemeinde, Neuausgabe der Sanskrit-Handschrift aus Gilgit, tibetischer Text und deutsche Übersetzung*. Marburg: Indica et Tibetica.

Yit Kin-Tung. 2004. *A Study of a Stereotyped Structure of the Path in Early Buddhist Literature: A Comparative Study of the Pāli, Chinese and Sanskrit Sources*. PhD thesis. University of Bristol.

———. 2008. "Remarks on Fixed Units of Wording in the Early Buddhist Canon." *Indian International Journal of Buddhist Studies*, 9: 267–91.

Zafiropulo, Ghiorgo. 1993. *L'illumination du Buddha, De la quête à l'annonce de l'éveil, essais de chronologie relative et de stratigraphie textuelle*. Innsbruck: Institut für Sprachwissenschaft der Universität Innsbruck.

Zhang Lixiang. 2004. *Das Śaṃkarasūtra: Eine Übersetzung des Sanskrit-Textes im Vergleich mit der Pāli Fassung*. MA thesis. München: Ludwig-Maximilians-Universität.

Zongtse, Champa Thupten. 1990. *Udānavarga, Band III: Der tibetische Text, unter Mitarbeit von Siglinde Dietz herausgegeben von Champa Thupten Zongtse*. Göttingen: Vandenhoeck & Ruprecht.

Zysk, Kenneth G. 2016. *The Indian System of Human Marks*. Leiden: Brill.

Index

D

About the Author

Bhikkhu Anālayo is a scholar of early Buddhism and a meditation teacher. He completed his PhD research on the Satipaṭṭhānasutta at the University of Peradeniya, Sri Lanka, in 2000, and a habilitation research with a comparative study of the Majjhimanikāya in the light of its Chinese, Sanskrit, and Tibetan parallels at the University of Marburg, Germany, in 2007. His over four hundred publications are for the most part based on comparative studies, with a special interest in topics related to meditation and the role of women in Buddhism.

What to Read Next from Wisdom Publications

Rebirth in Early Buddhism and Current Research
Bhikkhu Anālayo

"Bhikkhu Anālayo offers a detailed study of the much-debated Buddhist doctrine of rebirth and a survey of relevant evidence. He also investigates the Pāli chantings of Dhammaruwan, who at a very young age would spontaneously chant ancient and complex Buddhist suttas. I first met Dhammaruwan when he was seven years old, when my teacher, Anagarika Munindraji, and I visited him and his family in Sri Lanka. *Rebirth in Early Buddhism and Current Research* illuminates a complex topic with great clarity and understanding."—Joseph Goldstein, author of *Mindfulness: A Practical Guide to Awakening*

Superiority Conceit in Buddhist Traditions
A Historical Perspective
Bhikkhu Anālayo

"This book is a courageous call for integrity and self-reflection. Bhikkhu Anālayo argues that if Buddhism is to engage the modern world with any enduring success, it must abandon its own conceit and reckon with its internal prejudices. This book is a much-needed contribution that will help reshape the direction of the field."—Vanessa Sasson, professor, Marianopolis College

Buddhist Literature of Ancient Gandhāra
An Introduction with Selected Translations
Richard Saloman

"There is no doubt that this work will serve as a terrific guidebook especially for those who are interested in Buddhist philology. Therefore, it would not be surprising to find this book added to the curricula of many Buddhist studies programs as well as in the bookshelves of Buddhist scholars around the world."—*International Journal of Buddhist Thought & Culture*

In the Buddha's Words
An Anthology of Discourses from the Pali Canon
Bhikkhu Bodhi

"It will rapidly become the sourcebook of choice for both neophyte and serious students alike."—*Buddhadharma*

About Wisdom Publications

Wisdom Publications is the leading publisher of classic and contemporary Buddhist books and practical works on mindfulness. To learn more about us or to explore our other books, please visit our website at wisdomexperience.org or contact us at the address below.

Wisdom Publications
199 Elm Street
Somerville, MA 02144 USA

We are a 501(c)(3) organization, and donations in support of our mission are tax deductible.

Wisdom Publications is affiliated with the Foundation for the Preservation of the Mahayana Tradition (FPMT).